BANKRUPTCY INVESTING

How to Profit from
Distressed Companies

Fourth Edition

BANKRUPTCY INVESTING

How to Profit From Distressed Companies

Fourth Edition

by
Ben Branch
and Hugh Ray

Beard Books
Washington, D.C.

PREFACE

The first edition of this book was published in 1992, and several updates followed. With the passage of 14 years and a major revision in the Bankruptcy Code, a more comprehensive revision became necessary.

Frankly, we have been pleasantly surprised at the reception our book received. Its wide audience mirrors the substantial increase in interest in bankruptcy investing. The expanded interest of hedge funds and vulture funds in bankruptcy investment opportunities has led us to reconsider and revise some previous views and findings.

Large corporate reorganizations occurring under Chapter 11 of the Bankruptcy Code declined in 2006. Most observers expect that decline to reverse, as we explain below. A careful reader of the business news will have noticed a number of instances in which large organizations paid certain classes of creditors substantial dividends. Because people seldom recall minute details (such as isolated bond prices over a period of years), the corresponding investors' very attractive holding-period returns may have gone largely unnoticed. Indeed, many investors in distressed companies are reaping huge profits by carefully timing their investments in companies that others refused to touch simply because these companies were in public financial disgrace. We shall, in this fourth edition, show how it is done.

Defaults and economic ups and downs tend to revert to the long-term historical mean. For example, when default rates are experiencing new lows, high-yield debt issues increase. Historically, defaults surge later and bankruptcies follow. In 2005, for example, the default rate on high-yield bonds was a very low 2.4%. In 2004 it was 1.5%, a record low. (As this is written in 2006, the default rate continues to be abnormally low.) Only 80 public bankruptcies occurred in 2004 compared with 234 in 2002. By comparison, the default rate in 2001 was 9.8% and 12.8% in 2002.

In past economic cycles, the lower default rates, when coupled with an increase in high-yield debt, led to future bankruptcy investment opportunities. In light of this past experience, current low default rates (2006-07) may predict greater opportunities in the years that follow.

To amplify, more than $1 trillion in high-yield debt was outstanding in 2005. That is 33% more than was outstanding in 2002.

Looking ahead, more than $70 billion of high-yield debt is forecast to mature during 2006 and 2007, compared with $20 billion in 2005. All of that debt is unlikely simply to be repaid on schedule. Hence, the opportunity currently available.

As we pointed out in 1992, the active participants in major bankruptcy cases had long observed the investment opportunities available to the knowledgeable bottom-fisher. That hasn't changed in the slightest. Such investors understand that the investment quality of today's Chapter 11 debtor (in bankruptcy) is vastly different from the public failures of the past. We have updated our studies of the results of companies in Chapter 11 reorganizations and well-timed investments in those companies. Many investors still lose money in this area. But the investors – the apprentice vultures – who are willing to take the time to study the materials that follow and apply common sense can achieve substantial rewards.

Buying out-of-season goods has long been known to produce attractive bargains for the customers willing to wait to use them. So, too, with bankruptcy investing. Patience is the key. The average large Chapter 11 case takes 25 months to go from the initial filing to the point where a reorganization plan is confirmed. With the 2005 amendments to the Bankruptcy Code, that time is likely to shrink. Quick turnarounds are still rare, but becoming more common than a decade ago. Complete financial optimism remains rare. What we see is enough gloomy press and public proclamations to scare away the boldest of contrarians. What we see is an opportunity created by the interactions of economic theory and the legal entanglements of social legislation. Concepts of equality of distribution and price efficiency diverge and cross at several points. Fundamental concepts of risk and reward are skewed. At times, they are skewed in favor of you, the risk taker. At other times, the bias runs in the opposite direction. Our purpose is to advise you of when each of those situations is present. We are not giving specific legal advice, nor are we giving specific investment advice. We hope only to set out some more important rules of the contest.

Years after the publication of the first edition of this book, no other single comprehensive place now exists for the investor to look for advice regarding how to participate in the bankruptcy investments market. The current crop of players as have most traditional pioneers gained their experience and made their money by actually feeling their way as they went along from case to case. Much of what they learned came from trial and error, much from sheer luck. Almost all of the experience has been acquired since the "rules of the game" changed in 1979 with the enactment of the revised Bankruptcy Code. The public perceptions of bankruptcy acquired in previous decades became largely inapplicable. The authors, who were active in the area at the time, saw huge profits made by those early to the game. In the years that followed, certain factors have become more clearly defined. In the years to come, those factors will become clearer still. At this point we feel a structure and theme exists on which the reader can frame an investment program with some understanding of the substantial risks involved. As recent studies that we discuss show, the potential returns currently available are huge (assuming, of course, that the future will be like the past, always a somewhat questionable assumption).

The pages that follow remain the only extensive source material that effectively melds the legal and financial processes of bankruptcy investing into a coherent structure. Both areas must be generally understood if the bankruptcy investor can hope to exploit the available opportunities fully. Hopefully, this resource material will provide both the beginning investor and the experienced fund manager with a "Rosetta Stone" for translating the often-confusing lexicon of bankruptcy into a profitable investment program.

This book is designed for serious though not necessarily large-scale investors who would like to participate in the risky and potentially lucrative game of investing in the securities of troubled companies. Investments in both debt and equity securities are considered. Most discussion will focus on publicly traded instruments, but nonpublic securities also will be discussed.

Depending on the degree of distress, troubled companies may or may not go through any or all of the following: informal workout, formal workout, Chapter 11 bankruptcy (prepackaged or not) or Chapter 7 bankruptcy. The investment implications for the securities of firms in each of these stages of financial distress are considered in this book.

No specialized background is required to understand the material presented here. Although the book ultimately treats a number of rather advanced topics, everything needed to understand the issues is contained within these pages. Starting at an elementary level, the discussion moves on to whatever level of complexity is required to understand the concepts. Each step of that process is carefully explained. An extensive glossary of relevant terms is included in the book. This glossary constitutes a handy general reference, as well as a help source for the reader who needs a refresher on the meanings of some relevant terminology introduced earlier.

We offer a unique combination of knowledge and experience about bankruptcy and bankruptcy investing law and finance. We hope you will find it useful.

ABOUT THE AUTHORS

Ben Branch is a professor of finance at the University of Massachusetts. He has written books and articles, both popular and academic, on investing and has personally invested in the securities of a number of troubled companies. A well-known and respected academician in the areas of economics and finance, he has served on a number of creditors' committees and was chairman of the First Republic senior unsecured creditors' committee. He was elected Chapter 7 trustee for the Bank of New England Corporation, as well as chairman of the board of the reorganized First Republic Corporation.

Hugh Ray is a senior partner in the law firm of Andrews Kurth LLP. In that capacity, he has played a significant role in the legal proceedings of many major bankruptcy cases of the past 39 years, including those of Braniff Airways, Yukos Oil, Continental Airlines, Enron Storage Technology, Doskocil (Wilson Foods), Smith International, Denny's, ForcEnergy, Commonwealth Oil, Zale Corporation, Hunt Brothers, First Republic Bank, Adelphia, Columbia Gas, and Bank of New England. A recognized expert in the field of bankruptcy law and litigation, he has been certified as a Business Bankruptcy Specialist by the Texas Board of Legal Specialization. He has testified before Congress on several occasions concerning bankruptcy legislation and is former chair of the Business Bankruptcy Committee of the American Bar Association, as well as an elected member of the American College of Bankruptcy.

ACKNOWLEDGMENTS

We wish to thank numerous people for their help in producing this book. Glenn Atkins of Garner Asset Management read and made helpful comments on every part of the book. Moreover, parts of chapters seven and eight were adapted with permission from "High-Yield Bonds," by Glenn E. Atkins and Ben Branch, *AAII Journal* (October 1991), © American Association of Individual Investors, 625 N. Michigan Ave., Suite 1900, Chicago, IL 60611. Kathy Welton has served effectively as editor. Nancy Ediger has processed these words expertly and saved us much embarrassment. In addition, we would like to thank Jeff Spiers, Jim Donnell and Crawford Moorefield for their assistance in chapters one and three.

While the authors have sought to verify the accuracy of the information contained herein, no warranties expressed or implied are given. Investing is an inherently risky endeavor, and investing in the securities of bankrupt companies is particularly risky. The book should help reduce the risks. But nothing is guaranteed, and nothing in this book should be construed to constitute specific legal advice.

CONTENTS

Preface v

About the Authors ix

Acknowledgments xi

Chapter 1: Inside the Bankruptcy Process 1

Chapter 2: Investing in Bankruptcies 31

Chapter 3: Bankruptcy/Reorganization Examples 56

Chapter 4: First Republic: A Case Study 82

Chapter 5: Estimating Bankruptcy Values 113

Chapter 6: Quantitative Analysis of High-Yield Securities 135

Chapter 7: Qualitative Aspects of High-Yield Analysis 154

Chapter 8: Types of Securities 162

Chapter 9: The Determinants of Yields 191

Appendix: Investment Information Sources 217

Glossary 220

Index 308

CHAPTER 1

INSIDE THE BANKRUPTCY PROCESS

INTRODUCTION

What is the Bankruptcy Code? Often, you will hear references to Chapter 10s, Chapter 7s, Chapter 11s and the like. You will also hear references to the Bankruptcy Code or the Bankruptcy Act. All this technical mishmash can be simply explained, so an investor with absolutely no legal training can understand the bankruptcy process sufficiently to make intelligent investment decisions.

The Bankruptcy Act of 1898 (commonly referred to as the Bankruptcy *Act*) no longer exists. It was replaced by the Bankruptcy Reform Act of 1978, which applies to all bankruptcies filed since October 1, 1979. This current law is called "The Bankruptcy *Code.*" The Code was significantly amended as of October 17, 2005. Whenever we refer to a section number, the reference is to the Bankruptcy *Code.* Coincidentally, and confusingly, the Bankruptcy Code is codified at *11* United States Code beginning at section 101. Your primary interest as an investor will be in Chapter 11s. *11* United States *Code* includes a number of bankruptcy chapters, only one of which is called "Chapter 11." In other words, 11 United States Code (11 U.S.C.) divides up the substantive law of bankruptcy into several different chapters. Chapters 1, 3 and 5 are generally applicable to all bankruptcy cases (e.g., 7s and 11s) unless specific reference is made to a particular problem. The specific chapters are: Chapter 7 (liquidation), Chapter 9 (municipalities), Chapter 11 (reorganizations, the one you are most interested in), Chapter 12 (family farmers), Chapter 13 (wage earners), and Chapter 15 (international cases). Each of these chapters specifies particular treatments for particular types of cases. You can line up the chapters that make up part of 11 U.S.C. (not just *Chapter 11*) as follows:

generally applicable	Chapter 1 -	General provisions and definitions;
	Chapter 3 -	Case administration;
	Chapter 5 -	The relationship between creditors, the debtor and the estate in certain situations.

specific treatments	Chapter 7	Liquidations;
	Chapter 9	Municipalities;
	Chapter 11	Reorganizations;
	Chapter 12	Family farmers with regular annual income;
	Chapter 13	Individuals with regular income; and
	Chapter 15	Cross border cases.

In addition, the Code provides for a United States Trustee. Each district has a United States Trustee. This person is one of three different types of trustees that may be encountered in a typical bankruptcy proceeding. The U.S. Trustee is an employee of the Department of Justice charged with attending to some administrative matters, as will be explained in greater detail below. The other two types of trustees, the bankruptcy trustee and the indenture trustee, will be discussed shortly.

The United States Supreme Court has promulgated certain (procedural) Bankruptcy Rules. Most of these rules are well beyond the scope of your interest. Certain local rules differ from district-to-district. Thus each judge is able to govern that particular district's practice and procedure so long as such rules are consistent with the Bankruptcy Rules.

State laws are also incorporated into the bankruptcy laws. While the states are unable to supersede federal bankruptcy laws in most instances, the Bankruptcy Code often expressly recognizes the state laws where they can be incorporated in a non-conflicting fashion.

State law approaches bankruptcies differently from federal bankruptcy laws in several respects. Most state laws are designed to reward quick action by creditors. In other words, the first creditor to attach the debtor's property is the one most likely to be paid. Federal bankruptcy law, on the other hand, is social legislation that tries to emphasize equality of treatment and promote the opportunity for debtors to obtain a fresh start. The overall federal theme is to prevent an individual creditor from enhancing its position relative to other creditors by acting with alacrity, once the debtor files for bankruptcy. In addition, federal bankruptcy law places severe limitations on a creditor's ability to collect or secure repayment of its debts in the time periods just before the bankruptcy.

Probably the most unusual and valuable feature of U.S. bankruptcy law is the ability it provides a debtor to receive a "discharge," or the equivalent of a discharge, from its debts, thereby providing the debtor with the ability to get a fresh start.

THEORETICAL APPROACHES

The Two Types of Bankruptcies — Liquidations and Reorganizations: Chapter 7 is designed for liquidations. In most other countries when a person seeks protection under the insolvency laws, a receiver simply collects and liquidates all the debtor's assets and distributes the proceeds to the ever-hungry creditors. The debtor often receives a discharge and walks away without being legally responsible for most of the debts incurred prior to bankruptcy. A U.S. Chapter 7 bankruptcy is conceptually similar to the bankruptcy procedures of most other countries. This chapter was significantly changed in 2005 to be less lenient to Chapter 7 debtors. The Chapter 7 debtor's assets are placed in the hands of the appointed bankruptcy trustee (different from the *U.S.* Trustee described above), who liquidates them for the best price available and distributes the proceeds. This bankruptcy trustee is charged with administering the estate as the liquidation process proceeds. He or she performs the duties the debtor would have performed had the estate remained outside of bankruptcy. The trustee may be elected by the creditors and must be a qualified, disinterested person. This individual is customarily awarded a fee of 1% to 3% of the estate for his or her services. More will be said on this subject later.

By contrast, rehabilitation is usually the theme in Chapter 11. This chapter provides an opportunity for the reorganization of a debtor, rather than a liquidation of its assets. The social policy of fresh start is incorporated into this chapter. U. S. Chapter 11 cases are distinguished from the way insolvencies are handled in Chapter 7 and in most of the rest of the world in one primary way: In Chapter 11, the debtor retains control of its assets and continues its operations. While under this protection, the debtor seeks to pay off creditors (often at a discount) over a period of time, pursuant to a plan approved by a bankruptcy court. In other words, the creditors by law can be forced to look solely to the future endeavors of the debtor for repayment. A cynic would criticize the social policy implications of this approach: It appears to allow the persons who led the company into its present difficulties to continue doing whatever they were doing. And what they had been doing ran the company into the ground. On the other hand, many bankruptcies, particularly after the heady LBO days of the 1980s or the dot.com boom of the 1990s, resulted from piling too much debt on too few assets. The same trend continues in the 2000s with hedge funds extending credit to risky businesses destined to fail. In some cases, however, the core business and its management may be potentially quite viable. By allowing for this fresh start, jobs may be saved and productive resources kept operating efficiently rather than being scrapped or put to a less productive use. In any case, the credit system in the United States is wealthy enough to afford this fresh start concept. According to the Administrative Office of U. S. courts, however, in only one out of every eight cases that file for Chapter 11 is the debtor able to reorganize successfully. A debtor's estate may also be liquidated in Chapter 11, because it is frequently less expensive and more efficient to do so than through the use of Chapter 7 and a Trustee.

The bankruptcy arena's seven key players:

1. The Judge of the Bankruptcy Court: This is the judge who presides over the case. He or she is referred the case by the relevant United States District Court and is a judicial officer operating under that referred authority.

2. The Debtor: This is the entity seeking relief in bankruptcy court. This unlucky entity used to be referred as "the Bankrupt." As a part of the Bankruptcy Reform Act that became effective in 1979, the phrase "the Bankrupt" was expunged from the statute because of negative connotations. The term lives on, however.

3. Secured/Unsecured Claimant: A creditor that holds a lien on property that belongs to the debtor or has a right of setoff against property of the debtor holds what is called a secured claim. A creditor that has no lien on any of the debtor's property holds an unsecured claim. If property owned by the debtor on which the secured creditor holds the lien is not at least equal in value to the amount of the claim, then the claim can be partially secured (the value of the collateral) and unsecured (the difference between the value of the collateral and the amount of the claim). A creditor may be either senior or subordinated to other creditors. Several layers of subordination may exist.

4. The Bankruptcy Trustee or Trustee of the Estate: Unlike the U.S. trustee, a bankruptcy trustee is not an employee of the federal government. Rather, he or she is a private citizen who is often a lawyer. Every Chapter 7 has a trustee. Sometimes a trustee is appointed in Chapter 11 cases, although not often. The interim trustee is appointed by the United States Trustee, and at their initial meeting (the "341 meeting"), creditors can elect a trustee to replace the appointed trustee.

The trustee is charged with liquidating the assets of the debtor and overseeing their equitable distribution.

5. The United States Trustee: This employee of the Department of Justice appoints bankruptcy trustees and creditors' committees, and performs other administrative tasks that relate to the smooth operation of the bankruptcy case.

6. Debtor in Possession: The debtor in a Chapter 11 case, if still in possession of the company's property (no trustee has been appointed), is called a debtor in possession. This debtor in possession has certain fiduciary duties akin to those of a trustee requiring it to operate its business in an equitable and fair manner.

7. The Creditors' Committee: These representatives of the creditors in Chapter 11 cases are appointed by the United States Trustee or the bankruptcy judge to oversee the debtor in possession and assist in the formulation and confirmation of a plan.

In addition to the above-mentioned players, a number of legal representatives are almost always important participants in the case. Specifically, the debtor in possession or bankruptcy trustee is virtually certain to retain counsel to represent it in the proceedings before the court. The creditors' committees almost always will have counsel, and individual creditors may also retain separate counsel. Each creditors' committee will usually retain separate legal counsel. Other professionals, such as accountants and investment bankers, may also be retained by the various parties . The fees of these professionals contribute to making bankruptcies so expensive. A bankruptcy lawyer, for example, can easily cost $200 to $800 per hour. plus expenses. One interested party (e.g., the senior creditors) may retain one law firm to achieve one objective (maximum recovery for the seniors) while a second group (e.g., the juniors) may have their lawyers pursue a conflicting objective (maximum recovery for the juniors). In a Chapter 11 case, the estate picks up the costs of both lawyers' work. Moreover, the claims for fees are administrative claims and have the highest priority in settling the affairs of the estate. Professionals such as lawyers and accountants are unlikely to be willing to take on bankruptcy work unless they are relatively sure that they will be paid. Generally they are not only paid but paid well.

Chapter 7: As previously mentioned, in Chapter 7, the debtor's property is collected, sold, and the proceeds distributed to creditors by a trustee. Additionally, the debtor is normally discharged from its liabilities.

The independent bankruptcy trustee collects and liquidates the property of the estate in Chapter 7. This trustee is charged with selling or otherwise disposing of the debtor's assets. He or she is the source of information concerning what property the debtor has for sale, and how it is to be sold. The bankruptcy clerk's office for the district in which the bankruptcy case is pending will provide the name of the trustee. While this trustee can operate the business of the debtor for a limited period, his or her primary responsibility is to see that the assets are sold. Frequently, no equity remains as property of the debtor on which a lien has been placed. Accordingly, the secured creditor may be permitted simply to take the property back. When this type of settlement occurs, contact the secured creditor if you wish to purchase what had been the debtor's property.

Chapter 11: Chapter 11s typically involve a business that the debtor hopes can be rehabilitated via a plan of reorganization. This process requires persuading the creditors to accept, and the court to approve, the proposed plan. A Chapter 11 case can begin either voluntarily, when a debtor takes action, or involuntarily, when certain of the debtor's creditors or their indenture trustee take action. This indenture trustee is the third of the three types of trustees who may be involved in a bankruptcy case. The indenture trustee (usually a bank, trust company or other secure institution) is named in the indenture agreement (a contract between bondholders and the bond issuer) as the bondholder's agent charged with enforcing the terms of the indenture.

With an eye toward rehabilitation, generally under Chapter 11, the debtor will be allowed to continue to operate the business. Court supervision is usually restricted to transactions out of the ordinary course of business. Although optional provisions for bankruptcy trustees are provided in Chapter 11, they are seldom used. The debtor itself, as debtor in possession, has all the rights and duties of a trustee. Usually an unambiguous abuse of those duties is required before a trustee is appointed.

In most Chapter 11s, the debtor will work with its creditors (especially the creditors' committee) to formulate a plan of reorganization. This plan sets out for the creditors who will receive how much (in cash and/or securities) and over what period of time. An exclusivity period occurs at the beginning of each case during which time only the debtor can file a plan of reorganization. Once that exclusivity period expires, any party to the case can file a plan proposing how the estate's creditors are to be paid.

Typically, any plan will divide the various creditors into several classes of claims including unsecured claimants and secured claimants. As a general requirement, any claim in a particular class must be treated the same as all other claims in that class.

After a Chapter 11 plan is filed, the creditors and stockholders of the debtor will frequently be solicited in order to obtain their approval of the plan. As part of this approval process, a full disclosure must be made by filing a statement with the court, and the court must confirm that the statement contains adequate and accurate information before it can be sent to creditors for a vote. The disclosure statement is the best source of information outside of, or possibly including, an original prospectus, with respect to any particular company in which you may chose to invest.

The final state of a Chapter 11 case is the confirmation of a plan. Even if approved by a favorable vote of the creditors, the bankruptcy judge can still refuse to confirm a plan if it fails to meet certain other conditions: the plan must be proposed in good faith, feasible, and all creditors must receive no less than they would receive in a Chapter 7 liquidation. Moreover, the plan can be confirmed by the bankruptcy judge even though not every class accepts the plan. This overruling of a dissenting class is called a "cram-down." If one class of non-insider creditors does accept a plan, the court can still confirm the plan as long as it judges it to be "fair and equitable" and finds that no class of claims that is junior to a non-assenting impaired class receives anything until the non-assenting impaired class has been fully compensated.

Why would a debtor who has a choice agree to go through bankruptcy proceedings? The answer is that the debtor who emerges from bankruptcy obtains a fresh start. Corporations don't technically get a discharge in the traditional sense. Nonetheless, the confirmation of the plan effectively discharges the successful Chapter 11 debtor from its pre-petition debts except for those set out in the plan or the order of confirmation. Chapter 11 is a unique creation often taken for granted in the United States. Do not assume that it makes economic sense. Data indicates that its sole justification is as social legislation. The U.S. is hardly the only country that has a credit system healthy enough to place its legal system behind a statute that allows the people who ran a company into the ground to continue in control of the company. Some other countries, including Britain, Italy and France, are actually passing statutes with rehabilitative features. However, none came close to the U.S. statute's forgiveness and latitude.

Recall, however, that creditors in the aggregate must generally consent to any successful plan of reorganization. True, the debtor in possession manages the estate in Chapter 11 (at least at the outset). Eventually the creditors, particularly if they are assertive, tend to gain the upper hand. Only a reorganization plan acceptable to the creditor groups (especially the senior creditors) is confirmable. Still, a confirmed plan may or may not provide a favorable outcome for the creditors. Don't try to reinforce your investment decision with assumptions that the legal system will either guarantee the success or failure of your investment judgment. The social motivation of the debtor and his or her lawyer should have little to do with your decision; their ability to "pull off" a successful reorganization does.

HOW CASES GET STARTED

A bankruptcy case may commence in either of two general ways voluntarily or involuntarily. Voluntary cases begin when a debtor files a petition requesting relief in the appropriate district: the one in which for the 180 days or majority thereof immediately preceding the commencement of the case, the domicile, residence, principal place of business, or principal assets of the debtor were located.

Involuntary cases are commenced under either Chapter 7 or Chapter 11 by creditors having claims that are not contingent. Generally three unsecured creditors with claims totaling at least $12,300 must join in the filing of the petition. In the rare case of a debtor having fewer than 12 creditors, a single creditor having an unsecured claim of $12,300 or more is permitted to file.

A great deal of confusion exists over what happens when creditors file an involuntary bankruptcy petition against an obligor. In very simple terms all that has happened is that a lawsuit has been filed. The debtor is not automatically placed into bankruptcy. The debtor has the right to file an answer and litigate the issue of whether it should be in bankruptcy. While this litigation proceeds, the debtor receives all of the benefits of the automatic stay, yet is allowed to operate his or her business without having to file bankruptcy schedules or come to court for permission to conduct the business's affairs. The issue that is generally litigated is whether the debtor is paying its debts as they mature. The petition is likely to succeed if a creditor can establish that the debtor has failed to pay a valid debt when due (allowing for the passage of the grace period). The involuntary petition will also succeed if a receiver or custodian has taken possession of substantially all of the debtor's property. While this litigation wears on, the debtor continues to operate its business without a trustee, unless a court finds that one is necessary to prevent loss of the estate's property. Despite the technical freedom of operation that exists after a filing of an involuntary petition, the filing spells disaster for many businesses. Their reputations are severely impaired by the stigma of being forced into bankruptcy. For this reason, creditors who file unwarranted petitions may be held liable for serious consequential damages and attorneys' fees.

A debtor against whom an involuntary Chapter 7 is filed has a right to convert the case to a Chapter 11 proceeding. A Chapter 7 debtor that filed a voluntary petition can also seek the court's approval to convert the case to a Chapter 11 unless the case started as a Chapter 11. In addition, the bankruptcy court can convert a Chapter 11 case to Chapter 7 or dismiss the case for cause. One such cause would be the inability of the debtor to effectuate a plan.

The bankruptcy court may, at its discretion, abstain from hearing a bankruptcy case even if the technical requirements for such a case have been met. The bankruptcy judge's decision to abstain cannot be appealed. Courts have been known to overrule a bankruptcy petition when a debtor has shown substantial progress in reaching an out of court solution to its problems.

A bankruptcy court may, at any point in the case, dismiss a Chapter 11 case for cause. Such a dismissal would generally occur when the court believed it to be in the best interest of the creditors and the estate.

HOW CASES OPERATE – ADMINISTERING
THE ASSETS OF A CHAPTER 11 DEBTOR

Understanding the boundaries of how a debtor operates its business and disposes of its assets is critical to an understanding of the other chapters dealing with the timing of investments. The prime immediate benefit that debtors receive by filing Chapter 11 is an automatic stay of the acts of creditors to collect from the debtor. At the time this stay becomes effective, an "estate" is created. This bankruptcy estate is conceptually much like a probate estate. All of the debtor's property passes into this estate upon the filing. Not surprisingly, the use and sale of property of this estate is subject to court supervision.

The stay is designed to give a Chapter 11 debtor time to prepare and propose a plan. The stay ensures orderly administration of the estate while that process proceeds. This very broad stay cannot be taken lightly. For example, creditors cannot proceed to enforce their liens and cannot take steps to seize assets. Moreover, the stay has the effect of stopping the accrual of interest. Technically a claim for post-petition (post-bankruptcy filing) interest is allowable. As a practical matter, however, such claims are rarely collectible. They are subordinated to even the junior most creditor claims for principal and pre-petition interest. Very few actions are excepted from the scope of the stay. Creditors may request relief from the stay for specified reasons including situations where the debtor has no equity in the property and the property is not necessary for an effective reorganization.

What does the secured creditor receive in exchange for giving up the ability to look to its collateral? In recognition of the secured creditor's due process rights the creditor must be furnished what is called "adequate protection." This "adequate protection" can take many forms. Additional liens may be given, as well as numerous control protections relating to the use of the collateral. The relief may be broad enough to satisfy a secured creditor to the extent that the creditor may not care if the bankruptcy case ever ends.

Indeed, secured creditors are the one category that may be able to continue to receive interest payments during a bankruptcy proceeding. If their collateral is central to a business's operation (e.g., rolling stock for a railroad), the debtor may have little choice but to pay interest on the collateralized obligations (e.g., equipment trust certificates). The collateral trust bonds of Penn Central railroad, for example, continued to pay interest throughout the bankruptcy and reorganization process.

The restrictions on operation do not bar the Chapter 11 debtor from using or selling the property of the estate that has been created. However, notice and an opportunity for a hearing are required before property of the estate can be used or sold outside of the ordinary course of business. The court must evaluate a request to use or sell property of the estate outside of the ordinary course of business. In performing this evaluation, the court considers the concept of adequate protection, as well as whether the proposal constitutes a scheme to bypass the safeguards afforded to creditors under the provisions setting up the process for obtaining approval of plans of reorganization. In addition, the proposal by the debtor must prove to be within the sound exercise of good business judgment. After a consideration of these factors, the court may even order the sale of a secured creditor's collateral free and clear of the creditor's lien, with the lien then attached to the proceeds. A debtor is not obligated to administer all of the assets in the estate. It may simply turn the ownership of some or all of the pledged assets over to the secured creditors.

EXECUTORY CONTRACTS

A debtor that files under Chapter 11 may be in the midst of unperformed obligations (contracts, etc.) with third parties. The debtor must, at some point, decide whether to accept (assume) or reject these obligations. These incomplete transactions are called executory contracts. Leases make up a separate and special category of executory transactions. Usually, those executory contracts that are beneficial to the estate are assumed by the debtor and those that are not beneficial (e.g., burdensome union contracts, requirements contracts) are rejected. Under the 2005 amendments to federal law, the debtor is deemed to have rejected its leases of non-residential property if it does not assume them after 120 days (which a court may extend for an additional 90 days). Aside from the leases, a Chapter 11 debtor has no definite time deadline in which to make its decision to assume or reject many of its other executory contracts. Any third party to the obligation may seek a court order giving the debtor a definite time period to make a decision, however. The rejection of the executory contract or lease constitutes a breach. Generally the third party whose contract was rejected will have a claim against the debtor for its damages.

If a debtor wishes to assume a contract in default, it must cure the default, pay the damages and provide adequate assurance for future performance of its continuing obligations. Clauses in contracts stating that they cannot be assumed in bankruptcy are unenforceable. Court approval is necessary for acceptance or rejection; however, the standard is the debtor's business judgment. This rather subjective standard is quite easy to meet. Most of the controversy deals with whether a contract is executory or performed to the extent that it cannot be assumed or rejected.

Most importantly, if the debtor elects to assume the contract or lease but then fails to perform, the non-debtor party is entitled to a post-petition administrative priority claim. This claim ranks above unsecured claims and the like; generally, these claims are satisfied in full, although on occasion a debtor can be administratively insolvent. However, this is the exception in large bankruptcy cases.

When a trustee is appointed in a Chapter 11 case, the trustee takes possession of the estate. In a Chapter 7 case, a trustee always takes possession of the estate.

THE AVOIDING POWERS

The Bankruptcy Code is designed to ensure equality in the distribution of the debtor's estate. It also seeks to discourage pre-bankruptcy attacks by creditors attempting to obtain an advantage vis-à-vis the estate's other creditors. Congress also sought to discourage debtors from favoring selected creditors over others through the transfer of assets and other pre-petition actions. These discouragements are codified in prohibitions of preferential transfers, fraudulent transfers and invalid liens.

Preferences are transfers (payments) that enable a creditor to receive a greater percentage of its claim against the debtor than the creditor would have received if the transfer had not been made and the creditor had instead participated in the bankruptcy estate distribution. The key time period for this "look back" is generally 90 days prior to filing, while the debtor was insolvent. The look-back period is one year for those creditors who are insiders. One may be classified as an insider by being either a high-level executive of the company or a major investor having substantial influence over the direction of the company. Usually a 10% or greater ownership of the common stock will qualify one as an insider. This general precept relating to preferences and the look-back period has a number of exceptions and is subject to a number of complex rules of interpretation.

The Bankruptcy Code also invalidates liens against the debtor that are not properly recorded under applicable federal or state laws. In addition, tardily perfected liens are disallowed. In general, the concept of the bankruptcy estate places the debtor in the position of a hypothetical bona fide purchaser without notice of the actual facts. Accordingly, technical imperfections in the creditor's liens may be avoided without regard to the actual state of the relationship or understandings between the debtor and the creditor.

Transfers made by a debtor or for the benefit of the debtor with the actual intent to hinder, delay or defraud creditors are subject to avoidance as fraudulent conveyances. More controversial is the ability to avoid transfers in which the debtor received less than a reasonably equivalent value and was insolvent or became insolvent as a result of the transfer. This line of reasoning is the cornerstone of the attacks on LBOs, in which bankruptcy creditors contend that highly leveraged transactions (with the debtor's assets) defraud the existing creditors by leaving them unpaid.

HOW CASES SETTLE UP – PAYING CLAIMS AND DISTRIBUTING ASSETS

Claims must have been deemed to be allowed in order for the owner to receive any payment. A claim is deemed allowed once filed, unless a party with standing in the instant case objects. In general, post-filing interest on claims is effectively disallowed in many cases. Technically, these claims are subordinated to all other creditor claims. The amounts that can be asserted on claims for future rent payments are severely limited, as are claims arising from terminated employment contracts.

The Bankruptcy Code sets out some very exact priorities of distribution. In general, the expenses of administering the estate are paid first (the lawyers come out first). Certain employee claims and taxes are paid prior to the general unsecured creditors, who are paid in turn prior to holders who filed late claims and claims for fines and penalties. These priorities reflect deliberate decisions by

Congress to favor certain groups that might withhold their goods and services if their claims were not given special treatment.

The concept of subordination is expressly recognized in bankruptcy. The Bankruptcy Code states that contractual subordination arrangements – in which consideration otherwise payable to one subordinated class is thereby required to be paid over to its senior class until that class's full claim is satisfied – are to be honored in bankruptcy cases. In light of the numerous other contractual rights that are subject to avoidance in the bankruptcy court, this recognition is notable. This type of treatment is also well nigh essential for subordination to be meaningful. If subordination provisions were avoidable in bankruptcies, they would not accomplish the task for which they were devised: to allow a debtor to access additional capital while affording superior protection to those existing creditors whose prior advancement of credit diminished such protection. The treatment of those arrangements is also quite important for those who invest in bankruptcies. Most publicly traded investment opportunities for debtors with high-yield obligations have outstanding multiple "layers" of publicly held indebtedness. These obligations frequently contain provisions subordinating certain of those obligations to others under a variety of circumstances. Thus, one is likely to encounter terms like senior subordinated and junior subordinated debentures to the capital structure.

The Bankruptcy Code also recognizes, but does not spell out, the ability of the bankruptcy judge to subordinate claims based upon equitable considerations. Generally, equitable subordination is applied to a creditor who has committed fraud or other inequitable conduct that has given that creditor an unfair advantage over other creditors.

HOW CASES ARE RESTRUCTURED: THE CHAPTER 11 PLAN AND THE DISCLOSURE STATEMENT

In the early stages of a Chapter 11 case, the preparation and approval of the reorganization plan is under the absolute control of the debtor. The Bankruptcy Code gives the debtor an initial period of 120 days during which it, and it alone, can propose a plan of reorganization. Until the 2005 amendments, courts were usually inclined to extend this period indefinitely in major cases. Since 2005, exclusivity may not be extended beyond 18 months from the date the case was filed. At the end of the exclusivity period, any party in interest can file and seek to obtain approval of its plan.

The plan as proposed will classify claims that are substantially similar in the same class. Usually a plan proponent will try to create classes in such a way as to ensure a favorable vote on the plan. Secured and unsecured creditors will usually be classified separately, for example.

Parties whose legal equitable and contractual rights are unaltered will not be required to vote in favor of a plan for it to be approved. To be counted as favoring the plan, each class of those impaired parties, i.e., those whose legal rights are altered, must vote two-thirds in an amount of their claims and more than one-half in number of claims voting in support of the plan.

The court requires those who formulate the plan to prepare and distribute to the creditors a document called a disclosure statement. The purpose of this document is to provide creditors adequate information so that they can cast their votes knowledgeably. Its contents must be approved by the court before it is sent to the creditors voting on the plan. Adequate information means information both accurate and sufficient in detail to enable a reasonably able investor to make an informed judgment about the plan's acceptability.

Once the votes of the creditors have been received, the court holds what is called a confirmation hearing to consider the tally of votes and hear evidence on a variety of issues: (1) that the plan has been proposed in good faith; (2) that the claims have been classified properly; (3) that the plan is feasible; (4) that its acceptance has not been procured by any means prohibited by law; and (5) that certain other technical requirements specified in the Bankruptcy Code have been met. Whether the plan is in the best interests of creditors is usually the prime area of concern. To pass this best interest test requires that each impaired creditor receive more than the creditor would receive in a Chapter 7 liquidation.

Even if a class of claims does not accept the plan, the law permits the plan to be approved over the vote of the dissenting class. This process involves what is commonly referred to as the "cram-down." To accomplish this overruling of the dissenting class, the plan must be shown not to discriminate unfairly and to be fair and equitable with respect to impaired non-accepting classes. By not discriminating, the law generally means only that the holders of claims or interests with similar legal rights cannot be treated differently. To be fair and equitable to a class of dissenting secured creditors, the secured creditors must either receive the indubitable value equivalent of their claims or retain their liens and receive deferred cash payments of a value equal to their interest in the estate's interest in the property.

For a plan to be fair and equitable as to a class of dissenting unsecured creditors, the plan must provide either that the unsecured creditors receive property of a value equal to the allowed amount of the claim, or that the holder of any claim or interest junior to the dissenting class will not receive or retain any property on account of the junior claim. In other words, the classes below the dissenting unsecured class must receive nothing if the dissenting class is to be crammed down. This requirement is referred to as the absolute priority rule.

An exception to the absolute priority rule has been created, often referred to as the new value exception. This new value exception is used by equity holders seeking to retain all or a portion of their equity interest by making what amounts to a capital contribution. In exchange for this contribution they retain their interest, even in the face of a dissenting vote by a senior class of creditors.

THE CHAPTER 11 PLAN PROCESS AND THE ABSOLUTE PRIORITY RULE

Since the initial edition of our book, the United States Supreme Court has issued an opinion interpreting the Bankruptcy Code provisions relating to the "new value exception" to the absolute priority rule, under which equity holders of a Chapter 11 debtor might attempt to establish that their proposed contribution of new value permits them to retain their interest. The Court held that the "new value exception" does not permit contribution of such new value without competing bidding or some other mechanism to establish the adequacy of the contribution. This ruling benefits a bankruptcy investor. The Supreme Court observed that competing plans provide a better method for valuation of reorganized equity interests when new value plans are proposed. Among the advantages are the Code's disclosure requirements, which generate informed competing bids for the new equity. Before the Court's ruling, substantial uncertainty existed as to whether a lower class of creditors could receive a distribution under a plan of reorganization through the simple mechanism of contributing new value to the bankruptcy confirmation process. This uncertainty made the analysis of purchasing an interest in a Chapter 11 debtor more speculative than is currently the case.

After its approval in a confirmation hearing, the plan is consummated by the parties who exchange the documents and cash required to effectuate the reorganization described in the plan. Upon a report to the judge that the plan is consummated and the pending legal issues wrapped up, the case is closed.

HOW BANKRUPTCIES ARE EXPEDITED: PREPACKAGED CHAPTER 11S

The Bankruptcy Code permits potential candidates for Chapter 11 to solicit creditor approval of a reorganization plan prior to filing Chapter 11. These prepackaged bankruptcies ("prepacks") have gained some measure of popularity. Prepacks are designed to allow the debtor to obtain advance approval of what would amount to an exchange offer of public debt. But such prepacks, operating under the Bankruptcy Code, only require the two-thirds in amount and one-half in number requirement of creditor approval. Much more stringent requirements are usually found in the public indenture. Indeed the Trust Indenture Act prohibits changes in coupon rates, principal or maturity outside of bankruptcy without unanimous consent of the creditors.

The first advantage in the pre-bankruptcy solicitation vehicle is that a court-approved disclosure statement is not required. However, the solicitation must comply with applicable non-bankruptcy law. In particular, the securities laws must be complied with, or, if none are applicable, then the disclosure statement will be reviewed when the plan is submitted for approval.

The second and primary advantage of a prepackaged plan is its ability to squeeze those hold-out bondholders or minority creditors that attempt to obtain special treatment. Otherwise, such holdouts will seek to be paid off at a higher rate than those that are attempting to cooperate with the debtor. Individual bondholders do not have to accept an out-of-court exchange offer. On the other hand, the results of an approved reorganization plan apply to dissenting bondholders, as well as those who voted in favor.

The third advantage to this approach is the speed with which a debtor can go in and out of a Chapter 11 proceeding. In 2006, for example, one prepack was accomplished in a single day. The fast action tends to save substantial sums of money in administrative costs and lessen the adverse impact on the debtor's business. While the debtor still must comply with many technical requirements of Chapter 11, the advance approval process shortcuts much debate and acrimony because of the realistic advance communication that generally takes place before the filing.

2005 AMENDMENTS TO THE BANKRUPTCY CODE

In 2005, Congress passed a fairly sweeping set of amendments to the Bankruptcy Code. The vast majority of these amendments dealt with tightening the requirements for an individual or personal Chapter 7 bankruptcy. However, some amendments were directed toward perceived softness on the part of many bankruptcy judges in allowing the debtor in large reorganization cases entirely too much time and leniency to go through the Chapter 11 process. The primary change, as we noted above, is shortening to 18 months the length of time under which the debtor has the exclusive right to file a plan of reorganization. At any rate, the debtor is limited to no more than 210 days for assuming or rejecting its leases. A new section was added to prevent key-employee retention programs from being entered into between the debtors and insiders without a strong showing of need. Utility companies were given stronger rights for requiring deposits; certain administrative priorities were given for pre-bankruptcy sellers. The impact of these changes is to require a very large "war chest" for any debtor going into Chapter 11. Importantly, the Bankruptcy Code was bona fide to allow bankruptcy courts to order the U.S. Trustee to reconstitute creditors and equity committees. Previously, the court's ability to interfere with the decisions of the U.S. Trustee in this regard was unclear. The Bankruptcy Code was also amended to require the U.S. Trustee to move for the appointment of a Chapter 11 Trustee if reasonable grounds existed to suspect that the chief executives or current members of the debtor's governing body were engaged in fraud, or dishonest or criminal conduct. Presumably, this change is in response to the Enron and WorldCom cases, where no trustee was appointed.

BUYING AND SELLING CLAIMS AND INVESTING IN NEWLY REORGANIZED DEBTORS

Several specialist investment firms have sprung up to deal specifically in the claims of bankrupt companies. Note, however, that a purchased claim still has the same rights and disabilities that rested with the original seller. In other words, if the claim is based upon fraud, or an invalid document, its sale to a third party will not alter the debtor's defense.

More often than you might believe, creditors are anxious to sell claims for immediate cash. They choose to sell even though they must accept a steep discount rather than wait on the potentially higher recovery in bankruptcy. Many unfortunate creditors encounter the "domino effect" – a debt owed to them by a customer who files for bankruptcy imperiled their own companies as well. Accountants will often advise the creditor to sell a claim to capture its associated tax benefits rather than keeping it on the books and waiting to derive the tax benefits.

Additionally, certain financial institutions are restricted in their ownership of distressed securities. These institutions would prefer to avoid the regulatory hassles that might otherwise result from owning stock in a particular debtor company, in the event of a plan that proposes a stock-for-debt swap.

The purchasing of claims has also been accelerated by the use of purchased claims to obtain control of the debtor company. This was the motivation for a number of claims purchased in the case of ForcEnergy Inc., for example. Once it emerged from bankruptcy in February 2000, those who purchased ForcEnergy claims were able to exercise control. Purchasing of unsecured claims for takeovers raises several problems. Specifically, purchasers may need to comply with tender offer requirements or comply with securities laws, despite a general "safe harbor" from the securities laws.

An additional area for caution when purchasing claims is to make sure that the claim is not subject to attack on the basis that the seller received a preferential transfer or a fraudulent conveyance. Either objection can, if valid, be used to disallow a claim. However, the transferee of the claim would not be liable for the preferential payment. Rather the preferential payment or fraudulent conveyance would only be used to disallow the claim until the preference was returned.

The role of the bankruptcy court in connection with the purchase and sale of claims in bankruptcy is extremely limited. The rules are not intended to encourage or discourage the transfer of claims. If an objection is filed, the court's role is to determine whether the transfer is effective under non-bankruptcy law.

TRANSFER OF CLAIMS

The Federal Rules of Bankruptcy Procedure (Rule 3001(e)(2)) states that once a claim on which a proof of claim has been filed has been transferred, the transferee should file evidence of the transfer with the bankruptcy clerk. If a proof of claim has not been filed before the transfer is made and the transfer was not made for reasons of securing an obligation, only the transferee may file the proof of claim. The court procedures are designed to protect transferors and do not restrict transfers in any way.

The entire process of buying and selling claims is not generally subject to bankruptcy review, except in cases where the Debtor has been prejudiced or some sort of inequitable conduct on the part of the transferor or transferee has been alleged.

The law recognizes the recent emergence of what amounts to an auction market for claims after a bankruptcy case has been filed. The intention of the law is to restrict any inclination by particular judges to discourage such transfers.

The primary area of concern arises when members of creditors' committees who possess confidential information trade the securities. Customarily, members of creditors' committees are required to sign confidentiality agreements before debtors reveal sensitive information that would bear on the value and recoverability of claims in the particular case. Trading of the company's securities by those in possession of material nonpublic information is severely restricted. In general, one possessing such information is restricted to trades with other restricted investors and with non-restricted investors who are properly informed of the restricted person's possession of nonpublic information. This informing process is usually accomplished through documentation suitable to both parties prior to trade execution. When in possession of material, nonpublic information, many securities firms will inform parties that they are executing transactions on an agency basis only, not as a principal.

The Bankruptcy Code requires that all votes on a plan be made in good faith. Accordingly, claims acquired for the purpose of voting for or against a plan for reasons that amount to pure malice, strikes or blackmail, or for the purpose of destroying an enterprise in order to advance a competitor, will be disallowed. However, the mere purchase of claims for the purpose of gaining negative votes against a plan is not per se disallowable. On the other hand, purchasing claims in order to acquire control without filing a disclosure statement that reveals that interest may be restricted.

In connection with the LTV Energy Products bankruptcy proceeding, a corporation was formed offering to purchase unsecured claims for 33 cents on the dollar. More than 400 creditors accepted the offer. The corporation filed notices of transfer, as specified otherwise herein with the Bankruptcy Court. The debtor challenged the transfer as, in essence, a hostile takeover of LTV Energy. Judge Burton Lifland refused to approve the transfer, finding that the corporation had not disclosed that it was a front for another entity (Regal, Inc.) that was attempting to obtain control of LTV through the unsecured claim purchase mechanism. It was Judge Lifland's contention that Regal intended to propose a full 100 cents on the dollar recovery plan after acquiring all the claims (as cited in Stolts, "Trade Debt Buyers: Players Still Active Despite Variable Market and Judicial Objections," *Turnarounds and Workouts*, May 1, 1990). Judge Lifland held that the selling creditors had a right to an "informed judgment" before such a purchase could take place. He further required the claims purchaser to supply the selling creditor with a disclosure document. A similar order had been made, and rescinded, in the Allegheny International case, as well as in the Revere Copper and Brass case. These situations are the rare exception, rather than the rule, in claims-purchasing cases. They obviously represent an attempt to impose a judge-made rule of law in an area where no statutory authority is readily apparent for holdings of this nature.

Purchasers of claims and interests after a bankruptcy has been filed may find their activity viewed with favor by the relevant governmental agencies (bankruptcy court, SEC, other regulators, etc.), because they broaden the debtor's source of future capital through an enhancement of the public market for its Chapter 11 debt. In addition, the purchasing creditor is much more likely to be an active participant in the reorganization process and provide other creditors (who are willing to take a steep discount) a cash market for their claims.

INVESTMENT POTENTIAL

Experience has shown that selective purchases of non-equity securities of companies as they emerge from Chapter 11 can be profitable. Nonetheless an aversion to a company emerging from Chapter 11 still exists in the securities market. This aversion frequently causes the securities market to underestimate the potential of the reorganized company.

One bit of evidence on this matter comes from a JPMorgan study ("Post-Bankruptcy Equity Investing, the Chapter after Chapter 11," January 9, 2004). That study covered 117 companies that emerged from Chapter 11 over 15 years starting in 1988. They found an average return of about 88% in the first 12 months, far above any of the well-known benchmarks. The study does, however, add two important caveats. First, it finds that the volatility of these stocks is high and that the favorable performance is concentrated in particular sectors, especially telecommunications services. Moreover, as usual, past performance is no guarantee of future performance.

For example, when Amerco emerged from Chapter 11 in March 2004, it traded at 23.50. Within two years it traded at 106.25. This kind of performance has been going on for some time. The Itel Corporation confirmed its plan of reorganization in 1983, and its stock started trading late that year, at 1/8 bid, 1-3/8 ask. Six months later, the stock was trading at 3. Itel's preferred traded at 22 upon emergence from bankruptcy and six months later traded at 26.

These are not, however, buy-and-hold securities, in many cases. For example, when Braniff Airways emerged from its first bankruptcy in September 1983, its new common stock traded at 2. A year later it traded at 4. By early 1991 it was worthless.

Other favorable examples of this post-emergence upward swing include: Magellan Health, which emerged on January 6, 2004 at 27. By June 2006, it traded at 40.70. Seitel traded at 1.30 when it emerged on July 2, 2004; By June 2006, it traded at 3.92. When Allied Supermarkets emerged from bankruptcy in October 1981, its common stock traded at 7/16 bid. Three years later the stock sold for 2 3/4. Mego International confirmed its plan in late 1983 with its common stock at 20 cents; six months later the same shares traded at 2 1/8. Northwestern Corp. came out of Chapter 11 on November 1, 2004. Its stock went from 25.68 on that date to 34 within 18 months. HRT Industries confirmed its plan February 1984. The new common stock traded at 1 3/4. Six months later the stock was selling at 5 1/8. US Airways traded at 19.30 on September 27, 2005 when it emerged. Within a year, it hit 52.18. Some post-bankruptcy shares have been losers, however. Exide Technologies emerged from Chapter 11 on May 5, 2004. Two years later the stock was down from 22.01 to 4.57. Wilson Foods Corporation had been up and down after it confirmed its plan on February 28, 1984, with more negative trends. The company was acquired by Doskocil, Inc., which filed its own Chapter 11 in 1990. By late 1991, Doskocil common shares were traded at close to $1 per share. When Doskocil came out of Chapter 11 on October 31, 1991, its new common shares traded at $10 a share. By February 1992, the same shares of Doskocil were up 40% to $14 a share! The holders of the pre-bankruptcy common stock were virtually wiped out.

The above scorekeeping was inspired by a statement made in a law review article in 1983:

> At present, a substantial evidence as to the nature of the bankruptcy bargain does not exist. The lack of good empirical work is notable and lamentable. Even for reorganization of public companies, plans are often unreported.

Roe, supra at 537, n. 32.

Usually the official disclosure statement does not contain an estimate of the per-share valuation that is easily understood. Of the above examples, only one disclosure statement gave an estimate of per-share valuation: the Itel disclosure statement estimated a preferred-share value of 22 1/2 to 26 1/2, and a common share value of 1 1/2 to 2 1/2.

THE PURCHASE OF ASSETS OF AN INSOLVENT COMPANY IMMEDIATELY PRIOR TO BANKRUPTCY

Often everyone who is reasonably well informed will be able to conclude that a particular company is headed for protection under Chapter 11 of the bankruptcy laws. Frequently, opportunities will arise for an attractively priced purchase of stock or other assets from the insolvent company.

The two basic methods of purchase are stock acquisition and asset acquisition. With a stock acquisition, the purchaser becomes liable for all of the debts and obligations of the seller (in the event of the purchase of all of the stock). In an asset acquisition, the buyer purchases some assets of the insolvent company and, hopefully, limits its liability by virtue of the method of acquisition. Of course, when a purchase occurs after Chapter 11, many of the successor problems are eliminated. In addition to environmental concerns (asbestos problems, toxic waste, etc.) the purchaser of assets can become liable in four basic areas. These exceptions to the general rule are as follows:

  a. Where the circumstances surrounding the transaction warrant a finding that a consolidation or merger of the purchasing and selling corporation occurred;
  b. Where an expressed or implied agreement assumes the outside debts;
  c. Where the purchaser is a mere continuation of the seller;
  d. Where the transaction was, in fact, fraudulent.

Primary areas of concern in the purchase of assets of an insolvent corporation outside of bankruptcy exist in the areas of product liability and environmental liability exposure. These areas require due diligence and an audit of both environmental issues and possible product liability claims under the same product lines.

Assignments for the benefit of creditors are generally exempt under state law. Transfers in settlement of a security interest or lien are also generally exempt, as are sales made by executives, administrators, and receivers in the course of judicial or administrative proceedings.

Fraudulent Conveyance Problems

Purchasing either assets or stock at a bargain from a seller that needs fast cash is a well-known and widely practiced activity. However, aggressive bankruptcy lawyers now tend to attack such purchases as being for inadequate consideration. The fraudulent conveyance statutes of both state and federal Bankruptcy Codes provide the general legal basis to attack such sales prior to bankruptcy. Those statutes may make the purchaser personally liable for the value of the assets acquired. The Uniform Fraudulent Transfer Act and Uniform Fraudulent Conveyance Act, as well as Section 544(b) of the Bankruptcy Code, exist to protect the creditors of an insolvent seller, just as the bulk transfer laws exist to protect this group. Note that the purchaser need not have committed actual fraud for the transaction to be found to be a fraudulent conveyance. Indeed, all that may be necessary for a fraudulent conveyance finding is for the assets' negotiated price to be unreasonably low and certain other conditions to obtain. For example, the sale can be attacked if (1) insolvency of the seller follows the transfer for inadequate consideration; (2) the seller is left with inadequate capital to engage in business; or, (3) the seller is unable to pay its debts when they are due after the transaction. Understanding the facts and circumstances surrounding such questions like adequacy of consideration and insolvency require serious legal help, of a specialized nature. Obviously, caution is advisable with prospective pre-bankruptcy purchases when these factors appear to be present.

Methods of Purchase

Assuming and Paying the Sellers' Debts: In purchasing assets from a seller about to go into bankruptcy, part of the transaction will frequently contain a provision under which the purchaser agrees contractually to assume or directly pay off certain of the selling party's creditor claims. This type of transaction requires considerable caution. Paying certain creditors outside of bankruptcy while not paying others can result in an attack under the fraudulent transfer laws.

The payment of a debt that is not the seller's obligation, but is an indebtedness of an affiliate or an insider of the selling company, raises additional issues. Consideration or payment going to a creditor that holds an obligation from both the seller and the third party can be attacked after the transaction as not benefiting the seller directly. Thus, transactions of this nature require an inquiry as to whether any accommodation makers or guarantors are involved in the deal and whether the value being received is sufficient in terms of *just* the seller.

Purchases at Foreclosure Sales: Some courts have construed the Bankruptcy Code to require a certain percentage payment of the fair value of property sold at a foreclosure sale. Failure to make an adequate payment at a foreclosure sale has caused the sale to be set aside later as a fraudulent conveyance. The general benchmark figure thrown around in many jurisdictions, although certainly not universally adopted, is known as the "70% rule." While widely criticized, this rule has, on occasion, been stated to apply to foreclosure sales of all types of property. In other words, if the price bid at a foreclosure sale does not equal at least 70% of the fair market value, the sale may subsequently be attacked. Obviously, this creates a need for some reliable appraisal or estimate of the market value of the property prior to the purchase at a foreclosure sale. In short, a foreclosure purchaser needs to be prepared to justify the purchase in a subsequent attack if the seller ultimately goes into bankruptcy court.

Leveraged Buyouts ("LBOs"): A detailed discussion of the intricacies of this issue is well beyond the scope of this material. Nonetheless, LBO purchasers have provided a fertile field for litigation. An LBO in simple terms consists of a purchaser using the company's assets as collateral to finance the company's acquisition. The proceeds of the sale are paid over to the seller's shareholders. The selling company's unsecured creditors are left in place. This type of transaction typically creates a company that is heavily burdened with debt and/or undercapitalized. Frequently, the LBOed company becomes a likely candidate for bankruptcy. The transaction is also likely to be attacked after the fact as a fraudulent conveyance. While the purchaser's liability is a matter for discussion in the future, this type of transaction requires careful legal structuring and caution.

In any asset purchase prior to bankruptcy, as well as a purchase of substantial amounts of stock prior to its filing for bankruptcy, caution needs to be exercised. Several devices should be utilized to protect the purchaser from subsequent attack if and when the selling company eventually slides into Chapter 11. The best avenue for protection is to request that a portion of any purchase price be held in an interest-bearing escrow account. While this precaution does not provide an iron-clad assurance of protection, sufficient funds can be held to pay the legal expenses incurred in a subsequent attack. Another method of protection is to structure the purchase as an installment sale. Such a sale would provide for payments after the greatest risk of bankruptcy of the seller had passed.

Yet another method to protect the purchaser would be to request and obtain a lien on the unsold assets of the seller or the assets of an affiliate of the seller. This lien would secure an indemnity from the sellers, officers or affiliates in the event of a subsequent attack or breach of the agreement by the selling company. Any contingent arrangement with respect to structuring such a sale is advisable, in order to minimize the risk of doing business with an insolvent company outside of bankruptcy. As you can see, the myriad problems of purchasing assets from a shaky seller outside of bankruptcy lead to many bankruptcy filings motivated by a desire to protect the transactions from subsequent attack.

Holdouts: This activity involves the purchase of defaulted bonds that are subject to an exchange offer and an attendant strategy of holding out no matter how generous the offer, in order to receive payment at par (or restore the coupon). The risk for the holdout is that the defaulting company will simply file Chapter 11, and the involuntary bankruptcy threats will become meaningless, because two-thirds of the creditors class can vote down one-third of the class. However, holding more than one-third of the amount of outstanding bonds in a class frequently constitutes a block against any plan of reorganization, absent a classification scheme that dilutes the vote, or a cram-down on the class that also extinguishes the junior classes, absent a new investment by the junior classes.

TAX ISSUES

While tax issues play a major role in the overall estate valuation, they are much more critical to the value of the equity in the debtor. They will be of primary interest if you are contemplating an investment at that level.

Generally speaking, the plan of reorganization will seldom create a tax liability, alternative minimum tax considerations aside. In contrast with out-of-court restructurings, the cancellation of indebtedness can create ordinary income. When working with tax problems, remember that you are merely dealing with the logical manipulation of a self-contained system of artificial propositions. And those propositions are only principles that are not always applied the way you might expect.

The primary concern in most Chapter 11 tax considerations is a preservation of the net operating loss carry-forwards (NOLs). Preserving the NOLs of a bankrupt company through the reorganization process has become increasingly difficult. Section 382(a) of the Internal Revenue Code can eliminate or limit all NOLs if a change of control (as defined) occurs. In addition, Section 269 provides that tax-motivated acquisitions of control can cause the loss of NOLs. Discussing the detailed nuances of the term "change of control" is beyond the scope of this work because, among other things, the rules change frequently. In fact, they are so subject to change that they are published in loose-leaf binders and updated monthly.

Section 108 of the Internal Revenue Code, while excepting the forgiveness of debt in Chapter 11 from income, does eliminate tax benefits to the extent of the forgiveness. However, the exchange of equity for debt in a plan can preserve some NOLs under certain specific circumstances.

Many plans attempt to capitalize on the substantial tax losses that the companies have built up in their pre-bankruptcy years. Often payouts in plans will take into account the rationing of the rate of use of NOLs that is frequently required by Section 382(a). The desire for cash payouts post-reorganization is frequently pitted against a tax plan that seeks to preserve tax benefits through reinvestment in the reorganized debtor.

TRAFFICKING IN NET OPERATING LOSSES

In general, Congress and the Treasury Department do not look with favor upon trafficking in NOLs. Nor do they encourage Chapter 11s with no other goal than the preservation of NOLs. With proper and careful consideration, however, a reorganized Chapter 11 debtor may still be able to preserve the value of its net operating-loss carry-forwards. Preserving these NOLs would allow some or perhaps all of the profits generated from the newly reorganized debtor to be sheltered from taxation for a number of years.

The acquisition of control through purchasing claims in a Chapter 11 case can cause problems under Section 382 of the Bankruptcy Code to such an extent that the section's "Ownership Change Rules" can cause the loss of certain NOL attributes.

In general, when a company discharges indebtedness, income can be realized (cancellation of debt income) to the extent of the forgiveness of debt. Potential income of this nature generally receives the following treatment:

a. For a company in Chapter 11, any cancellation of debt will be excluded from income and will be applied to reduce certain tax attributes, and particularly any NOLs. Any cancellation of debt remaining after these reductions will continue to be excluded from income.

b. If a company is solvent and not in any chapter proceeding, the debt cancellation produces immediate taxable income and cancellation of debt income offsets net operating losses.

c. If a company is operating outside of Chapter 11 but is still insolvent, cancellation of debt income will be excluded from income only to the extent of the insolvency of the debtor, but also the tax attributes such as the NOLs will be reduced by the cancellation of debts so excluded.

d. For the typical insolvent debtor in Chapter 11, the rules relating to a discharge in Chapter 11 are fully applicable, meaning that cancellation of debt income should be excluded from taxable gross income.

In short, Chapter 11 companies have a tax advantage, because they are allowed to exclude from income any debt forgiveness that makes the debtor solvent. A company that is in Chapter 11 does not need to establish to the IRS that it is insolvent.

If the debtor's stock is issued in exchange for the debt discharged, the general debt discharge rules do not apply to the Chapter 11 debtor. Recognize that this exception applies only to insolvent companies during the period that they are insolvent, and not after the time that they are made or become solvent. The "stock for debt" exception applies to Chapter 11 debtors as well as to out-of-court workouts. The key factual issue is the fair market value of the stock issued in consideration of debt satisfaction. If the fair market value does not equal the tax basis of the outstanding debt, cancellation of debt income is created for the differences that might otherwise be used to offset existing NOLs. To the extent that the cancellation of debt income exceeds the NOLs, taxable income is generated unless the company remains insolvent.

THE EFFECT OF AN OWNERSHIP CHANGE

The change of ownership issue may come into play for a debtor that seeks to utilize its tax loss. A more than a 50 percentage point increase in the holdings of the stock of the debtor owned by one or more 5% shareholders (relative to the lowest percentage of stock owned by each such shareholder at any time during a rolling 36-month period) creates an ownership change under the applicable regulations. The amount of taxable income of such a debtor that can be offset by NOLs is severely limited by Section 382 of the Internal Revenue Code. This annual limitation is equal to a long-term tax-exempt interest rate multiplied by the value of the debtor's equity just prior to the ownership change. The number of complexities regarding non-voting straight preferred stock, warrants, options, convertible debt, and other similar interests are set forth. These complexities are far beyond the scope of the treatment of this subject herein.

A general limitation applies under which the amount of income that may be offset in each post-change year by a pre-ownership-change NOL is the fair market value of the debtor's stock prior to the ownership change, multiplied by the long-term tax-exempt interest rate then in effect. Since the value of a debtor's equity in bankruptcy will normally be at or close to zero, the general rule will normally eliminate virtually all NOLs. Accordingly, in Chapter 11 cases, certain exceptions are created for the Chapter 11 debtor. If immediately before the ownership change, the debtor is in bankruptcy court and the pre-reorganization shareholders have at least 50% of the voting power and 50% of all the total value of the stock of the debtor after reorganization, and the court approves the transaction, the general rule does not apply. The NOLs of the debtor are instead reduced by: (1) the interest paid or accrued by the debtor during the current taxable year prior to the change of ownership; (2) the interest paid or acquired during the three preceding taxable years on that portion of the indebtedness in respect of which the securities are issued under the plan of reorganization; and, (3) one-half of the amount of debt discharged for stock in the reorganization that would not otherwise reduce the NOLs, because of the stock-for-debt exception. Did you get all of that?

Unfortunately for the investor, the bankruptcy exception requires that if a second ownership change occurs within two years after the first ownership change, any accrued NOLs are lost for all time periods after the second change of ownership. Additional restrictions relating to the "old and cold" shareholders have the effect of providing a number of additional uncertainties for publicly traded claimholders.

In addition, an exception exists if the transaction involved can be characterized as an exchange of debt for stock or a Type G reorganization.

In summary, the operative feature of the bankruptcy exceptions to the extinguishment of NOLs appears to relate to a continuation of pre-existing ownership. Obviously, substantial shifts in ownership of a debtor, because of a trading of claims or equity interests, can impair the retention of NOLs.

STRATEGIES FROM A LEGAL STANDPOINT

Whether to be active or passive is one of a bankruptcy investor's first strategic considerations. The answer depends on the type and amount of resources available for investment. For instance, investing in equity, which is advisable primarily as a post-plan confirmation strategy, if at all, will normally be passive and reviewed periodically through available financial and market data. Investing in debt is the more interesting situation. The most advantageous timing for this investment will often be shortly after Chapter 11 has been declared. The prices of a company's debt securities tend to be severely depressed by the event of a bankruptcy filing. The market for the company's bonds is often in disarray. Some institutional investors are desperate to get out and avoid the stigma of being associated with this example of their poor investment judgment. Others will be assessing their options. They could cut their losses with a quick exit, or, alternatively, they could assign a workout specialist to the situation and ride it out. This latter approach is likely to be time-consuming and relatively costly. Such a strategy makes more sense for a larger investment (e.g., $10 million) than a smaller one (e.g., $1 million). Not only are the bonds likely to be depressed, they are often mispriced vis-à-vis each other (secured, senior unsecured, senior subordinated, junior subordinated, parent vs. subsidiary debt, guaranteed vs. unguaranteed debt, etc.). At this point, no one really knows what the bonds are likely to be worth in a reorganization. That uncertainty often brings out pessimism. All these factors tend to create buying opportunities. In this situation, not merely active, but aggressive, involvement tends to be rewarded.

Taking a proactive posture in debt investment often turns out to be both profitable and interesting. In early investments, however, the novice should be an active spectator as opposed to an active participant until he or she "learns the ropes." As in most areas, novices should be seen and not heard. Soon enough you can become more actively involved.

In your first investment the key will be patience. This is the common trait shared by many successful investors in distressed situations. In most market environments, plenty of investment opportunities are available for those interested in taking a flyer in the securities of a trouble company. The investor should first seek to determine the reason for the trouble. Is it industry-specific, company-specific, or related to a general economic downturn? In the case of distressed investment opportunities in an economy that is falling away from you, a longer holding period may be required. Financial difficulties attributed to the typical cyclical industry downturn may allow for a quicker profit. Company-specific difficulties are less well-defined in that the duration of their holding periods are determined by many factors external to both industry and economic conditions.

A useful strategy for those who are not yet ready to become active players is to diversify into several different situations. Such risk-spreading should give you the opportunity to become more familiar with the risks and rewards involved. To lower the risk further during this stage, senior debt obligations should be the primary type of investment. These could be either public or privately held securities. In fact, general outright unsecured trade claims might also be considered. Initially, the amount is not as important as it will be later. You can, and perhaps should, start small. If you become a major player, you will generally want to purchase at least one-third of the amount outstanding where possible.

To lessen the risk further, you should avoid startup companies and small, undercapitalized companies that are financially troubled. These longshots will usually require more attention than a novice can be expected to give. In the smaller company situation, as in the large company situation, you have to be prepared to fight for your fair share of the recovery. In the large company bankruptcy, however, you can usually rely on someone else to fight for your class. But not always, especially in Eurodollar situations. Moreover, only you can fight most effectively for your specific interests (e.g., earlier payout vs. higher payout, more debt or equity in your reorganization package).

The importance of patience cannot be overstated because of the poor liquidity of these investments. You will learn to think of your investment as a buy, hold and negotiate security, with rewards coming to those who display the most discipline. In general, equity tends to be a poor investment while a company is in Chapter 11, but not necessarily immediately after emergence. Even at this stage, the equity tends not to be suitable as a long-term investment. Debt investments tend to be preferable while a company languishes in Chapter 11.

As important as preferring debt over equity is the decision of which debt security or securities to purchase. Each type of bond will initially trade for a particular price or price range. The senior-most securities will have the highest absolute prices. The lower the priority, the lower the price. Which is the best buy will depend upon a number of factors. Assessing the relative risk-to-reward ratios is a very important aspect of bankruptcy investing. More will be said on this important topic.

CHAPTER 2

INVESTING IN BANKRUPTCIES

Large sums of money have a certain poetry and rhapsody. Judging from the numbers of investors stumbling into the world of investing in distressed companies, the romance of holding paper with face amounts in the millions of dollars is luring many novices to the bottom-fishing arena. Some make unprofitable investments, while other, more experienced investors have been earning substantial fortunes investing in insolvent situations and bankrupt companies.

How did the successful investors do it? By knowing what they were doing. For many years an investor in the securities of large publicly held companies emerging from bankruptcy could hardly lose.

Any observer of the comings and goings of major companies in and out of the bankruptcy courts has noticed a remarkable trend over the past decade or so. Often, all the publicly traded securities of a new debtor in possession drop precipitously in market price. . Frequently, this drop turns out to be an overreaction to the company's Chapter 11 filing. When all is said and done, many bankruptcies yield a much higher recovery for investors than the company's securities were selling for just after or even just before the filing. Not infrequently, the holding-period returns turn out to be extremely attractive. And yet, the results differ greatly from case to case and even from security to security within the same case. Which securities of which situations are the ones to buy? That is the key question for bankruptcy investors.

The distinction between successful investors and unsuccessful investors in insolvency situations comes largely from knowing both the rules of the game and how they are applied. Incredibly, many novices are willing to risk substantial sums of money without an adequate understanding of the natural process in which they are participating, much less an understanding of how to evaluate the available data specific to the particular situation. Both types of knowledge are needed to assess the relevant risks and rewards. The best place to start is usually the company's own website, which will frequently provide a link to all of the bankruptcy case filings.

Who Is the Judge?: One important variable in deciding whether to purchase the debt or, more rarely, the equity of a company enjoying the magnificent protections of Chapter 11 is the judge to whose court the case is assigned. To the Chapter 11 debtor, this person is God. From the moment the case is filed, no significant decision is made in the corporate offices or the boardroom without the question being asked: "How is the judge going to like this?"

Some judges are notoriously lenient with their debtors. Several reasons may account for this leniency. Such judges may believe that they will be viewed favorably by their peers (and those who might review their work in the process of selecting future United States district judges with lifetime tenure) if they show a measure of compassion to a debtor who is down on his or her luck. Other judges have suffered the trauma that occurs when a debtor and its counsel "throw the keys on the table": the bankruptcy judge is then faced with the chaos that must be resolved by having a trustee come in, while praying that not too many employees and creditors are destroyed in the process. Most experienced bankruptcy lawyers agree that bankruptcies, unlike wine, do not improve with age. You should beware if the bankruptcy judge allows the court to be used as a parking lot for a favorite debtor's counsel. The biggest enemy you have in this arena is time and its relation to the value of your investment. Asset values tend to deteriorate in bankruptcy. In addition, administrative (mainly legal) costs mount as time passes.

For a major bankruptcy, the press will report the name of the judge, as well as critique his or her past performance in previous bankruptcy cases. What if the press does not report the judge's name? To get a line on the judge, first call the company and ask the beleaguered switchboard where their bankruptcy case is filed. A trip to the company's website may prove worthwhile. It's one thing that they will know. Second, call directory assistance for the city in which the case is filed and get the number of the United States Bankruptcy Clerk's office. Give them a call. Eventually someone will answer the phone and can tell you the name of the judge to whom the case is assigned. Various publications and the Internet provide an ad hoc rundown on every sitting bankruptcy judge, but you don't need that much research. Call a bankruptcy lawyer and ask about the judge. If your lawyer does not know much about this particular judge, ask for the name of someone who does. Is this judge a take-charge jurist who will move the case swiftly through the process? Or is he or she an incompetent or a simple good-hearted soul who will give the debtor every extension of every deadline and grant every motion the debtor files and, in particular, every application for attorneys' fees (no matter how unnecessary or outrageous), without challenge? If you don't know a bankruptcy attorney, or those you do know draw a blank, look in the *Martindale Hubbell Directory* (available online at www.martindale.com) for the particular city where the case is pending. Every large library has this directory and almost every law firm has a copy. The directory contains a list of the law firms and their specialties for each major U.S. city, including the one where this bankruptcy is pending. Contact a bankruptcy specialist and ask him or her about the judge. Most will charge little or nothing for this information. If the judge assigned to the case is like most, you'll feel that he or she is a neutral factor in your investment. If the assigned judge has a reputation as an unsophisticated debtor-oriented do-nothing, think twice before committing capital.

Who Are the Creditors?: The next area of concern is the identity of the creditor group. Who, among the current holders, are the big losers who bought their bonds at much higher prices? Have any large investors recently entered the picture? Who is accumulating and who is selling out? At what prices? Are the large creditors mainly insiders or affiliates of the debtor, or is only one large institutional creditor involved? The two principal categories of major creditors are institutional investors (banks, insurance companies, mutual funds, college endowments, etc.) and large individual investors (arbitrageurs, vulture investors). Trade creditors constitute a third category that is important in some cases. The institutional investors generally purchased their bonds earlier at or near par, while the large individual investors are more likely to have acquired their holdings recently at a steep discount from par. The large individual holders will generally be more aggressive and more interested in a quick resolution and payout. They would like to turn their money over and go on to something else. The institutional investors, in contrast, are likely to be more patient and more inclined to work the situation for a higher ultimate payout, even if it takes a bit longer to achieve.

The major difference between the arbitrageurs and the institutional investors is their risk-return orientation. The arbitrageur sought out the risk and seeks a quiet commensurate return to go with that risk. The institutional investor, in contrast, is trying to salvage what is possible from an investment that didn't work out. Thus, arbitrageurs will be happy to buy at 10 and receive 30 in a year: that's a 200% return (annualized). The institutional investor might look at the same situation and say let's work the situation for another six months when we think we can get 36. To the institutional investor, that extra six points is clearly worth the wait. It amounts to a 20% greater recovery in six months or a 40% annualized return. Moreover, for one who bought at par, it represents a 36% recovery, as opposed to a 30% recovery. The arbitrageur will not disagree with the arithmetic but will be less impressed. Will the wait really be re-warded? More importantly, arbitrageurs often have other investments to pur-sue. They would prefer to extract the money from this deal now. The institu-tion-arbitrageur conflict does not always arise, and if it does, is not always fo-cused on the same issue. And yet the two types of investors do enter the bank-ruptcy investing arena from different directions with different expectations. The beginning investor should take these differences into account.

For most small, passive investors, debt widely spread over many creditors is preferable to a more concentrated set of holdings for all but the major players in the bankruptcy investing arena. The real "Big Boys" like to see one large holder of most of the debt when an inexpensive cheap acquisition is their goal. Even those very large traders prefer a diverse group of holders when their goal is simply to earn a quick profit. All too often, many creditors are each owed too little to care enough to exert much effort in the situation. This type of case presents both an opportunity and a dilemma. Disinterested creditors will usu-ally sell their claims for a song. When they don't, however, they invariably become dead weight later, when aggressive action becomes necessary to move a case out of Chapter 11 through the confirmation process.

How do you find out who the creditors are and how much they are owed? From your friends at the bankruptcy clerk's office. Many courts will be on the "Pacer" system, and they will refer you to that Internet resource for complete copies of everything filed in the case. When they finally answer the phone, they will tell you how to order either (1) a list of the debtor's 20 largest creditors, filed with the original petition for relief, or, (2) a complete set of the debtor's schedules and statement of financial affairs (extremely complete, detailed and lengthy – filed early in the case). Various services will supply you with this information in most large cases, but it's just as easy to find it yourself. Better yet, if you can, go to the clerk's office and have a ball reading a wealth of data about your investment target. Would that your local stockbroker knew half as much about the stocks he or she was touting with regularity. Most clerks will let you photocopy the pages you want. You can expect to find the complete name, address, and amount owed each creditor, and often the name of the contact person at the creditor's office. These items will eventually be posted on the court's website. Depending on the court, that may be the first place to look.

How Much Are the Assets Worth?: To put it another way, how in the world is this debtor going to be able to make its paper worth anything? If the schedules are on file, everything you can expect to know at this stage about the identity of the assets will be fairly well spelled out. The values given are another matter; these are generated by accountants from historical data. Such numbers may have very little relation to what can actually be derived, even in an orderly disposition of those assets. Moreover, the actual selling prices are likely to be quite sensitive to whether the sales take place in a strong or weak market environment; whether the bankruptcy filing has caused a deterioration of values, and whether the seller can be patient or must sell quickly, even if only distress-level prices are likely to be available. Uncertainty over asset values is one of the biggest risk factors early in the case.

As a case proceeds, more accurate data on the values of the various assets becomes available. For one thing, the marketplace is exposed to the saleable assets, and even for assets that are not advertised, buyers will usually appear. As time passes, the spread between the price of securities of a debtor in Chapter 11 and the actual recovery to be had on those securities will normally narrow. For this reason, most gains and most risks for investors in the securities of bankrupt debtors result from purchases early in the case. Since most investors want to achieve as high a return as possible, those not put off by gaps in the asset side of the equation are frequently rewarded for making their investments early in the case. The best time to buy is often before reliable data on assets are generally available and before market forces determine the outcome of a risk you never took. What? You mean buy a pig in a poke? No, of course not. Some information on the value of a company is available from other sources. You should immediately obtain the most recent pre-bankruptcy filing documents issued by the company. Specifically, you should obtain a 10K, 10Q, the proxy statement and the registration statements on the securities of interest. All can be found at the company's website or at the SEC's EDGAR site.

The Creditors' Committee: By moving quickly, you can make your purchase decision early enough in the case to be on hand for the organizational meeting of the official statutory creditors' committee. This event is usually within the first two weeks after a company files. The major players on the credit side are selected by the U.S. Trustees to become members of the official committee. Frequently, an equity securities committee is formed, as well. As of this writing, the U. S. Trustee in most districts around the country is appointing only one official creditors' committee. The additional expenses of operating multiple committees is usually given as the reason for forming only one committee; the bankrupt estate is responsible for paying the allowable expenses of the committee or committees. Each committee will almost always retain a law firm to represent its interest. It may or may not hire other professionals (accountants, investment bankers, economists, appraisers, etc.) as the need arises. Thus, the cost of two committees is likely to be approximately twice that of one committee, perhaps more (because they have to deal with each other).

The members of the committee are not paid for their work. They are, however, reimbursed for their out-of-pocket expenses (travel, hotel, meals) in attending meetings and doing the work of the committee. Note, however, that having creditors of different classes serve together on a single committee raises conflict-of-interest problems. For example, a creditor holding a debenture subordinated to senior bank debt has an interest different from the banks. Placing both categories of creditors on the same committee means these natural adversaries will have great difficulty agreeing on a common approach regarding whom gets what. The shifting alliances created by these inherent differences lead to Balkan intrigue and Byzantine plots among the various creditor groups. You may find these intrigues entertaining if you are fond of complicated interrelationships, but the delays caused by such conflicts are expensive.

Separate committees for different categories of creditors greatly reduce the likelihood of internal deadlocks on economic issues. Otherwise these deadlocks can paralyze, and thus delay, the "deal mattering" that is central to the process of reaching a consensual reorganization plan. Therefore, having different economic interests represented on the same committee is usually resisted by most experienced lawyers for the creditors. On the other side of the issue are the U.S. Trustees, keeping an eye on expenses, and the debtor's counsel, wanting to achieve the benefits that will flow from the delays that often result from stalemates among the creditors. Divisions among the creditors have often been exploited by the debtor. The committee relationship begins as an economic one and usually, after a while, grows into a personal one, as well. If different classes of creditors are placed on the same committee, personal relationships often sour, and the committee is all too likely to dissolve into bickering, deadlocked factions. The attendant delays will frequently cost the estate more than the superficial savings of having one committee and set of professionals. With separate committees, in contrast, each committee resolves internal differences among investors holding similar types of securities within that committee. Then the separate committees resolve their differences through negotiation, or, if that fails, through litigation.

If you have enough money and time invested, attending this organizational meeting of the committee(s) is a must. As previously explained, major decisions are being made in an information vacuum, and the die is often cast for the remainder of the case. At this meeting or later, take a look at the members of the committee. Are they owed enough money to provide them with an adequate incentive to ride herd effectively on the debtor? Is the committee made up of what appears to be contentious lawyers who seem more interested in proving a legal point rather than businesspeople who simply want to get their money back? What do you think of the professionals that the committee has retained? When you call the law firm that serves the committee counsel, does it return your calls? Have you or anyone else ever heard of the firm? Does the committee seem to have delegated all responsibility to the committee professionals? The U.S. Trustee is supposed to oversee all these matters, of course, but in practice you should not expect much from that quarter. The U.S. Trustee has no economic recovery at stake in the case.

You should plan on calling the members of the committee. Most of them will be happy to talk to you at least once. Remember, however, that these individuals assume a terrific responsibility and perform this public trust without pay. They, too, want to get their money back, but often they could have sat back and let some other similarly situated person do the job for them. They have stepped forward to serve on the committee for the benefit of all of the creditors. They will receive no more for their claims than those who do not serve. About one call (or perhaps one call per six months) per member is the most you should plan to make. What questions should you ask? What questions would you ask a stockbroker about a stock? Clearly, what you want to learn is how much is in the estate and what the likely recovery is for each category of creditors. You would also like to find out the probable timing of any distributions. Committee members are not necessarily going to know the answers and are usually limited by confidentiality rules in what they can say. You want to learn as much as you can without learning too much. If you are told material nonpublic information, you yourself become subject to the same restrictive rules for trading as insiders. Thus, you want to ask questions that are on the edge of the issues. Use existing public documents to fashion questions that help you understand what lies behind the number and statements. You want to use the public documents to sort out the assets' and liabilities' true worth and standings. But you want to be able to trade once you do achieve that understanding.

The First Creditors Meeting: Within the first two months after the case has been filed, a first meeting of creditors will be held. If you are still undecided about whether to make a purchase, here is your chance to ask the debtor anything your heart desires – within reason. Imagine that you are a large shareholder at a rather small annual meeting of stockholders; that will give you some idea of what the first meeting of creditors is like. Note one exception, however: these creditors are mad as Hell. The debtor's officers who have to stand and deliver are often to be pitied, but always prove more informative than at any previous time in their careers. What they say now is being recorded by an employee of the Department of Justice. Because a great deal is at stake, prudent debtor's counsel will usually make sure that someone is present who really knows the answers to the often hostile questions about the debtor's future finances.

Aside from the chance to hear the straight story from the horse's mouth, the first meeting of creditors is a fantastic opportunity to chat with the other creditors. Often, only a few will turn up, even in major cases. All too often, the creditors fail to take advantage of their chance to ask direct questions and turn this meeting into a non-event. Whether or not any questions are asked, those who attend get a chance to exchange rumors and tell each other who wants out of their investment in the debtor and who is buying the paper and for how much. Note that attending this meeting is not necessary. Many experienced investors do not do so. Adequate information on any major debtor is readily available in public records. The treat of seeing this event is nice, but not absolutely necessary.

In the days after the first meeting of creditors, the price of the debtor's investment paper may well move dramatically, up or down. These fluctuations are not trend-setting; they are probably just a reaction to the debtor's performance at the first meeting. Such fluctuations may also provide an attractive opportunity to buy on a downward swing, or to realize a modest profit if the price runs up.

The Action Slows Down: By now you are probably thinking that this sounds like a lot of work. Because these cases go on for a year or two or more, you may conclude that you don't have time to mess around with lawyers and committees and judges. Actually, at about this point in the case, the investor will have little to do until nearly the very end of the case. We have just taken you through the first few weeks of a typical case. Now someone else can do the work: the debtor in possession, the creditors' committee and the lawyers (unless, of course, you want to be on the committee yourself).

After the short initial period subsequent to the filing, the usual case settles in for a period of stabilization. You probably won't hear much about the debtor for some months. To the casual observer, mention a particular debtor five months or so into a case and you'll get a response like: "Didn't they go bankrupt or something?" Between the second and 12th month of the usual major reorganization, the people now running the debtor are getting into their business plan. Their plan may include divestment, slimming down the business, selling unprofitable lines, or liquidating. During this period, the value of your invest-ment, whether already made or being contemplated, is being established. For the four months following the filing, the debtor enjoys its basic exclusivity period. During these 120 days, only it can file a plan of reorganization. Thus, a breathing space is afforded for sorting out the problems that caused the Chap-ter 11 filing.

The lawyers continue to fight, the accountants continue to run manifold hy-pothetical projections, and the costs continue to mount. If nothing is done to move the case toward the plan confirmation stage, these expenses can totally de-plete the estate. The major creditors usually start to exercise their muscles behind the scenes. Clearly, they want to try to maximize the recovery value of the estate. You get a free ride. You have no need to hire your own lawyer unless you want someone to talk to as some perverse sort of entertainment.

Exclusivity: You may hear that the debtor has only four months when it alone can propose a plan of reorganization. This is superficially correct. Usually, in large cases, the bankruptcy judge is willing to extend this period for many months. The process became so abused that in 2005 Congress limited these extensions so the period of exclusivity can be no more than a total of 18 months. Not until the judge starts to express some reluctance about extending the time period will the case enter its most crucial phase – plan formulation. Having the exclusive right to propose a plan gives the debtor considerable leverage. Prior to 18 months, the judge may decide that the case has stabilized and that the interests of the creditors are being prejudiced by the continuation of the debtor's exclusivity period. Now things start to get serious. This point usually occurs about a year into the case. In most major cases, judges believe that more than 120 days is needed to give the debtor the opportunity to come up with a first cut at a plan. Terminating the debtor's exclusivity period allows any party-in-interest to file a plan. Such multiple filings give the judge the job of sorting out these competing plans, which is likely to be a lot of work. Nonetheless, the time always comes when the creditors come to the forefront, whether in com-pleting a plan or in negotiations under the threat of lifting of the exclusivity period, and negotiations begin over who gets what.

The Plan Phase: Most investors come away frustrated after they have seen the interplay among various factions at the stage when the gloves come off. That the estate's value is insufficient to satisfy the claims of the various constituencies is the primary source of most problems (except in the rare case of a solvent debtor). And why would a solvent debtor be put into bankruptcy? Actually, a company may derive enough from asset sales to pay off all of the creditors fully and still have something left over for shareholders (as in the case of the Chicago Milwaukee Corporation), but this is a rare event indeed. Most of the time liabilities far exceed assets. The tension is never greater than when the junior and senior bondholders go at it.

When these players first encountered each other, their goals were simpler and clear-cut. When the subordinated debt was created, the negotiating parties were seeking technical covenants that, while important at the time, have only slight pertinence at the stage of the case where the spoils are to be divided. At the loan documentation stage, the senior lenders sought to control the ability of subordinated debt holders to receive payments on account of their indebtedness. These provisions were written when the borrower was at an early stage of financial difficulty. At the same early phase of the lending process, the negotiators for the subordinated lenders expended great efforts to limit the term of the cessation of payments to their group when the borrower (now the debtor) ran into problems. The early debates are largely irrelevant in a negotiation that focuses on liquidation values. The true strength of the junior creditors arises from their ability to cause costly litigation and delay proceedings, holding up distributions to creditors. The economic loss arising from the delay and from the additional administrative and other costs of bankruptcy may exceed the amount the junior subordinated debt holders are seeking as a recovery.

One commentator observed:

> The United Merchants and Manufacturers bankruptcy has been offered as an example of an institutional rule of thumb that the seniors will give up 20% of their claim to avoid a 30% loss from litigation in the reorganization court (20% from receiving poor value, 10% from legal and other costs of a challenge). The Equity Funding case has been offered as an example of compromise to avoid complex litigation that would depress firm value and the value of the seniors' layer.

Roe, Bankruptcy and Debt: A New Model for Corporate Reorganization, 83 Col.L. Rev. 527, 543 n.49 (1983) citations omitted.

When and where does this plan get written? Largely out of the public eye. This stage is where committee membership becomes important for those who wish to participate in the negotiating process. Note that in the vast majority of cases an individual small investor need not perform this function. The "major players" in each class of creditors will normally do the negotiating, with the assistance of their bankruptcy counsel. On your initial foray into this arena, you probably will prefer to be a spectator to this frustrating spectacle. Term sheets and epithets fly among the various groups. These proposals usually are generated in the offices of the debtor, creditors' committees, and secured creditors. Only the representatives for those various key players are allowed to see the early drafts and play a role in their formulation. Of course, anyone can witness the show – they only have to buy their way in by purchasing enough of the claim of any of the players. When does this process occur? Remember the all-important discussion of the debtor's exclusive period for filing a plan. The bankruptcy judge and the creditors largely determine when the case should come to an end. The draconian possibility of a failure of the Chapter 11, conversion to Chapter 7 and the appointment of a trustee drives the parties to draw up an agreed-upon plan to present to the creditors and other claimants.

The Disclosure Statement: Frequently, the plan will be presented to the creditors with less than total unanimity on the part of those who helped draft it. Just as often, the combatants will iron out their differences on the eve of the hearing on the disclosure statement. This is the hearing on the document that will describe who gets what. It resembles a prospectus, and the typical investor is just about as likely to read it. But, as with most proceedings before the court, the judicial process subjects this document to careful scrutiny. Typically, a great deal of money is spent assuring the court that indeed the rights of the public creditors will be protected when they are allowed to vote on the plan of reorganization. The disclosure statement hearing's primary task is to determine the adequacy of disclosure in the proposed document (or documents in the case of competing plans of reorganization). After the court is satisfied with the adequacy of the information disclosed, the proponents of the plan send it and the disclosure statement to the various creditors and other parties that have requested copies. The main document in the mailing will begin with a summary and then offer a detailed exposition of the plan and its implications for the various categories of creditors. It is also likely to contain a number of exhibits, including historical financial statements. The mailing will also include the ballot that enables you to vote for or against the plan.

When you receive the disclosure statement and the plan, handle it carefully. If you are a creditor, you and your fellow creditors paid a lot of money to have this statement proposed. Lawyers and accountants and investment bankers are paid very high fees to undertake and apply the congressionally mandated process that places a complicated, convoluted document in the hands of someone who asks only that his or her debt be repaid. How do you analyze this document? To answer this question, we need to know what kind of an investor you are. Are you primarily concerned with the return on your investment? In other words, as long as you receive a satisfactory return on capital, are you satisfied? If so, you need only read the part of the disclosure statement that deals with what you get. Find out what class you are in. This will be right up front. Then read the section that describes the treatment that your class receives – what you get. Next, read the description of the assets in terms of what is on hand and what is expected to be received. Is your treatment (payout) enough for you?

Frequently, the distribution will be a package of different securities (cash, new debt, preferred stock, common stock, warrants of various categories). What is the package likely to be worth? The cash is easy to value, but all the paper will have uncertain market values. Most of the time, these securities will not have started trading. Each needs to be looked at separately in the context of the reorganized firm. The debt securities will have a face value and terms (coupon, maturity date). The investor needs to assess the risk and corresponding discount rate to apply. When issued, this paper will almost always be worth less than its face value. Preferred stock may also be evaluated as an income instrument. It will also start trading at a substantial discount from its par value. The common stock is the most difficult piece of the package to value. In theory, one values the reorganized company, backs out the senior claims (debt and preferred) and divides the value attributable to the common equity by the number of shares to be outstanding. Warrants are even more difficult to assess, because their value is dependent upon the chances of the common share's price rising high enough to make exercise attractive before the warrants expire. Warrants issued as part of a bankruptcy package are generally far out of the money (striking price much above the initial market price of the new stock). One should not normally place much value onto the warrant part of the package. Note that the package is not necessarily as complex as described above. A typical package may contain only two or three separate instruments (e.g., cash, bonds and common stock). In some cases, it will only contain one element (e.g., cash or common stock). Other cases, however, have offered more complexity. For example, Crystal Oil (a relatively small bankruptcy case) exchanged a package of securities including (1) zero-coupon bonds; (2) senior preferred stock; (3) junior preferred stock; (4) common stock, and (5) five different classes of warrants for its pre-bankruptcy securities. Adding further to the complexity, the zeros and preferreds were convertible into common stock and the warrants could be exercised, either with cash, with the zeros (at 110% of their face value), or with the senior preferred stock (at its liquidation value). The large array of convertibles and warrants made the potential common stock dilution exceedingly difficult to assess. Since no meaningful pre-issue market existed for these securities, placing a value on the package was no easy task.

What are the surrounding circumstances? Would a later payout be greater if the current plan is defeated? Is the window of opportunity so narrow as to prevent your class from holding out for the last dollar? In true democratic fashion, you and your class will generally get to vote based on what is in your own economic best interests. As is the American way, the majority rules.

If you are the kind of person who is not so much concerned with your own absolute return, but rather measures your results against the results that others receive, you will want to read the entire plan and disclosure statement. You will want to analyze the treatment of each and every class to see who, if anyone, is getting a better deal than your class. If you are this type of individual, you probably won't be very happy investing in this area. Small, hard-nosed creditors will often be found lurking in a plan with a disproportional recovery, because they possess some unique leverage (e.g., the particular creditor may be an indispensable business partner or customer). Another possible reason for reading the entire document is to decide whether you want to make additional investments. Maybe one or more other instruments is slated to be treated significantly better than the current market price recognizes. If so, perhaps you should try to buy it rather than add to what you already own. You want to buy the instrument that has the highest expected return relative to its risk. Which instrument holds this characteristic (greatest potential reward relative to risk) will vary over time, as information emerges and market prices change.

How Is the Pie to Be Divided?: The most crucial negotiation usually takes place over how much is left for equity. The inherent conflict that exists for management is apparent. Usually they have the shareholders' interest paramount in mind. Under normal (i.e., non-bankruptcy) circumstances, management is likely to see itself as working for the shareholders. After all, the shareholders are (or were), technically, the company's owners. The creditors are merely suppliers of the debt capital, not unlike some other supplier of the company (e.g., the electricity provider or the phone company). Moreover, the managers are frequently shareholders themselves. Finally, the board of directors is elected by the shareholders and, at least in theory, directs management in the shareholders' behalf. On the other hand, when a company is severely troubled, management is supposed to shift more and more of its attention to protecting the interests of the creditors. Indeed, once a company becomes insolvent (whether or not it has filed for bankruptcy), the creditors in effect become the owners. At that point, management should see itself as owing virtually its complete allegiance to the creditors (as opposed to the shareholders). Certainly, once a troubled firm files for bankruptcy, management should act as a fiduciary for the unsecured creditors. As a part of the reorganization process, these competing interests of shareholders and creditors are on a collision course. Equity, by law, is supposed to be in line to receive a distribution only once the secured and unsecured debt holders have been paid in full. And yet management would like to preserve some value for the old shareholders. How can this conflict be resolved? That is the subject of the basic negotiation in the plan. How much goes to the creditors and what, if anything, is left for the shareholders? The lawyers and accountants argue and threaten with notions of a litigated plan confirmation and "cram-down," and thousands of dollars are spent in posturing. The issue must be resolved either in or out of court.

If we assume that the issue of how much is to be divided among the creditors is resolved, and it will be, then the only other matter to be resolved is the most important one of how do the creditors divide the assets of the estate among themselves? The problem could also be approached from the other direction. The creditors can decide to divide the assets of the estate among themselves first, then decide what will be left over for equity. No matter, the negotiations that take place between the secured and unsecured groups will be intense and frequently acrimonious. In this era of junk bonds, most large businesses in Chapter 11 have various levels of unsecured indebtedness outstanding. In practice, a simultaneous solution will be achieved in iterative steps. Each party will be seeking the most advantageous treatment for its class. Alliances will form and dissipate and re-form among different groups. The process can be tedious and torturous, but eventually may reach a successful conclusion. Frequently, no one really likes the conclusion, but most are willing to live with it.

The significance of "subordinated debt" is critical. The Bankruptcy Code requires a plan to divide creditors' claims and equity holders' interests into separate classes; the economic rights of these classes are then dealt with under the plan. Each class can contain only claims that are "substantially similar." The claims within a particular class cannot be treated differently (absent agreements of a particular class member to being treated less favorably). For example, all unsecured trade creditors should receive the same pro rata payments. However, different classes of claims may receive disparate treatment, provided that the protections built into the Bankruptcy Code for non-consenting claims and interest are satisfied.

The Vote on the Plan: Holders of valid claims against and interest in a debtor are allowed to vote for the acceptance or rejection of a proposed plan. A class is deemed to have accepted a proposed plan if more than half in number and more than two-thirds in dollar amount of the members casting votes accept the plan.

A plan is still confirmable over the objections of a non-consenting member of a class that votes for the plan, if that class member receives or retains under the plan property of a value equal to or greater than what that member would receive or retain if the debtor were liquidated under Chapter 7 of the Bankruptcy Code.

If a class as a whole rejects the plan, a plan proponent may still have the court confirm that plan if the plan "does not discriminate unfairly" and is "fair and equitable" with respect to the dissenting class. This is the so-called cram-down of the Bankruptcy Code. With respect to unsecured creditors, the condition that a plan be fair and equitable includes the "absolute priority rule": no class junior to the dissenting class may receive any property until the higher dissenting class is paid in full.

A plan proponent facing a dissenting class and a contested confirmation hearing is placed in a difficult position. An enormous expense and delay is inherent in a judicial determination of whether the cram-down safeguards for dissenters are satisfied. A protracted delay can, and usually will, prove fatal to a company attempting to continue operations in Chapter 11 as a going concern. A dissenting class of creditors (such as subordinated debt) may be able to "veto" a plan provision providing for a continuing participation of existing equity when the dissenters are not satisfied. This ability enables such a class effectively to block confirmation of the entire plan. In cases requiring certain tax treatments or the participation of key debtor personnel, retention of a small equity position by management is often a *quid pro quo* for continued operations or for cooperation with an outside investor. In almost every case, creditors (whose rights are superior to equity interests) are receiving less than a 100% payout on their claims. Therefore, absent the agreement of each more senior creditor class, a plan providing that equity holders receive some distribution is not confirmable. For these reasons, most successful Chapter 11 reorganizations involve consensual plans.

A variety of factors combine to give subordinated debt holders considerable leverage (vis-à-vis senior creditors) in the bankruptcy negotiation process. In most instances, the classification scheme, voting requirements and class protections built into the Bankruptcy Code, the considerable court bias toward obtaining consensual plans and the frequent desirability of including existing equity in the distribution scheme all work to the subordinated debt holders' advantage. They will tell the seniors that they have relatively little to lose by blocking or delaying confirmation of a plan that provides them little or no recovery. Senior creditors, in contrast, will have much more at stake. Often, however, the seniors can achieve a recovery (of some positive, but perhaps lesser, magnitude) in a Chapter 7 liquidation, even if that process provides nothing for the juniors. Both sides may play a game of chicken, hoping the other one will blink.

Many otherwise viable companies are forced to file bankruptcy in order to reduce an overbearing debt burden. In effect they would like to shave off or at least shave down and convert to equity existing contractually subordinated debt. With less debt to service, the business may be able to operate quite profitably. Usually, this subordinated debt arises from unsecured junk bonds issued by the company.

The Subordination Issue: Most indentures (the stated contract between issuer and borrower) involving publicly issued subordinated debentures provide for "inchoate forbearance": the subordinated debt may be paid according to the terms thereof unless a default exists with respect to senior creditors. "Senior creditors" typically include borrowed money or particularly designated categories of debt owed by the borrower. In the real world, senior creditors typically do not include trade debt; that is, trade debt is neither senior nor junior to the debenture issue, but rather is characterized as "neutral," even though its proper place is usually more with the senior than the junior unsecured debt holders.

Just who is senior to whom and who is not is often in dispute. For example, the trade creditors will want to claim seniority to the subordinated debt, while the juniors will want to claim the contrary. The indenture may not be totally clear on the matter of just what other debt the subordinated debt is subordinated to. If, for example, the trade debt is clearly pari passu (on the same level as) with the senior unsecured bank debt, but the junior debt is only subordinated to senior bank debt, a complicated payout formula is called for. First, the available proceeds are allocated to the three categories of debt holders as if they were of equal standing. Then, the money tentatively allocated to the subordinated debt will generally be reallocated to the senior bank debt up to the amount of their shortfall. Any remaining monies are to be retained by the juniors. The trade debt distribution is not impacted by the transfer from the junior to the senior creditors.

Other formulas are applicable for other classifications. An example will help clarify this scheme. First, consider the result if the subordinated debt is only subordinated to the bank debt. This is the typical situation:

	Claims	*Available for distribution*
Bank debt	$ 50 million	
Trade debt	50 million	
Subordinated debt	50 million	
Total	$150 million	$99 million

	Initial Allocation	*% of Recovery*
Banks	$33 million	66%
Trade	33 million	66%
Subordinate	33 million	66%
Total	$99 million	

The banks' shortfall is $17 million which is taken from the subordinate holders' initial allocations. The final allocation would become:

		% of Recovery
Banks	$50 million	100%
Trade	33 million	66%
Subordinate	16 million	32%
Total	$99 million	

Now contrast this result with other possibilities. Suppose, for example, both trade and bank debt were classified as senior, with the debenture debt subordinated to both. For that situation, the initial allocation of the subordinated holders would be allocated pro rata to both trade and bank debt. The result:

		% of Recovery
Banks	$49.5 million	99%
Trade	49.5 million	99%
Subordinates	0	
	$99 million	

Now suppose both trade and debenture debt is subordinated to bank debt, but the trade and subordinated debt are pari passu. The bank's initial $17 million shortfall would be taken pro rata from both the trade and subordinate debt holders. The result for this (unlikely) situation would be:

		% of Recovery
Banks	$50 million	100%
Trade	24.5 million	49%
Subordinates	<u>24.5 million</u>	49%
	$99 million	

Finally, suppose the bank debt is senior to both and the trade debt is senior to the subordinated debentures. The result of this situation would be:

		% of Recovery
Banks	$50 million	100%
Trade	49 million	98%
Subordinates	0	0%
	$99 million	

Clearly, the way a subordination clause applies can have a major impact on the payout for the various classes of creditors.

The above results represent possible outcomes from what might be called for by the subordination provisions in the indentures. A consensual plan may tend toward one of these kinds of distributions (the one fitting the specific legal circumstances of the subordination clause). In the give and take of negotiations, however, the distribution is likely to depart from the appropriate formula at least somewhat. Generally the juniors will fare a bit better and the seniors a bit worse than the subordination provisions imply. On the other hand, if the case is converted to Chapter 7, the subordination provisions become fully enforceable. This threat is a potent weapon for the senior creditors.

Senior Strategy for Dealing With Subordinated Debt: Plan proponents may utilize any of several strategies in an attempt to limit the bargaining position of subordinated debt. First, plans have been structured so that subordinated debt is treated for voting purposes as in the same class as senior debt, even though that approach may seem technically improper. The subordination provisions of the two creditor classes are, however, left intact. If the amount and number of holders of senior and other debt in the same class is sufficiently high, the subordinated debt's vote can be diluted sufficiently to prevent it, by its own vote, to reject the plan. This result, in turn, takes the potent weapon of the absolute priority rule out of the hands of the subordinated debt. This approach may be useful in plans where distribution to existing equity is desired.

Advocates for this combined classification approach usually argue that the subordination agreement in question contained in the indenture is strictly between the senior and subordinated debt holders and does *not* involve the debtor. In other words, the senior and subordinated debt holders are similarly situated with respect to the debtor; they are just debts that happen to have a private (subordination) contract between them. On a consensual basis, senior creditors, which are able to enforce their subordination agreement against the subordinated debt, may be willing to accept a payout below what will assure a return to the subordinated debt, in order to speed confirmation of a consensual plan. Such senior creditors can then claim all the money allocated to themselves, plus all of the money initially allocated to those creditors subordinated to their position. Similarly, neutral creditors (typically trade creditors) might be willing to accept a lower payout in order to ensure the continued existence of a current customer.

Discussions often become heated over the classification issue for subordinated debt in workout scenarios both pre- and post-bankruptcy. Clear answers to the powers of the absolute priority rule are often absent. Of course, classification issues sometimes become moot if equity is not retaining an interest under a plan and the subordinated debt holders are "out of the money" (i.e., a situation where, under a liquidation scenario, no distributions would be available for the benefit of junior unsecured creditors in any event). In determining the position of unsecured debt under a liquidation analysis, investment bankers will sometimes allocate "relative values" to subordinated debt, particularly where multiple layers of subordinated debt exist. This analysis may assign value to subordinated debt issues even though all subordinated debt is out of the money (presumably, based on an analysis incorporating the results of the workout/bankruptcy "dynamics"). So, despite accounting results to the contrary, the "dynamics" of bankruptcy often yield returns to deeply subordinated and deeply out-of-the-money paper.

A plan proponent may also attempt to reduce the subordinated debt holders' leverage by enforcing indenture provisions assigning the right to vote subordinated claims to the senior debt holders. This technique has been attempted only where the underlying subordination agreement provides for the assignment of the subordinated claim to the senior creditor when senior debt is in default.

In a third approach, plan proponents are increasingly using what might be called the "alternative plan" or "either/or" plan to limit the leverage of subordinated debt. Under this scenario, proponents file a plan setting forth some modest payout for subordinated debt. However, the plan will also provide that, in the event the subordinated debt class rejects the plan, the class will receive a starkly different treatment:

(1) the subordination provisions of the subordination agreement, otherwise released under the plan, will remain in effect upon rejection by the subordinated class. Senior debt holders would then be able to enforce their subordination agreements against the subordinated debt holders (outside the bankruptcy court if necessary); *and*

(2) the subordinated debt holders and all junior claims and interest holders receive *no distributions* under the plan upon rejection by the class. Faced with this choice, consensual agreements often follow. Subordinated creditors are thereby faced with a Hobson's choice. Vote for the plan, and if it carries and is confirmed, receive only a very modest payout. Vote against the plan, and if the plan is confirmed over your class's objection, receive nothing. They can, of course, try to defeat not only the vote for their class but also the plan itself, and then hope that a new plan emerges that is more to their satisfaction. Usually, however, the lawyers who drafted the plan on behalf of the debtor and senior creditors have been careful to produce a confirmable plan. If the judge has approved the disclosure statement and allowed the plan to go out with the either/or provision as part, the plan is probably confirmable even over the subordinated creditors' objections. Moreover, even if the plan is defeated, the next plan may not treat them any better and conversion to Chapter 7 is almost certain to treat them worse. Faced with this choice, the subordinated creditors will frequently vote in favor of the plan even if they are very dissatisfied with their share of the pie.

In situations where appropriate, the plan proponent (such as a third-party investor) may also eliminate existing equity interests, thereby eliminating the threat of invocation of the absolute priority rule by the subordinated debt holders.

The single most important goal for subordinated debt holders in plans providing for distributions to junior claims is to be able to control the voting of a class. As you can see, considerable advantage exists in controlling 34% of the class, because the holder can work a consensual plan in many instances. Buying 34% of the bonds is the most straightforward approach to acquiring such veto power. Alternatively, one can form alliances with other holders to get to the 34% level. Even more desirable is an alliance controlling two-thirds of the vote. Such a group can usually deliver the class affirmatively (assuming they can also obtain a majority in number).

The general rule under bankruptcy law is that a claim against the debtor will not receive interest accruing after the petition date except in the (unlikely) event of a solvent debtor. An unresolved question is whether "senior indebtedness" under a subordination agreement such as an indenture for a debenture issue includes claims by the senior creditor for post-petition interest. The resolution is likely to turn on the specific wording in the subordination provisions of the relevant indentures. The senior creditor's ability to include post-petition interest in his or her senior debt vis-à-vis subordinated debt holders can become a significant factor in the leverage equation in bankruptcy cases lingering on for two or three years.

STRUCTURED FINANCE

Over the past decade, asset securitization, or structured finance, has become extremely popular in commercial settings and has led to new bankruptcy investment opportunities that have arisen from structured finance transactions. In particular, in the sub-prime lending area.

In a structured finance transaction, financial assets of an income-producing nature are pooled. In the ordinary structured finance transaction, these assets (e.g., loans) are converted into capital market instruments. A sponsor generally transfers a pool of these financial assets into a special purpose entity that, in turn, issues non-redeemable debt obligations or equity securities with debt-like characteristics. The repayment on the securities depends exclusively on the cash flows from the pooled assets. Generally the "lender" will be able to look only to transferred assets in the pool to pay the securities or debt obligations. The originator of the instrument will have no obligation to make up any shortfall. This type of structured financing vehicle enables companies to raise capital when they might otherwise have difficulty. The popularity of the structured finance transaction is understandable. This vehicle allows a company to leverage a pool of assets rather than having to rely on the company's own, usually weaker, credit quality for creditworthiness, thereby reducing its borrowing cost.

The common key feature of most of these transactions is the creation of a "bankruptcy remote" special purpose vehicle. In general, this type of investment has raised issues concerning "substantive consolidation" of the Special Purpose Vehicle (SPV) into the company sponsoring the transaction, should the sponsoring company go bankrupt. The relatively untested risks of substantive consolidation and "bankruptcy remoteness" have made this area tricky from the standpoint of an investor wishing to invest in one of these entities when bankruptcy looms for the sponsoring company. This situation requires a potential investor to investigate the likelihood that the SPV would be drawn into the bankruptcy case by being substantively consolidated with a debtor and the ability of the SPV itself to file bankruptcy voluntarily or have an involuntary bankruptcy filed against it. In short, this situation requires an investor to evaluate how likely the SPV assets are to become part of a bankruptcy estate of another entity. So, what do you need to know before you invest?

In general, where an SPV has been established, certain corporate governance and operational niceties must be maintained for an SPV to maintain its corporate separateness. An outsider is seldom able to make certain that these niceties have actually been satisfied. Enron abused these vehicles by having executives make false certifications of separateness. The requirements of an independent director and the like cannot be ignored by an investor who looks at the corporation from outside. Additionally, recent cases have raised a specter of the bankruptcy court's jurisdiction over cash collateral uses of an SPV if its affiliate is in Chapter 11.

In summary, while structuring financing transactions offers a number of advantages to a corporate sponsor, significant pitfalls exist in bankruptcy investing in this area, because post-closing operations can destroy the structure and "bankruptcy remoteness" of the transaction. This, along with the absence of a substantial body of law concerning the treatment of SPVs in bankruptcy, creates a highly speculative investment situation.

SPECIAL ALERTS

Landlords' Claims

Investors should be very cautious about purchasing a landlord's unsecured claim for damages resulting from lease terminations, whether by rejection or pre-petition termination. Such an investor should realize that a lease termination claim, while it might carry enormous face value, is subject to a legal cap. The cap is the greater of one year, or 15%, not to exceed three years, of the funds payable under the remaining term of the lease, along with any unpaid rent due under the lease, without acceleration.

Breach-of-Employment Contract Damages

The same caution applies to breach-of-employment contract claims. The Bankruptcy Code limits the allowed claim of employees for damages arising out of breach-of-employment contracts to one year's compensation.

Claims of Insiders

Claims of insiders for services rendered to the estate are generally subject to intense scrutiny. The Court will seek to determine the extent to which the claim exceeds the reasonable value of such services if any. A would-be purchaser should be aware that claims from an insider may be disallowed or only allowed in part.

Secured Claims

When purchasing a secured claim, five provisions of the Bankruptcy Code should be kept in mind:

(1) a debtor in possession can recover from a secured creditor's collateral the reasonable and necessary costs associated with preserving or disposing of the collateral if those costs demonstratively benefited secured creditor;

(2) a secured creditor's claim is secured only to the extent of the value of the collateral;

(3) a claim is unsecured to the extent that the value of the creditor's collateral is less than the amount of the creditor's claim;

(4) to the extent that the value of the creditor's collateral is greater than the amount owed to the creditor, the creditor may collect interest on its secured claim but only to the extent set forth in the agreement between the creditor and the debtor; and

(5) a secured claim that is successfully challenged and disallowed in the bankruptcy court is void.

Often the holders of facially secured claims will seek to sell them, as opposed to attempting to enforce them because of collateral avoidance issues and perfection issues. The use of an attorney is strongly recommended by a person seeking to purchase a secured claim.

From the standpoint of evaluating a secured claim, the most important issue (as it is in many areas of bankruptcy) is valuation of the property in question. This issue becomes important in adequate protection disputes, automatic stay disputes and plan treatment. Clearly, valuation can, and often does, become a very subjective matter. Since the first edition of our book, the Supreme Court has discussed the issue of valuation and stated that value is determined "in light of the purpose of the valuation and of the proposed disposition or use of such property . . . ." To many bankruptcy courts, this means that replacement value or its equivalent is the proper standard for valuing property.

Environmental Claims

In the last 15 years, environmental claims have become a much more prominent issue in bankruptcy cases. Debtors having substantial environmental claims are disadvantaged by the conflict between the Comprehensive Environmental Response Compensation and Liability Act ("CERCLA") and the Bankruptcy Code governing the discharge of environmental claims arising prior to the bankruptcy filing. Accordingly, a court will need to determine the nature of an environmental obligation and the time that it arose.

Making a Debtor-In-Possession Loan

Debtor-in-possession lending ("DIP financing") has become a major industry because of its profitability and the generally low risk of loss. This type of lending is primarily for the sophisticated lender and beyond the subject of this book. If DIP financing is of interest, it should be discussed with counsel and financial advisors. Providing such financing effectively requires the ability to undertake speedy due diligence and commit substantially large sums of money on very short notice.

Collusive Bidding and Other Collateral Attacks on Purchases in Bankruptcy Courts

The court can void (undo) a sale if the purchase is the product of bid-rigging. To avoid later claims of collusion, caution should be exercised in dealing with other bidders.

INTELLECTUAL PROPERTY BANKRUPTCIES

Beginning in the year 2000, the number of technology company insolvencies grew exponentially. Many of these companies owned very little other than intellectual property rights. Frequently, these companies' primary assets are groups of patent licenses and sublicenses that permit them to use the technology owned by equity owners or joint venture partners. With the commencement of a bankruptcy case, a debtor does not lose its trademarks. The issue becomes less clear in the instance of domain names.

Another area of uncertainty is intellectual property licenses. These contracts are generally deemed to be executory by bankruptcy courts. That determination makes these licenses subject to special provisions. A good bit of litigation arose in the dot.com era when a debtor in possession was a licensee and sought to assume and assign such licenses. A number of courts held that a debtor cannot assume or assign an executory contract when applicable law makes contracts non-assignable without the consent of the non-debtor party to the contract. This rule caused some debtors to become unable to assume and assign their non-exclusive patent licenses, because of the non-assignable nature of non-exclusive patent licenses. Not surprisingly, these holdings have tended to discourage investing in technology-related insolvency cases.

CHAPTER 3

BANKRUPTCY/REORGANIZATION EXAMPLES

What do bankruptcy plans look like in real life? How do all of these various factors that we have been discussing play out? Let's look at a few examples.

A. United Airlines (In re UAL Corporation, et al.)

On December 9, 2002, UAL, United Airlines and 26 other direct and indirect wholly owned subsidiaries filed voluntary petitions for Chapter 11 in the United States Bankruptcy Court for the Northern District of Illinois. United is one of the largest passenger airlines in the world. In 2004, United flew approximately 115 billion mainline revenue passenger miles and carried approximately 71 million passengers on more than 1,500 daily departures in 26 countries and two U.S. territories. Its operating revenue attributed to its North American segment was $10.5 billion in 2004, $10 billion in 2003 and $10.4 billion in 2002. Its underfunded pension obligations matched these whopping figures.

United's capital structure consisted of several components. First came aircraft-related guarantees on a number of aircraft that raised asserted claims based on such guarantees at $828 million.

UAL also had outstanding 3,203,177 shares of 12.25 percent preferred stock. This preferred stock was senior to all other preferred and common stock except for certain preferred securities.

UAL also had undergone a recapitalization in 1994 during which it provided a 55% equity in voting interest in UAL to most of its employees. Under these ESOPs, 17,675,345 shares of Class 1 and 2 preferred stock were allocated to individual employee accounts from 1994 to 2000. In addition, on June 30, 2005, UAL had 116,220,959 shares of common stock outstanding.

In December 1996, UAL Corporation had issued certain capital trust certificates (the "TOPrS Trust") preferred securities.

UAL had one fleet of 463 aircraft that was subject to secured aircraft financing arrangements of various types. This fleet was known as Section 1110 protection fleet because of the protection under Section 1110 of the Bankruptcy Code, requiring aircrafts covered by Section 1110 to receive current payments if they were used during a bankruptcy reorganization after a relatively short 60-day grace period.

United also had a series of six unsecured notes due between 2003 and 2021 pursuant to a trust indenture (junk bonds). The principal amount of these notes totaled $1,641,000,000. These unsecured debentures ranked *pari passu* with all of the existing senior unsecured indebtedness of United and senior to its subordinated indebtedness.

In addition, certain municipal revenue bonds were guaranteed by UAL that totaled $1,702,000,000.

After it filed Chapter 11, United negotiated two debtor-in-possession facilities. One was with Bank One for $300 million, and the second was what became known as the "Club DIP." The Club DIP was originally for up to $1.2 billion. Stage 1 draws only reached $500 million, while Stage 2 draws were anticipated to reach $700 million. They never did because the debtor-in-possession facilities each contained numerous financial covenants that United failed to meet on several occasions. Each time this occurred, United was required to obtain waivers and amendments.

On three occasions, United tried and failed to obtain a loan guaranty from the federal government. United was effectively forced to cease funding its pension obligations until the conclusion of its bankruptcy proceedings. The true reason for the Chapter 11 filing was finally confronted.

The United case became all about pension-funding obligations. The debtor-in-possession facilities had been amended numerous times, and numerous attempts were made to obtain government assistance. The pension obligations were just too great for UAL to survive, no matter what other financial restructurings were dreamed up for its other obligations. Finally, in entering into the eighth amendment of its DIP facilities (August 20, 2004), the debtors agreed, as part of their commitment to adhere to future projections, to cease funding their pension obligations until their exit from bankruptcy. This basically led to a war with organized labor about pension obligations. A number of employees had previously been given concessions to induce them to retire early under Section 1113. Then Section 1114 of the Bankruptcy Code was used to reduce their retiree benefits. Not surprisingly, the employees felt cheated. Turmoil ensued. Nonetheless, no more contributions to the pension fund were made by UAL until the end of the case. The United pension funds were taken over by the Pension Benefit Guaranty Corporation (PBGC).

Who got what? In exchange for assuming the horrendous obligations under the United pension funds, the PBGC wound up owning 23.4% of the equity in UAL. This happened because the PBGC's general unsecured claim of $10.2 billion was fixed under the plan of reorganization, and the plan provided that the PBGC would receive its pro rata share of common stock on account of this claim. Prior to confirmation of the plan of reorganization, United and the PBGC reached a settlement that had the effect of terminating the pension plan and transferring the existing obligations under the plan to the PBGC. In return, the PBGC received $1.5 billion in notes and preferred stock and an allowed general unsecured claim entitled to distribution under the plan. Hence, the claim for $10.2 billion became a settled amount.

The unsecured creditors received a recovery on their unsecured claims of 4% to 8% on the dollar, based on the projected $1.9 billion equity value of the reorganized entity and a total of other unsecured claims (aside from the PBGC) in the range of $20 billion to $35 billion.

Simple mathematics would show that the PBGC's 23.4% interest in the reorganized entity was worth $445 million, assuming the new airline entity would be worth $1.9 billion after Chapter 11. For a $10 billion claim, this represented approximately a 4.45% recovery rate as projected by the debtor at the time of the reorganization. The secured claims on the aircraft were handled through returns of collateral, refinancing, and restatements of loan agreements. This was an economic sideshow despite the enormous numbers. However, working through this "sideshow" consumed several years, leading to an emergence from Chapter 11 in early 2006.

The United case is an excellent example of how the pension fund issues are handled in Chapter 11. The quasi-governmental entity known as the Pension Benefit Guaranty Corporation in severe cases takes over the pension obligations. Generally the pensioners (particularly those with high levels of accrued benefits) receive reduced payments, and the PBGC receives a substantial equity stake in the reorganized debtor. Because of the acrimony involved in such a process, these cases are frequently lengthy.

B. Trump Hotels and Casino Resorts

Trump Hotel and Casino Resorts, "In re THCR/LT Corporation et al." dealt with issues created by a debtor that had been overleveraged, compounded by issues related to settling with a high-profile controlling shareholder. THCR was formed as a public company in March 1995. Until it was delisted (September 27, 2004), its common stock traded on the New York Stock Exchange under the symbol DJT. The debtors filed petitions for relief under Chapter 11 of the Bankruptcy Code on November 21, 2004. The plan of reorganization was confirmed on April 5, 2005. The case involved a series of general unlimited partnership interests. Approximately 63.4% of the debtor was currently owned by THCR, and approximately 36.6% was owned by Donald Trump and his controlled affiliates, as limited partners. Twenty-nine million nine hundred thousand shares of old THCR common stock were issued and outstanding, of which 9,960,000 were beneficially owned by Donald Trump and his affiliates. In addition, Mr. Trump owned options to purchase up to 1,800,000 shares of common stock. He also owned options to exchange partnership interests into 13,900,000 additional shares of common stock, giving him beneficial ownership of an aggregate of approximately 56.43% of common stock as of September 30, 2004, assuming his options were exercised. The debtor and its subsidiaries were the exclusive vehicle through which Mr. Trump, the chairman of THCR's board of directors, engaged in gaming activities. The debtors' business consisted primarily of five casinos and hotel properties that were owned and managed by THCR and its wholly owned subsidiaries: Trump Taj Mahal Casino Resort, Trump Plaza Hotel and Casino, Trump Marina Hotel and Casino, Trump Indiana Casino, and Trump 29 Casino. In addition, certain hotel casino resort properties were owned by the debtor.

The events leading up to Chapter 11.

The debtors faced increased competition and other challenges burdened by substantial debt service on their existing debt obligations. The debtors' core businesses did not generate the cash flow necessary to reinvest in the maintenance or expansion of the casino and hotel properties at levels consistent with those of their competitors.

To address these long-term needs starting prior to bankruptcy, the debtors began exploring ways to improve their operating efficiencies and develop a more suitable capital structure. They pursued and considered a number of overhead reduction possibilities, sale possibilities, and productivity improvements. Competition continued to increase. Clearly, the debtors needed to restructure their debts in order to extend their long-term longevity. Approximately 25 potential strategic and financial investors were contacted searching for someone willing to invest in the debtors. Extensive analysis and consultation with potential investors and investment banks revealed that additional capital could be obtained only if a significant de-leveraging of the debtors' balance sheet and a restructuring of the debtors' existing indebtedness took place. These concepts of de-leveraging led to pre-petition negotiations regarding possible sales of the Trump Taj Mahal Casino and the Trump Indiana Casino. Additional pre-petition negotiations with note holders took place.

Concurrently, pre-petition and post-petition negotiations with the majority shareholder, Donald Trump, took place.

Debtor's capital structure and recoveries.

Under the plan of reorganization, each public holder of the common stock retained its rights under the plan and received for each outstanding share one new Class A warrant to purchase an aggregate total of up to 3,425,000 shares of new common stock at a purchase price of $14.60 per share. As of the petition date, all of certain Class B stock was beneficially owned by Donald Trump. Under the plan, certain mergers and reverse splits took place in order to facilitate the debt reductions and conversions of debt to equity.

The plan set forth a significant settlement between Donald Trump and the debtors and the creditors.

Certain holders of the 11.25% first mortgage notes due 2006 (the "TAC Notes") and certain holders of 11.625% first priority mortgage notes due 2010 (the "TCH First Priority Notes") and the 17.625% second priority mortgage notes due 2010 (the "TCH Second Priority Notes", together with the TCH First Priority Notes, the "TCH Notes") came to a resolution of the issues that involved a restructuring of the TAC Notes, the TCH First Priority Note and the TCH Second Priority Notes, as well as a reverse stock split involving the current company's common stock. The agreement provided that the holders of the TAC Notes would exchange their notes (which aggregated approximately $1.3 billion in face amount) for approximately $773.3 million new notes and common stock equal to 63.69% of the shares of the recapitalized company on a fully diluted basis and an additional amount of cash equal to interest accrued on the $773 million new notes, at an interest rate of 8.5% from the last date on which their interest had been paid through the effective date of the plan. In addition, the holder of the TAC Notes would receive cash proceeds from the exercise of any of the new warrants issued under the plan.

The holders of the TCH First Priority Notes (which aggregated approximately $425 million) would exchange their notes for new notes equal to $425 million, $21.25 million in cash and common stock equal to 1.41% of the new recapitalized company on a fully diluted basis. In addition, they would receive cash equal to interest on their $425 million at a rate of 12.625% through the effective date of the plan. Unaffiliated holders of the TCH Second Priority Notes (which held a face amount of approximately $54.6 million) would exchange their notes for $47.4 million of new notes, $2.3 million in cash and approximately .35% of the shares of common stock of the recapitalized company. In addition, cash equal to interest on $54.6 million at an interest rate of

18.625% from the last interest payment to confirmation of the plan would be paid to these holders.

New notes would be issued by THCR Holdings and Trump Hotels and Casino Resorts Funding, Inc. with an 8.5% coupon and a ten year maturity. The new notes would be secured by an interest in substantially all of the debtors' real property and incidental personal property subject to liens securing a $500 million working capital and term loan facility to have entered into on the effective date of the plan. The company's existing common stockholders would receive nominal amounts of common stock with the recapitalized company (approximately .05% of the shares for all holders other than Mr. Trump. Such nonaffiliated holders would receive Class A warrants to purchase up to 5.34% of the recapitalized company's common stock. All existing options to acquire common stock in the company would be canceled. All the company's common stockholders, excluding Mr. Trump, would receive an aggregate of $17.5 million cash as well as proceeds from the sale of land.

On the effective date of the plan, the debtors would issue one-year warrants to purchase shares of the recapitalized company's common stock at an aggregate purchase price of $50 million. The company's common shareholders, *excluding* Mr. Trump, would receive new Class A warrants to purchase approximately 3% of the recapitalized company's common stock. Proceeds from any of its shares reserved for issuance of such warrants would be distributed to holders of the TAC Notes.

The result of the above arrangements was 14 months of working through numerous alternatives to de-leverage the balance sheet of the debtors. In addition, the debtors identified and negotiated with potential investors and eventually reached a consensus on the terms of the proposed restructuring with substantial majorities of the holders of the debtors' public indebtedness.

As part of the plan, the company would implement a reverse stock split. Donald Trump would reinvest $55 million in new cash and contribute approximately $16.4 million aggregate principal amount of the TCH Second Priority Notes beneficially owned by him.

Donald Trump also received new THCR Holdings Class A interests exchangeable for 3,700,000 shares of new common stock in exchange for contributing his $55 million in cash into the reorganized THCR Holdings. In addition, he received new THCR Holdings Class A interests exchangeable for 1,043,000 shares of new common stock in exchange for contributing all claims under the TCH Second Priority Notes beneficially owned by him. He received new THCR Holdings Class B interests exchangeable for 4,554,000 shares of new common stock. He received a new warrant valued at approximately $5 million to $10 million and his 25% beneficial ownership interest in Miss Universe LP, LLLP, valued at approximately $5 million and parcels of land in Atlantic City valued at approximately $7.5 million.

In addition, Mr. Trump retained the shares of old THCR common stock and old THCR Holdings LP interest beneficially owned by him, subject to dilution from the reverse stock split and the issuance of the new common stock. If Donald Trump exchanged all of the new THCR Holdings Class A interest and new THCR Holdings Class B interest beneficially owned by him in the new common stock and exercised the new warrant in full, then he would also beneficially own 10,836,000 shares of new common stock that would equal approximately 26.22% of the issued and outstanding new common stock.

So, what happened here? After a lot of hard-fought negotiations, senior debts were largely either reinstated or unimpaired. Lower levels of debt received some equity for their shortfall. Because Donald Trump began with a beneficial interest that constituted 56.43% of the company and wound up with a lesser amount of the new common stock and the option to better his position, after contributing new considerations and receiving other considerations, everyone came away fairly treated and the company had a capital structure that gave the debtor a chance to compete.

C. In re Enron Corp., et al.

From 1985 through mid-2001, Enron grew from a sleepy domestic natural gas pipeline company into a large global natural gas and power company with many attributes of a sleazy savings and loan, thanks to its management. During the last part of 2001, Enron lost access to the capital markets and had insufficient liquidity and financial resources to satisfy its current financial obligations. On December 2, 2001, Enron and 13 subsidiaries filed voluntary Chapter 11 petitions. The bankruptcy was important because of the sheer dollars involved, but a sideshow compared with the criminal activities.

The interesting part of this plan of reorganization is the way in which it addressed, in a measured way, a precipitous and disastrous fall of what was one of the five largest companies in the United States.

The market began to sense that something was not quite right when on August 14, 2001, Enron announced the resignation of Jeff Skilling as Enron's President and the assumption of the duties by its Chairman, the late Ken Lay. Both were later convicted by a Texas jury of criminal felonies. On October 16, Enron reported a net loss for the third quarter of $618 million, including a total of $1.01 billion for after-tax non-recurring charges. Of this, $287 million related to asset impairments recorded by Enron's water company, $180 million was associated with restructuring Enron Broadband Services, and $544 million related to losses concerning certain investments. Enron held a conference call on the earnings report and acknowledged a $1.2 billion equity reduction. Moody's announced the debt was being placed "on review" for downgrade.

On October 22, Enron announced it would cooperate fully with the SEC's request to provide information concerning certain related party transactions that had been occurring. On October 24, Enron announced that its CFO, Andrew Fastow (who later pled guilty to federal felony criminal charges), was taking a "leave of absence." That same day, Enron announced it had drawn on its committed lines of credit to provide cash liquidity in excess of $1 billion. On October 29, Moody's announced Enron's credit rating was downgraded to two notches above non-investment grade and placed it on review for further downgrading. On October 31, Enron reported the SEC had opened a formal investigation into certain matters that had been the subject of recent press reports. On November 1, Enron announced that some of its banks as co-arrangers had executed commitment letters to provide $1 billion of secured credit.

On November 8, Enron filed a form 8K discussing its $1.2 billion reduction in shareholder's equity, as well as adjustments based on certain "off-balance-sheet entities" that should have been included in Enron's consolidated financial statement. This led to the need to restate financial statements from 1997 through 2000 and the first two quarters of 2001.

On November 9, Enron and Dynegy announced the execution of a merger agreement and a $1.5 billion asset-backed equity infusion by Dynegy. This, clearly, was a desperation move by Enron.

On November 21, Enron announced it was in active discussions with its primary lenders on a restructuring of its debt obligations.

On November 28, Enron announced it received a notice from Dynegy that effective immediately, it was terminating the merger agreement. Enron also announced that S&P, Moody's and Fitch had downgraded Enron's credit rating to below investment grade.

On December 2, Enron announced that it, along with certain subsidiaries, had filed voluntary petitions for Chapter 11 reorganization in the United States Bankruptcy Court for the Southern District of New York. As of its initial petition date, the Enron companies employed 32,000 individuals worldwide. The debtors' business operations consisted of a hodge- podge of commodities, sales and services, assets, investments, electrical transmission and trading operations, as well as natural gas pipelines.

Debtors' pre-bankruptcy credit facilities consisted of $1.75 billion in 364-day senior unsecured committed revolving credit, through many of the major banks in the United States. This facility was fully drawn in October 2001. In addition, the debtors had $1.25 billion in a long-term senior unsecured committed revolving credit that was also fully drawn in October 2001.

Toronto Dominion Bank, as agent, had provided an additional $12 million, 13-month credit facility. Toronto Dominion resigned as agent in December 2001. In addition, Enron had borrowed $100 million on a revolving promissory note from Toronto Dominion. At the petition date, the principal balance under that note was $55 million. A $100 million revolving promissory note existed between Enron and Barclays as lender. The outstanding balance on that note on the petition date was $15 million.

Two Enron non-debtor subsidiaries had corporate revolvers at the petition date with a total commitment of $1 billion.

At the petition date, Enron had two syndicated committed letter-of-credit facilities, including *inter alia*, $166 million owed to WestLB; $290 million to a group of banks led by JP Morgan Chase Bank and various and sundry small letters of credit totaling approximately $651 million. In addition, an incredible amount of Enron junk-bond debt existed with various indenture trustees. Some examples were: a 7% exchangeable note through the Bank of New York as Trustee for $402 million; Wells Fargo Bank, as Trustee, for $700 million in outstanding obligations as indenture trustee; Chase Manhattan Bank as Trustee held $500 million in similar indenture debt; Wells Fargo Bank of Minnesota held convertible senior notes totaling $1.2 billion for one issue and at least twice this amount in other issues. At least four different preferred stock issues were outstanding. As of December 5, 2001, Enron had 764 million shares of common stock issued and outstanding and held 14 million shares of treasury stock. In short, billions were owed and the company had sunk like a rock.

Lawsuits flew in every direction during the bankruptcy, which consisted primarily of a liquidation of a business thought too big to fail.

The Plan of Reorganization

The plan consisted of a "rough justice approach" that involved a compromise and settlement of certain issues disputed by various groups of creditors, examiners, and other parties-in-interest. The plan was little more than a glorified liquidation, albeit a large one. Compromises were reached, including give and take on whether the estates of each debtor should be regarded separately for purposes of making payments to creditors, and whether the proceeds from liquidation of the assets should be combined. In the end, inter-company claims issues were settled in bulk, although many groups of creditors received larger payments based on the quality of the assets that supported their indebtedness.

A litigation trust and special litigation trust were set up to effectuate recoveries going forward. Enron's principal law firm, Vinson & Elkins, paid $30,000,000 in late 2006 to settle creditors' claims. The estates were not substantively consolidated for purposes of the plan. However, as part of the compromise and settlement embodied in the plan, the holders of various claims received their distributions based on a hypothetical pooling of the assets and liabilities of most of the debtors. Priority and tax claims were paid in full. A number of related party transactions were dealt with, including those known as "Chewco," the "LJM Partnerships," and "RADR." Examiners came and went, accusations were tossed around, and, at the end of the day, after hundreds of millions of dollars in fees and expenses were paid, assets were to be sold and the creditors were projected to receive less than 50¢ on the dollar.

D. Storage Technology Corporation

Storage Technology Corporation ("Storage Tech"), Storage Technology Leasing Corporation ("Storage Leasing") and 16 of affiliates filed voluntary Chapter 11 petitions in the United States Bankruptcy Court for the Southern District of Colorado in 1984. Storage Tech and its subsidiaries confirmed a consensual plan of reorganization in 1986.

Storage Tech designed, manufactured, marketed and serviced computer peripheral and retrieval subsystems used in information storage and retrieval. Its principal products were high-performance tape and disk storage subsystems and impact and non-impact printers. Storage Tech and its subsidiaries had approximately $800 million in pre-petition debt consisting primarily of senior unsecured debt, and $570 million in subordinated debt. The balance ($99 million) was held by various secured lenders and the Internal Revenue Service.

Storage Tech and one of its subsidiaries, Documation Inc. ("Documation"), had three outstanding issues of subordinated debentures: the 9% Subordinated Debentures due May 15, 20001 ("Storage Tech Debentures"); the Documation 12% Senior Subordinated Debentures due May 1, 1999 ("Documation Senior Debentures"), and the Documation 11 1/2% Subordinated Debentures due May 1, 1988 ("Documation Junior Debentures"). At one time or another all of these could be purchased at well below their ultimate recovery.

Under the joint plan confirmed by Storage Tech and its subsidiaries, creditors secured by assets of the debtors other than lease or installment sale agreements were unimpaired under the plan, while creditors secured with leases or installment sales contracts were issued five-year promissory notes.

Okay, how was the pie divided? When Storage Tech is characterized, as it often is, as a success for the creditors who bought into the problem, what did they see when the plan was presented to them?

Unsecured creditors with superior rights to the Storage Tech Subordinated Debentures (i.e., claims for funds due on borrowed money) received a *pro rata* distribution of approximately $83 million cash, $245.5 million in new debentures, and 138,637,726 shares (approximately 60%) of common stock in the reorganized Storage Tech. This distribution equated to a 14.4% cash payout, a 42.1% payout in new debentures, and a distribution of 228 shares of common stock per $1,000 claim. The value of the distribution (cash plus market value of the securities) totaled 100 cents on the dollar shortly after receipt.

Unsecured trade creditors received a 12.4% cash payout, a 39.1% payout in new debentures, and a distribution of 254 shares of common stock per $1,000 claim. Within a matter of weeks, this also proved to be a complete payout.

Under the joint plan, the three series of debentures were classified as separate subclasses within one class. The holders of claims pursuant to the Documation Senior Debentures received a *pro rata* distribution of $17.4 million in cash (of which $300,000 would be withheld by the indenture trustee pursuant to the indenture to satisfy the trustee's compensation and expenses claims), $12.76 million in new debentures and 6,471,047 shares (approximately 2.8%) of common stock. This distribution equated to a 5.4% cash payout, a 48.1% payout in new debentures and a distribution of 244 shares of common stock per $1,000 claim.

The holders of claims pursuant to the Storage Tech Debentures received a *pro rata* distribution of $500,000 cash, $22 million in new debentures and 34,459,643 shares (approximately 14.9% of the outstanding common stock). The debtors noted in the plan that substantially all of the cash portion of the distributions received by the indenture creditors were to satisfy the trustee's claims for compensation and expenses. This distribution equates to a 25.1% payout in new debentures and a distribution of 394 shares of common stock per $1,000 claim. While no cash was received, these holders also received a handsome return relative to the post-filing prices of their debentures.

The holders of claims pursuant to the Documation Junior Debentures received a *pro rata* distribution of $260,000 in cash (all of which would be retained by the trustee), $4.74 million in new debentures and 5,852,197 shares (approximately 5%) of common stock. This distribution equates to a 29.9% payout in new debentures and a distribution of 369 shares of common stock per $1,000 claim. Table 3.1 summarizes three various distributions.

Table 3.1
Storage Tech Distributions to
Unsecured Creditors per
$1,000 of Claims

	Cash	Debentures	Shares
Senior Unsecured Creditors	142	421	228
Unsecured Trade Creditors	124	391	254
Documented Senior Debentures	54	481	244
Storage Tech Debentures		251	394
Documation Junior Debentures		291	361

The point is that the interplay between the junior and senior creditors over what appeared to be not enough to go around was bridged by new paper that included realizable returns from the future of a reorganizable debtor. The securities issued proved to have a significant value after the plan was approved. In other words, you should not expect to be paid off in cash on confirmation of the reorganization plan. That is the exception, rather than the rule.

Suppose you were a holder of subordinated debt from Storage Tech. What would the Disclosure Statement you received from the bankruptcy court have looked like?

The Disclosure Statement stated:

4. Subordinated Unsecured Claims

a. *Class 4A (StorageTek Subordinated Debentures).* Class 4A consists of all claims based upon or which have been or could be asserted under the indenture or otherwise on behalf of the holders of the StorageTek Subordinated Debentures, other than claims, if any, in Class 6D (securities litigation claims). The aggregate amount of such claims is approximately $88 million. This amount includes the principal amount of such debentures, interest accrued prior to the filing date and the fees and expenses of the indenture trustee.

The Plan provides that on the Effective Date, the holders of Class 4A Allowed Claims will receive a pro rata distribution of $500,000 of Cash, New Debentures having a principal amount of $22 million and 34,459,643 shares of Common Stock representing approximately 14.9% of outstanding Common Stock on the Effective Date. Debtors are informed that all or substantially all of the Cash portion of the distributions received by the indenture trustee will be retained, pursuant to its indenture, by the indenture trustee to satisfy its claims for compensation and expenses, including compensation of any counsel or other consultants which may have been retained by the indenture trustee.

b.   *Class 4B (Documation Senior Subordinated Debentures).* Class 4B consists of all Allowed Claims against Documation and/or StorageTek based upon or which have been or could be asserted under the indenture, the supplemental indenture or otherwise on behalf of the holders of the Documation Senior Subordinated Debentures, other than claims in Class 6E (securities litigation claims). The aggregate amount of such claims, which include the principal amount of the Documation Senior Subordinated Debentures, interest accrued thereon prior to the Filing Date, and the fees and expenses of the indenture trustee for the Documation Senior Subordinated Debentures, is approximately $26.8 million.

The Plan provides that on the Effective Date, holders of Class 4B Allowed Claims will receive a pro rata distribution of $1.74 million Cash, New Debentures having a principal amount of $12.6 million, and 6,471,047 shares of Common Stock representing approximately 2.8% of the outstanding Common Stock on the Effective Date.

The amount of cash that will actually be received by the holders of Documation Senior Subordinated Debentures will be reduced by the amount of Cash withheld by the indenture trustee for such debentures pursuant to the indenture to satisfy claims for indenture trustee compensation and expenses, including compensation of any counsel or other consultant which may have been retained by the indenture trustee.

c.   *Class 4C (Documation Subordinated Debentures).* Class 4C consists of all Allowed Claims against Documation and/or

StorageTek based upon or which have been or could be asserted under the indenture, the supplemental indenture or otherwise on behalf of the holders of the Documation Subordinated Debentures, other than claims in Class 6F (securities litigation claims). The aggregate amounts of such claims which include the principal amount of the Documation Subordinated Debentures, interest accrued thereon prior to the Filing Date, and the fees and expenses of the indenture trustee for the Documation Subordinated Debentures is approximately $16.1 million.

The Plan provides that on the Effective Date, the holders of Class 4C Allowed Claims will receive a pro rata distribution of $260,000 in Cash, New Debentures having a principal amount of $4.74 million and 4,852,197 shares of Common Stock representing approximately 2.5% of the outstanding Common Stock on the Effective Date.

Debtors are informed that all or substantially all of the Cash portion of the foregoing distribution shall be retained by the indenture trustee for such debentures pursuant to the indenture to satisfy claims for indenture trustee compensation and expenses, including compensation of any counsel or other consultant which may have been retained by the indenture trustee.

In summary, the non-subordinated unsecured creditors received a cash payout of between 12.5% and 14.5%, a 39% "new debenture payout," and a 25.4% "share dividend." The subordinated debt holders (except for the Documation Senior Debenture holders) received a 0% cash dividend, a 20% to 25% "new debenture payout," and a 37% to 39% "share payout." The Documation Senior Debenture holders received a 5.4% cash dividend, a 48% new debenture payout and a 24.4% share dividend. Under the joint plan, equity retained about a 13% ownership interest.

The Disclosure Statement and joint plan each contain a detailed provision regarding the effect of confirmation on the release and satisfaction of claims, including the waiver of rights attendant to contractual subordination.

Do all cases involving several layers of debt work out as well as Storage Tech? Of course not. What does a failure look like? Here's one of our favorite examples.

E. MGF Oil Corporation

MGF Oil Corporation ("MGF") filed a voluntary Chapter 11 petition in the United States Bankruptcy Court for the Western District of Texas, Midland-Odessa Division. MGF confirmed a plan of reorganization three years later.

MGF was an oil and gas exploration and production company. MGF and its subsidiaries had approximately $287 million in pre-petition debt, allocated as follows: bank lenders (including deficiency claims), $145 million; general unsecured claims, $32 million; and subordinated debt, $110 million. The subordinated debt consisted of the following series of debentures:

(1) 6% Senior Subordinated Debentures due 1988 ("6% Debentures") issued by MGF;

(2) 14 1/2% Senior Subordinated Debentures due 1995 ("14 1/2% Debentures") issued by MGF.

(3) Class A and Class B Non-Interest Bearing Convertible Senior Subordinated Debentures due 1989 ("0% Debentures") issued by MGF International Finance N.V. ("International") and guaranteed by MGF;

(4) 8 1/4% Convertible Subordinated Guaranteed Debentures due 1995 ("8 1/4% Debentures") issued by International and guaranteed by MGF; and

The First Amended Plan filed by MGF classified the debtor's subordinated debt and senior unsecured debt in a single class. The trustee for the 14.5% Debentures objected to confirmation of this plan on that basis. Additionally, one bank filed a motion to enforce the subordination agreements contained in the indentures. The plan provided for a handsome (non-cash) return for the subordinated debt holders:

As a measure to permit distributions to holders of Public Subordinated Debt, it is a condition to Confirmation of the Plan that the Lenders and other holders of Senior Debt enter into the Subordination Enforcement Agreement. Under this agreement with respect to each holder of Public Subordinated Debt who does not seek to enforce any rights as a Senior Creditor against any other holder of Public Subordinated Debt, the holders of Senior Debt will limit the exercise of their rights as Senior Creditors to allow distributions to holders of Public Subordinated Debt as follows:

a. to holders of Class 4 Claims based upon 6% Debentures and 14 1/2% Debentures, 1.36 shares of Preferred Stock and 27.88 shares of New Common Stock per $1,000 face amount of such Debentures; and

b. with respect to Class 4 Claims based upon MGF's guarantee of the 0% Debentures and 8 1/4% Debentures, 0.88 shares of Preferred Stock and 19.72 shares of New Common Stock per $1,000 face amount of such Debentures. The remainder of the shares distributable with respect to such Class 4 Claims based upon subordinated debentures will be distributed to the Lenders.

(From the First Disclosure Statement)

This Plan failed. A sufficient number of the subordinated holders determined that they would hold out for more, and they voted accordingly. Many key players were more concerned with what the other guy was getting than with what they were getting. After further intensive negotiations, MGF filed its Second Amended Plan of Reorganization in December 1985.

In the Second Amended Plan, each debenture series was properly and separately classified in a subclass of its own. Under the Second Amended Plan, MGF's bank lenders would have received a controlling interest in the preferred stock of the reorganized debtor to be issued pursuant to the plan. Senior unsecured debt claimants would have received 1.83 shares of preferred stock for $1,000 of allowed claim, i.e., 00183 times the allowed amount of their claim. A paltry recovery it would seem.

The distribution to subordinated debt holders increased under the Second Amended Plan. The interests of existing equity holders were extinguished under the Second Amended Plan, with distributions of stock previously going to equity accruing to the benefit of the subordinated debt holders. The Class A and Class B 6% Debentures and the 14 1/2% Debenture claimants (debentures issued by MGF) received 1.36 shares of preferred stock for each $1,000 of allowed claim – i.e., .00136 times the amount of its allowed claim. The holders of claims pursuant to the 0% Debentures (issued by International) received 0.88 shares of preferred stock for each $1,000 of allowed claim – i.e., .00088 times the amount of their allowed claim. The senior unsecured and subordinated debt also received common stock under the Second Amended Plan in the following ratios: senior unsecured debt, 37.41 shares per $1,000 in allowed claims; 6% Debentures (Class A), 33.83 shares; 6% Debentures (Class B), 37.41 shares; 14% Debentures, 35.86; 0% Debentures, 21.52; and 8% Debentures, 21.82.

The Second Amended Plan also contained a provision stating that the plan gave effect and enforcement to subordination provisions and that no class would retain any right to any consideration received by another class:

> 9.0 The Plan shall be deemed to give effect and enforcement to all claims for consensual, contractual or equitable subordination pursuant to Bankruptcy Code 510. No class of creditors shall have or retain any right or claim to any consideration distributed under the Plan to any other class of creditors.

MGF did not seek confirmation of the Second Amended Plan because of a precipitous drop in oil prices. In other words, its core business fell apart because of market conditions while it languished in Chapter 11. The case dragged on. MGF subsequently submitted a Third Amendment Plan. Additionally, other parties in interest submitted plans for reorganization. Among those was a plan filed by Parker & Parsley Petroleum Company. A modified version of this plan was confirmed.

Under the confirmed plan, the bank lenders sold their secured debt position to Parker & Parsley for approximately $40 million, received certain MGF oil and gas interests and certain MGF accounts receivable. With respect to the bank lenders' unsecured claims, the bank lenders received 5,250,000 shares (10.5%) of common stock in the new much smaller reorganized debtor, or 70 shares of common stock for every $1,000 in claims.

Other secured creditors were paid in full or had the collateral securing their claim abandoned to them. Priority and small unsecured (less than $100) claimants were paid in full. General unsecured creditors received 4,550,000 shares (9.1%) of common stock, or 140 shares for every $1,000 in claims. The various debenture holders were classified in separate subclasses in a single class with no other members. Debenture holders collectively received 7,700,000 shares (10.5%) of common stock, or approximately 70 shares for every $1,000 in claims. Existing equity received no distributions under the Parker & Parsley plan.

The plan contained a provision that it should be deemed to enforce subordination in favor of general unsecured debt, as against the subordinated debt holders, and in favor of the 6% Debenture holders and 14 1/2% Debenture holders, as against the 0% Debenture holders and 8 1/4% Debenture holders. The Disclosure Statement stated:

Enforcement of Subordination. The Plan is to be deemed to enforce subordination of subordinated debt to senior debt, and no holder of senior debt, as such, shall have any claim against or right to obtain any property to be distributed to a holder of subordinated debt, as such, under the Plan. The Plan does not make adjustments to take into account seniority and subordination between the various issues of Subordinated Debt and does not purport to enforce subordination within Class 3, except in all cases as between holders of MGF Debentures and holders of Guaranteed Debenture. Holders of senior issues of subordinated debt may be able to enforce subordination against holders of junior issues of subordinated debt upon application to the Bankruptcy Court pursuant to the provisions of Bankruptcy Code §510.

The lesson was clear. After insisting on their "rights," the subordinated parties managed to preserve their "rights" to get less because of the diminished return available two years later. The case was a failure for all but the secured creditors.

Wait a minute, you say. You mean that I can invest in this area only to find that any one irate group can destroy, or for whatever reason delay, a case while the bankruptcy process consumes the debtor and any hope of a recovery for anything other than the senior and secured creditors? The MGF experience created among many of the same players a solution when the problem next arose. Enter the "either/or" plan.

F. Global Marine Inc.

Global Marine Inc. (GMI) and 11 subsidiaries filed voluntary Chapter 11 petitions in the United States Bankruptcy Court for the Southern District of Texas, Houston Division, on January 27, 1986. (Two other subsidiaries subsequently filed for Chapter 11 relief.) GMI and its subsidiaries (Global) confirmed a consensual plan of reorganization on February 2, 1989.

GMI was a publicly traded company whose subsidiaries engaged in offshore oil and gas drilling, exploration and extraction. Global had approximately $1.2 billion in pre-petition debt allocated as follows: secured drilling rig-related debt, $660 million; unsecured debt, $156 million; subordinated debt, $400 million.

The subordinated debt consisted of four issues of subordinated debentures issued by GMI: the 16 1/8% Senior Subordinated Debentures due 2002; the 16% Senior Subordinated Debentures due 2001; the 13% Convertible Senior

Subordinated Debentures due 2003, and the 12 3/8% Senior Subordinated
Debentures due 1998.

Under the plan confirmed by Global, the claims of all debenture holders
were treated in the same class. Under the plan, <u>all</u> holders of debenture claims
were allocated a *pro rata* share of common stock of the reorganized debtor and
receipts from any recovery of successful avoidance actions against affiliates of
Global. However, this distribution remained in the possession of GMI for distribution to the holders of unsecured claims that constituted senior indebtedness under the various debentures.

Nevertheless, under an "either/or" structure designed to promote a unanimous (each class voting yes) acceptance of the plan, the plan provided that if
the classes containing the claims of the debenture holders and equity interests
of GMI accepted the plan, then each holder of an allowed claim arising out of
the debentures would receive its *pro rata* share out of a pool of 7.5 million
shares of common stock, with warrants to purchase its *pro rata* share of an
additional 7.5 million shares. The Disclosure Statement provided:

> (i)   GMI Class 9 — Debenture Claims. GMI's subordinated bonds
> are in the aggregate face amount of $453,481,456 (including
> accrued pre-petition interest), resulting in Debenture Claims, net
> of any unamortized discount amount, totaling approximately
> $399,133,920. On the Effective Date, all bonds and other instru-
> ments evidencing a Debenture Claim will be cancelled, annulled
> and extinguished. Although the holders of Debenture Claims are
> allocated a pro rata share of Majority Common Stock and Affiliate
> Receipts, along with the holders of Unsecured Claims and Affili-
> ate Claims, they do not actually receive any of such property.
> Instead, such amounts of the Majority Common Stock and Affili-
> ate Receipts remain in the possession of GMI for distribution to
> the holders of Unsecured Claims that constitute Senior Indebted-
> ness.

Nevertheless, but only if the Plan is accepted by holders of Debenture Claims and Equity Interests at GMI, and is thus a Consensual Plan,
each holder of Allowed Debenture Claims will receive, upon tender to the
indenture trustee of the bonds and other instruments evidencing each
holder's Claim a pro rata share of 7,500,000 shares of New GMI Common
Stock ("Minority Common Stock") and GMI Warrants representing a right
to purchase 7,500,000 shares of New GMI Common Stock ("Minority

Warrants"). GMI estimates that each holder of a $1000 bond will receive the following amount of New GMI Common Stock and GMI warrants.

Issue

	13%	12-3/8%	16%	16-1/8%
% of Allowed Debenture Claims	30.385%	7.004%	24.509%	38.062%
New Shares	528,300	1,838,175	2,854,650	2,278,875
New Warrants	528,300	1,838,175	2,854,650	2,278,875
Number of Bonds	25,000	100,000	149,600	122,500
Per Bond:				
New Shares	21.13	18.38	19.08	18.60
New Warrants	21.13	18.38	19.08	18.60

As described in section G.2(d) herein, GMI may elect to cash-out New GMI Common Stock holdings of 100 shares or less.

11. *Equity Interests*

The Equity Interests that are treated under the Plan include the publicly held Common Stock and Preferred Stock interests at the GMI level and the Debtor-held stock interests at all other levels.

(a) Equity Interests in GMI. All Equity Interests in GMI, which include Common Stock and Preferred Stock holdings, will be cancelled on the Effective Date of the Plan. Under the absolute priority rule, the holders of Equity Interests at GMI are not entitled to retain or receive any property on account of their interests; however, the absolute priority rule will be invoked only if the classes containing Debenture Claims, Old Common Stock Equity Interests and Old Preferred Stock Equity Interests vote against the Plan. On the condition that such holders vote in favor of the Plan, the Plan provides for a distribution to the holders of GMI's Equity Interests. As described in more detail in sections E.1(1) and E.1(m), that distribution consists of 2,500,000 shares of New GMI Common Stock and 5,200,000 GMI Warrants.

With common stock of the reorganized debtor assigned a value of $1.50 per share in the Disclosure Statement, this distribution amounted to a 2.8% return on the debenture holders' claims. By contrast, the secured rig lenders received distributions equal to 77.5% of their claims, and senior unsecured debt received distributions equal to 39.3% of their claims.

The leaders of the subordinated debt holders had been able to muster the votes of a sufficient number of debenture holders to accept the plan, but they failed to obtain the requisite dollar amounts voting in favor of the plan. The subordinated debt holders, at great cost, managed to reopen the voting and get one major holder with a sufficiently large amount of debt to change his vote. The equity class then found a large amount of debt to change his vote. The equity class then found a large interest-holder who had not voted and voting approval was obtained. Clearly, *a fine recovery for the subordinated debt holders was achieved.*

G. In re Braniff Airways, Incorporated (Braniff)

Braniff International Corporation (International) filed for bankruptcy on May 13, 1982 in the United States District Court for the Northern District of Texas, Fort Worth Division. Braniff and International confirmed a consensual plan of reorganization on September 1, 1983.

Braniff was a certified air carrier engaged in the domestic and international air transportation of persons, property and mail. International was the holding company parent of Braniff and was also the parent for certain other wholly-owned operating subsidiaries.

Under the plan confirmed by the bankruptcy court, Braniff was reorganized. It was to engage in fixed-base operations at Love Field in Dallas, and, through a subsidiary to be formed, resume operation of a scheduled domestic airline route system with its hub at Dallas-Fort Worth Airport, using 30 Boeing 727-200 aircraft leased to such subsidiary by a liquidating trust established for the benefit of the holders of Braniff's senior debt. The reorganized operations would be funded principally by Hyatt Air, Inc., which would control the reorganized companies as a result of its investments (anticipated to total in excess of $10 million).

All of the debtor's aircraft, related engines and rotable spare parts, as well as certain of Braniff's other assets, would be transferred to or for the benefit of the Senior Creditors. Additionally, the Senior Creditors, the general unsecured creditors, and holders of certain of the debtor's preferred stock received an aggregate of approximately 12.3% of the common stock of Braniff, plus preferred stock convertible into 7% of the common stock of the reorganized Braniff. Further, the Senior Creditors received warrants to purchase 526,000 shares of common stock of the airline subsidiary formed under the plan, cash, and undivided interests in the liquidating trust.

In contrast, subordinated claims of Braniff (approximately $25 million) received 52,000 shares of common stock in reorganized Braniff, and subordinated claims of International received, along with certain other claims and interests that together aggregated approximately $145 million, 180,000 shares of common stock. By comparison, Hyatt received, among other things, 8,000,000 shares of common stock, and 1,402,000 shares were issued to other claimants under the plan.

The plan also provided that in the event the subordinated debt holders of Braniff did not accept the plan, the debtors would seek confirmation under 1129(b) (cram-down), and any recoveries by subordinated debt holders under the plan would remain subordinated to the rights of the Senior Creditors. The plan operated to release any and all claims from other creditors if accepted by the requisite majorities.

The Disclosure Statement provided:

> Class VII creditors are those holding subordinated claims against Airways, including publicly held 5 3/4% subordinated debentures, pursuant to a certain indenture dated as a December 1, 1966 and a certain subordinated credit agreement dated as of March 15, 1973 with Boeing. The Debtors estimate that the total amount of claims which will qualify for participation in Class VII will be approximately $25,000,000.

> Under the terms of the 1966 indenture and the 1973 subordinated credit agreement, any recoveries that such creditors make are subordinated to the rights of the Senior Creditors. Therefore, the Senior Creditors would have a right to any recoveries by such subordinated creditors. For this reason, the Class VII claimants would receive nothing in a liquidation of the debtors. The allegations made by OUCC, SBOCC and U.S. Trust in their lawsuits (described above under "Litigation Regarding the Indenture" and "Inter-Secured Creditor Litigation"), if established, might result in the elimination of subordination rights of certain Senior Creditors. If those rights were to be eliminated, the Debtors believe that Class VII claimants nevertheless would remain subordinated to the claims of the public secured

bond holders and the Class VII claimants would only be entitled to receive payments as Class VII claimants from the amounts remaining after the satisfaction in full of the claims of the public secured bondholders.

In recognition, on the one hand, of the Senior Creditors' subordination rights, and, on the other hand, in settlement of claims asserted by SBOCC, U.S. Trust, and the OUCC against the Senior Creditors, the Plan provides that the Class VII claimants will receive their respective pro rata shares of 52,000 shares of BA Common Stock free from any subordination rights of the Senior Creditors, but the Class VII claimants will not receive other distributions to which they would be entitled as Class VIA claimants. Class VII claimants and Senior Creditors will release any claims either have against the other including but not limited to Senior Creditors' subordination rights if and only if Classes V, VIA and VII vote to accept the Plan and the Plan is confirmed.

If the requisite majorities of Class VII creditors do not vote to support the Plan, the Debtors intend nonetheless to seek confirmation of the Plan over their rejection pursuant to § 1129(b) of the Bankruptcy Code. In that event, any consideration otherwise distributable to junior claimants against Airways would remain subject to the subordination rights of the Senior Creditors against the Class VII claimants as well as such defenses to those claims and their own claims as the Class VII claimants may have against the Senior Creditors. The result of the foregoing to the Class VII claimants is that they would not, in all likelihood, receive any distribution under the Plan if it is confirmed over their objection.

This means, on the one hand, that if the Class VII creditors vote in favor of the Plan, they will receive relatively prompt distributions of their pro rata shares of 52,000 shares of BA Common Stock, but no more. On the other hand, if the Class VII claimants do not vote in support of the Plan, they may receive distributions of approximately the same number of shares of BA Common Stock (assuming the Debtors' estimate as to the amount of Class VIA claims is correct) plus shares of Series AA Stock and possibly certain other distributions to which Class VIA claimants may be entitled, but (a) such distributions may be delayed for as long as two years and, as to the shares of BA Common Stock, may be less than would be distributed under Class VII because of the uncertainties with respect to the total amount of Class

VIA claims, and (b) such distributions would be subject to the subordination rights, if any, of the Senior Creditors.

The economic realities of the Chapter 11 reorganization process provides a backdrop that generally leads to the payment of some tribute to deeply subordinated debt holders in order to achieve a maximum return to the senior debt holders. The economic time-delay costs in bankruptcy usually lead senior debt holders to conclude that paying a modest recovery to the junior classes is preferable to exposing their own recovery to the risks involved in allowing the debtor to remain in Chapter 11 for the many months necessary to cram-down the subordinated debt holders.

The subordinated paper of Braniff could be purchased early on in the bankruptcy for a few cents on the dollar. Thus, the recoveries, while small in absolute terms, represented large returns to those who had the courage to buy.

THE LAST ACT: CONFIRMATION OF THE PLAN

It's now time to talk about the last act. The first scene in the final act of the bankruptcy process is the confirmation hearing. After the announcement of the voting classes' vote, the court verifies that the plan has met the requisite technical requirements of the Bankruptcy Code. A fantastic amount of momentum occurs at this hearing, with bluffing dissenters and holdouts clamoring to get on board the plan before the train leaves the station. Adamant dissenters who don't like the plan stage their last battle against it. In major cases, lone holdouts face long odds. Typically, they find themselves in front of a court that is inclined to follow the wishes of the great body of creditors and rule against a small number of dissenters.

The final scene of the bankruptcy process occurs, perhaps appropriately, behind closed doors. The consummation of the plan is quite similar to a closing of any other financial transaction. In some lawyer's office, the documents that implement the terms of the plan or reorganization are approved and signed by the parties. Then the various groups exchange their old paper for new paper and/or cash, and the debtor receives its fresh start.

What type of securities will the creditors likely receive at the closing of the bankruptcy case? A leading bankruptcy treatise gives insight into the reasoning usually utilized in that decision:

Consideration should be given in cases involving holders of public debt instruments to providing such holders under the plan with debt securities of a similar nature (except generally speaking, with respect to the principal amount or interest rate thereof). For example, such debt securities issued under the plan may be issued pursuant to an indenture and be marketable through public trading. In such cases, it might be easier for the plan proponent to obtain the acceptances of such holders of the plan if they are to receive thereunder consideration similar in form (if not substance) to the securities formerly held by such holders. To the extent that this raises separate classification issues and enhances the leverage of such class with respect to acceptance or rejection of the plan, careful consideration and evaluation would be desirable."

5 Collier Bankruptcy Practice Guide 90.06[5][b] (A. Herzog & L. King eds. 1984) (footnote omitted)

The authors of the treatise earmarked the following checklist of terms to scrutinize if you are to receive debt securities:

1. Principal amount
2. Interest rate
3. Maturity
4. Subordination provisions
5. Security
6. Sinking fund requirements
7. Mandatory and/or optional redemptions
8. Conversion rights
9. Variations in any of the foregoing characteristics based on various types of contingencies

For equity, the same authors give the following checklist:

1. Dividend rate
2. Cumulative dividend provisions
3. Liquidation preference
4. Mandatory and/or optional redemption provisions
5. Conversion rights
6. Preemptive rights
7. Voting rights
8. Registration rights
9. Restrictions on transfers

Our discussion thus far has highlighted a number of inefficiencies and imperfections inherent in the bankruptcy process. Accordingly, you should not expect the culmination of the reorganization process necessarily to provide any permanent cures for the companies that confirm plans of reorganization. Recidivist debtors are common, e.g., Braniff, Wilson Foods. Your goal is to profit from the process, take your profit and go on to the next opportunity. The reason for the inability of the bankruptcy courts to provide permanent cures is fundamental:

If a plan is particularly complex, bankruptcy courts might be unable to determine whether the level of debt in the plan is excessive. Except at the extremes, that question is highly speculative and would usually be grappled with by judging the relative credibility of expert witnesses and investment bankers. Thus, because of a lack of judicial expertise, a potential need to rely on the parties, and the ease with which bankruptcy litigation problems can be resolved by using complex structures, there is a substantial basis for concluding that action in the reorganization court seems unlikely to lead to a capital structure as sound as those ordinarily derived from marketplace bargains. More important, the reorganization court seems unlikely to lead to quick resolution of the problem of recapitalization.

Roe at 548 (footnotes omitted)

CHAPTER 4

FIRST REPUBLIC: A CASE STUDY

The bankruptcy of a large bank holding company is explored herein, a "blow by blow." This chapter provides a vivid example of the complexities that can be encountered from the start to the end of a case, and the economic rewards that can result.

THE FIRST REPUBLIC CASE: A MOSAIC OF AGREEMENTS*

This study reports on the experiences of two insiders (the creditor's committee chairman, Ben Branch, and his senior attorney, Hugh Ray) in tracking through the maze of a major bankruptcy case. This First Republic bankruptcy involved the failure of a $23 billion bank and led ultimately to the distribution of more than $400 million to creditors. The mosaic of agreements that had to be reached in the First Republic case resulted from both its basic nature and the incomplete documentation relating to its subsidiaries' assets and liabilities.

The First Republic Bank Corporation (FRBC) resulted from the merger of two very troubled Texas bank holding companies, and within a year it sought federal assistance. Soon thereafter, regulators seized the company's banks and Chapter 11 ensued. That began a complicated process leading to the resolution of many intra- and inter-estate claims and other disputes involving shifting economic alliances that, in turn, led to a successfully confirmed reorganization plan.

The Reorganization Process: When it seized FRBC's banks, the Federal Deposit Insurance Corporation took possession of the vast majority of the holding company's assets. FRBC retained all of its liabilities and certain nonblank subsidiaries. It also owned a number of causes of action (primarily against the FDIC) with potential affirmative recoveries and remained exposed to cross-claims from the FDIC and others. The result was a legal nightmare for the creditors and a field day for the lawyers. Let us outline the various interested parties:

---

* Based on: "The First Republic Case: A Mosaic of Agreements," *Annual Survey of Bankruptcy Law 1997-1998*, pp. 43-67

The Debtor in Possession: As in most Chapter 11 bankruptcy cases, the exist-ing management was left in place. The debtor was initially led by Albert Casey, later by Richard Carrington and still later by Susan Brown. After several other firms withdrew because of conflicts, the debtor retained the law firm of Gibson, Dunn & Crutcher. The debtor sought to liquidate most of the estate's assets and pursue its claims and causes of action. Later, it sought to lead the estate out of bankruptcy through the formulation of a reorganization plan. The debtor controlled the two primary debtor estates as well as a number of subsidiary corporations. The senior holding company, First Republic Bank Corporation, in turn owned the stock in the old Interfirst Bank (IFRB). Both FRBC and IFRB had their own individual sets of assets and creditors, as well as cross-claims and other disputes with each other.

The Bondholders and Their Committees: The bondholders and other creditors (exclud-ing the FDIC and NCNB) were divided into three primary categories, as well as several significant subcategories. Three principal committees were formed with approximately equal numbers of institutional investors (par purchasers) and bond arbitrageurs (who purchased their bonds at steep discounts). FRBC's senior credi-tors committee retained the firm of Andrews & Kurth, while the subordinated creditors committee retained the firm of Latham & Watkins. IFRB creditors formed a single committee of junior and senior bondholders and retained the firm of Weil, Gotshal & Manges.

The Guarantee Holders: Certain IFRB seniors and all of its juniors held guaran-tees, whose validities were in dispute, from FRBC. These parties at interest worked largely through the IFRB committee. Eventually the senior guarantee holders formed a subgroup and retained counsel, the firm of Shienfeld, Maley & Kay. Chemical Bank, as indenture trustee, protected the IFRB Juniors' in-terest through the McCutcheon, Doyle law firm.

NV Texas Finance: One of IFRB's subsidiaries, NV Texas finance (NV), had issued its own bonds. NV owned some assets directly, including some FRBC issued commercial paper, as well as a creditor claim against IFRB. IFRB had also guaran-teed the NV bond issue. The NV bondholders eventually formed a committee and retained the firm of Jones, Day, Reavis & Pogue to represent them.

The District Court Litigation: The debtor and creditors committees jointly filed suit against the FDIC in the district court. This suit alleged various claims against and offered various defenses to counter-claims of the FDIC. The firm of Shea & Gardner was retained to pursue this litigation.

The FDIC: This government agency eventually found itself engaged in both offensive and defensive litigation in both the bankruptcy and district court. Its bankruptcy court litigation was handled by the firm of Leonard, Marsh, Hurt, Terry & Blinn. At the district court level (after Haynes & Boone were conflicted out), it used Hopkins & Sutter.

NCNB: The FDIC indemnified NCNB against virtually every conceivable cause of action, including intentional torts, arriving out of its takeover of the FRBC banking system.   Nonetheless, NCNB was a party to many disputes between the debtor and creditors committees on one side and the FDIC and NCNB on the other.   NCNB retained the firm of Milbank, Tweed, Hadley & McCloy. Table 4.1 lists the players, claims and their law firms.

Table 4.1
The FRBC Case: The Players and Their Lawyers

Party in Interest	Claims Amount*	Against	Law Firms
The Debtor (FRBC and IFRB)	$1,630	FDIC	Gibson, Dunn & Crutcher
FRBC Seniors	$260	FRBC	Andrews & Kurth
FRBC Juniors	$264	FRBC	Latham & Watkins
IFRB	$490	IFRB	Weil, Gotshal & Manges
District Court Litigation	$1,600	FDIC	Shea & Gardner
NV Texas Finance	$105+	Comb.	Jones Day
IFRB Senior Guarantee Holders	$35	FRBC	Shienfeld, Maley & Kay
IFRB Junior Guarantee Holders	$107	FRBC	McCutcheon, Doyle
FDIC	$2,500	FRBC & IFRB	Leonard, Marth, Hurt, Terry & Blinn (bankruptcy court) Hopkins & Sutter (district court)
NCNB	various	FRBC & IFRB	Milbank, Tweed, Hadley & McCloy

* in $ millions

DISPUTES BETWEEN THE COMMITTEES

Initially, the creditors committees were able to agree only on their common differences with the FDIC and NCNB. Who owned and owed what and the validity of various guarantees were disputed. Other disputes involved alleged fraudulent conveyances, preferences and the typical differences of opinion over subordination provisions. The IFRB-FRBC disputes were particularly complex.

The IFRB-FRBC Disputes: FRBC and IFRB did not agree on the shared ownership of three significant assets (worth $120 million): The Services Companies (two subsidiaries involved in the back office processing for FRBC/NCNB banks); The Pension Fund Surplus; and a $19 million tax refund. In addition FRBC had sizable creditor claims against IFRB that were partially offset by IFRB creditor claims. Complicating this situation further were commercial paper claims against FRBC held by IFRB subsidiaries (assets) that were exposed to significant third-party claims. Other disputes revolved the validity of cross-corporate guarantees, as well as causes of action alleging fraudulent conveyances and preference claims. Figure 4.1 illustrates the structure of these disputes.

Figure 4.1
FRBC-IFRB Disputes

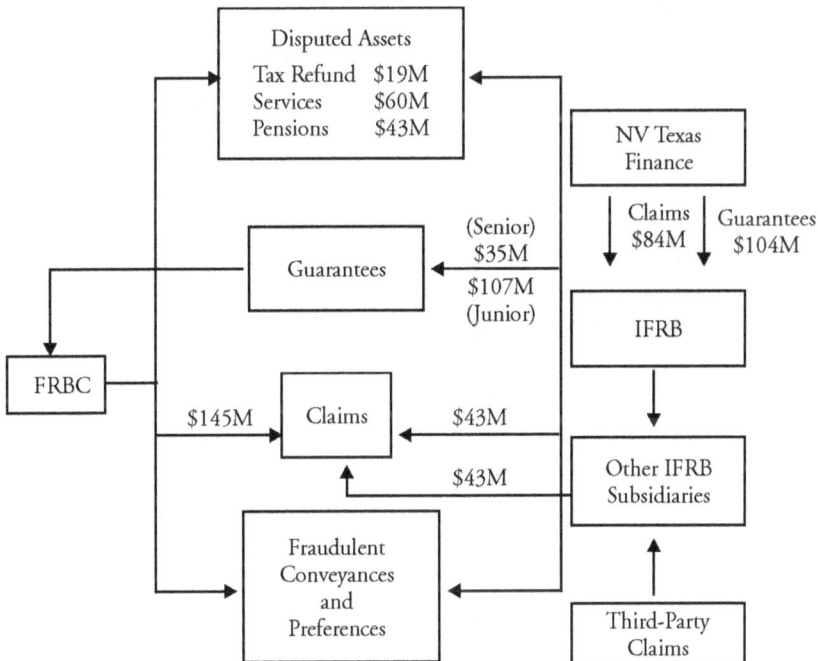

IFRB-NV Disputes: N.V. Texas Finance, an IFRB subsidiary, had issued about $104 million in IFRB guaranteed bonds. In addition, IFRB owed NV $84 million. Finally, NV owned about $20 million of FRBC commercial paper, as well as other assets worth about $20 million. NV's outstanding bonds ($104 million face) could look to creditor and guarantee claims of $188 million against IFRB, creditor claims of $20 million against FRBC and another $20 million in NV held assets. Not surprisingly, the IFRB senior bondholders were not anxious to share their estate with the NV bondholders. Moreover, the FRBC bondholders wanted NV's commercial paper positioned where it could be offset by FRBC's IFRB claims.

NV Balance Sheet

Assets*		Liabilities and Net Worth	
FRBC Commercial Paper	$20	Bond Issue (IFRB Guarantee)	$104
IFRB Loan	$84		
Other Assets	$20	Equity (on paper)	$20
Total	$124	Total	$124

*in millions

OVERFUNDED PENSION PLAN

One of the debtor's major contingent assets was the potential reversion of surplus assets from the FRBC and IFRB pension plans, estimated to be in excess of $100 million. NCNB Texas and the FDIC challenged the debtors' rights as plan sponsors to all of this asset. Accordingly the debtors effected amendments and restatements to clarify the meaning of various plan provisions in a manner which protected the Debtors' interest. Immediately prior to Congress' October 1988 adjournment, however, NCNB Texas and the FDIC sought an amendment to the Technical Corrections Act of 1988 purporting to affect the debtors' right to the surplus. Through extensive contact with key members of Congress and their staffs, debtors, with the assistance of counsel, consultants and lobbyists for individual creditors, were able to obtain a revision in the proposed language that significantly lessened its impact. Instead of attempting to transfer almost the entire surplus to NCNB Texas, the revised version purported to affect no more than half the surplus. Once Congress passed the amendment to the Technical Corrections Act, debtors expeditiously implemented their strategy to retain control over their plans. Literally overnight, the debtors mailed over 15,000 termination notices to preempt NCNB Texas and the FDIC from attempting to prevent the debtors from terminating the plans and realizing the surplus. These events led to negotiations and a final agreement with NCNB Texas and the FDIC that provided for an immediate $43 million settlement payment to debtors' estates.

FIRST REPUBLIC BANK SERVICES CORPORATION AND FIRST REPUBLIC BANK INTEGRATED PROCESSING CORPORATION

First RepublicBank Services Corporation and First RepublicBank Integrated Processing Corporation (the "Services Companies") were wholly-owned subsidiaries of the debtors. When FRBC and IFRB filed for bankruptcy, the Services Companies were providing data-processing services and bank operations services to their affiliate banks (NCNB Texas) and 136 correspondent banks. Services supplied to NCNB Texas accounted for 94%. Moreover, substantial questions existed regarding the ownership of various assets necessary to perform such services. Accordingly, both valuing and realizing value from the Services Companies was extremely difficult. This situation was exacerbated by the intermingling of the affairs of NCNB Texas and the Services Companies, the negotiations between NCNB and the FDIC concerning the ultimate ownership of the various assets of the FRBC banking system, and the implications of a Services Companies' sale upon the debtors' other assets.

On August 15, 1988, shortly after the bankruptcy filing, the Services Companies and NCNB Texas under an Interim Management Agreement agreed that certain management services would continue until October 31, 1988, and that NCNB Texas would pay a specified amount for these services and could not hire any Services Companies employees. Contemporaneous with the expiration of the Interim Management Agreement, NCNB Texas hired the Services Companies' data-processing employees, technicians and operations personnel.

FRBC was concerned that NCNB Texas might create data-processing systems that would duplicate those provided by the Services Companies. If NCNB Texas completed such a duplication or converted the data-processing operations to another system, NCNB Texas would have no further need for the services supplied by the Services Companies. Without NCNB Texas' business, the Services Companies would be left with a skeletal staff and only 6% of their former business. As such, the situation was highly volatile, with the debtors negotiating with NCNB Texas on one front, while trying to preserve the Services Companies' value.

The Services Companies prepared a comprehensive offering memorandum. The offering memorandum, containing detailed information regarding the Services Companies and the correspondent bank business, was distributed to potential purchasers.

The negotiations finally resulted in the sale of most of the Service Companies to NCNB Texas for $55 million. The Debtors' representatives were also meeting with potential purchasers of the correspondent bank business, the remaining 6% of the Service Companies' business. Four parties submitted bids that resulted in the sale of the correspondent bank business for approximately $12.7 million.

TAX REFUND COMPROMISE

One substantial contingent asset of the debtors' estates was a tax refund attributable to significant net operating losses (NOLS) incurred in 1987. As the parent of an affiliated group of corporations (including both the bank and non-bank subsidiaries), FRBC was required to file a consolidated federal income tax return for 1987. A consolidated return combines the separate taxable income and loss figures for each member of the affiliated group into one return.

The FRBC and IFRB 1987 returns were due on or before September 15, 1988, only a few weeks after the bankruptcy. Only days before this date, debtors learned that NCNB Texas expected debtors to make certain elections relating to the carry-back of the NOLs and the recapture (i.e., the taking into income) of the banks' loan loss reserves. As the parent corporation filing the returns, FRBC and IFRB had the authority to make these elections. The debtors also learned, shortly thereafter, that the FDIC intended to take actions that might preclude the debtors from receiving any portion of the refund being generated from the NOLs. After extensive negotiations, a Tax Allocation Compromise was reached that provided the debtors would be guaranteed $18 million of the refund (approximately $4 million greater than the estates might otherwise have been entitled.)

Texas Franchise Tax Dispute: The State of Texas assessed a franchise tax deficiency against the debtors for approximately $1.7 million. Deloitte & Touche tax professionals began an investigation and review of the issues underlying the assessment and advised the debtors that refunds might be available based on a variety of theories, unique applications of tax law and regulations, and novel applications of previous tax cases in Texas. Hampered by a short window of opportunity in which to obtain a refund from the state, the debtors negotiated a $9.4 million franchise tax refund rather than an assessment of $1.7 million, an improvement to the estates of more than $11 million.

FIRST REPUBLIC LIFE INSURANCE COMPANY AND FIRST REPUBLICBANK LIFE INSURANCE COMPANY

First Republic Life Insurance Company and First RepublicBank Life Insurance Company (the "Insurance Companies") offered credit life and credit accident and health insurance in connection with installment loans provided by debtors' former bank subsidiaries. An offering package was prepared and distributed to interested parties. Two preliminary proposals were presented to the Bankruptcy Court. The proposals were, however, subject to higher offers received in a bidding process to take place at the Bankruptcy Court hearing scheduled to approve the sale. Four potential buyers arrived, and after a number of bids were offered and raised, NCNB Texas was the successful bidder, offering to pay in excess of $15 million for the Insurance Companies' stock.

Junior Senior Disputes: As in any bankruptcy, the expected recovery was substantially less than the total amount of the creditors' claims. Under the absolute priority rule, the allowed claims of senior creditors are to be paid in full before any money flows to subordinated creditors. A consensual reorganization, however, generally provides for some recovery to the juniors even when the seniors receive less than a full recovery. How much goes to the juniors is usually controversial. For both IFRB and FRBC, the junior and senior bondholders initially had very different opinions on the appropriate sharing formulas.

The Guarantees: When Republic and Interfirst were merged, FRBC guaranteed certain Interfirst debt instruments. Those guarantees' validities were, however, subject to challenge. Not surprisingly, the FRBC and IFRB bondholders differed on whether those guarantees should be recognized.

Disputes with NCNB: The debtor and its various creditors committees had a large number of disputes with NCNB. Some disputes were first and foremost with the FDIC, with NCNB named as a codefendant. Still, the estates and NCNB were linked in a variety of interesting ways, including the Services Companies relationships. Additionally, the debtor and NCNB jointly owed a variety of assets and the debtor had legal possession of a variety of other assets for which NCNB was the logical buyer.

Disputes Involving the FDIC: The FDIC's seizure of the FRBC banks created a number of legal disputes. The FDIC claimed the billion dollars that it "loaned" to the Dallas bank and was "guaranteed" by the holding companies (both FRBC and IFRB). This "loan," known as the "note purchase agreement," had been made, with many strings attached, only a few months before the banks were seized. The FDIC also asserted a variety of other (largely receivership) claims against the two estates. In addition, the FDIC claimed to own the assets or be owed money by several of FRBC's non-bank subsidiaries. Finally, the FDIC claimed the Delaware credit card bank sale proceeds. This FRBC bank, having no depositors and a substantial positive net worth, was seized by the regulators a few days after the initial FRBC bank seizures. It was subsequently sold for $230 million in excess of its liabilities, a sum that, with interest added, eventually grew to $280 million.

For their part, the debtors, bondholders and other non-FDIC creditors of the two estates claimed that the guarantees under the note purchase agreement were invalid. Thus, the FRBC and IFRB creditors laid claim to all of the money in the estates, their respective shares of the credit card bank proceeds and compensation for the solvent country banks that the FDIC had seized. Figure 4.2 illustrates this array of disputes.

Figure 4.2
Estates FDIC Disputes

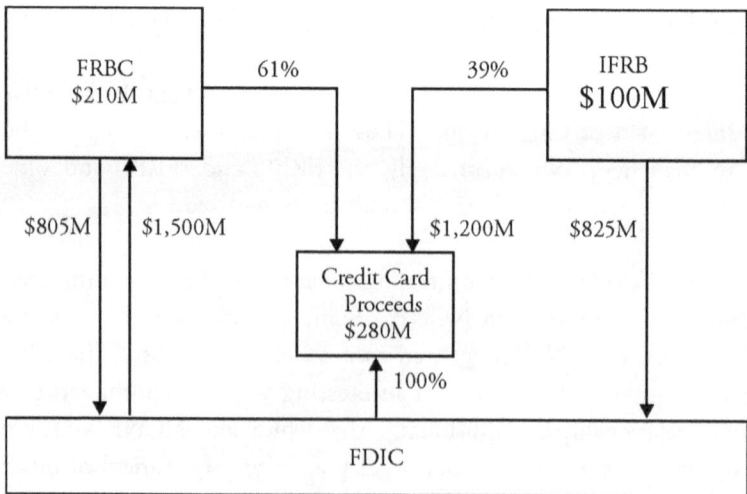

A MOSAIC OF AGREEMENTS

With so many different parties at interest, law firms and issues in dispute, the situation seemed hopeless. Commentators reported that the creditors were wiped out. On the date of bankruptcy, both estates held a total of less than $20 million in cash. Several law firms expressed a lack of interest. A consensus existed that insufficient funds were on hand for administrative expenses. How could all of the conflicting claims ever be sorted out? The parties had retained at least 10 different law firms to represent them. Moreover, the bondholders were divided into seven distinct categories, each of which sought advantageous treatment for its own class at the expense of the other classes. Each estate also had trade creditors. The separate existence and differing interests of the debtor, FDIC and NCNB further complicated the picture. Nonetheless, step-by-step agreements were reached.

DEBTOR-CREDITOR AGREEMENTS

As is often the case, the debtor was initially very protective of its presumed prerogatives. The creditors' committees, particularly the FRBC senior committee, saw the creditors as the estate's rightful owners. Conflicts among the creditors further complicated debtor-creditor relations. The first step toward an understanding involved information-sharing. Eventually the creditors were asked to sign a confidentiality agreement after which the debtor agreed to begin sharing nonpublic information. Starting in November 1988 and continuing throughout 1989, almost weekly meetings between the debtor and its counsel were held with representatives of the creditors' committees and their counsel. Initially, the debtor claimed to be quite busy managing the affairs of the estate and professed not to have full access to all of the needed information, much of which was under the physical control of NCNB. The creditors saw the debtor as unnecessarily uncooperative. Slowly, however, the debtor and creditors began to trust, understand and work better with each other. Toward the latter part of that year, work began on a reorganization plan. An important step in that plan's development was an agreement that the creditors (especially the FRBC senior and IFRB committees) would be proponents having the major role in drafting their estates' plans. An effective plan, however, required resolving the intra-creditor disputes (or at least the non-FDIC creditors' disputes).

FRBC-IFRB CREDITOR AGREEMENTS

The two committees (IFRB and FRBC senior) began to discuss their differences in early 1989. The undisputed (with each other) hard assets in the FRBC and IFRB estates amounted to about $155 million and $60 million respectively. About $120 million of solid assets were in dispute. Additionally, FRBC asserted creditor claims of about $145 million against IFRB. IFRB and its subsidiaries had creditor claims of about $85 million against FRBC. Still other issues involved dispute guarantees, as well as fraudulent conveyances and preference causes of action.

Separate meetings were held for each disputed asset category, as well as for the general category of claims. Each side stated its position. Neither seemed ready to compromise sufficiently to reach a deal. Eventually, however, both groups came to appreciate the importance of two considerations. First, a court-ordered resolution of their various disagreements would take years and incur legal fees in the millions. Second, the ultimate resolution of the case, and the resultant distribution to creditors, depended upon a successful resolution of the estates' disputes with the FDIC. A satisfactory resolution was much more likely to emerge if the intra-estate disputes could be sorted out first. If any doubt remained on this point, Bankruptcy Judge Steven Felsenthal's urgings of the parties to get together made it clear. If the relevant parties could not agree on a reorganization plan, the case was likely to be converted to Chapter 7. Only the FDIC seemed to want that. Most, if not all, of the bondholder groups believed that conversion to Chapter 7 would cause the creditors to lose influence, delay the process and ultimately increase the legal and administrative costs.

The FRBC senior committee proposed that each estate release all claims against the other and agree upon a percentage sharing of the disputed asset sale proceeds. The IFRB committee also liked the proposed structure. Not surprisingly, however, the two sides differed on the percentage split. A further problem involved IFRB's lack of control over some key subsidiaries. In particular, two subsidiaries, FUBI and NV Texas Finance, together owned about $42 million of the $85 million in FRBC-issued commercial paper. Significant third-party creditor claims against FUBI and NV outranked IFRB's equity interests. FRBC did not want to remain exposed to these debts while releasing IFRB from its FRBC debts. Moreover, FRBC expected its senior claims to receive a substantially higher payout than senior claims against IFRB. FRBC wanted IFRB to acquire direct control over all of their subsidiaries' commercial paper. That task proved to be difficult.

The initial agreement provided that the disputed assets would be split on a 55-45 basis in IFRB's favor and all claims between the two estates were to be released. IFRB agreed to seek court approval to purchase the FUBI- and NV-held commercial paper. This initial agreement soon began to unravel. FRBC believed the mutual release included IFRB's bondholder guarantee claims. The IFRB committee claimed to be powerless to execute such a release. A second problem arose when IFRB attempted to acquire the FUBI- and NV-held commercial paper. The debtor had to petition the court to allow the transaction. By the time the debtor got around to doing so, opposition to the transaction had emerged and a higher purchase price was expected. IFRB wanted FRBC to share in that higher cost. FRBC wanted the guarantee issue clarified in its favor. The result was a new round of negotiations and eventually a new agreement that looked very much like the earlier one. IFRB again agreed to acquire the FUBI and NV commercial paper (even if it cost more than earlier expected) and the split remained at the 55-45. IFRB did agree to contribute $1.8 million toward a fund to be used for the resolution of the guarantee issue.

The initial agreements were between the FRBC senior committee and the IFRB committee (which represented both junior and senior bondholders). If the agreement was to bind FRBC, the FRBC junior committee also had to agree. For that to happen, however, the FRBC junior and senior committees needed to resolve their own differences. Similarly the IFRB junior and senior bondholders' representatives needed to reach an agreement.

IFRB-NV Agreement: To implement its deal with FRBC, the IFRB committee needed to obtain control of NV's FRBC commercial paper. The NV bondholders wanted IFRB to accept the validity of their claims. After negotiations, NV agreed to contribute its commercial paper to IFRB, and IFRB agreed that both the creditor and guarantee claims of NV would be recognized. Realizing $20 million from other assets left the bondholders with $84 million in outstanding claims ($104-$20=$84). This was represented by a $188 million claim ($84 million as a creditor and $104 million as a guarantee holder) in the IFRB estate. Thus a 40% recovery for the IFRB senior claimholders would result in a 100% recovery for the NV bondholders: Approximately 20% from their other assets plus 40% x 2 from the IFRB estate.

IFRB Junior Senior Agreements: That both junior and senior bondholders were represented on the IFRB committee did not mean they could easily agree. Nonetheless, an effective reorganization plan required their agreement. After a number of fits and starts, as well as a threat by the seniors to convert the IFRB case to Chapter 7, the two parties reached an agreement. The agreement assigned to the juniors a modest upfront payment, equal to about 2.6% of their claim, plus a 20% share of the estate in excess of the point where the IFRB senior bondholders recovered 40%. The IFRB junior bondholders were also looking to a recovery from FRBC via their disputed guarantee.

FRBC Junior-Senior Agreements: Once an initial agreement with IFRB was reached, attention turned to the junior-senior economic split issue. The two sides started out miles apart. The juniors finally indicated a willingness to accept a 10% share of the FRBC estate. The seniors proposed to begin sharing with the juniors on a 95-5 basis when they recovered 70% of their claim.

While the junior-senior negotiations were taking place, the debtor and creditors' committees were beginning to draft a reorganization plan. One of the plan's agreed-upon goals was to preserve the estates' net operating loss carry-forwards. Achieving that goal requires meeting a number of criteria, including allocating a certain minimum percentage of the reorganized corporation's equity securities to the subordinated bondholders. This need placed a lower boundary on the juniors' upfront consideration.

After some very hard bargaining, a tentative agreement emerged that provided for about $10 million in upfront money to the juniors (amounting to about 3.4% of their claim), plus a sliding scale formula that began sharing when the seniors recovered 70% of their claims. One key unresolved issues involved the disputed guarantees of the IFRB junior and senior bonds. The junior committee had filed a lawsuit seeking to disallow the guarantees. The senior committee believed its initial agreement with the IFRB committee had caused guarantee claims' release. Later the guarantee holders indicated that they would reject the plan treatment, even after significant compensation from the FRBC estate was offered to both groups of bondholders. Eventually this issue caused the FRBC junior and senior committee agreement to break down.

Agreement Between FRBC and IFRB Senior Guarantee Bondholders: FRBC had at the time of the merger arguablyassumed contingent liability for a $35 million private placement. The relevant legal considerations were:

1. The full amount of the claim is applied against the guarantor if   the original obligor defaults (joint and several liability).
2. Guarantee holders can collect no more than 100% of their claims.
3. A guarantee can be held invalid if:

   a. both the guarantor and obligor were either insolvent at the time the guarantee was issued or rendered insolvent by the granting of that guarantee, and
   b. inadequate consideration was given for making the guarantee.

A full determination of the financial condition at the time of the Republic-Interfirst merger and accompanying guarantee was not conducted. Such an accounting investigation would have been costly and depending upon the outcome of certain legal issues, could have gone either way. Accordingly, most parties thought compromise was the far better approach. The IFRB committee claimed that it had no authority to bind the guarantee holders. Nonetheless, representatives from the two committees met and agreed to establish a fund to compensate the guarantee holders. The fund would have provided for a payment from the FRBC side of about 20% and 1% of the claims for the senior and junior guarantee bondholders, respectively, added to the recoveries derived from the bondholders' claims in the IFRB estate. At least a two-thirds majority of the bondholders of each class would have to accept the proposed terms.

While the guarantee holders (senior and junior) initially seemed inclined to accept, later most of those who expressed an opinion rejected the proposed treatment and threatened to oppose the reorganization plan. Everyone realized that to come out of bankruptcy most of the non-FDIC creditors would need to support the plans (FRBC and IFRB). Counsel for the debtor strongly advised the relevant parties to compromise. Because the senior guarantee holders had formed their own informal committee, the FRBC senior committee at last could negotiate with someone. Eventually, the two sides agreed that FRBC would pay 23.5¢ in cash and recognize a claim of 24¢ for allowed senior guarantee claimants. Issues involving both the FRBC junior bondholders and the guarantee issue at the junior level remained unresolved.

FURTHER NEGOTIATIONS BETWEEN THE FRBC SENIORS AND JUNIORS

The FRBC junior committee had counted on the IFRB-FRBC compact to resolve the guarantee issue. When that did not happen, they demanded to retrade the economic split. The seniors, for their part, wanted both the guarantee and the junior-senior split issues resolved in a way that minimized the adverse impact on the seniors' distribution.

The seniors asked the FRBC juniors to reach an understanding with the IFRB juniors on the guarantee and then jointly come to the seniors to negotiate. The FRBC juniors agreed to try. However, the two groups of junior bondholders could not agree on a sharing arrangement. At that point, the FRBC juniors and seniors tried to reach an understanding but that, too, failed. The juniors were asking for a major increase in their share; the seniors were only prepared to absorb the dilution resulting from the addition of the IFRB to the junior class. In exchange for that absorption, the seniors wanted some other changes in the plan that benefited their group. Unless they could agree, the plans would go out for a vote with the junior committee in opposition. Had this opposition resulted in a negative vote at the subordinated debt level, the court might well have refused to confirm the plan. Alternatively, the juniors might have been subject to a cram-down that would have created other problems. The FDIC had moved to convert the case to Chapter 7. Such a conversion would probably have meant delays, increased expenses and no distribution at all for junior creditors. Unless the bondholder groups could agree on a plan, conversion to Chapter 7 seemed likely.

NEGOTIATIONS BETWEEN FRBC SENIORS AND IFRB JUNIORS

When the FRBC seniors concluded that they could not reach an agreement with the FRBC juniors, they turned to the IFRB juniors who, holding disputed FRBC guarantees, had already been seeking a dialogue. If the FRBC seniors and IFRB juniors could agree, they might be able to prevail over the opposition of the FRBC junior committee. To be confirmed in its entirety, a reorganization plan requires a positive vote of 2/3 in dollar amount and a majority in number of each class of voting creditors. If any class votes no, the plan might still be confirmed under the cram-down provisions that apply the absolute priority rule to all creditors at and below the dissenting impaired class. The IFRB juniors represented about a third of the total dollar amount of the combined FRBC and FRBC guaranteed subordinated debt. With the IFRB juniors' support, the plan might obtain a favorable overall sub-debt vote. The seniors were quite prepared to try using the argument that the plan, if confirmed, provided something for the juniors, while neither cram-down nor conversion to Chapter 7 (the likely outcomes of a negative vote) were likely to produce any junior recovery. This Hobson's choice put the junior committee under tremendous pressure. The seniors also needed to deal.

REACHING A REVISED JUNIOR-SENIOR FRBC DEAL

At about this point, Judge Felsenthal unexpectedly allowed the debtor's exclusivity period to expire. A Chapter 11 debtor initially has a 180-day exclusivity period during which only it can propose a reorganization plan. The judge will generally extend this exclusivity period at least a few times at the request of the debtor. After several extensions, Judge Felsenthal sought to force a resolution of inter-creditor disputes by not granting a further extension. That event allowed other interested parties to file their own plans. The IFRB Committee, FRBC senior committee and debtors were all working together in the plan process.

The FRBC juniors had ceased to be plan co-proponents as a result of the guarantee dispute.

Both the FRBC juniors and the FDIC were now free to file their own plans. Only the juniors did so. Their plan closely paralleled the FRBC debtor/senior draft except that it contained a substantially more generous economic split for the juniors. In the meantime, the FRBC debtor/senior plan had been revised to recognize the IFRB juniors as allowed claimants. The FRBC juniors could continue their objection to the IFRB junior guarantee claimants. Other minor changes were made, including beginning the juniors' sharing threshold where the seniors received 55%. The seniors waited. The juniors filed a plan that had little prospect of confirmation. A reorganization plan cannot be confirmed over the objections (i.e., a negative vote) of impaired senior creditors. Moreover, the judge ruled the junior plan would be sent out only if the debtor/senior plan failed, if at all.

Because of fast-approaching plan mailing and other deadlines, any junior-senior FRBC agreement had to be reached quickly or the plan would go out as then drafted. At this point, the juniors agreed to talk on terms that the seniors had indicated all along they were prepared to give. The basic change was to gross up both the upfront and sharing formula to absorb the inclusion of the IFRB juniors. One non-FDIC intra-creditor dispute remained to be resolved.

INTRA-FRBC JUNIOR DISPUTE AND AGREEMENT

With the inclusion of the IFRB juniors, the FRBC seniors' three distinct categories of debt were defined: two issues of FRBC junior debt plus the IFRB juniors' guarantee debt. The three groups disagreed on their relative status. The bond indentures were far from clear on that subject. Representatives of the two junior issues had been working on the matter for some time, without success. The plan provided for pari passu treatment unless the relevant parties agreed. Any party could litigate their treatment. At the last possible minute, the three groups agreed that the Manufacturers Hanover (Indenture Trustee) issue of $105 million was established as preferred; the Eurodollar bonds of $159 million were allowed a relative claim of 80% of the Manufacturers Hanover issue; and the IFRB guarantee debt of $107 million was allowed a relative claim of 80% of the Eurodollar bonds.

CONTINUING THE LIQUIDATION

As disputes were being resolved and a reorganization plan formulated, asset liquidations continued.

Republic Money Orders, Inc: Republic Money Orders, Inc (RMO), formerly a wholly-owned subsidiary of FRBC, provided money orders through a nationwide network of selling agents. Many of RMO's current agents had terminated or had expressed their intent to terminate due to FRBC's Chapter 11 status. Prospective agents were refusing to enter into agency arrangements for the same reason. Thus the debtor decided to sell RMO. The debtor, aided by Lazard Freres & Co., produced and distributed a comprehensive offering memorandum. Lazard then solicited non-binding indications of interest from potential purchasers. The debtor spent approximately two months negotiating with interested parties before selecting from five final offers the bid of Travelers Express Company, Inc.

Immediately prior to the Bankruptcy Court hearing to approve the sale, a controversy arose between the debtor and NCNB Texas over a purported assignment of the capital stock of RMO by FRBC to RepublicBank Dallas, now part of NCNB Texas. NCNB Texas claimed the alleged assignment indicated that it either owned or had a security interest in RMO's capital stock. The dDebtor investigated the alleged assignment and began negotiating with NCNB Texas in order to settle the dispute, or arrange a solution that allowed the sale of RMO while limiting the dispute to the issue of who was entitled to the RMO sale proceeds. These negotiations resulted in an amendment to the Stock Purchase Agreement that enabled the sale of RMO to Travelers Express to close as contemplated, but did not affect the claims of either FRBC or NCNB Texas to the sale proceeds. The sale of NCNB Texas closed on April 21, 1989. The proceeds were placed in an escrow account.

In preparation for RMO's sale, FRBC personnel contacted the NCNB Texas Safekeeping Department to obtain the RMO stock certificate. NCNB Texas informed FRBC that the stock certificate had been removed from the account (without FRBC's knowledge or consent) and refused to deliver it to the FRBC. The debtor, insisting that the certificate had been removed in violation of the automatic stay, demanded that the RMO stock certificate be returned. At some point during this dispute, NCNB Texas assigned its interest in RMO, if any, to the FDIC. The FDIC asserted ownership of RMO based on the D'Oench, Duhme doctrine, which gives the FDIC broad rights in a failed bank situation.

FRBC was forced to litigate its claim to the RMO proceeds. Almost exactly one year after the RMO sale, the court held that RMO was the property of FRBC both before and after the filing of FRBC's petition, and that the sale proceeds were FRBC's property. In reaching this conclusion, the court flatly rejected the safekeeping contract FRBC had with FRB Dallas. Rather, the court accepted FRBC's argument that the RMO ownership issue depended on the facts and applicable law prior to July 29, 1988. The FDIC filed a motion for a new trial, which was later denied. The FDIC's subsequent appeal was dismissed as a result of the FDIC settlement.

Republic of Texas Properties, Inc: Republic of Texas Properties, Inc. (RTP), a wholly-owned subsidiary of FRBC, owned and managed several Texas office towers and undeveloped tracts of land. The properties' book values totaled approximately $120 million, compared with a fair market value of $70 million. NCNB Texas held $140 million in mortgages secured by pledges of certificates of deposit and an alleged $40 million FRBC guarantee against the properties.

The debtor considered a number of alternatives, including putting RTP into bankruptcy with the goal of successfully disputing NCNB's right to the alleged $40 million FRBC guarantee. If allowed, this guarantee would have resulted in a senior claim against FRBC. The debtor agreed to cooperate with the lender and transferred the real property to NCNB in complete satisfaction of its debt. After paying approximately $1 million owed a sister subsidiary, approximately $2 million of value was preserved in RTP for the estate and FRBC was released from the $40 million guarantee.

AGREEMENT WITH NCNB

Initially the FRBC complex (debtor and creditors committees) found themselves in an antagonistic position vis-à-vis NCNB. The old FRBC system had been careless in keeping track of who owned what. Some assets were owned jointly by the Dallas bank and the holding company. Others appeared to be owned by one, but the other asserted a claim. Still other claims flowed back and forth between FRBC and NCNB. Early on, disputes arose over the relative percentage of ownership of an overfunded pension surplus and tax refund, as well as money management and the Service Companies. Eventually the two sides agreed on a $55 million price for the Services Companies. Both IFRB and FRBC claimed most of the proceeds. To preserve its option, the FRBC committee sued to block or reverse the sale. The existence of this suit was one issue between FRBC and IFRB that was ultimately resolved by their compact.

The other major unresolved issue between NCNB and FRBC involved assets that FRBC owned outright or jointly with NCNB. The largest of these was a participation in a portfolio of foreclosed properties resulting from a defaulted loan to Vantage Properties. As the reorganization plans were moving close to the hearing stage, NCNB and FRBC reached an overall agreement to release most claims and transfer assets. In May 1990, the general terms of a global settlement were reached by the debtors, the creditors' committees, NCNB Texas, NCNB Corporation, and the FDIC. Once the initial drafts were prepared, approximately two more months of lengthy negotiations and redrafting of the proposed settlement documents were required before the parties were ready to sign. Under the settlement's terms, NCNB Texas, in exchange for a general release of all claims among the debtors and NCNB Texas, agreed to purchase the vast majority of FRBC's remaining real assets and a limited number of IFRB assets for approximately $25 million. This settlement effectively ended NCNB Texas' involvement in the bankruptcy, removing it as an adversary to plan confirmation, and left FRBC with very few significant non-cash assets to liquidate. As a result, NCNB withdrew as an objector to the reorganization plan.

CONFIRMING THE REORGANIZATION PLAN

The mosaic of agreements were ultimately reflected in the FRBC and IFRB reorganization plans. The plans could only be confirmed, however, if a positive vote was obtained and the judge ruled in favor of the plans.

The FDIC had been invited to participate in the plan drafting. It offered criticism on various aspects of the plan but never became plan proponents or co-proponents. Nonetheless, the plan was revised in a number of ways to reflect the FDIC's input. Once the creditors agreed, the only major obstacle to plan confirmation was the FDIC's objection. In addition to its billion-dollar note purchase agreement claim, the agency asserted several hundred million dollars of receivership claims. One claim was based on the theory that the Dallas bank improperly dividended money to the holding company while it was insolvent and therefore such payments should be reversed. This theory is inconsistent with the FDIC's assertion that the billion-dollar loan provided value to the Dallas bank. Another FDIC claim went against the proceeds of the Services Companies sale. Still other claims were based on tax and pension issues. For its part, FRBC had claims for compensation for the seized banks, as well as claims against the FDIC in its capacity as the banks' receiver.

To litigate these various claims fully would have required years of further delay. Still, a preliminary determination was needed for voting purposes. If most or all of the FDIC's claims were allowed to be voted, no plans could be confirmed without FDIC approval. On the other hand, a nearly unified vote of the non-FDIC creditors could be sufficient to confirm a plan if the FDIC's allowed vote were small enough. Almost all of the FDIC claims were in dispute.

To determine which FDIC claims could vote, the bankruptcy judge needed to evaluate the likelihood that the claims would ultimately be allowed. Thus, lengthy hearings on the voting issues were held. The judge ruled that the FDIC could vote $113 million in the FRBC estate and $71 million in the IFRB estate. For voting purposes, the FDIC's billion-dollar claim was totally disallowed. Judge Felsenthal agreed with the non-FDIC creditors that the claim was probably a fraudulent conveyance.

IFRB senior bondholder claims could outvote the FDIC's $71 million vote with relative ease. In contrast, the FDIC's $113 million vote was a major obstacle for FRBC's other creditors. Senior non-FDIC claims in the FRBC estate only amounted to $275 million. To win the vote the proponents needed at least $226 million (twice the FDIC's $113 million). Additional positive votes would be needed to offset any non-FDIC negative votes. Creditors that were not expected to vote included those that: sold their bonds after the record date; did not get the voting materials because of address changes or other confusions, and would choose not to vote for individual reasons. If creditors holding as much as $50 million of the $275 million of the non-FDIC creditors voted no or did not vote, the FDIC's $113 million negative vote might well prevail. To be approved, a reorganization plan requires a favorable vote of two-thirds of the dollar amount of the allowed claims.

The delays in reaching a final agreement between the FRBC seniors and juniors left a very short solicitation period. The judge was unwilling to move the voting deadline. After a vigorous solicitation by the debtor, creditor committees and the firm of Hill & Knowlton, enough positive votes were obtained to overcome the FDIC's negative vote. But obtaining a favorable vote is only the first step in confirming a plan. The judge must determine that the plan is feasible and consistent with relevant law. Those hearings promised to be contentious. At the same time, the FDIC's motion to convert the case to Chapter 7 would also be heard.

The FDIC first objected to the vote on a variety of procedural grounds. The agency challenged the authority of those who signed the vote card, whether those who voted with facsimile could be counted, etc. Attention then turned to the provisions of the plan itself. Key issues concerned whether the plan provided for at least as high a recovery for the creditors as would conversion to Chapter 7 and whether the FDIC was fairly treated.

In Chapter 7, the absolute priority rule applies and the company's net operating loss carry-forward is preserved. Such a conversion almost certainly meant delay and loss of the creditors' committee influence over the FDIC litigation. The FDIC probably saw converting the case to Chapter 7 as a simple way to blunt FRBC's legal offensive. The judge, however, needed to be shown specifically why the creditors would be better off with this confirmed plan. Showing that the junior creditors were better off was relatively easy. Under this plan they would get some payments, while in Chapter 7 they would likely get none. The non-FDIC seniors clearly expected to get more through the plan as more than 98% of them voted for the plan. The plan proponents mounted several arguments designed to show the plan gave the senior creditors more of a recovery than they would get in Chapter 7. Perhaps the most telling argument related to the advantages gained from the agreements embedded in the plan. Most of these agreements, and specifically the FRBC-IFRB compact, were contingent upon a plan's confirmation. If the agreements went away, each estate's trustee would be expected (at substantial additional expense) to revisit these otherwise resolved issues.

The proponents also argued that the opportunity to manage the estates' money would facilitate achieving a higher risk-adjusted return. They noted that hiring Chapter 7 trustees would require the payment of costly fees. Additionally, they argued that their control over the estates was a valuable intangible asset. Finally, the creditors attempted to draft a plan that preserved the tax loss carry-forward. Even if this tax benefit was lost, however, the plan proponents argued that the plan provided greater value to the creditors than would a conversion to Chapter 7.

To protect the FDIC's interests, the plan provided for a holdback for the FDIC claims if ultimately allowed. Additional funds were retained to pursue the various categories of litigation with the FDIC and others.

On October 30, 1990, Judge Felsenthal entered an order confirming the FRBC and IFRB reorganization plans. On November 6, 1990, he set the plan's effective date for November 30, 1990. The district court, however, granted an indefinite stay on November 27, 1990 while the FDIC appealed the confirmation order. Oral argument on the appeal was days away as 1990 drew to a close.

NEGOTIATIONS WITH THE FDIC

The FDIC, facing a confirmation plan against its objections, and the FRBC and IFRB committees, facing years of additional litigation, recognized a mutual interest in negotiating a settlement. Millions of litigating dollars had already been spent. A settlement would end that drain while providing for substantial distributions to allowed creditors. The confirmed plan would have permitted the undisputed creditors to receive a modest initial distribution. Most of the money, however, would be left in the estates to protect the FDIC's interest should its claims ultimately be allowed. Moreover the Delaware credit card proceeds remained in an escrow account.

As with many negotiations, both sides started out miles apart. The creditors committees claimed all of the FRBC, IFRB and credit card bank money plus compensation for the value of the FDIC-seized solvent country banks. FRBC also asserted various receivership claims against the FDIC in its capacity as receiver of the former FRBC banks. The FDIC, in contrast, claimed all of the credit card bank proceeds and asserted other claims against the two estates while rejecting all of FRBC's affirmative claims. Negotiations had occurred intermittently as reorganization plans were being put together. While each side moved toward the other's position, no deal was struck prior to the confirmation order.

THE ISSUES

The basic issue in the FRBC-FDIC dispute was whether the FDIC had the right to force FRBC and all of its subsidiaries to agree to the terms of the note purchase agreement. When the "loan" was extended, the Dallas bank was already hopelessly insolvent. The primary beneficiary of the "loan" appears to have been the FDIC. It did provide the agency with time to explore its options and ultimately decide to sell the FRBC banks to NCNB. The FDIC, however, extracted major commitments from FRBC in exchange for making the "loan." As a result of those terms, most of the value that had been available to protect the uninsured creditors, especially the bondholders, was attached by the FDIC. Moreover the "loan" itself only provided some of the funds that ultimately would be needed to cover losses that the FDIC had already guaranteed. Ingenious as the FDIC "loan" terms were, they could very well have been illegal. Judge Felsenthal had already disallowed the FDIC's "loan" claims for voting purposes. A private lender almost certainly could not have gotten away with such a maneuver. Actions designed to move a creditor up relative to other creditors just prior to a bankruptcy filing are always highly suspect. If the FDIC lost on this issue, the estates could recover substantial value (i.e., the solvent banks). The FDIC, in contrast, contended that not only was it entitled to seize all of the FRBC banks, but that the holding companies owed it still more money. If the FDIC prevailed, relatively little would be available to satisfy bondholder claims.

Accordingly, on December 18, 1990, after months of seemingly fruitless negotiations, the FDIC, the FRBC Senior Committee and the IFRB Committee worked out a settlement at the Washington, D.C., offices of Andrews & Kurth. The agreement settled all of the FDIC claims against FRBC and IFRB.

The debtors and their subsidiaries agreed to pay or cause to be paid to the FDIC $142.5 million in cash from the Delaware bank escrow and all the cash or assets in the Tax Interpleader Trust Custody Account, one of the myriad side disputes referenced earlier. The FRBC Senior Committee and the IFRB Committee separately agreed that of the $142.5 million to be paid to the FDIC, $105.875 million was to be paid by FRBC and $36.625 million would be paid by IFRB. In exchange, the FDIC released its claims against First Republic and IFRB and Texas Finance N.V. and committed to various undertakings relating to the assets of the First Republic Credit Card Delaware Receivership.

Second Renegotiated Agreement Between the FRBC Senior and FRBC Junior Creditors' Committees: The FRBC junior committee, having witnessed an unanticipated, timely settlement with the FDIC, threatened to object. The FRBC seniors might arguably receive more than 100 cents on the dollar. Additional negotiations between the seniors and juniors ensued. To wrap up the case consensually, avoid a number of expensive and time-consuming settlement/ arbitration mechanisms set forth in the lengthy plan of reorganization, and simply to make a distribution at consummation, the terms of the FRBC junior-senior settlement agreement were once again revisited. Certain disputed assets (with the FDIC) in a grantor trust were uncovered that had not previously been included in some of the asset calculations. These assets were resolved in FRBC's favor in the settlement. These "found" sums of approximately $6,350,000 were assigned to the junior creditors. This adjustment still allowed the senior bondholders a recovery close to par – ultimately more than par – while awarding the juniors a bit more than the plan had heretofore provided.

Implementing the Settlement Agreement: Once approved by the bankruptcy court, the agreement with the FDIC had to be implemented and certain matters resolved. In particular the Delaware Credit Card bank escrowed money needed to be allocated between the FDIC and the FRBC/IFRB estates. First, however, the FDIC needed to facilitate its release by giving notice and allowing a 90-day period to elapse for third-party claims. That process did not begin until March 1991. As a result the money could not be released until June. The closing was set for July 2, 1991. Upon the closing the FDIC released its objection, and the FRBC and IFRB approved plans of reorganization were allowed to proceed. Both FRBC and IFRB emerged from bankruptcy on July 15, 1991.

Settlement with Old Officers and Directors: Once the FDIC settlement was approved, and the reorganization plans became effective, only the indemnity claims of FRBC's old officers and directors remained to be resolved. While they had not yet been sued, these former officers and directors were vulnerable. The FDIC, in particular, could bring suit seeking to recover some money to put toward its cost of assisting the old FRBC banks. If, for example, these officers or directors acted improperly, thereby causing FRBC losses, the FDIC might be able successfully to assert a claim against them. The officers and directors were, however, "arguably" indemnified by the FRBC itself. Many of these officers and directors had filed presentation claims in the estates to collect on their indemnities. The plan provided for holding back money for unresolved claims. Thus, an FDIC claim against FRBC officers and directors could find a back door into the FRBC estate. Accordingly, the estates needed to settle this indemnity issue or ask the court to estimate the claim and provide a holdback. That process, however, would take time and incur the risk of a substantial estimate. A settlement was the preferred path.

The vehicle around which a settlement might be fashioned was a class action suit by old FRBC investors (stock and bondholders). This suit alleged, among other things, that the pre-bankruptcy financial disclosures were inadequate. FRBC itself had a potential cause of action against the old officers and directors for their involvement in such matters as financial reporting, the Republic-IFRB merger and the note purchase agreement.

An agreement in principle was structured in which the insurance companies would fund a settlement of the class action suits with $20 million. Of this sum, $500,000 would be allocated to the FRBC (with its lawyers taking one-third) and FRBC, and its old officers and directors would not assert their indemnity claims. An agreement in principle was reached months before the FRBC-FDIC closing. When the FRBC-FDIC closing occurred, the officers and directors settlement remained only an agreement in principle. Attention soon turned to converting the understanding into a formal, signed agreement. Fifty-one pre-bankruptcy officers and directors had asserted indemnity claims. Some of these individuals were represented by law firms; others were unrepresented. Each law firm and each individual needed to execute a mutual release with the estates.

By July 15, 1991, when the reorganization plan became effective, the D & O agreements were well on their way to being signed, but many loose ends remained. Moreover, the signed agreements and releases had not been blessed with court approval. A hearing on the agreement(s) was scheduled for August 6, 1991.

Everyone connected with the case had hoped to see an initial distribution occur immediately upon the plan becoming effective. Without a fully signed and approved D & O settlement, however, an initial distribution was difficult to make. The D & O settlement might not ultimately obtain court approval, in which case the indemnity claims would remain a live issue. If most of the estates' money had been paid out to allowed creditors, those responsible for making the distribution would be vulnerable. Accordingly, the initial distribution was deferred pending the court hearing on the D & O settlement. While the FDIC filed suits against certain officers and directors of the former Dallas and Houston FRBC banks in late July 1991, all of the needed releases were obtained. The settlement itself was presented to the court as scheduled on August 6, 1991, and was approved from the bench.

The Initial Distribution: With the D & O settlement approved, nothing stood in the way of making an initial distribution from the estates. Well over $400 million was distributed on August 7, 1991. Table 4.2 reports the results.

Table 4.2
Initial Distribution
First Republic Bank Corporation

	Class 2	Class 4A	Class 4B	Class 4C
Percentage of Allowed Claim*	100.0%	11.0%	9.2%	6.0%
Percentage of Par Value				
Class 2:				
11 1/4% Notes due 1989	108.0%			
Floating Rate Notes due 2004	101.9%			
9 1/8% Debentures due 2001	105.5%			
Class 4:				
8 1/4% Notes due 1999		11.6%		
Floating Rate Notes due 1997			9.5%	
7 3/4% Notes due 2005				6.2%
10% Notes due 1992				6.2%

IFRB CORPORATION

	Class 2	Class 2A	Class 4
Percentage of Allowed Claim*	48.2%	48.2%	7.3%
Percentage of Par Value			
Class 2:			
12 3/4% Notes due 1989	50.3%		
9 3/4% Notes due 1999	51.6%		
NV Floating Rate Notes due 1989	49.8%		
Class 4:			
7 3/4% Notes due 2005			7.5%
10% Notes due 1992			7.5%

*Allowed claim includes interest accrued through Petition Date.

Note FRBC class 4C and IFRB class 4 are for the same bonds. Thus their total recovery is the sum of the two distributions, or 6.2% + 7.5% = 13.7%

The three classes of senior bonds had different amounts of pre-petition interest and thus received somewhat different payouts (ranging from 101.9% to 108% of par). The junior FRBC issues got differing amounts based on the plan provision and their post-petition interest. The two straight FRBC issues received around a 10% payout. The junior IFRB guaranteed debt got about 6% from the FRBC estate and another 7.5% from the IFRB estate. The IFRB seniors received approximately 48% of their claim corresponding to slightly different percentages of par depending upon their pre-petition interest. Note that two categories of IFRB debt did particularly well. The NV debt collected on two claims against IFRB, plus from its own estate. The result was a payout well over par. The IFRB senior guarantee debt received close to a 50% payout from both the IFRB and FRBC estates, thereby achieving a recovery close to par. While these results, particularly for the FRBC senior, NV and IFRB senior guarantee debt, seem quite favorable, one should not ignore the cost (in terms of lost interest) of having to wait more than three years for a payoff.

Second Distribution: After the initial distribution, small sums of held-back money, as well as unliquidated and contingent assets, remained in the estates. Tax returns needed to be filed; remaining assets needed to be sold; final fee applications needed to be heard by the court and the estates needed to be administered as the final affairs were being resolved. Reserves had been set aside for those needs. At year-end 1992, FRBC distributed $5.5 million and IFRC $2.5 million. Because the senior FRBC creditors had already received 100% of their claim, the split shifted to 75%-25% in favor of the juniors. On average, the FRBC juniors got a bit over 1% of their claim while the seniors received about 0.6%. The IFRB distribution amounted to about 0.6% of the senior and 0.5% of the junior claims.

Third Distribution: The estate had set aside reserves for defense against any potential litigation. After the statute of limitation had run without litigation being brought, these funds were available for distribution. Additional monies unclaimed by the creditors were returned to the estate. Still other funds were derived from remaining asset liquidations. As a result, the FRBC estate had about $5 million available to distribute in late 1993. Overall these distributions produced the sums contained in Table 4.3.

Table 4.3
Total Distributions
First Republic Bank Corporation

	Class 2	Class 4A	Class 4B	Class 4C
Percentage of Allowed Claim*	101.11%	13.65%	11.31%	7.39%
Percentage of Par Value				
Class 2:				
11 1/4% Notes due 1989	109.20%			
Floating Rate Notes due 2004	103.03%			
9 1/8% Debentures due 2001	106.60%			
Class 4:				
8 1/4% Notes due 1999		14.28%		
Floating Rate Notes due 1997			11.69%	
7 3/4% Notes due 2005				7.63%
10% Notes due 1992				7.63%

IFRB CORPORATION

	Class 2	Class 2A	Class 4
Percentage of Allowed Claim*	48.8%	48.8%	7.8%
Percentage of Par Value			
Class 2:			
12 3/4% Notes due 1989	50.9%		
9 3/4% Notes due 1999	52.2%		
NV Floating Rate Notes due 1989	50.4%		
Class 4:			
7 3/4% Notes due 2005			8.0%
10% Notes due 1992			8.0%

*Allowed claim includes interest accrued through Petition Date.
'Again, these bonds received a combined distribution (15.63%).

When the FRBC estate closed, approximately $1 million in cash and un-liquidated assets were transferred to a five-year trust that had been set up to defend the post- reorganization officers and directors from any potential litiga-tion. At the end of that period, one final, very small additional distribution was made.

The Price Performance of the Bonds: The market reaction to the case is an interesting story in itself. Table 4.4 reports the price history of the three pri-mary bond categories from January 1988 to May 1991.

Table 4.4

Monthly Price History for Selected FRBC and IFRB Bonds

		FRB 11¼	IFRB 12¾	FRB/IFRB junior
	Jan 88	92?	74	46
	Feb	86?	60	39½
FDIC Assistance	March	43¾	47	27½
	April	36	28	17
	May	26	24	17
	June	28	27	17
FDIC Seizure	July	23	23	17
	Aug	12	10	3
	Sept	12	10	3
	Oct	9	9	3
	Nov	10½	10½	2
	Dec	12	13	2
	Jan 89	15	15	2
	Feb	17	16	3
	March	18	17	3
	April	16	15	2
	May	15	14	2
	June	15	14	3
	July	16	15	3
	Aug	17	16	3
	Sept	19	18	4
	Oct	17	15	3
	Nov	18	17	3
	Dec	21	20	3
	Jan 90	24	22	3
	Feb	25	23	3
	March	28	24	3
	April	30	25	3
	May	33	24	3
Reorganization Plan	June	37	24	4
Vote	July	56	33	7
	Aug	57	33	7
	Sept	56	32	7
Confirmation	Oct	55	31	7
Hearing	Nov	55	31	7
	Dec	49/72	31	7½
FDIC Settlement	Jan 91	77	35	8½
Court Approval	Feb	93	41	8
	March	96	41	8
	April	98½	42	8
	May	100½	44	7

We see that in January 1988 the FRBC and IFRB senior bonds were priced as non-distressed high-yield securities (i.e., junk bonds). By March, however, the market was clearly anticipating trouble. FRBC had announced that it expected to experience huge losses and would seek FDIC assistance. The note purchase agreement was signed. The bonds' prices continued to decline from March to July/August, when the FDIC seized the banks. Curiously, the FRBC and IFRB senior bonds both fell to about 10 and then traded for very similar prices for quite some time thereafter. The senior bond prices stayed in the teens throughout the remainder of 1988 and 1989, as most of the estate's assets were liquidated and the various intra-creditor disputes were sorted out. The junior bonds traded at the 2-3 level during this period. By early 1990, the FRBC and IFRB senior bonds had moved into the 20s and the market began to recognize the greater recovery potential of the FRBC seniors. By April 1990, the FRBC seniors were at 30 while the IFRB seniors were at 25. The junior bonds still traded around 3. During this time frame, the proposed reorganization plan was filed and the disclosure statement approved for distribution. In June, the plan went out for a vote. By then the FRBC senior bonds had risen to 37 (IFRB seniors were at 24 and junior bonds traded around 4). In July, the apparently positive vote came in. The FRBC senior bonds reacted by rising to 56, while IFRBs seniors moved to 33 and juniors started trading in the range of 7. The confirmation hearing occurred and on October 30, 1990, Judge Felsenthal ruled in favor of the plan, but that ruling was appealed by the FDIC. The district court granted an indefinite stay on November 27, 1990. The FRBC senior bonds dropped to 49, but on December 18, 1990, the committees and the FDIC reached an overall settlement agreement. The FRBC senior bonds then shot up into the 70s. That agreement was approved by the bankruptcy court in February 1991, and the senior FRBC bonds moved into the 90s. The other bond categories also moved up. The rise continued through April and May.

Cost of the Case: Between July 29, 1988, when the voluntary Chapter 11 petitions were filed, and November 1990, when the plans were confirmed, First Republic incurred about $30 million in expenses for operating in Chapter 11, largely in litigation costs in battling with the FDIC. The FDIC and NCNB spent many millions more. The ultimate settlement, while paying modest dividends to subordinated creditors, did provide for the FRBC seniors, at least, substantially close to complete payout (after about three years, without taking into account the lost interest).

CONCLUSION

This case illustrates the potential complexities of the bankruptcy process rather well. The incomplete nature of the First Republic and Interfirst mergers and incomplete and careless documentation of asset ownership (as between the estates and FDIC/NCNB and within the estates) led to numerous intra-creditor disputes. The unusually complicated capital structure (seven bondholder categories alone) made the case even more difficult to resolve. Efforts to resolve these disputes cost the estates and their creditors a lot of money. Still, the end result was a total settlement of all the myriad of issues. Such settlements could not have been reached without the cooperation and hard work of numerous people representing many diverse interests. Indeed three major creditors committees, as well as four other sub-groupings of bondholders, ultimately had to accept a distribution formula. The creditors, debtor, NCNB and the FDIC all had to come together on a final set of settlements. Had different personalities prevailed and insisted upon their positions, this case might still be in the courts. Alternatively the cases could easily have been converted to Chapter 7 and very different outcomes emerged, no doubt after far more in legal expenses. What lessons might be learned from this case?

First, the precise nature and amounts of the assets and liabilities (including guarantees) attributed to the various parts of a large commonly owned set of corporations need to be carefully documented as transactions such as mergers and restructurings are occurring. Much of the cost of dealing with a case like this involved sorting out which part of the system owned which asset and/or was on the hook for which obligation. Far better documentation should have been in place. While bank (and other types of) holding companies may not expect to be shorn of their principal assets (i.e., their banks), they should be prepared for such possibilities. Second, those who participate in such a process need to put aside petty issues of price and take into account the big picture. Reaching an acceptable closure on troublesome issues is far more important to the interest holders than fighting over the last dollar or point of principle. Third, some mechanism is needed to reduce the level of debtor-creditor conflict. Under current law, the debtor is initially granted substantial latitude (e.g., exclusivity and control of operations). Debtors may exploit the divided nature of the creditor class or classes for their own advantages. And yet these are the same debtors who stood watch as the firm became distressed. As the new owners, these creditors deserved a strong voice in the running of their now bankrupt firm. Fourth, tension between bankruptcy, corporate and banking law need to be addressed with an effort toward reducing the areas of conflict. Fifth, a system is needed for resolving senior subordinated creditor disputes that neither place a premium on the negotiating and/or legal skills of the respective parties nor encourage one party to try to delay progress.

Monthly Price History for FRB Senior Bonds

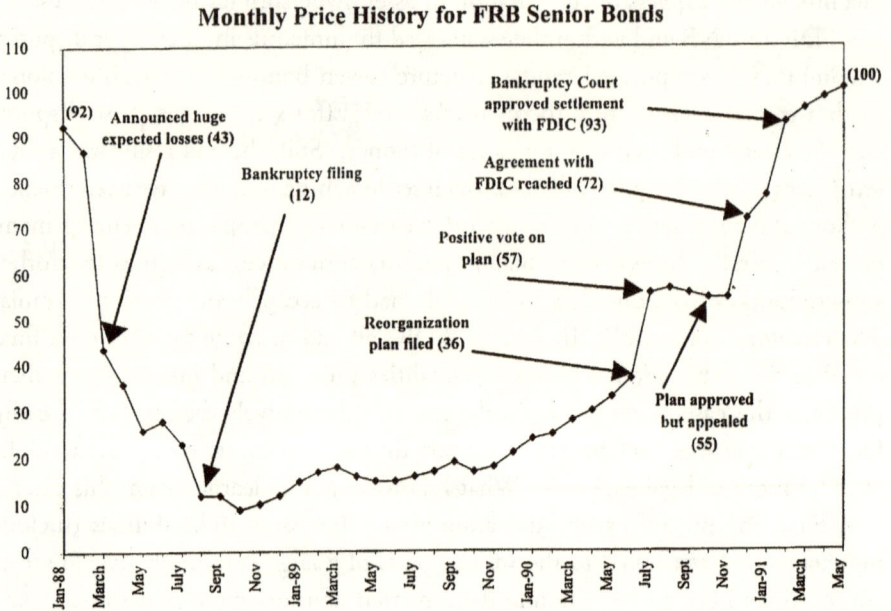

CHAPTER 5

ESTIMATING BANKRUPTCY VALUES

The key to successful bankruptcy investing is assessing the likely outcome (value of the estate and relative distributions to claimants) and then identifying those securities (or other claims in interest) that are most underpriced relative to that prospective outcome. One can, and often should, perform this type of analysis at any point in the case: pre-filing; immediately after the filing; while the plan is being formulated; while the plan is out for a vote; at the confirmation hearing stage; just before or just after the effective date; or even just before or just after distributions are made. Significant profit opportunities may be available at any of these points. Frequently, however, the greatest profits are earned by those who make early commitments. Moreover, once you are involved, you can adjust your position as circumstances warrant. Accordingly, let's start the analysis just before a bankruptcy filing. What is happening?

A Company Gets Into Trouble. If the company is large (e.g., WorldCom, Delphi, UAL, or Enron, for example) the press is full of stories of its problems. Each earnings report is anticipated with foreboding. First common, and then preferred, dividends are suspended to conserve cash. Will the company be able to avoid or put off a bankruptcy filing once the next installment of bad news is out? Losses mount. The company's net worth account is eroded. Various plans are discussed. Mergers, employee givebacks, asset sales, informal workouts with creditors, equity infusions from abroad or elsewhere, even federal assistance (Chrysler and Lockheed). These ideas are mostly pipe dreams. Occasionally, one of them will be tried and, very occasionally, such an effort will work. On other occasions the attempt at least buys a little time. The effort, however, only puts off the inevitable. The decline continues relentlessly.

As the trouble worsens, the securities markets react. All of the company's securities suffer. The more junior the security, the greater the decline. Any outstanding warrants become virtually worthless. The common stock falls ever lower. A year earlier the stock may have sold for a double-digit price. Now, it qualifies as a penny stock (priced under a dollar). The preferred stock, if any, also suffers, but perhaps not quite as much, particularly if it is cumulative. The dividend is, or soon will be, suspended, but an accrual may be being built up. If the situation turns around short of bankruptcy, the preferred holders will have a shot at a major recovery. And they will get that recovery before the common holders see any cash. On the other hand, a bankruptcy filing is just about as likely to wipe out the preferred as the common equity. All equity's priority, particularly in a bankruptcy, is behind that of all of the debt.

The Bonds. The debt securities also decline. Under normal conditions (a healthy and profitable company), the different categories of debt securities will tend to sell for a relatively high percentage of their par or face value. Different coupon rates and maturity dates will, of course, apply to the different securities, thus causing some price differentials. The most secure investments with adequate collateral backing them will be able to be issued for the lowest interest cost to the issuer, say within one percentage point of the yield on equivalent Treasuries. If 20-year Treasuries are yielding 6.5%, well-collateralized 20-year corporate bonds might be priced to yield around 7.5%. Senior debentures of a financially secure company would be priced similarly. If the company has plenty of unpledged assets to cover the senior indebtedness, coupled with more than sufficient cash flow to cover all of its debt service, the bonds should also sell at a price that would result in a yield within about one percentage point of Treasuries. If the collateralized bonds are priced to yield 8.5%, perhaps the senior debentures would be priced to yield 8.75%. The senior debentures are slightly less secure, and in a liquidation would tend to receive a lower recovery. If, however, the company has not issued any collateralized bonds, its senior debentures should be very nearly as well protected as they would have been if they themselves had been collateralized. Subordinated debentures, in contrast, are much more at risk than either the collateralized or the senior debentures. Their subordination clause calls for them to pay over to the seniors any consideration that would otherwise have been allocated to them up to the point where the senior creditors recover their full pre-petition claim. Depending upon the relevant indenture, the subordination may also be applied to post-petition interest. Only after the seniors have been made whole are the subordinated creditors allowed to retain any of their initial payoff allocation. While a Chapter 11 reorganization plan usually treats the juniors less harshly than absolute priority would imply, they are exposed to a much bigger hit than more senior creditors. Accordingly, even under healthy conditions, the subordinated debt will be priced to yield appreciably more (a larger risk premium) than senior debt. If the company is relatively healthy and the senior debt yields 8.75%, the subordinated debt might be priced to yield 10%. If both senior and junior subordinated debt are outstanding, the junior subordinated would require a still higher yield to be marketable. If, for example, the senior subordinated yields 10%, the junior subordinated might need to yield 11% to be saleable, even for a relatively healthy company. The less healthy the company, the greater the penalty for subordination and the greater the differential penalty for deep subordination. Each lower level of priority would tend to cost the issuer about one rating grade. Thus, we might see the collateralized bonds rated AA, the senior debentures A, senior subordinated debentures BBB and the junior subordinated debentures BB. Lower levels of subordination would have still lower ratings and require higher yields.

These differentials are likely to be accounted for in the coupon and original issue price. Thus, as the firm issues more debt of lower priority, it will set the coupon rates higher and higher, so the issue price will still be near par. If market conditions remain similar and the company's financial condition remains healthy, all of its different priority bonds will sell for prices near par. Only the coupons will differ, with-ever higher coupons set for the lower priority issues.

In a more realistic situation, the bonds will have been issued at different times under different market (interest rate) conditions, requiring different coupon rates at issue. They will also have different maturities. Their market prices will reflect these differences. Nonetheless, most of the bonds will probably sell within a range of about 20 points. Thus, some bonds might sell near par and other in the 80s, but all are selling into a market that expects them to continue to pay interest and repay principal at maturity. Characteristics such as a conversion option, call feature, sinking fund provision or different maturity date may impact the pricing on specific issues. This situation is typical before the firm starts getting into trouble. All of its bonds are selling for relatively high prices (close to par), but with different coupons and yields to maturity that reflect their different priorities (and other differences).

Problems Begin to Surface. Now the company starts encountering some financial difficulties. Initially, perhaps all that is observable from the outside is that reported earnings are declining. As long as they remain positive, things may seem satisfactory for those who don't look too closely. Under the surface, however, cash is becoming increasingly scarce. Perhaps accounting tricks can hide the problem from the investment community for a while. Inventories are probably building up, but little or no markdown is taken on the older (out of style, technologically obsolete) items. Perhaps depreciation rates are reduced (the useful life estimate is extended, straight line rather than accelerated depreciation is used). Other assets may not have been written down to their economic value. Some operations are discontinued, but the reserves established for the shut facilities are inadequate or nonexistent. Other money-losing operations are kept going to avoid calling attention to the company's festering problems. Payments to creditors are slowed and payables begin to accumulate. Spending for R&D, marketing and product development is cut back. Support staffs are reduced. Service and quality deteriorates.

Consequently, a very short-term focus emerges. The company is robbing Peter to pay Paul. Paul is a squeaky wheel, while Peter can be put off. But even Peter eventually demands his due. Sooner or later, the firm has to acknowledge two major, related problems. First, the enterprise is suffering substantial economic losses and the consequent erosion of its net worth. Second, and of more immediate concern, the company is running short on liquidity and, consequently, is having trouble paying its bills as they come due. Credit sources are drying up, and the bills keep mounting. Large interest payments become increasingly difficult to make. Any scheduled principal payments become more and more of a challenge to refinance or roll over. Trade creditors get nervous and may start demanding cash on delivery or increases in letters of credit.

As all of this bad news is coming out, what happens to the bonds? Clearly they react negatively to the news that their issuer is getting into deeper and deeper financial difficulty. The various categories of bonds do not decline proportionately. Rather, the lower is the priority, the greater is the decline. Prior to a bankruptcy filing, the typical price decline for a troubled company might be as follows: Collateralized bonds are down 30%; senior debentures are down 50%; senior subordinated debentures are down 80%, and junior subordinated debentures are down 90%. Obviously reactions can be varied. These figures are reasonably representative.

What about the rating agencies (Standard & Poor's, Moody's, etc.)? What are they likely to be saying about the troubled company's bonds? The ratings are likely to be downgraded, but with a bit of a lag. Investment-grade bonds (BBB or higher) may be downgraded to Junk (BB or lower), as the firm's problems worsen. But the downgrades typically occur after the market itself has already recognized and reacted to the problems (i.e., the bond price has already declined to reflect the greater default risk). Investors should not rely upon the rating agencies to warn them of trouble. By then, it is likely to be too late to dodge the bullet. Downgrades are more of a validation than a warning. On the other hand, one can use a downgrade as a signal that further trouble is possible.

A bond that is downgraded by one level is much more likely to be downgraded again than it is to be upgraded.

Chapter 11 Filing. Next, the company files for Chapter 11 protection. While the market probably anticipated the filing, the confirmation of the need to file is a further negative for the company and its creditors. Prior to the filing, some chance for an out-of-court workout may have remained. With a bankruptcy filing, the expenses of a bankruptcy proceeding are unavoidable. Thus the market prices for the firm's bonds are likely to decline further. Moreover, in Chapter 11 or 7, all creditors' interest (except for well-secured, collateralized debt) effectively stops accruing.

Consistent with our previous discussion, just prior to filing we may have seen the following price structure: collateralized bonds 80; senior bonds 50; senior subordinated 20, and junior subordinated 10. To complete the picture, the preferred stock was trading at 2 (par of 50) and the common stock at 1/2 (down from 40). Again, these numbers are only illustrative.

Immediately following the Chapter 11 filing price reaction is as follows: The collateralized bonds fall to 65; senior bonds to 40; senior subordinated to 10; junior subordinated to 3; the preferred stock to 1 1/4; and the common to 3/8. Even at these low prices, the stock is probably overpriced. A scenario that provides any upside for the stock will make the bonds worth a lot more than these prices. On the other hand, many other scenarios wipe out the shareholders entirely while leaving something for the bondholders (often a handsome recovery) who may buy at these knock-down prices. On a risk-return basis, the bonds are almost certainly a better buy than the stock. But at this point are they a good buy? That is the key question.

Assessing the Initial Situation. Suppose you have been following the situation, and now you are ready to act. What do you do? You need to try to assess the worst-case scenario and what it means for each security. Does the situation offer promise, and, if so, which security is most attractive? This is where some real detective work is called for. Reliable information is scarce. However, you have to make do as best you can with what information is available.

You should quickly collect all of the publicly available information. Start with the most recent 10K, 10Q, proxy statement and any 8Ks and news releases they have issued in the last six months. You may also want to see the registration statements on any recently issued securities. You may be able to obtain the information quickly by visiting the company's website (if it has one) or through the SEC's Edgar system. Expect to find some holes and some dated materials. Still, these various reports may provide the best information available initially. Later, you can start accessing the court filings. At the outset, however, pre-filing documents will be all you have to work with.   You want to understand the publicly available information as well as you can. Remember that in the land of the blind, the one-eyed person is king. Once the case is filed, you should be able to obtain the pleadings from the bankruptcy court's website.

Evaluate the Assets. Once you have these documents, what do you do? Realize that you will probably have three to six inches of material, perhaps more. Do not become overwhelmed. Most likely, much of it is out-of-date anyway. What you really want is to be able to assemble a realistic balance sheet for your potential investment. Start with the balance sheet contained in the company's last report (probably the 10Q filed the quarter before it failed). Now, make some quick adjustments. First, focus on the asset side. If you see an entry for goodwill or deferred organization cost, mark through it. A company that finds itself having to file for bankruptcy is almost certain to have no goodwill (and perhaps some ill will). Similarly, mark through any capitalized expenses or other intangibles (excise over book value paid for organized assets, capitalized tax characteristics, franchises and licenses, etc.). Most such intangibles have little or no value in a bankruptcy, particularly in a liquidation.

Now, examine the other asset categories one by one. Take a hard-nosed view of each. What are they really worth in a liquidation? Cash is cash; the real value of everything else is suspect. Even the cash number is suspect if the balance sheet is relatively old. Much of that money may have gone out the door (paying the most immediately pressing bills) as the bankruptcy filing approached. Accounts receivables are probably worth close to their stated value, but only if the obligators are solvent. Look for any problems. Trouble often breeds more trouble. For example, in 2005 Delphi was having problems and one of its biggest customers, General Motors, was being squeezed. If manufacturers are in trouble, those who supply them will also be affected. Thus Delphi's relationship with GM was a very questionable asset. Look for these special situations and make appropriate adjustments.

Next, examine marketable securities. If not contained in the body, the footnote will report the market price. The footnotes, by the way, are a key part of a financial statement. They should be read carefully for the information they contain. Always use market, not book, values. If the company provides a breakdown as to what specifically is owned, check current prices. Total it up and compare it with the end-of-quarter report. Use the most recent value. Mark that number down by some percentage for the cost of liquidating the position. If the hold-ings are Treasuries or some other easy-to-sell portfolio of securities, the selling costs will be modest. On the other hand, if company X owns 10% of the outstanding shares of company Y, realize that such a large block of Company Y's stock may not be easy to sell. To be conservative, mark down the current price by some substantial discount. Circumstances differ, but perhaps a 10% to 20% haircut would be reasonable in typical situations, with deeper dis-counts appropriate for real estate and partnership interests as discussed below. In other situations, however, the position may be saleable at a premium, particu-larly if the position is controlling. Sometimes the company itself or another large shareholder will be interested in the block. Find out what you can about this other company.

Now, move on to notes and mortgages receivable and the like. These are valued on the balance sheet on a going-concern basis. They were probably executed to facilitate an earlier transaction. What would their value be in a forced sale? Again, a discount is usually called for. Are the note and mortgage originators sound? How good is the collateral, if any? Are the interest rates at market levels? Are the instruments in economic units that are sufficiently large to be attractive to a buyer? Does a meaningful secondary market exist for such assets? If so, how liquid is it? A discount of 5% might be appropriate in some situations, while a markdown of 30% or more is needed in other circumstances.

Inventories are another tricky area. Make separate analyses of raw materi-als, work in process, and finished goods. Raw materials inventory may well be worth close to its cost if the market is active, well defined and easy to buy and sell in. The more commodity-like the raw material is, the more saleable it is (i.e., steel, copper, etc.). The raw materials may even be worth a premium over their book values if LIFO is used and materials prices have gone up. On the other hand, every case is different. Evaluate the market itself. Raw materials are always easier to buy than to sell. Finished goods inventories are usually much more difficult to evaluate. Growing inventories represent a problem for a cash-short company. Liquidating them is sure to require a markdown. Perhaps fire-sale prices will be required to move them. For example, we could be deal-ing with a farm implements manufacturer in the midst of an agricultural de-pression. On the other hand, some highly-sought-after finished goods invento-ries may be worth close to their balance-sheet values. Again, check the market. What does the trade think? Is technological or stylistic obsolescence a prob-lem? If so, big markdowns are in order.

Work-in-process inventories and incomplete projects (for example, a half-built shopping mall) are among the toughest assets to value. A bankruptcy filing is likely to cause all sorts of problems for such incomplete projects or production runs. Such assets are likely to have relatively little value in an intermediate stage, but many barriers stand in the way of their completion. To place a realistic value on them you need to estimate what the market value would be if incomplete, the cost of completing them, their market value if complete and the likelihood of completion. If completion is unlikely, their value in a sale is likely to be minimal. If turning them into a finished product or project offers the greatest chance of reasonable recovery, you need to make three estimates: the value of the finished items, the cost of completing them, and the time required. Be conservative with each estimate. Every task tends to be more difficult to perform when operating in bankruptcy.

Next, assess real estate holdings. First check for prior or senior mortgages. These can be troublesome. A building could be carried on the books for $10 million. You might wonder to yourself how bad could things get? Maybe it is worth $7 or $8 million, or at least $5 million. But suppose the book value on the building is $50 million with a $40 million mortgage against it. That $10 million in recorded equity is at a much greater risk with a lot of debt in front of it. In bankruptcy, the owners may not be able to service the mortgage. The same circumstances that put the owner into bankruptcy may have caused the building's value to deteriorate. The company's equity in the building could quickly evaporate. The same principle applies to any other assets with prior liens, such as airplanes or railroad rolling stock having equipment trust certificate liens. If liens represent a large percentage of an asset's book value, only a small decline in its market value is needed to make it worth less than the debt against it. Undeveloped land is another tough category to evaluate. In a distressed sale, such property may have very little value. With time and money to develop it, the value could be substantial. Bankrupt companies, however, rarely have the resources to develop risky ventures.

Now, take a look at the plant and equipment category. Plant and equipment usually has rather specialized uses. It may be essential to the (now bankrupt) company's operations, but in a distress sale, it may have little value to anyone else. Again, the same problems that brought the company down could be hurting the market for its specialized assets. For example, when the oil market collapsed, so did the market for drilling rigs. When crude dropped to $10 to $12 a barrel, rigs weren't even worth scrap.

Raw undeveloped land, mineral rights, closed-up mineshafts, discontinued facilities and any other unproductive assets are likely to be worthless, or nearly so. Facilities associated with toxic-waste dumps and buildings with as-bestos problems are likely to have negative values. If you have any hint of such problems, check into them. Such exposures can turn into major liabilities.

Investments in subsidiaries and affiliates must be evaluated on a case by case basis. Sometimes the parent experiences financial difficulty and the subsidiaries continue to prosper. At other times the parents' problems are reflected in the subsidiaries as well. What does the P&L statement for the subsidiary look like? Does the subsidiary depend upon the parent for capital, or as a customer or supplier? Can the subsidiary enterprise stand on its own? Each case is different. Realize, however, that a bankrupt estate seldom receives top dollar even for its crown jewels.

Did we miss any odds and ends? Patents and trademarks are intangibles that usually have little value in a liquidation. But let's not go too fast. Some assets' values are hidden or understated. Some things are worth far more than their book values. Airlines, for example, may have gate rights or landing slots that are not reflected on the balance sheet yet are quite valuable. Television and radio stations have allocated broadcast frequencies that may be worth far more than the values carried on the books. Similarly, cable TV and cellular phone franchises have considerable value based on their rights to operate. Note, however, that if recently acquired, these types of rights and franchises may conversely be carried on the books at inflated values. Railroads may own land (from 19th century land grants or downtown terminal sites) worth far more than their book valuations. Oil and gas companies may be carrying their proven reserves at $10 or $15 a barrel when the market is several times that level. Some very old historical real estate values may be only a small fraction of their actual market values. Long-term leaseholds may be at rental rates well below the current market. If so, they may have considerable value in a sale if they are transferable. Pension funds may be overfunded and contain a substantial surplus. Some troubled companies may have applications filed for large tax refunds. Net operating loss carry-forwards may have some value if they can be preserved and eventually utilized to offset subsequent income. Franchises (e.g., a Coca-Cola bottling company or a McDonald's restaurant) are another potential source of value. But each case is different.

First, take a hard-nosed view of assets, and then look for upside. Come up with a valuation range. Under a fire-sale liquidation, the assets would bring in X. With a better market environment, viewed as a going concern the company would be worth Y.

Evaluate the Liabilities. Now let's evaluate the liability side. Be careful. Don't let any contingent liabilities go unnoticed. Unfunded pension obligations could be a big overhang. Expect legal and other administrative fees and taxes to take a big chunk off the top. Check for guarantees as well as damage and other claims arising from unresolved lawsuits. Now line up all of the ordinary creditor claims. Pension claims; bank debt; senior bond debts; trade credits; employee claims; subordinated debt; debt to subsidiaries; tax claims; lease obligations. Put each debt in its proper order of priority.

Now compare the asset range with the liability range. Under absolute priority who would get paid what? If the going-concern value is used, what percentage of total liabilities is covered?

Estimate the Payout. This is the point at which the really tough call must be made. What is the probable outcome of the case? If the company is likely to be liquidated, the analysis is relatively straightforward. How much would the senior-most creditors be slated to receive in a simple liquidation? Suppose it is 90% of their claim. This means that the rest of the creditors are out of the money. They may negotiate some consideration but shouldn't count on much. Take a hard look at the senior and subordinated obligations. What is the ratio of the market price to the expected outcome? Suppose the seniors trade for 65, and your analyses predicts they should receive 90 in a liquidation. Is that a buy? Probably not, at least not early in the case. Realize that you will receive no interest (or accrual of interest) on your investment while you wait. The junior debt holders may make enough noise to get something (thereby reducing the senior recovery), and markets for the company's assets could deteriorate. Paying 65 cents on the dollar to get a possible 25 cent appreciation is probably not worth the risk and wait (unless the risk is minimal and only a short wait is expected.) Moreover, a costly administration of the estate could erode recovery values substantially. On the other hand, if bonds sell for 30 or 40 cents on the dollar, the price may be right. Investing 30 or 40 cents on the dollar to get possibly double or triple that amount back in, say, a year is an attractive potential return given the risks. Assess the likely wait and risks and then act accordingly.

The case becomes much more complicated when you consider the going-concern scenario. Suppose that as a going concern the company is worth 80% of its outstanding (pre-bankruptcy) debt obligations. How you might come up with this assessment is a story in itself. Suppose, however, that the reorganized firm can produce operating income of some amount Z dollars, and otherwise similar firms sell for a multiple of five times their operating income. Then, this firm might have a valuation of perhaps four Z dollars. The lower multiple (four rather than five) is appropriate because of the higher risks associated with projections for a firm coming out of bankruptcy. In fact, a multiple of three times operating earnings might be more realistic.

Now look at the classification of creditors. Suppose the total creditor claims break down as follows: seniors are 30%, trade creditors 10%, senior subordinated 30%, and junior subordinated 30%. How is the pie likely to be divided? If this were a liquidation accomplished within Chapter 7 with absolute priority applying, the results would be obvious. First, administrative and tax claims would be paid in full. These are the claims arising out of administrating and liquidating the estate. Lawyers, accountants, appraisers, trustees and the like will each reduce their fees. Moreover, in a liquidation the sale will not bring in as much as the firm might be worth as a going concern.

Assume that the firm sells for 75% of its going-concern value. That works out to 60% of creditor claims (.75 x 80 = .60). Depending upon market conditions and the effectiveness of the selling effort, the actual discount required to sell the company could be more or less than this 25% we have assumed Administrative claims will come off the top. These claims could easily take an amount equal to 10% of creditor claims. That leaves 50% (.60 - .10 = .50) to go to the creditors. The seniors get their 30%, leaving 20% for the trade creditors and senior subordinated creditors. If trade creditors are also judged to be fully senior, they will get their 10%, while the senior subordinated creditors will get the remaining sum. Since they had claims equal to 30% of the total of creditor claims, but only 10% of this amount is left for them, their recovery equals one-third of their claims. You should also take into account the likelihood that the liquidation process will be time-consuming. Unsecured creditors usually do not accrue post-petition interest while they wait for the last move through the courts. Creditors and equity holders that are junior to the senior subordinated creditors would receive nothing under absolute priority.

Negotiating a Consensual Plan. Now rather than a liquidation in Chapter 7, let's see what might happen in a reorganization coming out of Chapter 11. A consensual plan will probably need to provide something for all of the creditors, and perhaps even something for the shareholders in order to succeed in obtaining the necessary approvals of each creditor class. If the net operating loss carry-forward is to be preserved, the shareholders will have to be left with more of the common stock of the reorganized firm than their priority would often indicate. The seniors will, at the same time, insist on coming out whole or nearly so, and the shareholders will also demand something. The tough question is determining how well the intermediate debt will fare. Those investment categories in the middle are probably where the reward/risk ratio tends to be highest. Go back to our earlier case. The senior bonds are at 40, senior subordinated at 10, and junior subordinated at 3. These prices are totally hypothetical but useful for illustrating the analysis.

Again we assume a valuation of the company equal to 80% of its creditor claims. Rather than a liquidation sale, however, we assume that the company's debt and equity securities are distributed to the old investors (bondholders and stockholders). We might see a negotiated plan provide something like the following: Administrative expenses, which are less for reorganization than liquidation, take the first 5% (of the 80% that we start with). That leaves 75% for the claims of pre- petition creditors. Senior bondholders receive consideration equal to 95% of the amount of their (pre-petition) claim (95% of 30%, or 28.5% of the total value of the claims in the estate). That leaves 75% - 28.5%, or 46.5% for the rest of the investors. Shareholders (who must be left in place to preserve the net operating loss carry-forward) might be able to grab 3%, which now leaves 43.5% for the trade creditors (10%), senior subordinated creditors (30% of total claims), and junior subordinated (30% of total claims). At this point we have 70% (.10+.30+.30 =.70) of total claims to be satisfied out of value equal to 43.5% of total claims. On the average, these intermediate categories of creditors are slated to get value equal to 43.5/70 = 62% of their claims. The trade creditors have the highest priority after the senior creditors and thus might be able to demand a recovery equal to 90% of their claim. Take this 9% (.90 x 10 = .09) away from our 43.5%, and we are down to 34.5% for the senior and junior subordinated debenture holders to divide. Suppose the senior subordinated are able to negotiate an 85% recovery of their claim (85% of 30% is 25.5%). Subtracting 25.5% from 34.5% leaves 9% for the junior subordinated. This corresponds to a recovery of
9/30 = 30% of their initial claim.

Now, you ask, why did we end up here with senior subordinated receiving 85% of their claim and junior subordinated 30%? Why not 90-25, 95-15 or 80-35 or even 70-45? All of those outcomes would have been possible. Recall that in a Chapter 7 liquidation, the senior subordinated would have gotten 33% and the junior subordinated nothing. Clearly, any of the above outcomes in a reorganization gives both categories of subordinated creditors more than they would receive in a liquidation. This unwritten feature is the dynamic that makes successful Chapter 11's. All groups have a strong incentive to agree to a consensual plan. And yet each knows that the other also has a lot to lose if the case is converted to Chapter 7. In the give and take, the senior subordinated group has the better bargaining position. They can say to the junior subordinated creditors that they (the juniors) are to be awarded something in reorganization that is surely better than getting nothing in a liquidation (Chapter 7). The junior subordinated group can threaten to torpedo the entire deal, but everyone knows that doing so hurts them more than it harms the other creditors.

At the end of the day, the resulting split will turn on a number of factors: personalities, specific indenture provisions, characteristics of the two groups of creditors, how well their lawyers represent them, etc. The result presented here is one of many possible outcomes. Assuming this assessment is correct, which security is the better buy? Let's look at the expected outcome to price (payoff to cost) ratios:

Seniors	= 95/40	237.5%
Senior Subordinate	= 85/10	850%
Junior Subordinate	= 30/3	1000%

Clearly, in this example, the junior subordinated has the greater expected payoff as a percentage of current cost. However, it also has the greatest risk. Our analysis is based on a number of assumptions, any of which could prove to be too optimistic. Many things could go wrong. For example, the senior creditors could demand most or all of the available consideration. If they stand firm, the juniors may be forced to blink. The 80% of creditor claims estimate for the value of the reorganized firm could turn out to be too high. In either case, the junior subordinated creditors could receive much less than our estimates, or even be wiped out. If the case is converted to Chapter 7, they are almost certain to be entitled to nothing under the absolute priority that applies in such situations. Thus the senior subordinated bonds (which would get something in a Chapter 7) could offer the better combination of security and return. If the situation ends up as a liquidation, the seniors still come out close to whole (although they would have a longer wait without receiving any interest, which is not really as good). Our earlier projections show the senior subordinated would achieve a recovery equal to 33% of their claim in a liquidation (again with a longer wait). This result would correspond to a ratio of payoff to cost of 330% (33 vs. 10). Thus in Chapter 7 and Chapter 11, our projected outcomes become:

	Liquidation Reorganization	(longer wait)
Seniors	250%	237%
Senior Subordinated	330%	850%
Junior Subordinated	0	1000%

Another factor to consider in a reorganization is the form of the payout. The more senior your claims, the more likely your payout will be in the form of higher quality (more senior) securities. Thus, in the above scenario, the senior creditors are likely to receive a package heavily weighted toward cash and senior debt instruments. The junior creditors' package is more likely to be weighted toward junior paper (warrants, common stock, preferred stock and deeply subordinated debt instruments). Just after the company comes out of bankruptcy as a reorganized firm is usually a disadvantageous time for an investor to liquidate his or her position. After all, everyone has only recently received their package of securities. Most of those who invest in distressed securities are not likely to want to hold these particular securities long term. The senior securities are easiest to sell for a price close to their intrinsic (underlying) values. Moreover, a quick sale is likely to have adverse tax consequences (subject to taxation as a short-term holding) for one who bought in at a distress level price. Thus, even though the junior subordinated debentures appear to offer the greater upside potential, their risk and potential illiquidity may offset that potential.

Clearly, each case is different. At times the senior-most security offers the best prospects. At other times, the intermediate or junior most security offers the highest potential reward relative to the risks.

In the above analysis, we considered investing early in the case with a projection for the ultimate outcome in hand. Realistically, one is unlikely to have more than a vague idea of that outcome until the case is well under way. By then, however, prices of securities are likely to reflect the underlying values much more closely. Still, opportunities may remain.

Evaluation at the Disclosure Statement Stage. Suppose we are now at the stage where a disclosure statement has been sent out and a plan is up for a vote. If the plan is truly consensual, all of the creditor groups will have agreed to support it. A favorable vote is likely. Moreover, if a favorable vote does occur, it is quite likely to result in confirmation of the plan itself. While such circumstances remove some of the uncertainty, a business (as opposed to legal) risk remains. Specifically, the reorganized company's worth and how this worth is to be divided up among its various categories of securities remain uncertain. You can refer to the disclosure statement to see what the company's balance sheet is expected to look like and what kind of package of securities will be issued to you. At this point (before the plan is confirmed and takes effect) you have a number of options: you can sell your position at current prices, buy more of the security (e.g., senior subordinated) that you already own, or switch or diversify into something else (say a combination of senior and junior subordinated debentures). What should you do?

First, find the section of the disclosure statement that reports what the firm's anticipated (pro forma) balance sheet will look like coming out of bankruptcy. Mark out any intangible assets like goodwill, and assess the rest of the assets. What does the company really have to work with? Next, determine what they projected for income and cash flow. Do those numbers appear adequate to service debt and other fixed costs going forward? They should, or the reorganization process has not been done properly. The plan should be feasible. No one is offering any guarantees, but the court should not approve a plan that will put the company right back into trouble once it comes out of bankruptcy.

Suppose that in our example the company has $100 million in debt when it went into bankruptcy. After reorganizing and paying administrative claims, it emerges with $75 million in properly valued assets. It also has a going-concern value of $75 million. What kind of capital structure makes sense? The creditors will want to be paid, if not in cash, in senior claims, while the debtor will want to limit the company's ongoing exposure to fixed charges, particularly interest. Suppose this $75 million can generate operating income that should average $15 million a year. Realize that this money must first go to pay overhead, taxes (to the extent not sheltered by an NOL), and debt service. These are contractual or other legal obligations that must be paid. Anything left over would then be available for reinvestment in the company, and eventually something might be available for preferred and common dividends. Also, the company's capital structure should contemplate that some years will be better than others. Fifteen million dollars of operating income may be a reasonable estimate for an average year, but by its very nature an average is composed of the results from both good and poor years. If the company operates in a volatile industry, operating income might have a range of $5 million to $25 million. With fixed overhead of $2 million, that kind of range implies that in a poor year only $3 million is available for debt service and everything else. Reserves (if any), or additional borrowings (if possible), would then have to be tapped to make up any shortfall.

The Securities Packages. With this information as background, we see that the firm should not have a reorganization plan that overburdens the firm with debt, at least not debt that requires a lot of cash interest. Still, the creditors will push for what they can get. In this give and take, the seniors are in the best position. They had $30 million in claims. They will demand and probably get $30 million face amount of new debt. They will, however, have to give up something. To make the deal work, they agree to accept relatively long-term bonds (10-year) with a 10% coupon. They insist that it be senior to all other debt. Still under current market conditions (a high interest rate environment), these bonds will trade at less than their face value. To determine what the seniors are getting, one must consider the likely risk and returns and compare this issue with the market. Suppose otherwise similar bonds are trading for prices that yield 11%. This bond would need to be priced at about 95 in order to offer a similar 11% yield. You can check these figures in a bond book or use a financial calculator.

Next, consider the trade creditors. They did not start out as investors and are very likely to have no interest in being long-term investors in the reorganized company. Still, the firm is not in a position to pay them off with cash. Whatever securities they receive are likely to be quickly sold for whatever they will bring. In this instance, the trade creditors are given $5 million of the same bond as the seniors and another $5 million in senior subordinated debt. The senior subordinated debt also has a 10% coupon, but it has a 15-year maturity and is subordinated to the senior issue. The company wants to stretch out any need to refinance its debt. The senior debt comes due in 10 years, but the senior subordinate debt runs another five years. Again you have to estimate this (senior subordinated) instrument's value. Because of its longer term and subordinated status (but equivalent coupon), this bond will surely sell for a larger discount from par than the senior bond. Using a similar methodology as with the earlier issue, you estimate it to command a 12% discounted rate and thus trade in the market for about 85% of its face value.

At this point we have $35 million of senior bonds and $5 million of the senior subordinated issued. By themselves, these bonds would require debt service of $4 million each year. The reorganized firm has only $75 million in hard assets. Thus, the company must satisfy the remaining claims, without issuing too much more debt.

The senior subordinated creditors are to receive the following: $10 million in senior subordinated debenture, $10 million in junior subordinated (optional 12% PIK) 20-year debentures (10% coupon), $10 million in preferred stock (10% non-cumulative dividend) and common stock equal to 35% of the outstanding shares of the company coming out of bankruptcy. The junior subordinated debenture holders are to receive $5 million of the junior subordinated debentures; $5 million in preferred stock and common stock equal to 14% of the outstanding stock of the reorganized company. Managers are awarded 10% of the new shares. The old common shareholders retain 4% of the new stock. To evaluate these packages we must value each of the parts in the context of the firm's pro forma balance sheet and income statement.

Pro Forma Balance Sheet
(in millions)

Assets	Liabilities and Net Worth	
	Liabilities	
$75	Senior debt	$35
	Senior subordinated debt	15
	Junior subordinated debt	15
	Total liability	60
	Net worth	
	Preferred Stock	15
	Common Stock	0
Total $75	Total	$75

Pro Forma Abbreviated Income Statement

Operating Income	$15
Overhead	3.0
	$12.0
Senior debt interest	3.5
	$8.5
Senior subordinated interest	1.5
	$7.0
Junior subordinated interest	1.5
	$5.5
Taxes*	2.0
	$3.5
Preferred dividends**	1.5
Retained earnings	$2.0

*Taxes may not be due if the NOL is preserved in the reorganization.
**Preferred dividends may not be paid in the first several years.

What can we make of all of this? If the senior subordinated 10% debentures are priced at 85, the junior subordinated must be priced even lower. Moreover, the junior subordinated debentures have a feature that allows the company to pay the interest in more bonds (at a 12% rate) if the company chooses. This PIK (payment in kind) feature allows the company to conserve cash when times are bad. But the feature reduces the bond's value to the investor. Cash always beats paper. After some analysis, you conclude that these junior subordinated PIK bonds should be discounted at about a 15% rate and therefore, are worth around 70% of face.

The preferred stock's dividend is payable only at management's discretion. It is not cumulative. Management does not expect to pay the dividend for at least the first two years. Again you check around. With a great deal of luck the company will be able to start paying its dividend in about three years. Your analysis suggests that the preferred will be worth about 60% of its face value.

Now, what about the stock? No hard assets on the balance sheet appear to lie behind this junior-most security. In a liquidation, nothing would be left for the common. Additionally, no common dividends can be paid until after the preferred dividend is resumed. In all likelihood, the company will conserve cash and pay no common dividend for at least the first five years. And yet, as the residual owners, the common shareholders do have a claim to any upside beyond what is necessary to service the debt and preferred. In an average year, the common shareholders should have $2 million of retained earnings accrue to their ultimate benefit. If they could receive that money as a cash distribution, it would make the stock like an annuity with considerable value. They cannot, however, gain access to those retained earnings, at least not initially. The company must build up its equity position if it is ever to be in a position to pay a common dividend. The $2 million is only a projection and even if it is realized, will be retained by the firm to accumulate as a cushion against harder times. Thus. at the outset, the common is a relatively low-value high-risk security, with some upside potential. And yet the common shareholders are the residual owners. If the above projections are correct, value will build up over time. Perhaps the stock is worth a multiple of three times its projected retained earnings (and because no common dividends are expected to be paid, retained earnings are equal to total earnings attributable to common) or $6 million. This amount would be divided, with approximately $2.5 million to old common shareholders, $2 million to senior subordinated and $1 million to junior subordinated creditors and $0.5 million to management.

So what do the senior and junior debenture holders receive?

Senior Subordinated		New Senior Subordinated	New Junior Subordinated	Preferred Stock	Common Stock
$30 million in claims	Amount	$10	$10	$10	35%
	value par	85%	70%	60%	
value in $ millions		8.5	7	6	2

Total $23.5 (8.5 + 7 + 6 + 2)
% Recovery 23.5/30 = 78%

Junior Subordinated		New Junior Subordinated	Preferred Stock Subordinated	Common Stock
$30 million in claims	Amount	$5	$5	14%
	value par	70%	60%	
Value in $ millions		3.5	3	1

Total 7.5 (3.5 + 3 + 1)
% Recovery 7.5/30 = 25%

At this point of the analysis, we have the seniors, senior subordinated and junior subordinated slated to receive packages of securities with estimated values equal to 95%, 78% and 25% of their claims. These amounts are close to but not precisely the same as our earlier projections (95, 85 and 30). If we had made these initial projections early in the case, we could consider ourselves very close to the mark with this outcome. Suppose that just after the disclosure statement is released, the bonds themselves are selling for 80, 50 and 15. Again, which is the better buy and are any of them attractive instruments?

First, look in the disclosure statement to see when the plan is expected to become effective. How long must you wait? Time is money. The longer the projected wait, the less each package is worth. Also look to see what they say about the anticipated markets for the securities. Will they be listed on an exchange or NASDAQ? Realistically, in the above example, markets for these new securities are likely to be thin. Thus, trading could be a bit of a problem for a seller. Again the senior-most securities are likely to be the easiest to sell. All of them, however, will require the owner to incur selling costs if he or she wants to realize a quick cash recovery.

Take Account of Trading Costs. As always, specific circumstances will vary from case to case. Still, bid-ask spreads are likely to increase as the quality and amount outstanding of the instrument decreases. Perhaps the senior bonds will cost 5% to sell (spread plus commissions) in modest quantities. Similarly, the senior subordinate bonds may cost 8%, junior subordinated bonds 9%, preferred stock 10% and common stock 15% to trade. As a result the realizable value for the seniors would be 95% - (.5 x 95%) = 90%. The senior subordinated bondholders would see their realizable recovery reduced as follows:

$$
\begin{array}{rcll}
8.5 \times & .92 & = & 7.82 \\
7 \times & .91 & = & 6.37 \\
6 \times & .90 & = & 5.40 \\
2 \times & .85 & = & \underline{1.70} \\
\text{Total} = & & & 21.29
\end{array}
$$

$$\frac{21.29}{30} = 70.97\% \text{ or approximately } 71\%$$

Similarly the junior subordinated recoverable value (after deducting selling costs) equals:

$$
\begin{array}{rcll}
3.5 \times & .91 & = & 3.18 \\
3 \times & .90 & = & 2.70 \\
1 \times & .85 & = & \underline{0.85} \\
\text{Total} = & & & 6.73
\end{array}
$$

$$\frac{6.73}{.25} = 26.94\% \text{ or approximately } 27\%$$

Thus, taking account of selling costs we have the following:

	Market Price	Realizable Value	Market Price Realizable Value
Senior	80	90	112.5%
Senior Subordinated	50	71	142%
Junior Subordinated	15	27	180%

Suppose the projected effective date, assuming the plan is confirmed, is four months away. All three securities seem to offer a potentially attractive return. Nothing, however, is ever that simple in investing particularly investing in distressed securities. First, we need to consider the cost of purchasing the securities. This cost could be large or small, depending upon the nature of the market and the size of the trade. Second, we have to consider the risk that the plan might not be confirmed. That is a much greater problem for the junior than the senior debt. If the plan is not confirmed, a revised plan may be drafted or the case could be converted to Chapter 7. In either case, the recovery for the senior creditors is much more reliable. Third, we should note that our value estimates for the securities are only educated guesses. Indeed, the more junior the security, the more uncertain the estimate.

On the other hand, we are at a stage of the case where many uncertainties have been narrowed. If our plan is confirmed, and if our value estimates are accurate, and if the securities can be bought for close to the current market prices, the potential annualized returns are quite attractive. Indeed, the returns for the more junior securities seem particularly appealing.

Assessment. We have tracked through a hypothetical troubled company from the stage when it gets into serious financial difficulty to the point where it comes out of bankruptcy as a recognized firm. Every real life case will be different. The example was constructed to illustrate the kinds of issues that tend to arise at various points in the case. One is always trying to evaluate the overall situation and apply that analysis to the specific securities. Thus, one wants to assess the likely returns for each instrument and compare that with its corresponding risk. The process is neither easy nor precise. Many uncertainties lurk in the weeds. Thus the successful distressed/defaulted securities investor will assemble a well-diversified portfolio. One can diversify within a case by buying securities of various categories (secured, senior subordinated, junior subordinated, preferred, and common). This spreading of the money hedges one's bets regarding how the pie is split. One can diversity across cases by purchasing distressed/defaulted securities in a variety of cases. To be most effective, such diversification should be across types of cases. For example, the companies should be in different industries (e.g., banking, retailers, oil, real estate, etc.) and should be subject to a variety of different environmental influences (government regulations for some and not others, highly interest rate sensitive for some but not others, high tech vs. low tech; hard assets for some and iffy contingent assets for others, etc.) One can even diversify internationally, but that topic is beyond the scope of this book.

CHAPTER 6

QUANTITATIVE ANALYSIS
OF HIGH-YIELD SECURITIES

Effective high-yield credit analysis involves a number of carefully executed steps. Each step is specifically designed to limit the risk to invested capital, enhanced total portfolio returns and differentiate between actual and perceived value. This type of analysis includes in-depth valuations of assets and their coverage of total indebtedness, market multiples and their relationship to liquidation values, differing interpretations of cash flow coverage of interest expense and the write-up of assets and increased depreciation expense (or, in rare instances, a writedown of assets and a corresponding decrease in depreciation expense) brought about through purchase accounting adjustments.

Quality research is an elusive commodity. Similarly, the visible differences between an outstanding credit and a terrible one are often relatively small. The margin for error can be very thin. Subtle differences in credit quality can be compounded into enormous opportunity, and conversely, enormous capital losses. Indeed, an entire book could be written on the topic of high-yield credit analysis. We shall focus here on those (credit-specific) analytical avenues that warrant particular attention.

The discussion is divided into several parts. The first part treats certain quantitative techniques that are important in the financial analysis of high-yield securities. The second part deals with those aspects of high-yield credit work that are qualitative in nature, and hence more subjective and dependent on careful interpretation. Both types of analysis must be incorporated into the larger context of high-yield security analysis. Sources of investment information are covered in the final part.

FINANCIAL ANALYSIS

We have divided financial analysis into four primary areas: 1) Asset values, 2) Cash flow (defined as Earnings Before Interest, Taxes, Depreciation and Amortization, or EBITDA), 3) Liquidity and balance sheet analysis, and 4) Leverage.

Without sufficient levels of the first three attributes, a high-yield company cannot survive. With burdensome levels of the latter, survival is also questionable.

Asset values, if in excess of total debt, allow for some cushion in the event of bankruptcy. Furthermore, such values represent an excellent appraisal of enterprise value on a private-market basis. However, negative cash flows will dilute the protection provided by asset values that may at an earlier time have appeared high. Indeed, sufficient cash flow is needed for the timely payment of interest and principal, as well as for the business expansion. Moreover, sufficient cash flow is the key ingredient if the overall levels of credit quality are to improve.

With the possible exception of certain real estate/asset-intensive businesses, however, most high-yield credits should be evaluated on the basis of their going-concern values, rather than by their estimated liquidation values. Liquidation analysis does, however, afford a certain degree of comfort, particularly if the going-concern assumption turns out to have been substantially in error.

FINANCIAL POSITION

An attractive industry environment, strong competitive position, and effective management are all important components of a company's fundamental position. Only companies with adequate financial resources can fully exploit their opportunities, however. Thus, much of fundamental analysis involves assessing the company's financial strengths and weaknesses.

BASIC ACCOUNTING CONCEPTS
USED IN FUNDAMENTAL ANALYSIS

Accounting data are utilized extensively in financial analysis. Accordingly, we shall briefly review the principal types of financial statements. First, a balance sheet provides an instantaneous picture of a company's resources and obligations. Balance sheets are set up in a particular way. A classified listing of assets appears on the left. Plant and equipment are valued at historical cost less accumulated depreciation, whereas most other assets are valued at the lower of either cost less accumulated depreciation or current market value. Liabilities (both long- and short-term debts) and net worth (the residual ownership position) appear on the right. Net worth is by definition equal to assets minus liabilities. Thus, the two sides of the balance sheet are always equal: hence its name.

The income statement provides a picture of business performance over a particular time period. It begins with total revenues at the top. Various expenses are then subtracted until only the company's earnings remain. The income statement helps answer questions such as: How much money did the company make or lose in the recent period? How much of its earnings went to its stockholders? How do current earnings compare with past results? Every year (unless the company sells or buys in its stock), the company's net worth will change by that year's retained earnings (profit after taxes less dividends). The income statement and balance sheet are thus connected by changes in net worth.

The statement of cash flows, the third of the principal accounting statements, is designed to help one analyze the company's liquidity/cash flow position. Figure 6.1 summarizes the three types of statements.

Figure 6.1
Types of Accounting Statements

Balance Sheet	Income Statement	Statement of Cash Flows
Instantaneous picture of resources (assets) and obligations (liabilities)	Revenues less expenses equal earnings	Liquidity/Cash Flow position

Preparing accounting statements necessarily involves many subjective judgments. That subjectivity opens up opportunities for abuse. Such temptation may be too great for some managers, particularly if the actual underlying economic results are poor. Permissible accounting conventions are frequently misused in order to alter a company's financial appearance, for example, decreasing depreciation expense by extending the estimate of the useful life of assets for no apparent economic reason other than to report an increase in current earnings. Nevertheless, the vast majority of accounting statements probably reflect a consistent and meaningful financial picture.

RATIO ANALYSIS

Relative magnitudes of financial data are generally more revealing than absolute levels. A company with a bank balance of a million dollars could be very rich (local retailer) or very poor (Fortune 500 Company), depending upon its overall size. Clearly, such a number needs to be compared with the overall size of the enterprise. Accordingly, *ratios* of financial aggregates have long been used to assess the financial positions of various sized companies.

Ratios may be grouped into three categories. *Liquidity ratios* measure the company's ability to meet its short-term obligations. *Debt ratios* measure the company's long-term strengths and weaknesses. Finally, *profitability and efficiency* ratios are designed to reflect the firm's productivity.

Liquidity and Liquidity Ratios: High degrees of financial liquidity allow for advantageous and timely realization of business opportunities. Additionally, financial flexibility provides a cushion during times of economic crisis or a sudden and unexpected downturn in a company's business. Financial liquidity is measured primarily in three ways: 1) balance sheet analysis and working capital projections, 2) available bank lines, and 3) cash flow.

Liquidity difficulties are usually encountered in conjunction with one of three problems: 1) Slow Working Capital Turnover; 2) Insufficient Credit Availability; 3) Insufficient Cash Flow Generation

Working capital is obtained either from internally generated funds or, in the case of many high-yield companies, through periodic drawings against available working capital facilities. Working capital is comprised of cash, accounts receivable and inventory, along with smaller components. Projections of peak seasonal borrowing needs must be evaluated against currently available borrowing lines. Bumps against current line limits may be indicative of future sales constraints.

Three ratios are of utmost importance in evaluating working capital efficiency: Accounts Receivable Turnover, Inventory Turnover, and Inventory to Sales. They are calculated as follows:

$$\text{Accounts Receivable Turnover} = \frac{\text{Net Sales (1) on Credit}}{\text{Average Accounts Receivable (AR) (2)}}$$

(1) Generally assumed to be on credit unless otherwise reported.
(2) Calculated as beginning plus end of period AR, divided by two.

$$\text{Inventory Turnover} = \frac{\text{Cost of Goods Sold (COGS) (1)}}{\text{Average Inventory (2)}}$$

(1) Cost of Goods Sold is normally used to reduce calculation bias caused by fluctuations in gross margins. If COGS is unavailable, use sales.
(2) Averaged by the same method as Accounts Receivable, see #2 above.

$$\text{Inventory Sales} = \frac{\text{Ending Inventory}}{\text{Yearly Sales}}$$

From the company and its investors' standpoints, the higher the level of Inventory and Accounts Receivable Turnover, the better. In fact, many supermarkets turn over inventory in excess of 12 times per year. Think of it this way: If they have to pay their suppliers no more frequently than every 30 days and their inventory turns in excess of 12 times, they will be able to finance their entire inventory needs with their supplier's money, consequently freeing tremendous amounts of working capital for other purposes.

The lower the ratio of Inventory/Sales, the better, assuming levels are sufficient to meet current demand and maintain adequate sales growth. Lower inventory as a percentage of sales equals higher turnover and consequently lower financing costs.

The inventory turnover ratio equals the cost of goods sold divided by average yearly inventory. Although monthly inventory figures are generally unavailable to external analysts, yearly averages may be successfully calculated from quarterly, or even yearly, inventory balances. The ideal inventory level differs by industry and, in some cases, with the season and business cycle. A high turnover suggests brisk sales and well-managed inventories. A very high ratio might indicate an inadequate level of inventories, however. A low turnover, in contrast, reflects idle resources tied up in excess inventories and/or a large obsolete inventory component.

The average collection period (ACP) is the weighted average life of outstanding accounts receivable. It should be compared with the company's stated credit policy. For example, a manufacturer might have a credit policy based upon an expectation of receiving payments within 30 days of billing. An ACP longer than 30 days indicates the firm may have a problem with credit extensions. Perhaps the firm's credit standards are too lax or its collection policy is too loose. The presence of one or more large, slow-paying customers in financial difficulty would also lengthen the ACP. Although not indicative of a lax collections policy per se, the reliance on one or several large customers can inflict financial stress on a company if the customers themselves experience financial difficulty.

The current ratio is an index of the short-term picture. It is defined as current assets (cash, short-term investments, accounts receivable, prepaid expenses, and inventories) divided by current liabilities (accounts payable, notes due in one year, and the current portion of long-term debt). According to conventional wisdom, the current ratio should be two or greater. As with all ratios, however, the optimal value varies from company to company, industry to industry, and over time. Stable incomes and reliable sources of short-term credit lessen the need for liquid assets and therefore reduce the optimal current ratio level. Indeed, a high current ratio may indicate that resources are being tied up unnecessarily. A relatively stable ratio below two is generally less worrisome than a sustained major decline in the ratio.

The quick, or acid test, ratio is defined as liquid assets (current assets less inventories) divided by current liabilities, including interim debt. Inventories, which may be relatively difficult to liquidate, are part of the current ratio's numerator but are excluded from the quick ratio. Most analysts recommend a quick ratio of one or more. The appropriate level, however, varies from industry to industry, over time, and with special characteristics of the company.

Unless substantial losses or a major adjustment (i.e., a large merger) have clouded the picture, short-term financial conditions of most established companies will be found to be satisfactory. Small, less-experienced companies, in contrast, frequently encounter short-term financial difficulty either because of poor capitalization or poor rates of profit/cash flow.

Borrowing Capacity: Ideally, one should prefer to invest in companies that have adequate credit availability even during times of peak seasonal borrowings. Additionally, an investor should prefer a company to have either a relatively long term (three to five years) revolving credit facility or one that can be converted, at the option of the company, into a term loan. Long-term bank loan agreements allow for a substantial amount of flexibility; they also enable management to focus on the operation of the business rather than being interrupted periodically to procure bank lines. The relatively permanent nature of long-term credit facilities helps to prevent banks from withdrawing a company's access to credit without warning. Such protection is critically important to issuers of high-yield securities.

Additionally, prospective investors should look for consistency and conservatism in the application of generally accepted accounting principles (GAAP). Extreme and frequent policy changes (e.g., depreciation or inventory accounting assumptions) can be indicative of an attempt to manipulate earnings. Such changes should be highly scrutinized. As many GAAP decisions are ultimately the responsibility of management, consistency and conservatism over long periods of time may be used as one proxy for management's attitude toward the operation of its business. Also look favorably upon low volatility of earnings and cash flow and a high degree of stability in cash flow itself. The degree of volatility is reflected in the range of historical patterns. The stability of cash flow can be measured by analyzing the percentage of the depreciation component of cash flow in relations to total EBITDA (Earnings Before Interest, Taxes, Depreciation and Amortization). From the company's standpoint the higher the percentage the better, as the depreciation rate will almost certainly vary less than earnings, financing costs, and tax policy.

Leverage and Debt Ratios: Leverage is analyzed in a number of ways, including debt to capitalization, debt to equity, and degrees of operating leverage. One interesting and important measure is "cash flow leverage." Cash flow leverage is defined as Long-Term Debt (LTD)/EBITDA. As with other leverage indicators, the lower the better. In contrast to the "Years to Pay Off Debt," this ratio attempts to measure the degree of leverage inflicted on cash flow, or conversely, cash flow's ability to support a given debt level, rather than measuring deleveraging potential.

The actual degree of leverage, in and of itself, is not particularly important, and in many cases should not be of great concern to creditors. In fact, many defensive recapitalizations result in high degrees of negative equity, due to the nature of the accounting treatment of the transaction. When book equity is negative, no meaningful leverage ratios may be computed. For perspective, keep in mind that the majority of new home loans reflect 80-95% leverage when initially written. More important than a mechanical ratio such as debt/assets, however, is the intent, and particularly the ability, to service a given level of debt. Consequently, cash flow analysis and coverage ratios are much more important to the financial health of a company than are the static measures of debt levels.

Debt-equity and times-interest-earned ratios are used to assess the prospects for a company's continued success and stability. The "Times Interest Earned" or cash flow coverage ratio is defined as EBITDA divided by interest expense. It measures how many times the cash flow generated by the company is in excess of required interest payments. Although cash flow coverage of interest is extremely important, investors should not overlook the importance of being able to make principal payments when they come due. Keep in mind that required principal payments must either be paid out of cash flow or refinanced. Large, looming principal payments generally create some degree of concern, particularly during restrictive financing environments. In order to assess a company's ability to repay principal, many analysts subtract from EBITDA such items as cash interest, working capital changes (or add working capital savings), and capital expenditures. Cash interest is deducted from

EBITDA because it must be paid currently. Sustainable growth cannot occur without additions to working capital or increased turnover.

Therefore, net increases in working capital (working capital in period two, minus working capital in period one) are subtracted from EBITDA. Likewise, working capital savings (a decline in net working capital), either from increased turnover or decreases accompanying sales declines, are added to cash flow. As revenues cannot increase indefinitely without investments in plant and equipment, capital expenditures are also subtracted from EBITDA. The amount remaining, after subtracting these items, reflects the amount of EBITDA available for principal payments. The amount available for principal payments is the amount that should be compared with actual principal payment requirements. Although a company may exhibit excellent EBITDA coverage of interest, large capital expenditures and uneven principal payment requirements may hamper future financial flexibility. Ideally, a high-yield company's capital structure should be self-amortizing. That is, projected EBITDA after subtracting cash interest, working capital changes, and capital expenditures, should be sufficient to retire debt as it comes due. The ability of a firm's cash flow to exhibit this self-amortizing feature significantly reduces its need to rely on external sources of funds and greatly enhances its financial flexibility.

Debt-equity ratios (liabilities divided by net worth) vary considerably from industry to industry, company to company, and over time. A public utility with highly predictable earnings, a bank with very liquid assets, or a construction company that undertakes very large projects relative to its equity base may have quite a hefty ratio (2:1, or even 20:1). Companies with volatile earnings (e.g., automobile manufacturers) may need and choose to have a much lower target ratio, such as 1:10.

Companies generally take on debt in an effort to increase their profit rate relative to their net worth (i.e., return on equity). This is the principle of leverage. A company that can borrow at X% and earn (X + Y)% on the borrowed money, gains the difference (Y%). So, for example, if you can borrow at 8% and earn 15%, you are ahead by the difference or 7%. If every dollar of your own money is matched by a dollar of borrowing, you would earn 15% on your own funds, plus 7% on the borrowed funds for an overall return on equity of 15% + 7% or a total of 22%. Leverage is, however, a two-edged sword. The company that borrows has thereby incurred debts that must be serviced regardless of the returns earned with the borrowed funds. Thus, companies planning to be heavy borrowers need to be relatively confident that the return they earn will exceed their borrowing costs. Moreover, interest payments, unlike dividends on common and preferred stock, are legal obligations that must be made when due whether or not a profit was made in that period.

Accordingly, a company with a stable return is better positioned to borrow than one with a similar average profit rate that is less stable. Burdensome debt obligations may, in difficult times, force a company with favorable long-term prospects to liquidate needed assets and, in an extreme case, to file for bankruptcy. Thus, a substantial amount of leverage (high debt-equity ratio) is both potentially profitable and risky. The more secure the company, the greater the percentage of debt that may safely be accepted.

The appropriate debt-equity ratio for a company varies directly with its earnings stability. A comparison of debt-equity ratios over time and within the industry may help one assess the adequacy of the current debt burden. A rapid rise in the ratio suggests potential problems. If the increased debt leaves the firm with a substantial cushion of equity and profitable operations, no immediate concern need be shown. The company may simply be taking advantage of heretofore unused debt capacity. If the firm is experiencing losses or only modest profits, however, its increased reliance on debt suggests possible problems. The company may well be taking on additional debt in order to finance a risky strategy. Such debt may, for example, be designed to finance a program that the borrowing firm hopes will eventually show profits. Such hopes, however, may not be realized. Even if the firm's greater debt is accompanied by increased profits, the investor needs to be cautious. The recent growth in profits may not be sustainable. At a minimum, further growth would be difficult to finance if it required a still greater proportion of debt.

Debt is not the only type of fixed payment obligation that a company must make. In particular, leases, which also represent fixed payment obligations, may further complicate accounting statement analysis. Purchasing assets with borrowed funds increases the debt-equity ratio, whereas leasing the same assets does not increase debt per se. The resulting long-term obligations are very similar, however, whether the assets are leased or purchased. Thus, debt-equity ratios do not always accurately reflect a company's financial commitments. Investors need to look beyond the debt ratios of companies that lease a large fraction of their operating assets. Companies must report their capitalized long-term lease obligation on their balance sheets. Leases that call for payments of less than 80% of the asset's value need not be capitalized. However, these off-balance-sheet obligations must be properly recognized and thus included in a company's overall debt level when they are recurring in nature or excessively large in relation to reported debt.

The absence of an allowance for unfunded pension liabilities can distort a corporation's reported financial picture, as can rising values on pension liabilities. Rising values on pension fund portfolios are expected to pay a substantial part of the promised benefits. When the funds invested in the portfolio do not produce the expected gains, these resources may be inadequate to cover pension obligations, particularly under defined-benefit plans where pension risk is shouldered by the employers. Moreover, many pension plans have been underfunded by the corporation. Pension reform legislation now requires that many benefits be paid even if the employee leaves well before retirement age (vested benefits) or the company leaves the industry. These unfunded pension liabilities have a high priority claim in any bankruptcy proceeding. Over the next several decades, companies are required to set up reserves to cover such liabilities.

Some financial analysts prefer to use the debt-asset ratio rather than the debt-equity ratio as a leverage ratio. Assets equal debt plus equity. Thus, the two ratios are closely related. They have the same numerator. Moreover, both have equity in the denominator. The debt-equity ratio's denominator is equity, whereas the debt-asset ratio's denominator is assets, which is the sum of debt and equity. Therefore the debt-asset ratio's denominator is increased by the same number that appears in each ratio's numerator. The main difference in the two ratios is in their scales. Equity can be a small or large percentage of assets or something in between. Therefore the debt-equity ratio can vary from a number close to 0 (almost no debt) to a very large number (almost no equity). Because the debt-equity ratio varies over a larger range, some analysts prefer it to the debt-asset ratio.

Profitability and Efficiency Ratios: Six important and related profitability-efficiency ratios are: 1) return on equity (ROE); 2) return on assets (ROA), also sometimes called return on investment (ROI); 3) return on sales (ROS), also sometimes called profit margin; 4) asset turnover; 5) debt margin and 6) gross profit to selling, general and administrative expense.

Annual averages are generally used to compute profitability and efficiency ratios. One can, of course, use a shorter time frame, but seasonal influences may distort the results.

1.   ROE = After-Tax Profit / Shareholders' Equity
2.   ROA = Before-Tax Before-Interest Profit / Total Assets (also called ROI)
3.   ROS = After-Tax Profits / Total Revenues (also called profit margin)
4.   Asset Turnover = Total Revenues / Total Assets
5.   Debt Margin = Total Assets / Shareholders' Equity
6. TT/SG&A = Gross Profit/Selling, General and Administrative Expense

Note that ROE is the product of ROS, asset turnover, and debt margin:

ROE = ROS   X Asset Turnover X Debt Margin

$$\frac{\text{After-Tax Profit}}{\text{Shareholders' Equity}} = \frac{\text{After-Tax Profit}}{\text{Total Revenues}} \times \frac{\text{Total Revenues}}{\text{Total Assets}} \times \frac{\text{Total Assets}}{\text{Shareholders' Equity}}$$

Thus, one can examine the source of profitability or profit problems by looking at these components of ROE. ROE as a measure of profitability relative to shareholders' equity is a major determinant of share prices. Because its denominator (equity) is smaller and more variable, ROE tends to be more variable than ROA.

ROS is also called the profit margin. ROS tends to vary inversely with inventory turnover. A high turnover operation, such as a supermarket, tends to have a low profit margin, whereas a high margin operation, such as a jewelry store, tends to have a low turnover.

Profitability and growth prospects are forward-looking concepts. Is the past profit and growth record likely to improve or get worse? An examination of past results helps assess various possible scenarios.

High growth rates resulting primarily from increased debt, higher capacity utilization, accounting changes, cost cutting or price increases must eventually reach a barrier that is likely to limit further growth. Earnings forecasts should only project earnings growth that relies upon a more favorable margin, debt-equity ratio, output-asset ratio, or depreciation rate if the projected change seems likely to take place.

Gross Profit to Selling, General, and Administrative Expenses is another important ratio. It is a measure of management's efficiency in generating gross profit dollars. In other words, how many dollars does management have to spend in order to generate a dollar of gross profit. Generally, with this ratio, the higher the better. However, too high a ratio might be unattainable, and thereby invite other companies to enter the industry and lead to more competitive pricing unless entry was blocked by patent protection or high capital costs. A declining ratio would be indicative of a cost structure that was inflating relative to the level of sales.

OTHER RATIOS

In addition to liquidity, debt, profitability, and efficiency ratios, investors may find several other ratios useful. Earnings per share (EPS) are the company's total earnings (less any preferred dividends) divided by the number of shares outstanding. Several different earnings numbers are often reported.

Fully diluted EPS gives effect to the exercise and conversion of any outstanding warrants and convertibles. Earnings figures may include or exclude extraordinary items and the results from non-continuing operations. As we have already seen, the P/E ratio or ratio of the per-share market price to EPS is a measure of relative stock price. The current annual dividend rate (usually four times the quarterly rate) divided by the price per share is the current yield. The total return reflects both capital gains and dividends. The dividend-payout ratio equals dividends per share divided by EPS. A very low payout may indicate a substantial need to finance internal growth, management's desire to expand, or abnormally high current earnings. A very high ratio may suggest few attractive investment opportunities. Cash flow per share is the sum of operating earnings and depreciation divided by the number of shares outstanding. When reported depreciation is overstated (understated profits) or depreciating assets are not replaced (funds available for other uses), the cash flow per share figure reflects an important source of discretionary funds. Many high-yield companies often report net losses due to high interest and depreciation expenses. For such companies with negative earnings, the P/E ratio is not meaningful. In this instance, investors should use the ratio for the per share market price to cash flow per share as the measure of relative stock price.

Book value per common share equals the company's net worth (after subtracting that attributable to preferred shareholders) divided by the number of its common shares outstanding. One would typically compare the per share book value with the current stock price. A high book value relative to the stock's price may indicate either unrecognized potential or overvalued assets on a book basis. Railroad book values, for example, have often been many times the market price of the stock. Unless the assets can be sold for close to their book values, however, the rails' modest profit rates justify their low stock prices. Alternatively, the per share price of the stock may reflect some hidden or undervalued assets, such as highly recognizable consumer brand names, patents or real estate valued at historical costs. Because book values that diverge appreciably from stock prices suggest that securities may be misvalued, further analysis could be indicated. Table 6.1 summarizes the various ratios discussed herein.

Table 6.1
Types of Fundamental Ratios

	Liquidity Ratios
Accounts Receivable Turnover	*Net Credit Sales* Average Accounts Receivable
Inventory Turnover	*Cost of Goods Sold* Average Yearly Inventory
Inventory Sales	*Ending Inventory* Yearly Sales
	Debt Ratios
Average Collection Period × 360	*Accounts Receivable* Credit Sales (Total sales if credit sales not available)
Current	*Current Assets* Current Liabilities
Quick, or Acid, Test	*Current Assets - Inventories* Current Liabilities
Cash flow Leverage	*Long Term Debt* Earnings Before Interest, Taxes, Depreciation & Amortization
Debt-Equity	*Total Debt* Shareholders' Liability
Times Interest-Earned	*Earnings Before Interest, Taxes, Depreciation & Amortization* Current Interest Payment
Debt-Asset	*Total Debt* Total Assets
	Profitability and Efficiency Ratios
Return on Equity (ROE)	*After-Tax Profit* Shareholders' Equity
Return on Assets (ROA)	*Before-Tax Before-Interest Profit* Total Assets

Return on Sales (ROS)	*After-Tax Profit* Total Revenues
Asset Turnover	*Total Revenue* Total Assets
Debt Margin (Leverage)	*Total Assets* Shareholders' Equity
Gross Profit to Selling General and Administrative Expenses	*Gross Profit (Sales - Cost of Goods Sold)* Selling, General and Administrative Expenses

Other Ratios

Earnings Per Share (EPS)	*Profits After Taxes - Preferred Dividends* Number of Shares
Price Earnings (PE)	*Price Per Share* EPS
Market Price/Cash Flow =	*Market Price* Cash Flow Per Share
Current Yield	*Indicated Annual Dividend* Price Per Share
Dividend Payout	*Dividends Per Share* EPS
Cash Flow Per Share	*Earnings Before Interest, Taxes, Depreciation & Amortization* Number of Shares
Book Value Per Share	*Net Worth Attributable to Common Shareholders* Number of Shares

Sources of Ratios: A company's ratios are most effectively analyzed by comparing them with those of similar companies. Thus averages of industry-wide ratios would be helpful to one analyzing a company's ratios. Robert Morris Associates collects data and computes ratios for a large group of industries. Other sources include Dun & Bradstreet and Standard & Poor's. Individual industry ratios may be computed with appropriate data from several similar companies.

ASSET VALUES & CASH FLOW: AN EXAMPLE

Estimated asset values may be derived in a number of ways including multiples of earnings and book value and discounted cash flow (DCF) analysis. We rely herein almost exclusively on DCF analysis which we believe is generally more reliable than other approaches.

Credit analysis, and particularly high yield credit analysis, may be effectively illustrated through an example. The following hypothetical illustrates how a company may be valued. Determining the value of, in this case, Company A, involves a number of steps: the expected cash flows are valued; the future sales price of the enterprise is estimated; the two expected cash flows are then discounted to a present value (PV) and other factors (net working capital and long term debt) are factored into the analysis.

A key variable in this analysis is the rate used to discount the expected cash flows. The appropriate rate will depend upon a number of circumstances, especially current credit market conditions and the risk associated with the cash flow estimates. The 15% rate that we use in this example is not unreasonable in a typical market situation. However, any actual valuation is quite sensitive to the rate used in this analysis. The following example illustrates a number of interesting points relevant to high-yield analysis:

Table 6.2
Expected Cash Flows ($$ Millions) for Company A

	Year 1	Year 2	Year 3	Year 4	Year 5
Net Income	$ 27.11	$ 37.27	$ 51.23	$ 70.43	$ 96.82
Interest Expense	100.00	89.17	79.51	70.90	63.22
Taxes	37.41	45.95	56.43	69.31	85.13
Depreciation & Amort.	92.94	99.48	106.48	113.98	122.00
EBITDA	257.46	271.87	293.65	324.62	367.17
Capital Exp. (CAPX)	98.62	105.56	113.00	120.95	129.45
Free Cash Flow (FCF)	158.84	166.31	180.65	203.67	237.72

Company A also has the following attributes at Year 1 ($$ Mill.):

Total Debt	$875	Other Working Cap.	$-66.50
Cash	$4.5	# of Shares	38 Million
Current Market Price:	$23.00		

To determine asset value, calculate the present value of the Free Cash Flows as shown in Table 6.3.

Table 6.3
Present Value of Free Cash Flow for Company A ($$ in Millions)

	Year 1	Year 2	Year 3	Year 4	Year 5
Free Cash Flow	$158.84	$166.31	$180.65	$203.67	$237.72
× Present Value Factor	.8696	.7561	.6575	.5744	.4972
= Present Value of Free	$138.12 +	$125.75 +	$118.78 +	$116.99 +	$118.18
Cash Flow (at 15%)					
Total Present Value of $617.82.					
Calculated as 1 + (1 + Discount Rate)					

Assume that the business is to be sold in Year 5. How much will it sell for at that time? One approach is to apply our 15% discount rate to Year 5 EBITDA. A 15% discount rate corresponds to a 6.667× multiple of EBITDA, or 6.6667 × $367.17 = $2,447.80. The multiple is derived by dividing Year 5 EBITDA by the discount rate, or $367.17 / .15 = $2,447.80, and dividing this number by $367.17 (2447.80 ╷ 367.17 = 6.6667). By applying a 15% discount rate to Year 5 EBITDA, we are thereby assuming, very conservatively, that EBITDA remains constant after Year 5. To account for the possibility that EBITDA would continue growing after Year 5, one would divide Year 5 EBITDA by the discount rate minus the expected growth rate, or $367.17 / (.15 - Growth Rate).

Note the rapid growth in net income (shown in Table 6.2), compared with the relatively slower growth in depreciation expense. This apparently anomalous discrepancy in relative growth rates is a function of the rapid deleveraging that is expected to take place (shown in Table 6.5). The buyer that purchases this company in Year 5 may choose to realize another round of de-leveraging in subsequent years, assuming growth continues.

Discount this selling price ($2,447.80) to its present value by multiplying it by Year 5's PV Factor of .4972, or $2,447.80 × .4972 = $1,217.05. This result is the Residual Asset Value. Add the PV of FCF ($617.82) to the Residual Asset Value ($1,217.05) to derive a total Fixed Asset Value of $1,834.87.

Continuing:

Table 6.4
Calculation of Net Equity Value

Fixed Asset Value	$1,834.87
Add: Cash	4.50
Add: Other Working Capital	–66.50 (1)
Equals: Enterprise Value	$1,772.87
Subtract: Total Debt	875.00
Equals: Net Equity	$ 897.87

(1) Negative due to the cash nature of the Company's business. For example, no accounts receivable.

Enterprise value covers debt by 2.02x ($1772.87 / $875). Interest coverage as measured by EBITDA/Interest Expense is 2.57x in Year 1 ($257.46 / $100) and is expected to grow to 5.83x in Year 5 ($367.17 / $63.22). This is an example of the "cash flow coverage" ratio.

Additionally, cash flow of $58.84, $77.14, $101.14, $132.77, and $174.50 after interest expense and capital expenditures during the next five years will allow for meaningful debt reductions. For example:

Table 6.5
Expected Deleveraging

Beginning Debt	$875.00				
	Year 1	Year 2	Year 3	Year 4	Year 5
Cash Flow after Interest and CAPX (1)	$ 58.84	$ 77.14	$101.14	$132.77	$174.50
Ending Debt (2)	$816.16	$739.02	$637.88	$505.11	$330.61
Years to Pay Off Debt (3)	14.87	10.58	7.30	4.80	2.89

(1) Termed in this example "Excess Cash Flow", or ECF.

(2) Assumes excess cash flow is applied to debt reductions.

(3) Calculated as beginning debt divided by next year's projected Excess Cash Flow, or Total Debt/ECF.

A prospective investor should be sure to determine whether the company being evaluated is reducing capital expenditures below levels needed to meet maintenance spending on plant and equipment or below levels necessary to meet expansion and sales projections. Some companies will seek to make current cash flow appear to be stronger than it actually is likely to be on a sustainable basis. In effect, they are robbing Peter to pay Paul. If done on a short-term basis in reaction to severe economic distress, such a policy is a simple matter of survival. However, such a short-term focus, if kept up for extended periods of time, can be devastating to sales and ultimately fatal to the enterprise.

You, as an investor, would be willing to pay $897.87 ($23.62 per share), the net equity value (private market value) and assume the debt of $875 for Company A, assuming you could control the disposition of its cash flow, and further assuming that your required rate of return for similar investments of comparable risk is 15% (discount rate).

DCF analysis is an easily applied concept of valuation. The trick comes not in the math itself, but in the projection of cash flow statements, the choosing of an appropriate discount rate, and the assignment of exit-year cash flow multiples. Recall that in our example EBITDA was not projected to continue growing past Year 5. Had we factored in such growth, the valuation would have increased and Company A would appear undervalued.

Company A is a relatively high-quality issue (among high-yield credits). Most of its debt securities are trading above par with yield levels in the 12.60% range. As illustrated above, the company is expected to have very strong cash flows and is expected to de-lever rapidly. The market is very comfortable with Company A's prospects, as evidenced by the trading levels of its debt securities and by the equity market's confirmation of its true asset value.

In addition to the ratio of Total Debt/ECF, the EBITDA margin is also very important, particularly in identifying underlying trends and cash flow strength. EBITDA margin is calculated as EBITDA/Sales and is an indicator of the percentage of cash flow per dollar of sales. In general, the higher the level of EBITDA margin the better. Declines over time in this margin generally indicate inefficient levels of cash flow generation.

QUANTITATIVE ANALYSIS: CONCLUSION

We have focused herein on four important areas of financial analysis for high-yield securities: asset values, cash flow, liquidity, and leverage. Asset values are critical in high-yield research work. Indeed, most high-yield securities can be viewed as a coupon instrument in conjunction with a short position in a put option on the equity value of the company. In other words, if a company defaults on its interest obligations, many holders of high-yield bonds ultimately end up owning (equity holders exercise their put) a substantial equity stake as the company emerges from bankruptcy. Hence, we see the need to value assets properly in advance. Internally generated cash flow is necessary for any measurable degree of credit quality improvement. Additionally, liquidity is important for the simple reason that many companies of less-than-investment-grade status cannot borrow with the ease of most double-A rated firms. Leverage is an important consideration in virtually all security analysis.

Thorough financial analysis plays a key role in the overall analysis of high-yield securities. However, unlike many other types of securities, the values of high-yield issues are very sensitive to qualitative characteristics as well. Such characteristics would include covenant provisions, financing structure, type of transactions and the nature (quality) of management. Indeed, such characteristics are distinctly separate from the actual numbers-crunching, but they must be included in the overall context of high-yield credit research work. Granted, the numbers themselves must be acceptable, but the risk goes beyond cash flow coverage and other financial measures. We shall now visit these qualitative topics.

CHAPTER 7

QUALITATIVE ASPECTS OF HIGH-YIELD ANALYSIS

Compared with the quantitative aspects, qualitative issues are less well defined, and tend to be left to professional judgment and interpretation. Qualitative analyses is, by its very nature, less subject to quantification. And yet in today's very competitive high-yield market, acceptable financials alone are not adequate to make most issues a success. To be sure, the numbers must be convincing. For high-yield security analysis to be truly successful, however, one must go beyond the numbers. For example, prospective investors need to do what they can to evaluate management's intent. In particular, one should analyze the specific issuer's covenant package, taken as a whole. These topics, and many others, fill in the unquantified "gray" area of thorough high-yield analysis. We shall now focus on some of the more important subjective qualities of high-yield security analysis.

COVENANTS

Always important, financial indenture covenants have become even more so over the last several years. This increased emphasis results from the propensity of many issuers to re-lever their balance sheets in order to pay out huge dividends to stockholders, or to use their companies as acquisition vehicles. Such activities greatly increase the amount of debt relative to assets. These types of actions tend to work to the detriment of existing bondholders. In a few isolated instances, where both the intent and history of management is understood, some restrictive covenants can be relaxed or eliminated altogether. Generally, however, the market is now demanding that tighter restrictions be placed on management, particularly financiers.

Many types of covenants have been written, including change-in-control "puts" that enable bonds to be sold back to the issuer if the ownership of the company changes significantly. Additionally, one rating agency has begun to assign certain event risk ratings to a number of issuers.

Protective covenants are more likely to be found in recently written inden-tures than in indentures of bond issues that have been outstanding for some time. An investor needs to be particularly careful with older issues. Such issues are less likely to contain covenants designed to protect against such actions as re-leverag-ing, large dividend payouts, and changes in control. One might obtain informa-tion about the presence or absence of covenants by reading brokerage house reports. However, with many covenants, the strategic placement of an "and" or an "or" can make a tremendous difference in the actual effectiveness of the cov-enant. Therefore, successful covenant analysis almost always involves an examina-tion of the registration statement itself. Indentures are much more difficult and costly to obtain. The registration statement generally contains the covenant lan-guage as written in the indenture. Some of the more important types of cov-enants are:

Net Worth Requirements: This covenant generally requires periodic monitoring of net worth and usually contains provisions that require repurchase of bonds by the company if net worth falls below stipulated levels. Ideally, we look for the definition of net worth to read "tangible net worth," thus excluding good-will from the calculation. As noted in the section on leverage, the stated amount of equity, or net worth in this case, is not a particularly reliable indicator of financial health. Therefore, this covenant is not vitally important. Be aware that some companies have intentionally violated this covenant in order to create a situation whereby they were required to purchase bonds at their par value that were previously trading at premiums (above par). In other words, by violating the covenant the issuers were able to trigger a provision that forced the owners to sell the bonds back to the company for less than what had been their market value.

Limitation on Restricted Payments: Restricted payments provisions usually apply to dividends, distributions on, or requirement of, capital stock of the company. This type of covenant is extremely important, as it attempts to constrain equity holders from substantially re-leveraging the company and paying out undue amounts of dividends, while at the same time maintaining voting control. The restricted payment itself is generally limited to the sum of 50% of cumulative net income from some specified date, plus the proceeds realized from the sale of equity in the company. Ideally, this covenant should exclude profits derived from asset sales and other gains generated outside of the ordinary course of business from the calculation of net income, thus preventing the company from, in effect, being liquidated through overgenerous dividend payments.

Limitation on Indebtedness: This covenant usually limits indebtedness to debt existing at the time of the offering, plus a defined amount of additional debt, subject to the maintenance of maximum debt ratios or minimum cash flow coverage of interest expense. These minimum acceptable financial ratios generally escalate upward over time, in order to provide increasing levels of credit protection. In other words, a company that meets its escalating coverage tests may incur additional debt. Increasingly stringent financial tests are in place to provide for gradual credit improvement, while at the same time allowing for the financing of some level of continued growth. Thus, this type of covenant is designed to accomplish two goals simultaneously; growing credit protection and business expansion. In a few instances, a fixed dollar amount is placed on additional debt incurrence.

Typically, certain levels of capital spending and increased borrowings under existing bank facilities are "carved out," or excluded from this test. Rather than causing alarm, this carve-out, if reasonable, should generally be viewed as facilitating necessary or at least desirable business growth. The existence or absence of this covenant is a key determinant of whether a company will be continually used as an acquisition vehicle or whether it will gradually de-lever as its cash flow situation improves. Again, this covenant should ideally be based on cash flow coverage tests rather than static debt measures. Such cash flow tests are more indicative of credit quality. Anti-layering clauses are also beneficial, as they prevent debt from being inserted (layered) junior to bank debt and senior to existing bondholders. Such anti-layering clauses are also called the "me first" rule.

Restrictions on Mergers/Asset Sales: This type of covenant is designed to prevent the company from merging with or selling substantially all of its assets to another company unless the following conditions are met: 1) the surviving company is a United States corporation, 2) it expressly assumes the obligations of the company under a supplemental indenture, 3) no event of default would occur as a result of the merger. To provide the bondholders with any meaningful protection, this covenant must include some type of financial test, such as an "offer to repurchase" bonds or the maintenance of net worth.

Change in Control: This covenant generally provides for a "put" back to the company at a predetermined level (usually par plus accrued interest) in the event the ownership of the company changes significantly. Most covenants of this type exempt a "friendly" (with the board of directors' approval) change in control from the definition of a significant ownership change. Virtually every significant transaction that has occurred in the last several years has ultimately been approved by the board of directors, and consequently deemed "friendly." Thus, unless some financial test is attached, this covenant is virtually worthless to the bondholders.

Financing Structure: The advent of increasing financial creativity in the capital markets led to a dramatic increase in the types of high-yield securities. In addition to straight coupon bonds, many issues have been structured as zero coupon bonds, payment-in-kind (PIK) bonds that pay interest in like securities, increasing rate notes, floating-rate notes, and a myriad of others. Due to their ease of analysis and relative market stability, most investors prefer the straight coupon debt obligations. The overall demand for them tends to be greater and they provide a significantly higher level of actual cash income than do the other types of bonds.

Clearly the actual type of security that is issued is an important consideration for the investor. The "use of proceeds" is also very important. Specificity is to be preferred. Ideally, the company should have stated a reasonable use for the money, rather than simply issuing bonds for future acquisition possibilities or for the general corporate purposes. Investors should rarely, if ever, participate in any kind of blind pool offering. Investing is risky even when you know what is being done. Additionally, many companies issue high-yield bonds in amounts that exceed the company's actual need for funds. The company's cost of carry is almost always negative, and many times management chooses to invest excess proceeds in risky, high-yielding securities in order to minimize this adverse spread. This need for the company to cover its interest spread can be a tremendous distraction, particularly in times of tight cash flow in the early stages following a high-yield financing. To be effective, management needs to be fully focused on the operation of its business, rather than on the pressing need to cover carrying costs.

Type of Transaction: Five different situations give rise to high-yield financing needs and/or high-yield securities.

1) Strategic acquisitions or financings
2) Financial leveraged buyouts (LBOs)
3) Defensive recapitalizations
4) Broker-based buyouts
5) Fallen angels

Strategic acquisitions or financings involve the purchase of a similar or complimentary company by a strategic buyer. A strategic purchaser generally has in mind such objectives as expanding market share in a given product, expanding into complementary businesses that have similar distribution channels to the company, or some type of vertical or horizontal integration. The ultimate goal of the acquisition is to expand the business and capitalize on real or imagined economies of scale.

Financial LBOs refer to acquisitions or restructurings that are strictly motivated by financial considerations. They involve a very large amount of leverage, are usually hostile in nature, and generate huge amounts of press coverage as the debate rages about the net economic benefit of such transactions. Compared with strategic acquisitions, financial LBOs should lead creditors to seek significantly tighter covenants.

Defensive recapitalizations typically involve a company that is initially approached on a hostile basis and subsequently re-levers and pays a special, one-time dividend. Historical owners thereby maintain their equity interest in the company. Provided management was competent in the first place, a defensive recapitalization can actually be a positive step for the company and its high-yield investors. Such a recapitalization provides enormous incentives for efficient operation and refocuses management on the maximization of cash flow rather than on increases in short-term earnings that would otherwise be needed to satisfy a demanding investment community.

Broker-based buyouts are much like financial LBOs, in that they are typically initiated by investors largely motivated by the financial returns. Many of these entities trade portfolios of entire companies instead of portfolios of stocks. In most cases, a large brokerage firm will own nearly all of the equity of the company in question. Again, covenants need to be relatively strict for this type of transaction to be attractive.

Fallen angels are those companies that were once rated investment grade and have subsequently been downgraded to high-yield status. Most often, this fall from grace is caused by ineffective management and poor operating performance over long periods of time. Such fallen angels may or may not come to the market with new high-yield securities (for example, to refinance existing debt as it comes due). In any case, the company's existing issues will be priced as high-yield securities.

Competitive Position: While more difficult to evaluate than its financial strengths and weaknesses, the company's competitive position is nonetheless an important performance determinant. How able is the firm to withstand competitive pressures? How vigorous are its rivals? What is the government's attitude? Clearly, these are important questions.

A company's ability to compete within its industry depends upon how its resources compare with those of its rivals. Scale economies in production, marketing and distribution generally give larger companies an advantage over their smaller rivals. On the other hand, difficulties in exercising effective control increase with size. For example, U.S. Steel has, since its inception, been described as a lumbering dinosaur too large for effective control. Antitrust vulnerability is yet another disadvantage of size. Every competitive move of high market share companies such as Microsoft, Kodak, and IBM risks antitrust action. Mere size does not constitute an offense, but a company whose own sales represent a very large percentage of its served market has difficulty competing aggressively while simultaneously avoiding being charged with illegal actions. Kodak, for example, sought to avoid antitrust suits by sharing new product technology with its competitors. Antitrust pressure led the old AT&T to agree to spin off its operating companies in 1984. (More recently it has been partially put back together with acquisitions). Even when within-market expansion is legal, a dominant firm has little opportunity to grow other than in line with its industry, unless it diversifies. For the giants, even diversification-inspired mergers may provoke an antitrust suit. Procter & Gamble's acquisition of Clorox and General Foods' acquisition of S.O.S. were both undone by government action. Thus, some companies may be too small to compete effectively, whereas the existing size of others may limit further growth. Within a wide range of viable sizes, however, other factors have greater impacts on differential performance.

Management: Evaluating management is largely an analysis of qualitative characteristics. Useful proxies for management's ability are such measures as return on equity or assets over an extended period of time and the overall growth and profitability of the business. Even these data, however, do not adequately address the largely unquantifiable nature of managerial effectiveness.

Therefore, critical variables when judging management are such factors as number of years with the company/industry, actual success in past ventures, and existing commitments that would potentially distract a member of management from the task at hand. A serious investor may even go so far as to verify the educational degrees of certain management members when deemed relevant. Ideally, management should have a significant share of ownership in the company (10% or so), one that is backed by actual invested cash. This level of ownership provides appreciably more incentive to manage effectively than does more modest amounts of equity obtained gratis, or with funds borrowed from the company itself. Additionally, management should devote 100% of its available time to the operation of the business, rather than being involved in various personal business ventures throughout the country.

Although a great number of bright, young individuals have been put on a fast track upward, they may not have adequate experience to occupy the uppermost posts in the majority of companies. Accordingly, the presence of extremely young executives in the top-most positions should be carefully scrutinized. Additionally, companies in which the top executive makes as much as four or five times that of the No. 2 person may be indicative of a one-person show. Significant dependence on one person sometimes causes a great deal of difficulty in the case of their sudden death or departure, particularly when a successor has not been fully groomed.

A perceptive, aggressive, forward-looking management enhances the odds of realizing a company's full potential. The classic investment textbook by Cohen, Zinbarg, and Zeikel (*Investment Analysis and Portfolio Management*, McGraw-Hill, 1986) lists the following as relevant: motivation, R&D activity, willingness to take reasonable risks, success in integrating required firms, effectiveness in delegating authority, information systems, use of a board of directors, relations with financial analysts, and social responsibility. Others have noted that managers who are especially interested in stockholder welfare generally outperform those more concerned with their own well-being. Still other studies imply that highly rated managements do not always produce unusually high returns for their shareholders. They do, however, tend to limit risk, so that the risk-adjusted returns to shareholders are attractive. A broad array of information on managerial quality is probably relevant, but few investors/analysts have the resources to evaluate most of these factors effectively. Past performance is one useful guide. Such performance is, however, of less help when needed most – when leadership shifts. Investors can normally do little more than read the financial press. A few may contact some managers directly (particularly those of small local companies), however.

QUALITATIVE ANALYSIS: SUMMARY AND CONCLUSION

High-yield credit research is very labor-intensive. The process is especially demanding for the analysts or individuals who undertake it. The margin for error is always very thin, and, in many cases, nonexistent. Subtle deviations in minor detail can result in the loss or gain of millions of dollars, many times in the blink of an eye. What is most important, however, is that no relevant question be left unasked, or, more importantly, unanswered. Quality research must diligently cover all of the topics mentioned here and a host of others and ultimately an investment decision must be made. The best that we can strive for is to make a reasonably informed, intelligent decision, and through constant monitoring and refinement of our investment outlook, adjust our opinions as economic, market and credit-specific environments change.

CHAPTER 8

TYPES OF SECURITIES

Fixed income securities (bonds and other types of debt instruments) provide the principal investment alternative to common stocks. The same brokers and similar markets are used to trade them. Many companies issue both types of securities. Their similarities notwithstanding, many stock market investors largely ignore the bond markets. Such neglect may have been understandable at one time. But times have changed. Far from being a mundane backwater, fixed income securities have become much more competitive with common stocks. Their volatility, market attention, diversity of types, ways of participating, and small investor involvement have all increased in recent years. Bonds may not belong in every investor's portfolio, but all serious investors should at least consider them.

We explore herein the characteristics of the various types of short- and long-term debt instruments.

TYPES OF DEBT SECURITIES

The federal government, state and local governments, corporations, foreign governments, and international organizations all issue fixed income securities. The standard type of debt security (bond) promises to pay a fixed periodic coupon amount and return its face value at a pre-specified time. Bonds vary in a number of ways, including length to maturity, coupon rate, type of collateral, convertibility, tax treatment, and restrictions placed on the borrower.

Particular debt instruments compete with other similar-maturity debt instruments. Securities maturing in a year or less are considered short term. High-quality, short-term debt obligations trade in what is called the money market.

The vast majority of the components of the money market never or almost never default (e.g., Treasury bills and government guaranteed certificates of deposit). One category of money market instrument that has been known (on rare occasions) to enter the category of distressed and defaulted securities is commercial paper. A second money market category of potentially risky securities is the banker's acceptance.

THE MONEY MARKET AND OTHER SHORT-TERM DEBT SECURITIES

Money market instruments are highly liquid, quite marketable, and very secure. The principal money market instruments are large bank CDs, Treasury bills, commercial paper, bankers' acceptances, and Eurodollar deposits. Very short-term lending and borrowing in the federal funds market, repurchase agreements, and the Fed's discount window round out this market. In addition, money market mutual funds, short-term unit investment trusts, short-term municipals, and certain securities and accounts of banks and other financial institutions also compete in the short end of the debt security market.

Commercial Paper: Many large corporations with solid credit ratings issue commercial paper in order to finance short-term needs. The paper is secured only by the issuer's good name and promise to pay. The issuer does, however, usually have a backup line of bank credit. Such a credit line is available to repay the maturing commercial paper issue if the existing market environment prevents refinancing via sale of new paper. Commercial paper issuers are generally able to raise funds in this market that cost slightly less than the prime rate. They will, however, incur a fee on their backup credit lines. Even adding in this fee, the commercial paper issuer's borrowing costs are typically below the alternative cost of bank borrowings. Similarly, eliminating the intermediary's (i.e., the bank's) need for compensation allows those that issue commercial paper to pay investors a slightly higher rate than they would receive by buying a bank's CDs.

Commercial paper is rated, but as a practical matter only high-grade issues are likely to be saleable. Conditions can, however, deteriorate rapidly. Thus, what was initially marked as high-grade paper can move into the distressed category before it matures. Paper is marketed in round lots of $250,000 and is seldom available in smaller than $100,000 denominations. Some paper is registered; most is payable to the bearer.

Bankers' Acceptances: A banker's acceptance begins with the creation of an obligation to pay a certain amount of money at a specified time. For example, a company may have purchased some equipment and is thereby obligated to pay for it. Payment is to come due at some point in the future. Once the obligation is accepted (guaranteed) by a bank (which is familiar with the credit status of the obligor), it becomes an *acceptance*. The acceptance is a contingent liability of the bank. As such, the bank is required to redeem it whether or not the issuer funds the redemption. With this possibility in mind, banks are inclined to check out carefully the credit standing of the issuers of these obligations. Acceptances usually arise in the course of foreign trade, although they may also result from domestic transactions. Because the owner can look to both the obligor and the accepting bank, acceptances are considered to be about as secure as the bank that accepts them.

LONG-TERM DEBT INSTRUMENTS

A wide variety of types of long-term debt securities are also available to investors. Most such securities fall into three categories: government bonds (including agencies), municipals, and traditional corporate bonds. Other categories include mortgage loans and mortgage-related securities, bank CDs, bond funds, income bonds, floating-rate notes, zero coupon bonds, Eurobonds, insurance company debt securities, and private placements and Payment In Kind or PIK bonds. Preferred stock also competes for the same income-oriented investor dollars that might otherwise go into long-term debt securities.

Not since the days of the Civil War and its aftermath have U.S. government securities been considered the least bit risky. While some municipal issuers have indeed gotten into the distressed category and even defaulted, such issues are not a focus of this discussion. Our attention will center on corporate issues.

CORPORATE DEBT OBLIGATIONS

Corporations constitute one of the three principal categories of bond issuers (in addition to governments and municipals). Both convertible and nonconvertible corporate instruments, like government bonds, bear interest and mature. In addition, convertibles may at the owner's option be exchanged at some fixed rate for stocks of the issuing corporation.

Most bond purchases involve a payment of both the market price of the bond and an adjustment for accrued interest. The buyer pays and the seller receives a sum to reflect the portion of interest that has already been earned but not yet paid. Thus, a bond that is quoted at 93 would initially cost the buyer $930 principal plus the prorated amount of accrued but unpaid interest. If the bond has a 10% coupon and made its last coupon payment three months ago, unpaid interest would have accrued as follows: $3/12 \times .10 \times \$1,000 = \$25$

Interest is paid to the one who holds the bond on the day of record. The issuer will pay the entire coupon to the new owner.

A relatively small number of bonds are traded flat. Typically, bonds that are in default or whose interest payments are considered very uncertain trade flat. Such bonds are traded without any adjustment for the impact of accrued interest. If such bonds do make their interest payments, they make the payments to the holder of record on the record date. Thus the owner of such bonds on the day of record receives all of that period's interest payments regardless of length of ownership. In the quotation tables, bonds that trade flat have an "f" in italics following the abbreviation for their name.

Many more actively traded corporate bonds are listed on an exchange (especially the NYSE), but most of the trading takes place in a much more active (Over the Counter) OTC market. Investors wishing to buy or sell a large dollar value of bonds should instruct his or her broker to obtain several quotations to see which market maker offers the best price.

High-Risk Corporates: Bonds were once thought of as very secure low-risk investments. More recently, however, many bonds have come to be viewed as potentially very risky. Such bonds bear commensurate yields. One observer reports that 93% of low-rated issues have paid off and the substantial yield-premiums of such issues tend to offset their default risks. Indeed, junk bond speculators have often done quite well.

Table 8.1 illustrates some mid-1982 yield differentials. Mid-1982 was a period of relatively high rates. Risk premiums also tended to be high at that time. For comparison, some rates for January 18, 1988, March 15, 1991, July 2, 2001 and May 3, 2006 are also shown.

Clearly, these substantial indicated yield differentials reflect appreciable differences in perceived risk. Indeed, the higher the "promised" yield, the greater the default risk is likely to be. Although junk bonds are ill-suited to the needs of cautious investors, many risk-oriented investors are attracted to them. Risk and potential returns can be as great as with many stocks. Indeed, a risky firm's bonds sometimes offer a more attractive way of speculating than does its stock. To realize a profit the bond investor only

Table 8.1.
Differential Bond Yields

May 19, 1982				
Company	Coupon	Maturity	Price	Current Yield
Very Secure:				
AT&T	13 1/4	1991	96 1/4	13.7
GE Credit	13 5/8	1991	97	14.0

Risky:

Eastern Airlines	17 1/2	1998	92 7/8	18.8
Rapid American	11	2005	57 5/8	18.9
World Airlines	11 1/4	1994	52 7/8	22.3

Very Risky:

International Harvester	9	2004	28 1/2	31.6

In Default:

Braniff	10	1986	32	30.8
				(if paid)

January 18, 1988

Very Secure:

AT&T	8 5/8	2026	89 1/2	9.6
General Motors	8 5/8	2005	91 1/2	9.4

Risky:

Beth Steel	8 3/8	2001	74 1/2	11.3
Commonwealth Edison	11 3/4	2015	103 1/2	11.4

Very Risky:

Texas Air	15 3/4	1992	94 1/2	16.7
Resorts International	11 3/8	2013	62	18.3

In Default:

LTV	8 3/4	2004	25	35.0
				(if paid)

March 15, 1991

Very Secure:

AT&T	8 5/8	2026	933/4	9.2
General Motors	8 3/4	2001	98	8.9

Risky:

Beth Steel	9	2000	9 3/4	10.7
Commonwealth Edison	10 5/8	1995	103	10.3

Very Risky:

RJR Nabisco	17	2007	109 5/8	15.5
Resorts International	11	1994	50 1/2	21.8

In Default:

LTV	8 3/4	1998	11 1/2	76.1
NV Ryan	13 3/4	1997	5 1/8	268.3
				(if paid)

July 2, 2001				
Very Secure:				
Bell South	7	2025	99 3/4	7.0%
GMAC	6	2011	93 1/2	6.4%
Risky:				
Lucent	6 1/2	2028	58 1/2	11.1%
Budget	9 1/8	2006	52	18%
Very Risky:				
Trump AC	11 1/4	2006	67	28.88%
Level 3	9 1/8	2008	43	26.50%
In Default:				
Genesh H	9 3/4	2005	11	88.6% (if paid)

May 3, 2006				
Very Secure:				
HSBC Finance	5.25	2011	98.53	5.6%
DuPont	6.875	2009	104.23	5.5%
Risky:				
Bausch & Lomb	7.125	2028	94.10	7.6%
Clear Channel	7.25	2027	97.39	7.4%
GMAC	8.00	2031	94.45	8.5%
Very Risky:				
SunCom	9.375	2011	74.50	17.5%
CCH	11.00	2015	89.00	13.0%
In Default:				
Calpine	8.50	2008	48.75	53.5% (if paid)
NW Air	10.00	2009	45.81	47.2% (if paid)

needs for the troubled firm to avoid bankruptcy or to maintain a substantial value in a reorganization. The stockholder's return, in contrast, may not be attractive unless the company becomes relatively profitable. A study by Chandy and Cherry strikes a cautious note for would-be investors in junk bonds, however. The authors found that, while the average realized yields on junk bonds generally exceeded that for high-grade bonds, volatility was proportionally even greater. Moreover, in periods of rising interest rates investment grade bonds offered both less volatile yields and higher realized returns.

While always a worthwhile investment strategy, diversification is particularly important for those who hold junk bond portfolios. A defaulting issue may eventually pay off but the wait can be long and tedious. Having a well-diversified portfolio tends to dilute the advise impact of individual defaults. Such risk-spreading is especially advisable for junk bond investors. Junk bond funds do provide small investors with an effective diversification vehicle.

Corporate Bond Funds: Corporate bond funds have existed for many years. With the stock market depressed and interest rates at historic highs, bond-fund yields became increasingly attractive in the early 1970s. The very high interest environment of the early 1980s further enhanced their yields and attractiveness. Markets are, of course, always changing. Later in the 1980s, interest rates fell, making bonds and bond funds somewhat less attractive. Bond funds' relative attractiveness waxed and waned throughout the 1990s, as interest rates moved up and down. By the early 2000s rates had fallen to quite low levels, but short rates were so low that many fixed income investors were again looking at bond funds. Investor interest in bonds continued into the mid-2000s even as short-term interest rates rose to the level of longer-term bonds.

As with other types of securities, bond funds may be load or no-load, open-end or closed-end, and managed or unmanaged (unit trusts). As with stock funds, most investors will generally find the no-load type of fund to be the preferable way of buying into a bond portfolio. Most closed-end funds sell at a discount from their Net Asset Value, or NAV. Bond funds offer diversification, convenience, and low-denomination purchase. On the other hand, the expenses incurred in marketing and managing the funds reduce their effective yields somewhat. As with other types of funds, unmanaged funds have lower expenses. Thus, more of the portfolio's yields flow through to the unit holders.

OTHER TYPES OF DEBT INSTRUMENTS

In addition to the most important types of debt instruments (money market, governments, municipals, and traditional corporates) a number of other types bear mentioning: long-term CDs, floating-rate notes, zero-coupon bonds, Payment in Kind (PIK), and yield curve notes, Eurobonds, insurance company debt instruments and private placements.

Floating-Rate Notes: In 1974, Citicorp introduced a novel type of variable-rate security. Soon thereafter, several other corporations offered their own floating-rate notes. For example, Citicorp issued a "floater" that matured in 2004. Its coupon was adjusted every six months to yield approximately 1% over the six-month

Treasury bill rate. The floating-rate feature of such bonds tends to cause their prices to remain relatively close to their par values. The bonds are structured so that their yield adjusts to market conditions. Thus, their market price will usually stay relatively close to their par value as interest rates fluctuate. The more distant maturity of most ``floaters'' does, however, make them more risky to hold (because of greater default risk) than otherwise similar short-maturity debt instruments.

The volume of new issues of floating-rate notes has varied substantially. The student loan programs in Kansas, Kentucky, and Minnesota have issued intermediate-term notes with tax-free interest pegged at approximately 70% of the T-bill rate. Similarly, the Student Loan Marketing Association (Sallie Mae, a government-chartered but privately owned corporation) has sold notes backed by government-guaranteed student loans whose interest rates are adjusted weekly to .75% above the 91-day T-bill rate. Floating-rate issues are also relatively common in the international market, especially in Asia. Moreover, a few companies have issued floating-rate preferreds.

Zero-Coupon and Other Types of Original Issue Discount Bonds: Most coupon rates are initially set so that the bond will be priced close to its face, or par, value. Original issue discount bonds are sold for appreciably less than their value at maturity. These bonds have either a zero-coupon rate or a coupon rate that is well below what would be the market rate for the issuer's level of risk. As a result, such bonds initially sell for a market price that is substantially below their face values.

Bonds that do not pay a coupon are called zero-coupon bonds, or zeros. The return on such securities is derived from the difference between their purchase price and maturity value (or sale prices if sold prior to maturity). Treasury bills and certain other securities such as U.S. Savings Bonds have long been sold on a discount basis. For example, a one-year T-bill might be priced at 95. This means that a bill with a $10,000 face value would initially cost $9,500 and pay an additional $500 at maturity. More recently, a number of long-term corporate zeros have been issued.

Instruments equivalent to zero-coupon bonds may also be created from coupon bonds. The coupons are simply separated from the principal portion, and the two components sold separately. Most bonds pay interest to the registered owner, but some have attached coupons that may be clipped and sold to an investor seeking periodic income. The bond without its coupons attached is called a strip bond.

Merrill Lynch created yet another type of zero-coupon security that it called Treasury Investment Growth Receipts (Tigers). A pool of U.S. government securities is purchased and used to guarantee the issue. Like other zero-coupons, Tigers pay no coupon. They are sold at a discount and mature at face value. Other brokerage firms offer similar instruments, also bearing feline names (Cats, Lions, Cougars, etc.).

These various categories of zeros have precisely identifiable maturity values (usually $1,000). This feature has an appeal for IRA and Keogh accounts. Investors in zeros know at the outset exactly what the compounded value will be at maturity (absent a default). The end-period value of funds invested in coupon-yielding bonds, in contrast, is not nearly so certain. The actual compounded value of such a stream of income will depend upon the rate earned on the reinvested coupon payments.

The uncertainty associated with the return on reinvested coupon payments is called reinvestment risk. Because they do not pay a coupon that needs to be reinvested, zeros have no reimbursement risk. Thus, their lack of reinvestment risk, coupled with their relative scarcity, cause zero-coupon bonds to tend to sell for somewhat lower yields than equivalent-risk coupon bonds.

Like other long-term bonds, long-term zero-coupon bonds lock both the buyer and the issuer into a debt instrument having a fixed long-term rate. If rates go up after the purchase, the buyer will end up receiving a below-market return. The issuer, in contrast, will pay an above-market rate if market interest rates decline after the issue is sold. Moreover, for a given change in interest rates, the prices of zeros change proportionately more than do those of similar maturity coupon bonds. Owners of coupon bonds are at least able to reinvest their coupon income at higher rates when market interest rates rise. Owners of zeros receive no coupon payments and thus have no payments to reinvest.

Not only do zeros pay no coupons; they impose an annual tax liability on their owners (assuming the investors are subject to the income tax). Special tax rules apply to original issue discount bonds. Such bonds either pay no coupon (zeros) or pay coupon that is well below the corresponding market rate at the time that they are issued. As a result, they are issued at a substantial discount from their par value. To determine the tax liability, one first needs to determine the relevant amount of imputed interest. This is the amount that the government calculates is earned but not received each year. The imputed interest rate is computed as if the bond made annual coupon payments equal to its yield-to-maturity rate computed at the time of its purchase. Thus, a zero-coupon bond that was sold to yield 10% would be treated for tax purposes as if it actually yielded 10% each year. Because of the affect of compounding, the amount of the imputed interest income will rise each year. The issuer is allowed to deduct each year's imputed interest cost while the owner incurs an equivalent amount of taxable income. As a result the issuer obtains an early tax deduction, while the owner must pay out taxes prior to receipt of the associated income.

The tax computation on coupon-paying original issue discount bonds is even more complex. The owner is, of course, liable for taxes on the coupon payments. In addition, taxes are assessed on the appropriate imputed interest as the bond moves closer to maturity. The basis on both types of original issue discount bonds is increased each year by the amount of the accumulated imputed interest. Thus, the basis on an original issue discount bond would equal the initial purchase price plus the sum of the imputed interest amounts.

Payment in Kind or PIK Bonds: Payment in Kind bonds also have unusual payment characteristics. They pay their coupon, not in cash, but in additional securities. PIK bonds are encountered many times in conjunction with lower-rated issuers. They might also be issued or exchanged by a company emerging from bankruptcy in order to ease initial cash interest requirements. PIK bonds incur many of the same tax consequences as zeros.

They are, however, different from zeros in one important aspect. Unlike zeros, PIKs do not accrete interest, but make coupon payments in the form of additional securities. For example, a 10% PIK would issue $100 in fresh bonds annually for each $1,000 bond. These securities may be sold in the open market as a way of monetizing interest income. The trading market for many PIK bonds is quite limited.

Eurobonds: Eurodollars are dollar-denominated accounts held by individuals, companies, or governments domiciled outside the United States. Eurobonds, in contrast, are denominated either in dollars or in some other currency but traded internationally. U.S. and foreign bonds, in contrast, are traded in only one country. The Eurobond issuer benefits from the wider distribution and the absence of restrictions and taxes that are placed on national bonds. Eurobond buyers may obtain greater diversification than from U.S. bonds alone. Moreover, bonds denominated in a foreign currency offer investors an opportunity to speculate against the dollar.

One of the most attractive features of Eurobonds, at least for some investors, is the ease with which they allow investors to evade taxes. Two features of Eurobonds facilitate such activity. Unlike domestic bonds, no withholding is applied to Eurobond interest and principal payments. Moreover, such bonds are issued in bearer (unregistered) form. Without either registration or withholding, Eurobond owners find that taxes are relatively easy to evade. As a result, Eurobonds appeal to investors wishing to evade taxes. Because of this appeal, Eurobonds tend to yield less than similar-risk domestic bonds.

Most Eurobonds are issued by multinational corporations, governments, and international organizations, and most are denominated in dollars or marks. They may take on any of the forms of regular bonds: straight bonds, convertibles, floating-rate notes, zero-coupon bonds, and so on.

Private Placements: Approximately one-third of the debt instruments sold are placed privately. Such issues are sold to a few large buyers (often insurance companies) and publicly announced in the financial press. Such announcements are generally referred to as "tombstones" because of the large white spaces and small amount of lettering. The large size (tens of millions of dollars) of typical private placements rules out direct purchases by most individual investors. Nonetheless, individuals may participate indirectly through one of the closed-end funds that specialize in assembling portfolios of such securities.

Private placements generally yield 1/2% to 1% more than equivalent-risk bonds but lack marketability. Private placements offer issuers greater flexibility. They can be tailored for specific buyers and do not require the issuer to produce a prospectus. Moreover, the underwriting cost savings largely offset their somewhat higher coupon. Finally, the relatively small number of owners makes terms easier to renegotiate when need be. Table 8.2 summarizes the various types of (non convertible) long term debt instruments.

Table 8.2.
Long-Term Debt Securities

Primary Types	
Issue Type	Characteristic
Treasury Notes and Bonds	Lowest risk category
Agency Issues	Slightly higher risks and yields than Treasuries
Mortgage Related Securities	
FNMA	Mortgage-backed [VA and FHA]
GNMA	Mortgage pass-throughs [VA and FHA]
Freddie Mae	Conventional mortgages with Freddie Mac guarantee

Bank Issued	Conventional mortgages, often with a private guarantee
Direct Mortgage, Seller Financing	Risk varies, seconds are usually quite risky
Municipals	Tax-free, risk varies
Municipal Bond Funds	Diversified, may be open- or closed-end
Corporates	Vary greatly in risks and yields
Corporate Bond Fund	Diversified, may be open-or closed-end
Junk Bond Fund	High-risk portfolio

Specialized Types	
Floating-Rate Notes	Coupon varies with market rates
Zero-Coupon	Sold at a discount, pays no coupon
Eurobonds	Traded internationally
Payment in Kind Bonds (PIK)	Pays interest in like securities Large and flexible
Private Placements	80% tax-sheltered to domestic corporations
Preferred Stock	

CONVERTIBLES AND OTHER COMBINATION SECURITIES

Several types of securities add option features to other types of instruments. The two primary types of combination securities are convertible debentures and convertible preferreds. A host of much rarer types include hybrid convertibles, equity notes, LYONs, payment in kind (PIKs, may be either bonds or preferreds), commodity-backed bonds, and stock-indexed bonds. Convertible preferreds and PIK preferreds are equity securities. Convertible debentures, hybrid convertibles, equity notes, LYONs, PIK bonds, commodity-backed bonds, and stock-indexed bonds are all debt securities. Each type of combination security has a close relationship to another type of security or other asset. Most combination securities may be exchanged for a set number of common shares or, in the case of commodity-backed and stock-indexed bonds, their redemption value or coupon rate is indexed to the price of some other asset. PIKs pay their owners a return in the form of more units of the security that is now held. Except for equity notes, conversion of the combination security is at the security owner's option.

The Appeal of Combination Securities: Combination securities derive value from their current return (coupon payments or preferred dividends) and also as potential common stock or some other type of asset (into which they may be convertible). If the price of the underlying common stock rises sufficiently, the convertible owner can either acquire stock at a below-market price or sell the combination security at a price that reflects the increased value of its underlying stock. If the stock's price does not rise sufficiently to make conversion attractive, the owners will still receive income and the eventual redemptions of the securities in their roles as preferreds or debentures, assuming the issuer remains solvent. Convertibles offer an attractive combination of upside potential and downside protection. The convertibility feature, however, usually comes at the cost of reduced interest or dividend income.

Convertible Terminology: A number of specialized terms are encountered with convertibles: (Table 8.3)

Table 8.3
Convertible Terminology

Conversion Ratio:	Number of shares into which the security is convertible.
Conversion Price:	Face value of the security divided by its conversion ratio.
Conversion Value:	Current stock price times the conversion ratio.
Straight-Debt Value:	Market value of an otherwise-equivalent bond lacking a conversion feature.
Conversion Premium:	Bond price less its conversion value.
Premium over Straight-Debt Value:	Bond price less its straight-debt value.

To explore the use of these terms consider a (hypothetical) convertible bond (CVD). It has a $1,000 face value, 12% coupon, and is convertible into 50 shares of CVD stock (its conversion ratio) any time over the next 20 years. For a price of $20 a share, the conversion value of the convertible equals the face value of the bond ($20 x 50 = $1,000). Thus, the conversion price is $20 per share. If the stock sells for $15 a share when the bonds are issued, the bond's initial conversion value equals $750 (15 x 50 = 750). Such bonds will generally trade at a price that more closely reflects their value as bonds (the straight-debt value of their 12% coupon rate). Thus, if the market rate on similar-risk long-term bonds is 14%, this bond should sell for at least $860

(12%/14% = .86). It actually should sell for a bit more so that its yield to maturity equals 14%.

Suppose the price of the underlying stock rose sufficiently for the conversion value to approach the convertible's straight-debt value. In that price environment, the bond's price fluctuations would begin behaving more like that of its underlying stock. Assume the stock rose to $25 a share. At that price level, the convertible would have a conversion value of $1,250 (50 x $25). The market price would be at or a bit above the conversion value. Thereafter, it would tend to move up and down more or less proportionately with the stock's price. Thus, if the stock's price next moved to 26, the conversion value would rise to $1,300 and the bond price would be at least that high.

Conversion and straight-debt values tend to place a floor under the market price of convertibles. Because of their "equity kicker," they normally yield appreciably less than otherwise-similar non-convertibles. Thus, a convertible with a 10% coupon would typically command a somewhat higher price than a similar-quality 10% non-convertible. The difference between the bond's conversion value and market value is known as the conversion premium. The difference between the convertible's market price and straight-debt value is called the premium over the straight-debt value.

Suppose the CVD bonds sold for $950 when the stock traded at 15 and similar coupon, maturity, risk level non-convertibles were selling for $875. The conversion premium would be $200 ($950 - $750) and the premium over straight-debt value would be $75 ($950 - $875). Table 8.4 contains data on some real-world convertibles.

Because convertible bonds are often almost as risky as stocks, the same margin percentage is required: in 2006, 50% vs. 30% for straight bonds. Thus, $10,000 worth of marginable convertibles could be purchased with $5,000 of investor's equity and $5,000 in margin borrowing. The convertible's coupon payments may offset part or all of the interest cost of a margin purchase. Buying convertibles on margin may be appealing if the (short-term) margin rate is low relative to the (longer term) bond rate. Indeed, low conversion value convertibles often pay relatively high yields and sometimes even return to life.

Table 8.4
Selected Convertible Bond Data for February 1, 1983 and December 31, 2000

Convertible Issue yield, maturity	S & P Rating	Conversion Ratio	Stock Price	Conversion Value	Estimated Straight-Debt Value	Market Price
February 1, 1983						
AVCO 5 1/2 93	BB-	18.52	27.625	$ 512	$500	$ 670
GELCO 14 01	BB-	22.13	42.375	$ 938	$950	$1,010
GTE 5 92	BBB	22.98	40.75	$ 936	$560	$ 962
Life Mark 11 02	BB+	30.30	34.875	$1,057	$840	$1,215
Ramada Inns 10 00	B-	129.03	5.75	$ 742	$710	$ 960
December 31, 2000						
Adv6Micro15Dev	CCC+	54.05	13.81	$ 747.50	$ 450	$925.00
Centocor 4 3/4 15	AAA	12.97	105.06	$1363.70	$ 875	$1363.70
Lowes Corp 3 1/8 07	A+	15.38	40.00	$ 616.20	$ 725	$875.00
Nextel Corp 5 1/4 10	B	13.44	24.75	$ 538.70	$ 650	$725.00
August 10, 2006						
Nextel Corp 5 1/4 10	BBB+	17	16.83	$286.11	$982	977.50

Note that the Advanced Micro Device, Centocor and Lowes convertible bonds were all called.

The Advantages of Convertible Bonds: Convertible bonds offer both a fixed coupon (usually a bit below the market rate on equivalent-risk straight-debt securities) and the possibility of a capital gain. They should not be bought either as income securities (straight bonds almost always offer a higher risk-adjusted yield) or as pure stock plays (the stock itself will usually rise proportionately more in a strong market). Rather, convertibles appeal to investors who find the prospects of the related stock attractive but desire the income and protection of the convertible's straight-debt value.

Investing in convertibles has two basic advantages over investments in the underlying common. First, the security's current return is usually higher and certainly more reliable than the corresponding common's dividend yield. Second, their fixed coupons provide convertibles some resistance to the adverse effect of downward moves in the common's price. Convertible prices do tend to move inversely with interest rates, however. Moreover, they normally yield less than otherwise-similar nonconvertible debentures. Finally, the conversion feature will have value only as long as the stock price has a reasonable potential of rising enough for the conversion value to exceed the straight-debt value.

Busted Converts: When the underlying stock's price falls so low that conversion is viewed as highly unlikely, the bond is called a busted convert. Such bonds generally trade at about the same prices as they would command if they did not have the conversion feature. In essence, you get the conversion feature for free. Occasionally such busted converts come to light when the underlying stock recovers. Even if it doesn't, you still have the coupon return of the bond.

Convertibles' Call Risk: While most debt securities are callable, the call feature (and corresponding call risk) is especially relevant to convertible holders. In theory, corporations should force conversion whenever the bond's conversion value is safely above the call price. Such a call would force the owners to exchange their convertible bonds for common stock and thereby reduce debt and strengthen the firm's balance sheet. Rigidly following such a policy would severely limit convertibles' upside potential. Thus, they may only offer attractive returns (vis-à-vis nonconvertibles) if the conversion value rises above the call price relatively soon after the security is issued. Moreover, calling to force conversion generally depresses the price of the underlying stock. Most companies, however, do not call their convertibles as quickly as the theoretical model predicts.

The Theoretical Value of Convertibles: Because they contain both debt and equity elements, convertibles' theoretical values are relatively difficult to define. Debt values will depend upon the coupon, default risk, maturity date, and other indenture provisions. The value of the conversion feature is affected by the firm's risk and capital structure, dividend policy, calling policy, conversion terms, and the current stock price.

As with call valuation, a convertible's theoretical value should not offer assured arbitrage profits to either buyers or short sellers. Values derived from the Black/Scholes contingent-claim pricing model (used to derive theoretical values for options) have been applied to convertible pricing.

Calculating the price that the stock must reach in order to make the returns on investments in convertibles equivalent to that of their associated stocks is also much more complex than with warrants. Both the premium over conversion and the difference between interest and expected dividend income must be considered.

Hybrid Convertibles: Convertible bonds and preferreds are the primary types of convertible securities, but other types of combination securities also bear mentioning. Unlike traditional convertibles, hybrids (also called exchangeable debentures) are convertible into stock of different companies from those that issue them. For example, in 1980 Textron sold debentures convertible into Textron-owned shares of Allied Chemical (at 66). At about the same time, Mesa Petroleum sold a security convertible into General American. Companies with substantial stock portfolios may find hybrids a useful source of funds.

Hybrids are about as attractive to investors as the straight convertibles of the underlying company. The bond's default risk depends on the issuing company's financial position, however. Moreover, the conversion of a regular convertible is a tax-free exchange, whereas any profit realized when a hybrid is converted is immediately taxable.

Equity Notes: Equity notes (also called mandatory convertible notes) were developed to meet the capital needs of banks. Such notes are issued as debt instruments that yield a fixed coupon until maturity, when they are automatically converted into common.

LYONs: One of the most complex of these convertible instruments is the Liquidity Yield Option Note, or LYON. LYONs differ from ordinary convertibles primarily in being zero-coupon convertibles. In addition, they are callable and redeemable. Making the security even more complicated, both the redemption and call prices escalate through time. The first two of these issues were brought out by Merrill Lynch in 1985.

Commodity-Backed Bonds: Commodity-backed bonds are debt instruments whose values are potentially related to the price of some physical commodity. For example, in 1980 Sunshine Mining (silver) sold $57.5 million in 8 1/2% bonds whose redemption value was tied to the price of silver. For prices below $20 per ounce, the bonds mature at face, but at higher prices the bond's redemption value rose proportionately. Thus such bonds allow the owner to speculate on a silver price rise while earning a modest return. The bond's price has moved up and down with variations in both the silver price and market interest rates. When the bonds were issued, silver sold for $14 to $15 per ounce. At year-end 1982, silver was down to $10. Still later, silver fell as low as $5. In May 1991 silver was trading for about $5.00 per ounce, a substantial amount below the $20 price envisioned by the bond. Ten years later, in July 2001, silver was around $4.50 per ounce. By August 2006, silver was trading at around $12.50 per ounce. Other examples include the energy bonds of Petro Lewis and the gold bonds of Refinement International and the copper-indexed bonds of Magma Copper, which are also PIKs under some circumstances.

Stock-Indexed Bonds: In 1981, Oppenheimer & Co. marketed a $25 million stock-indexed bond. The coupon rate was indexed to stock trading volume, with a maximum of 22% compared with an initial rate of 18%. High stock volume should result in booming business for Oppenheimer. Thus, they should be able to pay a higher interest rate when stock market volume is strong. Similarly, Salomon issued S&P Subordinated Index Notes, or SPEIs, whose interest was indexed to the market return. Chase issued a CD with similar features. An interest rate of 4% is guaranteed with an additional return equal to one-fourth of the rise in the S&P 500.

Both commodity-backed and stock-indexed bonds were designed to appeal to speculative investors with options that specially positioned issuers can offer. Additional types of innovative combination securities will probably be devised as time passes. Table 8.5 lists the various types of combination securities.

Table 8.5
Types of Combination Securities

Convertible Bonds	Debt securities that may be exchanged for common stock at a fixed ratio
Commodity-Backed Bonds	Preferred stock that may be exchanged for common stock at a fixed ratio
Hybrid Convertibles	Debt securities of one company convertible into the common of another company
Equity Notes	Debt securities with a mandatory conversion
LYONs	Zero-coupon, convertible, callable, redeemable bonds
Commodity-Backed Bonds	Debt securities whose potential redemption values are related to the market price of some physical commodity such as silver
Stock-Indexed Bonds	Debt securities whose yields are related to stock market volume

EQUITY INSTRUMENTS

Unlike debt instruments, equity securities represent proportional ownership in an asset such as a corporation. The owners have a residual claim on its assets and earnings. Equity-related assets include publicly traded common stock, preferred stock, options, convertibles, and equity mutual funds, as well as ownership positions in small firms and venture capital investments. Each investment represents direct or indirect ownership in a profit-seeking enterprise. Equity holders' claims are junior to those of all debts but encompass all residual value and income in excess of the claims of the senior securities.

Common Stock: By far, the most important type of equity-related security is common stock. Approximately one hundred million U.S. investors own stock directly while many more participate indirectly in the stock market. Such vehicles as mutual funds, trust funds, insurance company portfolios, and the invested reserves of pension funds all provide indirect access.

As the residual owners, shareholders are paid dividends that are generally financed out of the company's profits. The portion of profits not paid out (retained earnings) is reinvested in the company, helping it grow and increase in value. Growth in sales, assets, and particularly profits and dividends should lead to a higher overall value for the company. The benefit of any appreciation in the company's value accrues to its owners, the stockholders. A company's stockholders theoretically control it by electing its board of directors. The board, in turn, selects upper-level management and makes major policy decisions. Most stock ownership groups are, however, widely dispersed and unorganized. Existing management generally fills the resulting power vacuum by nominating and electing friendly slates of directors. This practice has continued despite the era ushered in by Sarbanes-Oxley. More care is now taken by these outside directors, who seem to exercise more due diligence than in the past.

The long-term average returns of stocks compare favorably with those of most bonds and depository accounts. On the other hand, returns on particular stocks over particular periods have differed greatly from the average. Furthermore, the returns on most stocks were well below these long-term averages during many recent periods (e.g., 2000-2003). Managing a portfolio of stocks effectively is not an easy task. Many books have been written on the subject and no doubt many, many more will be written. "Playing" the stock market is and always will be a very challenging "game."

Dividend payments are not assured, and common stock never matures. Thus, shareholders are particularly dependent on their company's future profitability and market acceptance. Companies that reduce or eliminate their dividends are likely also to see a dramatic decline in the values of their stocks. Bond prices generally fluctuate much less than stock prices. Moreover, their promised interest must be paid regardless of the company's profit picture. Accordingly, bonds almost always have less downside risk than the stocks of the same or similar-risk firms.

Stocks can be bought and sold effectively in increments of as little as a few thousand dollars. Thus, the relatively low minimum cost of a stock portfolio makes stocks relatively accessible to small investors. Commissions, however, are disproportionately high on very small transactions (less than about $1,000 and/ or less than 100 shares).

In summary, common stock offers somewhat higher but more risky expected returns than bonds. Stocks are not very liquid, but those of most large and medium-sized firms are quite marketable. Small investors can begin assembling a stock portfolio with relatively modest sums. Informed stock selection requires considerable skill and time, however.

Preferred Stock: While preferred stock is also a type of equity security, it has much in common with debt instruments. The indicated dividend payment rate is generally fixed. The issuer is not required to declare preferred dividends. Payment is required, however, if common dividends are to be paid. Moreover, most preferreds are cumulative, which means that accumulated dividends (accrued, but unpaid) must be made up before the common dividend can resume. Thus the preferred dividends of many companies are almost as dependable as their bond interest. The preferreds of a weak company may, however, be almost as risky as its common. Some preferreds (participating) may receive an extra dividend payment if the issuing firm's earnings or its common dividends are high enough.

Preferred stockholders are residual claimants only one step ahead of common stockholders. Unless the creditors' claims are fully satisfied, nothing will be left for either class of stockholders. Unlike corporate interest payments, preferred dividends paid by domestic corporations (incorporated in the United States) to domestic corporations are 70% tax free. That is, only 30% of dividends that one domestic corporation receives from another is taxable. This tax preference is available only to holders that retain ownership of the preferred for at least 46 days. For a corporation in the 34% tax bracket, a 9% preferred yield is equivalent to an after-tax yield of 7.98%. A fully taxable yield of 12.1% would, in contrast, be needed to generate 7.98% after taxes. Preferreds have become very popular with corporate investors – particularly banks and insurance companies.

Preferred stocks vary greatly in risk but, as a class, tend to be more risky than most types of debt securities. While also a form of ownership, preferred stock is a generally less risky investment than is common stock. Preferred dividend yields are usually below the average long-term total return (dividend plus capital gains) on common stocks. As relatively fixed income securities, preferreds are subject to interest rate risk much like bonds. Moreover, most preferred shares have relatively little long-term appreciation potential. The preferred of a weak company may, however, be riskier and have a higher expected yield than the common of a stronger company. The prices of preferreds vary inversely with interest rates. Like common, preferred stock tends to be relatively marketable. Assembling a diversified portfolio of preferred requires a modest amount of time, funds, and effort.

Convertible Preferreds: While less popular than convertible debentures, convertible preferreds have become much more numerous in the past few years.

Convertible preferreds promise, but do not guarantee, to pay a fixed dividend. Like convertible bonds, they can be converted into a stated number of common shares within a pre=specified period. The convertibility feature may eventually expire, at which time the stock becomes a normal fixed-income preferred. As with convertible bonds, convertible preferreds behave more like the underlying stocks when the market price is close to their conversion values and more like straight preferreds when the conversion value is well below the value as a preferred.

The number of common shares that can be obtained by converting is called the conversion ratio. Thus, a preferred convertible into four common shares would have a ratio of 4.00. This conversion ratio may change with time. For example, an issue might be convertible into four shares for the first 10 years after its issue, two shares for the next 10 years, and then may become a straight preferred, thereafter.

A preferred's conversion value is the current price of the common stock multiplied by the conversion ratio. A preferred convertible into four shares of common stock selling at $10 would have a conversion value of $40. A market price of $50 would reflect a conversion premium of $10. The conversion premium is normally expressed as a percentage:

$$\text{Conversion Premium} = \frac{\text{(Market Price of Preferred - Conversion Value)}}{\text{Conversion Value}}$$

The conversion premium in the above example is: ($50 − $40)/$40 = $10/$40 = 25%

Knowing the size of the conversion premium should help an investor determine whether the convertible preferred or the common is the more attractive investment. For example, one might have a choice between a company's 10% convertible preferred selling at $50 and its common stock bearing a 5% dividend yield selling for $20. If the conversion ratio is two and the conversion value is $40, the conversion premium is 25%:

	CVP	Common
Price	$50	$20
Dividend	$5	$1
Yield	10%	5%

For the 25% premium, an investor buying the 10% convertible preferred receives a higher current yield (10% versus 5%), a more stable dividend (a characteristic of preferreds), and the option of converting the issue into common at a later date when the common stock price could be a lot higher. Of course, the higher the conversion premium, the more remote will be the chance of an attractive conversion and the lower the amount of the gain, even if conversion does become profitable. Moreover, convertible preferreds are exposed to the same kind of call risks and interest rate risks as are convertible bonds.

Small Firm Ownership: Most people who invest in companies (e.g., as individual shareholders) own very small stakes in relatively large firms. Other investors, however, may hold a relatively large stake in a small company. The company may be organized as a sole proprietorship, partnership, or closely held corporation. Such investors may or may not take an active role in the company's affairs. Those who take an active role in their enterprise are much more involved in the management side of the business than the investment side. This management commitment may cut deeply into the time for other activities. Moreover, joint ownership can lead to troublesome policy disputes, and nonexpert part-time owner-managers may be at a disadvantage relative to specialist-competitors. Finally, valuating and ultimately selling a small business can be especially difficult. Silent-partner owners have different problems. A suitable manager may be difficult to find and/or keep. Managers may misuse their positions (legally or illegally) and, unless given a share in the company's profits, may have less incentive than the owners to operate the business profitably. Moreover, the owners are personally liable for the unpaid debts of a partnership or sole proprietorship, and many creditors require the owners of a small corporation to cosign its loans.

Limited Partnerships and Master Limited Partnerships: Most businesses are organized as partnerships or corporations. The corporate form provides limited liability for owner's (shareholders), but its income is first taxed at the corporate level and its shareholders are taxed again on the income that they derive from the company (dividends and capital gains).

Unlike that of a corporation, the income of a partnership is only taxed once. Partnership profits, whether distributed or retained by the partnership, are treated for tax purposes as the imputed income of the partners. Partners are, however, individually and collectively liable for all of the partnership's obligations. Limited partnerships provide an alternative way of organizing business enterprises. They combine the benefits of a corporation's limited liability with the single taxation advantage of a partnership. A single general partner, who is usually the organizer, does have unlimited liability. The limited partners, however, are not liable for the partnership's debts and obligations beyond their initial capital contribution. Most limited partnerships have one major drawback. Because they are relatively small, their ownership units trade in very thin markets. The master limited partnership (MLP) is designed to overcome this drawback. Most MLPs are relatively large (compared with limited partnerships). Their ownership units are designed to trade actively in the same types of markets as stock.

MLPs have generally been organized around oil and gas holdings. Others are designed for real estate. Mesa Limited Partners (oil and gas) is one of the best known of the MLPs. Investing in MLPs involves many of the same advantages and disadvantages as investing in common stock. Note, however, that the stated current yields on MLPs have often been inflated and unsustainable. The managers of these MLPs have been depleting assets to make what appear to be attractive payouts.

Venture Capital: Venture capitalists provide risk capital to otherwise undercapitalized companies that they believe have attractive growth prospects. In exchange, the venture capitalist receives a ground-floor equity position in what may turn out to be a highly lucrative venture. For example, Georges Doriot invested $70,000 of American Research and Development's (ARD) money into what eventually grew into several hundred million dollars worth of Digital Equipment common stock when Textron acquired ARD.

Options: Calls, Puts, Warrants, and Rights: Options are an interesting and relatively complex type of security. Most options provide the holder with the right to acquire or dispose of an equity-related security. The owner of a call contract has an option to buy something. The call writer sells the call buyer the right (but not the obligation) to purchase an asset, such as 100 shares of a particular stock. The contract will specify the price (called the striking price) at which, and the period over which, the call may be exercised. Similarly, a put is a sell-option contract for a particular security, price, quantity, and period. Exercising the option privilege is solely at the owner's (not the seller's) discretion. The option buyer and option writer in effect have a wager on what will happen to the market price of the asset on which the option is written. For example, the call buyer will earn a profit if the price of the associated asset rises sufficiently. Call writers, in contrast, usually profit on the transaction if the relevant price does not rise to or much above the exercise level. In that case, they can generally earn the option premium without having to deliver the stock or other optioned asset.

Suppose an investor pays $200 for an option to buy 100 shares of stock at 20 ($20 per share). If the stock's price subsequently rises to 30, the investor can exercise the option (buy the stock) at 20 and then immediately turn around and sell that same stock at 30 for a gain of $1,000. Subtracting the $200 paid for the call would yield a profit of $800 (before commissions) compared with the initial cost of $200 for the call. That corresponds to a profit of 400% ($800/$200). A similar profit would be made on $200 invested in a put if the price subsequently fell from 20 to 10. The same $200 could, in contrast, have only purchased 10 shares at 20 producing $100 gain for a 10-point price rise (50% profit). An adverse stock price move can, however, lead to a total loss for the option holder. The shareholder's potential loss is, in percentage terms, generally much lower.

Standardized option trading began with the 1973 opening of the Chicago Board Option Exchange (CBOE) and soon spread to other exchanges. Options are now listed on a large number of different stocks. Other options are listed on stock indexes and commodities futures contracts. Most options have relatively short lives (nine months or less) and their prices are dominated by random market fluctuations. Accordingly, option trading is largely the preserve of relatively sophisticated investors.

Warrants and rights are traded in the same markets that trade the stocks that underlie them. Warrants, like calls, permit their owner to purchase a particular stock at a pre-specified price over a pre-specified period. Unlike calls, warrants are generally exercisable for relatively long periods (e.g., several years). Furthermore, warrants are issued by the company whose stock underlies the warrant. If the warrant is exercised, the issuing company simply creates more shares. In contrast, existing shares are used to satisfy the exercised of a call. Thus warrants are company-issued securities whose exercise results in additional shares and generates cash for the issuer. Calls are contracts between individual investors that do not involve the underlying company.

Rights, like warrants, are company-issued options to buy stock. Rights differ from warrants in two ways. First, rights are issued for very short periods. They expire in a few weeks or at most a few months from time of issue. Also, rights are generally exercisable at a price that is substantially less than the current market price of the stock. The issuer sets the strike price low enough to make near-term exercise attractive. Thus, most rights are exercised while warrant exercise is more uncertain. For example, a right might be issued to allow an investor to buy stock at 40 when the market price is 45. Failure to exercise or sell such rights is like throwing away $5 for each right that is allowed to expire. Rights are normally issued to existing shareholders on the basis of their current holdings. Thus shareholders might receive a right to purchase one new share for each 20 shares that they owned.

Option prices tend to move with the underlying common stock but at a considerably greater magnitude. As a result, options are generally considered relatively risky securities. On the other hand, option writing may reduce a portfolio's risk and increase its income.

In summary, most listed options are quite marketable, whereas unlisted options are generally traded in thin markets. Most types of option trading are relatively risky. At least as much expertise and time are required for profitable option trading as for trading common stock.

HEDGING AND ARBITRAGING

As markets have become more sophisticated, security types more diverse, and takeover activity more widespread, hedging and arbitrage trading have risen markedly. Both brokerage firms and individual investors have gotten into the act.

Hedging involves taking opposing positions in related assets to profit (or reduce losses) from hoped-for relative price movements. For example, the hedger might buy convertible bonds and short corresponding shares of stock, or vice versa. Arbitrageurs, in contrast, simultaneously buy and sell equivalent securities in separate markets, profiting from temporary price differences. Arbitrageurs will generally take advantage of any appreciable price disparities for securities traded on both the Pacific Stock Exchange and the NYSE or any other combination of exchanges. In addition to their use in debt- and equity-related securities trading, hedging and arbitraging also take place in a wide variety of other markets including those for currencies and commodities. Both hedging and arbitraging may be classified into risk and pure forms.

Table 8.6
Equity-Related Securities

Direct Ownership of a Company	
Common Stock	Residual ownership of corporations
Preferred Stock	Preferred to common in dividends and Liquidation
Small Firm Ownership	May be organized as corporation, partnership, or sole proprietorship
Master Limited Partnerships	Combined with tax advantage of a partner-ship with the limited liability and ease of trading of a corporation
Venture Capital	Risk capital provided to start-up companies
Options	
Call	Private option-to-buy contract
Put	Private option-to-sell contract
Warrant	Company-issued buy option
Rights	Short-term company-issued option to buy
Indirect Equity Ownerships	
Convertible Bonds	Debt securities that may be exchanged for a pre-specified amount of stock
Mutual Funds and Closed-End Investment Companies, Unit Investment Trusts, and Variable Annuities	Pooled portfolios of securities and other types of interest

Hedging: A pure hedge is designed to reduce risk per se. For example, silver mining companies generally have relatively stable extraction and processing costs. The risky part of their business stems largely from the volatility in the market price of silver. The price has, for example, ranged from over $50 to under $4 per ounce in the 1979-2006 period. Establishing a price for its planned production well ahead of time would substantially reduce the risk that a silver mining company faces due to price fluctuations. Hedge trades in the futures market would establish a price for the sale of the mine's output well before the silver is ready for sale. Mining companies that hedge each projected output increment largely insulate themselves from subsequent silver spot (immediate delivery) price fluctuations. Similar types of hedge trades may be made by a variety of enterprises. Pure hedging is often advisable whenever establishing a forward price reduces an important business risk. Such pure hedges are incidental to hedgers' main spot-market business.

Risk hedges, in contrast, are designed to yield a profit. Rather than reduce the impact of potentially adverse price moves, risk hedgers seek to profit from potentially favorable relative price movements, while limiting their exposure to potentially adverse moves. Put and call spreads and ratio positions are examples of risk hedges.

Arbitraging: Pure arbitrageurs assume opposite positions on equivalent (or convertible to equivalent) assets when prices in separate markets diverge sufficiently. Pure arbitrage produces a quick certain profit. Risk arbitrageurs, in contrast, take offsetting positions in potentially equivalent securities. The shares of an acquisition candidate and its proposed acquirer are the primary types of potentially equivalent securities. An exchange for debt or equity securities may or may not be hedged by the arbitrageur. A tender for cash does not require the arbitrageur to make an offsetting trade, however.

A proposed merger involving an exchange of shares will generally leave the relative prices of the two stocks somewhat out of line with the merger terms. For example, XYZ may offer two of its shares for each share of UVW Corporation. If pre-offer prices of XYZ and UVW were 50 and 75, immediate post-offer prices might move to 52 and 85. At these levels, the UVW stock would still be underpriced relative to the XYZ offer. Assuming the merger agreement takes effect, the UVW stock is worth 104 (two times the per share price of XYZ). That is, the arbitrageur would buy in the ratio of one share of UVW at 85 while shorting two shares of XYZ for a total of 104. The net result would be a gain of 19 (104 - 85) times the number of shares of UVW purchased. The risk the arbitrageur would lock in this gain, by entering into a combined long and short position.

SUMMARY AND CONCLUSIONS

Security market investors should at least consider the wide variety of risks, returns, marketabilities, liquidities, and tax treatments offered by the bond market. A well-diversified portfolio containing both equity and debt securities is likely to be less risky than a well-diversified portfolio of stocks or bonds alone. Investors should have little difficulty finding issues bearing risks corresponding to their own preferences.

The money market provides relatively attractive short-term rates on high-quality securities such as T-bills, commercial paper, large bank CDs, bankers' acceptances, and Eurodollar loans. Small investors can participate in this market through money market mutual funds, short-term unit investment trusts, and the money market certificates and accounts of commercial banks and savings institutions. Larger investors can assemble their own money market portfolios.

Treasury and federal agency securities make up a large part of the long-term debt security market. Most such issues are untaxed at the state and local level. The agencies tend to offer slightly higher yields, but are somewhat less marketable than Treasury issues. A large part of the agency security market is mortgage-related. The various bonds, pass-throughs, and participations of FNMA, GNMA, Freddie Mac, and the large bank pools offer high, safe, monthly income combined with a somewhat uncertain maturity.

State and local issues, whose interest payments are untaxed at the federal level, form another major segment of the debt security market. Most municipals offer relatively low before-tax yields. Such securities primarily appeal to those in high tax brackets. Municipal bond funds and municipal unit investment trusts provide small investors various ways to enter this market.

Corporate securities vary greatly in risk. Some high-risk issues offer very high yields. Corporate bond funds (including high-risk bond funds) and closed-end bond funds permit small investors to own part of a diversified debt security portfolio.

Other types of debt securities include, floating-rate notes, zero-coupon bonds, Eurobonds, privately placed issues, and preferred stock (an equity asset priced primarily on its stated yield). Each of these securities appeals to specialized segments of the marketplace.

Thus, the debt security market offers a wide array of risk-return tradeoffs, maturities, and tax treatments. Moreover, in the past few years a variety of new instruments have enhanced the access of small investors to these markets. A number of mutual funds, closed end funds and short-term unit trusts facilitate investing in money market, municipal, corporate, high-risk corporate, and various other more specialized types of debt securities. Access is therefore no longer restricted by the difficulty of diversifying across a variety of high-denomination securities.

Combination securities include convertible bonds, convertible preferreds, hybrid convertibles, equity notes, commodity-backed bonds, and stock-indexed bonds. Each combines a fixed income security with an option (or in case of the equity note, an obligation) to convert the security to common stock or some other asset. Thus, such securities offer some of the upside potential of a common stock coupled with the downside protection of a bond or preferred stock.

Combination securities are priced to reflect their profit and risk characteristics. Thus, buyers usually obtain the upside potential at the cost of a lower yield than otherwise-equivalent straight debt or straight preferred securities. Moreover, the call risk further limits the upside potential. Pure and combination option security positions are often combined with each other and/or with non-option securities to create hedges and arbitrages. Clearly, investors considering investments in some company's common stock should also weight the pros and cons of taking a position in its other securities.

CHAPTER 9

THE DETERMINANTS OF YIELDS

The prices of all investments, including debt securities, are affected by the general level of interest rates. That general level is. in turn. related to such factors as the supply and demand for credit, the economy's strengths and weaknesses, inflationary expectations, and the state of the world economy. The discount rate applied to an individual debt security's promised income stream will vary with a number of other characteristics.

We explore herein the impacts of a variety of factors that affect individual debt security yields. Default risk, a primary determinant of yields, is given considerable attention. Near-default workouts, Chapter 11 and Chapter 7 bankruptcy proceedings, and bond ratings are each considered. We also explore the impacts of term structure, duration, coupon effect, seasoning, marketability, call protection, sinking fund provisions, me-first rules, usability, industrial classification, condition of collateral, and listing status.

DEFAULT RISK

Some investors achieve high yields from diversified portfolios of bonds in or near default. Other investors prefer simply to collect their principal and interest when it is due and not have to worry about defaults. Such investors should avoid bankruptcy investing. Regardless of whether a lower but safe or higher but riskier yield investment is your preference, you need to be able to evaluate the underlying security. What are you buying? The issuer's promises to the bondholders is one place to start this inquiry.

Indenture Provisions: Bond indentures contain a number of provisions, the most important of which relate to each issue's interest and maturity obligations. The borrower agrees to a specified coupon payment until maturity, when principal is to be returned. The indenture will also contain a number of other provisions. For example, some debt obligations are backed by specific collateral. The indenture for such a security will specify the nature of the collateral obligation. The provision will typically state that the issuer agrees to maintain any pledged assets or acceptable substitutes in good repair.

The equipment trust certificates of railroads and other transportation companies (especially airlines) constitute a major portion of the collateralized corporate bond market. Even weak companies can issue relatively low-risk (and, therefore, low-yielding) equipment trust certificates. The collateral's quality protects the owners in the event that the issuer of the equipment trust certificates goes into default. For example, under Section 1110 of the Bankrupt Code, Braniff I and Continental I continued to pay interest on equipment trust certificates in order to maintain use of certain aircraft in their fleets throughout their bankruptcy proceedings.

Most corporate bonds called debentures are not backed by any specific collateral. Rather, such debentures are backed by "the full faith and credit" of the issuer. Such backing amounts to nothing more than a promise by the issuer to pay. In most instances, the issuing company has a strong enough credit rating not to need to specify any collateral to back up its debt issue. In other cases, the issuer may not have any unencumbered collateral. Debentures can be subordinated to other debentures and/or to other debt. Senior (unsubordinated) debentures generally have the same standing as the firm's other general creditors. Thus, in a bankruptcy filing senior debenture holders and other general creditors could be treated equivalently.

In addition to interest, principal, collateral, and liquidation requirements, a bond's indenture may provide for subordination to other debts, a sinking fund, and call privileges. as well as restrictions on dividends and certain other matters. A subordination provision provides that when the issuer is in default, the subordinated debt issue will not receive any liquidation payments until the claims (usually pre-bankruptcy filing) of other specified debt issues are fully satisfied. Any monies that would have been paid to the subordinated debt holders are paid to the senior creditors until their claims are paid in full. Sinking funds require that a portion of the issue be retired periodically. To satisfy this provision, bonds may be bought in the open market, they may be called, or funds may be set aside in an escrow account for the issue's eventual retirement.

A call privilege permits the issuer to redeem the securities before maturity at a pre-specified price. The call price normally exceeds the bond's face value by an amount that declines over time. The call price usually approaches par as maturity nears. For example, 10 years before maturity, the bond might be callable at 105 with the call premium declining by .5 per year thereafter.

Falling interest rates encourage issuers to call and refinance their debt at lower rates. The no-call feature of some bonds prohibits calls for part or all of the bond's life, however. Investors should be wary of bonds with call rights. High-coupon bonds often trade for substantial premiums over face. An early call for such a bond would cost the bondholder the difference between the pre-call market price and the call price. Thus, a bond selling for 115 that is called for 105 would cost the investor $100 (10 points) per bond, compared with what the bond could have been sold for prior to the call.

Restrictions on dividend payments are designed to preserve the company's capital and thereby protect the creditors. A firm that pays out too much in dividends could conceivably threaten its solvency and put its bondholders' claims in jeopardy. Thus, dividend payments might be limited to a certain percentage of profits unless and until the company's net worth exceeds some specific level. A minimum current ratio may be set and me-first rules may restrict the future borrowing level. All of these features are designed to protect the creditors. An indenture trustee, usually a bank, is charged with enforcing each indenture provision. Table 9.1 summarizes the typical indenture provisions. Because the value of these provisions to the bondholder depends on how they are enforced, we need to consider what usually happens in a default.

Table 9.1
Indenture Provisions

Provision	Nature of Provision
Principal and Maturity	Specifies amount and timing of required principal payment
Coupon	Specifies amount and timing of each coupon payment
Collateral (equipment trust certificate or other collateralized bond)	Identifies pledged collateral and specific obligation of issuer to maintain collateral's value
Full Faith and Credit (debenture)	Backs promise to pay principal and interest on the bond with the "good name" of the issuer
Subordination	Provides liquidation priority to other specified debt issues
Sinking Fund	Requires periodic redemption and retirement over the life of the bond issue
Call Provisions Schedule	Specifies length of no-call protection and the call premiums payable over life of the bond
Dividend Restrictions	Restricts dividend payments, based on earnings and amount of equity capital

Current Ratio Minimum	Requires that the ratio of current assets to current liabilities not fall below a specified minimum
Me-First Rule	Restricts the amount of additional (non-subordinated) debt that may be issued
Trustee	Identifies the institution responsible for enforcing the indenture provisions
Grace Period	Specifies the maximum period that firm has to cure a default without incurring the risk of encountering an involuntary bankruptcy filing

Defaults and Near-Defaults: Companies almost always pay required interest and principal when they are capable of doing so. Sometimes, however, they have no choice. Indeed, the 1980s and 1990s saw a large number of financially troubled companies: Braniff, Chrysler, AM International, Lincoln Savings, First Republic Bank, International Harvester, Saxon Industries, Wickes, Mego, Manville, World Airways, LTV, Bethlehem Steel, A.H. Robins, Texas Air, Pan Am, Continental Illinois Bank, Continental Airlines (twice), First City Bank, TWA, Texaco, Bank of New England, Drexel Burnham, First Executive, Columbia Savings, Pacific Gas and Electric, Lucent Technologies, Xerox, KMart, and Sunbeam. Still others followed in the 2000s: WorldCom, Enron, UAL, Delphi, U.S. Air, Delta. The experiences of these companies heightened interest in the default issue and led to consideration of investing in the bonds of defaulting and bankrupt companies.

A company is in technical default whenever any indenture provisions of its bonds are violated. Similarly, a violation of any terms of its other debt agreements constitutes a technical default. Many, even most, debt contracts contain cross-default provisions. Such provisions trigger a default in the subject instrument when a default occurs in another instrument of the same issuer. Most defaults, however, involve relatively minor matters. For example, if the working capital ratio fell below the stipulated minimum, the company would technically be in default of the relevant debenture provision. Rarely, if ever, would a default in such a matter, in and of itself, lead to a bankruptcy filing. The indenture trustee may grant a waiver for the violation, or the matter may be quickly cured. A monetary default differs from a technical default in that some form of required payment has not been made.

Informal Reorganizations: Even a failure to pay stipulated interest and principal will not automatically or immediately force a bankruptcy proceeding. A late payment may quickly rectify the default. The indenture usually provides a grace period (e.g., 30 days) for curing such a default. Even after the expiration of the grace period, the trustee may not institute legal proceedings right away. Indeed, most defaults do not lead to bankruptcy filings, and many bankruptcies do not lead to liquidations. Rather, defaults (and indeed many near-defaults) usually result in a formal or informal reorganization that stops short of a long and costly liquidation.

When a few large creditors (such as banks that have extended substantial loans) can be identified, the troubled borrower may seek concessions that will give it a reasonable chance of avoiding a bankruptcy filing. Big lenders have an important stake in their creditors' survival. An interesting oversimplification of the borrower-lender relationship is seen in the following two sentences:

A borrower who owes $10 and cannot pay is in trouble. A borrower who owes a million dollars and cannot pay puts the lender in trouble.

The weakness of a troubled borrower is, in fact, a strength in any negotiations with the lender. Lenders with large exposures are likely to be asked to accept a payment stretch-out, interest rate reduction, swap of debt for equity or tangible assets, reduction in loan principal, and a change or waiver of certain default provisions. Lenders can often be persuaded to agree to such restructurings in the expectation of eventually recovering more than they would in a formal bankruptcy.

Obtaining concessions from all of the numerous bondholders would be difficult. Accordingly, they are only rarely asked to make them. Thus, the bondholders may be able to obtain the benefit of the large lenders' concessions without making any corresponding sacrifice. If the effort fails, the bondholders still retain their priority in formal bankruptcy proceedings.

Exchange Offers: The Trust Indenture Act (1940) prohibits a change in principal, coupon or maturity provisions in a bond indenture without unanimous approval of the bondholders. That provision effectively bans such changes. As a result, the only way to effectuate this type of change is with what is called an exchange offer (voluntary). The company may offer existing bondholders a package of securities in exchange for their existing bonds. Such a package may contain a combination of cash, new bonds, preferred stock, common stock and warrants. The exchange is structured to reduce the cash flow burden of the existing debt structure, especially the short-term burden. By reducing principal and coupon, and partially offsetting it with equity, the company seeks to avoid a bankruptcy filing. Staying out of bankruptcy is usually in everyone's interest, including the stockholders'. The company therefore seeks to convince its bondholders to accept the exchange "voluntarily." Some bondholders, however, will hold out. They thereby may achieve the benefit from the exchange while retaining the benefit of their existing bonds. Each individual bondholder is likely to be best off if he or she chooses not to exchange, but everyone else does. Too many holdouts, however, will kill the deal and may force the troubled company into bankruptcy. Thus, the holdout problem is the Achilles heel of exchange offers. Many are tried, but few succeed.

Bankruptcy Filings: Some financially troubled companies cannot or should not be reorganized in an out-of-court workout. The alternative is usually a bankruptcy filing. Many troubled companies would be financially viable if their debt loads were sufficiently reduced. Thus, a major objective of most bankruptcy reorganization proceedings is to reduce the amount and interest burden of the company's debt. Bankrupt companies generally have little or no excess cash to distribute to creditors. Indeed, bankruptcy filings are often triggered by a shortage of available cash needed to pay bills as they come due. As a result, most creditors are prevailed upon to accept lower-priority securities of the reorganized firm. Senior creditors may receive debentures or preferred shares; junior creditors could be allocated common stock and warrants. In some instances, the bankrupt company may accumulate cash through asset sales and continuing operations while under court protection. Recall that once a company is put into bankruptcy, its obligation to pay interest and principal on its pre-petition debts is deferred. Indeed, post-petition interest has a very low priority claim in a bankruptcy/reorganization. Rarely are funds sufficient for such claims. To the extent that the debtor's cash is not required for working capital, it may be available for distribution. The senior creditors generally demand that most or all of that cash go to them. In such circumstances, the senior creditors are likely to receive a package containing both cash and various categories of securities (subordinated debentures, income bonds, preferred stock, common stock, warrants, etc.). More junior creditors receive little or none of the cash. Their package tends to be heavily weighted toward the more junior securities (stocks and warrants). The going-concern value of a company going through a bankruptcy process is quite subjective. The securities to be issued by the reorganized company will not have an established market price until the company emerges from bankruptcy. Thus, the relevant values are rather uncertain when, in the course of the bankruptcy proceeding, the securities distribution is being set. Not surprisingly, the ability of these securities to satisfy claims is often subject to dispute.

Generally, the lower priority claimants will argue for a higher overall valuation for the company and its securities. In this way they seek to increase the assumed value of the securities that are available for distribution to their priority class. The greater the overall estimated value of the company, the greater is the proportion of the estimated value available to satisfy the lower priority claimants. Suppose, for example, the high-priority claimants have claims of $95 million the company's value is estimated at $100 million. The high-priority claimants would, under absolute priority, be awarded securities representing 95% of the company's value. Only 5% would be available to the lower-priority claimants. Now suppose that the lower-priority claimants are able to have the company's estimated value raised to $110 million. At that valuation. the higher-priority claimants would receive about 86% (95/110) of the company's value. The lower-priority claimants would, in contrast, see their share rise to about 14% (15/110). Clearly, the lower-priority claimants would be awarded more of the company's value under the higher-valuation estimate (14% vs. 5%). The higher-priority claimants, in contrast, would see their share fall from 95% to 86% under the higher valuation. Accordingly, senior creditors will argue for a more conservative valuation. They want to limit the distribution of the securities so that it goes largely to the senior claimants.

Additionally, the legal status of each issuer may be subject to attack. Senior creditors may be challenged by the representatives of more junior issues on the theory that their alleged priority is invalid or subject to differing interpretations. A given credit's relative priority is not always clearly established. For example, a subordinated debenture may be clearly junior to some senior credits (e.g., bank lenders), but its status vis-à-vis others (e.g., trade creditors) may be unclear. Similarly, the validity of guarantees may be objected to by other creditors. Any transactions entered into shortly before a bankruptcy filing may be attacked as fraudulent conveyances by anyone disadvantaged by them. Similarly, distributions to creditors shortly before the bankruptcy filing may be attacked as preferences. Whenever any uncertainty attaches to a credit's priority, the junior creditors are likely to try to take advantage of the situation. Unless the low-priority claimants are given some meaningful consideration, they may choose to use various legal maneuvers designed to delay and tie up the proceedings. The bankrupt estate is obligated to pick up the legitimate legal expenses of the various creditor classes as they seek to sort out their claims and agree upon a reorganization or liquidation plan. Thus, the junior creditors can litigate with money that would otherwise be available for distribution to the creditors (most of which would have gone to the seniors). Not only can they delay the distribution, their actions can actually reduce the senior's recovery. As a result of this potential weapon, most informal workouts and reorganizations ultimately allocate lesser-priority claimants somewhat more than the absolute priority of claims that principle requires. In practice, unsecured and subordinated creditors can generally make enough noise to obtain some share of the assets, even when senior creditors' claims exceed the company's remaining asset value. The reduced debt burden generally permits the reorganized company to remain solvent. New equity holders may have a long wait before receiving any common or preferred dividend payments, however.

Bond Ratings: The default risks of both municipal and corporate bonds are evaluated by several rating services. The best-known are Standard & Poor's and Moody's. Fitch Investors Service also rates bonds. Each service's ratings is based on its evaluation of the company's financial position and earnings prospects. Table 9.2 on the following page describes the primary rating categories of the two principal agencies. Pluses and minuses are used to discriminate within a broader rating category.

The agencies do not release their specific rating formulas or analyses. A number of studies do, however, reveal a rather predictable pattern. Ratings tend to rise with profitability, size, and earnings coverage. They decrease with earnings volatility, leverage, and pension obligations; they vary with industry classification. Ratings sometimes differ between the rating agencies, usually reflecting a close call on fundamentals. Moody's tends to be the more conservative of the two primary rating agencies. Several researchers have found that the market price and yield of such issues is much more closely related to the lower than the higher ratings.

For issues of the same company, a subordinate issue will usually receive a lower rating than a more senior security. The rating agencies follow the fortunes of issues over time, but rating changes occur relatively infrequently and often take place long after the underlying fundamentals change. Accordingly, several services (including S&P's Creditwatch) offer more up-to-date analyses, including a prediction of rating changes. Moreover, many brokerage firms are paying increasing attention to bond analysis.

Investors can use financial ratios and bankruptcy-prediction models to perform their own bond analysis. Such an examination would probably include an analysis of the level and trend in a variety of financial ratios: current, quick, debt-equity, return on equity, times-interest-earned, and other relevant ratios. These ratios would be compared with industry and national averages in an effort to reveal current deficiencies and/or significant long-term risks. Clearly, high debt-equity ratios and low times-interest-earned percentages are not reassuring. Unfortunately, such historical analysis can only provide part of the story. Bondholders should also be interested in the company's prospects. For example, the negative perspective associated with a seemingly shaky current financial position may be offset by the positive outlook for an upcoming product introduction. Alternatively, a company with a solid financial position may be trapped in an industry slowly being eliminated by a changing technology.

TABLE 9.2
Bond Rating Categories

	Moody's	Standard & Poor's	Definition
Highest Grade	Aaa	AAA	An extremely strong capacity to pay principal and interest.
High Grade	Aa	AA	A strong capacity to pay principal and interest, but lower protection margins than Aaa and AAA.
Medium Grade	A	A	Many favorable investment attributes but may be vulnerable to adverse economic conditions.
Minimum Investment Grade	Baa	BBB	Generally adequate capacity to pay interest and principal, coupled with a significant vulnerability to adverse economic conditions.
Speculative	Ba	BB	Have only moderate protection during both good and bad times.
Very Speculative	B	B	Generally lack characteristics of other desirable investments. Interest and principal payments over any long period of time are not safe.
Default or Near Default	Caa	CCC	Poor quality issues in danger of default.
	Ca	CC	Highly speculative issues that are often in default.
	C		The lowest rated class of bonds.
		C	Income bonds on which no interest is being paid.
		D	Issues in default with principal and/or interest payments in arrears.

Adapted from: *Bond Guide* (New York: Standard & Poor's Corporation, monthly); *Bond Record* (New York: Moody's Investor Services, monthly).

Avoiding Bankruptcy Candidates: Avoiding or perhaps even shorting the securities of companies that are likely to go bankrupt may be a profitable strategy. Altman's model for bankruptcy prediction (Edward Altman is a senior finance professor at New York University who has written extensively in the bankruptcy area) facilitates such a strategy. His early warning system identifies companies with a high bankruptcy probability. Subsequent work indicates that bankruptcies are relatively predictable events. Moreover, the Altman formula seems about as accurate at forecasting failures as most of the alternatives. Whether one can profit from accurate bankruptcy predictions depends on the securities' pre- and post-bankruptcy performance.

Various researchers have found significantly negative risk-adjusted returns for holding periods of up to four years prior to a bankruptcy filing. Others have reported that shareholders experienced large losses during the month of a bankruptcy filing, with much of the losses concentrated during the three days surrounding the announcement. Taking advantage of such observed tendencies depends on having lead time relative to the market.

Using one form of risk adjustment, Altman and Brenner found predictable subsequent negative performance associated with deteriorating financial data, but the relationship disappeared when a second risk adjustment procedure was applied. Thus trading signals of bankruptcy prediction models may or may not be helpful. Those who want to try them may find a simplified form of the Altman model useful. It involves the calculation of a Z-score value of creditworthiness and financial viability from the following financial data:

$$\text{Altman Z Score} = 1.2A + 1.4B + 3.3C + 1D + .6E \text{ where:}$$
$$A = \text{working capital/assets}$$
$$B = \text{retained earnings/assets}$$
$$C = \text{pretax earnings/assets}$$
$$D = \text{sales/assets}$$
$$E = \text{market value of equities/liabilities}$$

A firm scoring less than 1.81 is classified as troubled.

A further refinement of the Altman formula has been developed by a consulting firm called Zeta Services, in Hoboken, New Jersey. Although the output of the proprietary model is sold primarily to institutional subscribers, its results sometimes appear in publications such as *Forbes*. The Relative Financial Strength System of *Value Line* provides similar output to subscribers.

Contrary Opinion: Investing in Troubled Firms: Far from avoiding troubled firms, some investors seek them out. Indeed the so-called "theory of contrary opinion" advises investors to concentrate on issues that are out of favor, and, therefore, presumably undervalued. The market will eventually return to the former favorites that are now being neglected, so the argument goes. Contrarians may contrast their concept with what they despairingly refer to as the "greater-fool" theory. Those who follow fads often bid prices up to unrealistic levels hoping that still greater fools will pay even more.

Like many investment concepts, contrary opinion investing is easier to discuss in the abstract than to reduce to practice. Those who favor investments in stocks with low P/Es or small capitalizations, in stocks neglected by analysts, or stocks with low per share prices are practicing a contrarian approach. Concentrating on currently unprofitable companies is another possible approach.

Conceptually, the most appealing contrary opinion approach is to target (or seek to identify before the market does) troubled companies that are about to turn around. In this regard, Katz, Lilien, and Nelson examined a trading strategy based on whether, according to a bankruptcy model such as Altman's, a company was moving toward health or distress. They found that the stocks of companies moving from distress to health exhibited positive abnormal returns. The abnormal returns of firms moving in the other direction were negative. These findings suggest that the changes in a firm's Z scores may offer useful trading signals.

An even more daring contrary approach concentrates on one of the most out-of-favor groups: the bankrupts. Thus a *Barron's* author argued, "Equity Funding, Penn Central, Interstate Stores and Daylin all have sought the shelter of bankruptcy. But like corporate Lazaruses, each has risen form the dead." Although bankrupt companies usually decline severely around the time of their filing, a few eventually come back handsomely. Many are total or near-total losses, however. One who wishes to invest in bankrupt companies, may, however, find their bonds a more effective vehicle than their stocks.

Bond Ratings and Performance: How well do bonds of the various risk classes perform? Bonds in the top four rating categories (Aaa, Aa, A, or Baa) are considered investment grade. Bonds with ratings below investment grade are referred to as junk bonds. No bonds that Moody's rated investment grade defaulted in the 1950s or 1960s. A small number of railroad bonds rated Ba or less did default, however. The experience of the 1920s and 1930s is rather different, to be sure, but Pye, in a frequently referenced academic study, argued that major companies seldom go bankrupt except during major depressions. Moreover, economists and government officials now know how to avoid such depressions.

More recently, however, a number of large companies have gone under: Enron, WorldCom, Delta, UAL, U.S. Air, W.T. Grant, Franklin National Bank, Penn Central, Braniff, AM International, MCorp, First Republic Bank, Bank of New England, Continental Airlines, and Manville (with close calls for International Harvester and Continental Illinois Bank). Moreover, government bailouts were required to save Lockheed and Chrysler. Clearly, large companies are not immune to bankruptcy.

The issues are less clear for lower-rated bonds. The realized (after-default loss) yield experience of below-Baa bonds is of considerable interest in light of the growing numbers of such issues. Many institutional investors and fiduciaries are prohibited from owning below-Baa bonds. Their absence in the market place may tend to depress the price of such issues. Accordingly, such securities may well offer superior risk-adjusted yields. Excluding a major category of investors from the market place may distort supply-demand relationship and thus make pricing less efficient. Therefore, diversified portfolios of medium- to high-risk bonds might outperform similarly diversified high-quality bond portfolios. Diversification across industries would spread the default risk, and the higher indicated yield might more than offset the impact of any default losses. A number of researchers have found that the yield premium on junk bonds has substantially exceeded the loss from default. Such results, however, are derived from studies covering relatively prosperous times. Experience during severe recessions might be quite different. Indeed the experience of the late 1980s and early 1990s, as well as the early 2000s, appears to have been quite a bit less favorable for the high-yield bond market than the immediately preceding period.

The Term Structure of Interest Rates: Its term or length to maturity is one of three major determinants of a debt security's yield to maturity. (General credit conditions and default risk are the other two.) Yields to maturity tend to vary systematically with length to maturity. This relationship can be illustrated with what is called a yield curve. This curve emerges when yield is plotted versus term to maturity for issues with otherwise-similar characteristics (risk, coupon, call feature, etc.) The yield curve reveals a pattern that at various times rises, falls, does not vary, or rises and then falls.

Term Structure Hypotheses: The segmented markets, preferred habitat, liquidity preference and unbiased expectations hypotheses have all been advanced to explain the term structure of interest rates. Each is capable of accounting for the various shapes of the yield curve. The segmented-markets hypothesis asserts that supply and demand within each market segment determine interest rates for that maturity class. According to this hypothesis, the yield curve simply reflects the supply and demand for each maturity class for that particular time frame. Some investors are thought generally to prefer to lend short, whereas many borrowers prefer to borrow long. Thus, rates are often lower for short maturities.

A related but somewhat less restrictive form of the segmented-markets hypothesis is called the preferred habitat hypothesis. According to this form, borrowers and lenders prefer certain maturities. They can only be induced to buy or sell other maturities by more attractive rates. As with the segmented-markets hypothesis, preferred habitat assumes that most investors prefer the short end and most borrowers prefer the long end of the market.

The liquidity preference hypothesis assumes that markets are not segmented, per se, but that some lenders (especially commercial banks with their short-term capital sources) generally prefer to lend short. Similarly, many borrowers are thought to prefer to borrow long term. Thus a rising yield curve is generally needed to compensate lenders for their greater time commitment.

The unbiased expectations hypothesis asserts that long rates reflect the market's expectation of current and future short rates. Thus the one-year rate is simply the geometric average of the current six-month rate and the expected rate six months hence. Suppose the 12-month rate is Y%. The unbiased expectations hypothesis asserts that current rates have embedded within them the market's anticipated six-month rate six months from now. That anticipation is in fact the rate necessary when coupled with the current six-month rate to yield a 12-month return of Y%.

Consider, for example, six-month and 12-month yields of 8% and 9%, respectively. Taken together such yields imply a specific value for the expected six-month yield for a security whose life begins in six months. Thus, the rate for the second six months will cause an investment that yields 8% for the first six months to generate an overall 12-month return of 9%.

An (annualized) 8% return that is earned for six months corresponds to a return relative (ratio of beginning and ending values) of 1.04. A 9% return that is earned for 12 months corresponds to a return relative of 1.09. Thus, we first seek the return relative for the second six months that will produce the appropriate 12-month return relative. Once we obtain the return relative, the corresponding annualized return is easy to compute. The appropriate formula is:

$$1.04 \times ? = 1.09; \text{ Solving for } ? \text{ yields: } ? = 1.09/1.04 = 1.048$$

A yield of 1.048 for six months corresponds to a 12-month return relative of 1.098. This, in turn, corresponds to an annualized return of 9.8%. Thus, the implied yield for the second six months is 9.8%. In other words, an investment that earns 8% in the first six months must earn 9.8% in the second six months in order to produce an overall 12-month return of 9%.

The unbiased expectations hypothesis asserts that the market signals its expectations for future interest rates by the rates it establishes for debt securities of various maturities. According to this view, potential arbitrage activity always drives the yield curve into the shape appropriate for that set of expectations.

If long rates seem too high vis-à-vis expected future short rates, some short-horizon investors will move toward longer-term issues, while some longer-horizon lenders will switch toward shorter-term borrowing. Such activity should quickly drive rates into the appropriate relation. All four hypotheses recognize the existence of such arbitraging activity but only the unbiased expectations hypothesis asserts its overriding power. Table 9.3 summarizes the four term structure hypotheses.

Table 9.3
Term Structure Hypotheses

Segmented Markets	Yields reflect supply and demand for each maturity class.
Preferred Habitat	Investors and borrowers can be induced out of their preferred maturity structures only by more attractive rates.
Liquidity Preference	Lenders generally prefer to lend short and borrowers prefer to borrow long, tending to produce an upward sloping yield curve.
Unbiased Expectations	Long rates reflect the market's expectation of current and future short rates.

Each hypothesis explains the various yield curve shapes slightly differently and has somewhat different implications. According to liquidity preference, yield curves are typically rising because, on balance, lenders prefer the short end and borrowers the long end. Segmented markets and preferred habitat are also consistent with a tendency for yield curves to rise. Lenders may be relatively more numerous at the short end.

The unbiased expectations hypothesis, in contrast, asserts that yield curves only rise when interest rates themselves are expected to increase. A flat yield curve indicates neutral expectations. A falling yield curve reflects an expectation that rates will fall. Such an expectation causes borrowers (bond issuers) to rely on short-term financing until the expected fall occurs. Accordingly, borrowers anticipating a decline in interest rates tend to shift demand from the long- to the short-term market. As a result, short rates tend to be bid up relative to long rates. Lender expectations have a similar impact. Lenders (bond buyers) want to profit from the expected interest rate decline by owning long-term bonds. Falling rates would cause their prices to rise relative to shorter-term issues. Thus, investors who expect rates to fall will tend to favor the longer maturities, thereby pushing downward on long rates and upward on short rates. In summary, when rates are expected to fall, the actions of both lenders and borrowers will tend to twist the yield curve downward, causing short-term rates to exceed long-term rates. The very tight monetary policy in 1974 and again in 1980-1981 created just such circumstances: very high short-term rates with lower long-term rates.

None of the term structure hypotheses has gained overwhelming acceptance or been completely ruled out of contention. On theoretical grounds, unbiased expectation is generally favored. Liquidity preference may have a slight edge in explaining the data. Most academicians believe that modern debt markets are not segmented, per se, but that appreciable numbers of borrowers and lenders may have preferred habitats. From the investor's viewpoint the relative strengths and weaknesses of the hypotheses are less important than an understanding of the empirical relationship between yield and maturity.

The Investment Implications of the Term Structure: Yield curve relationships may provide bond traders with two opportunities. First, securities whose yields are some distance from curves plotted with otherwise-similar issues may well be misvalued. Thus, bonds whose yields exceed their respective yield curve values may be underpriced. If their market prices adjust more quickly than the curve itself shifts, the strategy would produce an above-market return.

A second bond strategy involves what is called riding the yield curve. A steeply rising yield curve may offer an attractive trading opportunity. Suppose, for example, that one-year T-bills yield 7%, compared with 5% on six-month securities. Both the six-month bill and a 12-month bill sold six months later would generate a six-month return. Suppose that six-month T-bills are still yielding 5% six months later. Under that scenario the six-month return on the 12-month bill will be quite a bit higher than 5% and, indeed, above 7% as well. To yield 5% with six months to go, the 7% one-year T-bill must return approximately 9% in the first six months (1.025 x 1.045 = 1.07). Undertaking a strategy of riding the yield curve incurs the risk of an adverse interest rate move, however. Should six-month rates rise to 10%, the six-month return on the 12-month bill would only be around 3% (1.05 x 1.02 = 1.07).

Duration: Up to this point, we have discussed debt securities as if the maturities of such securities were easy to determine. A 12-year bond is a bond that promises to return principal in 12 years. Not all 12-year bonds are alike, however. The payment patterns of debt securities vary all the way from zero coupon bonds to fully amortized mortgages. Zeros make only a single payment, which is paid at maturity. Mortgages make levelized, periodic payments over the life of the instrument. The final payment of a mortgage is no larger than any other payment. Clearly, a 12-year zero and a 12-year mortgage have very different payment profiles. The differences are less pronounced for traditional coupon-yielding bonds. Still, measuring the length of a bond by the amount of time remaining before principal is to be repaid may be misleading. Bonds can have very different coupon rates even when their maturities and other characteristics are similar. The term to maturity does not fully reflect the timing of a debt security's total payment stream. The final payment on a debt security is only one of the promised payments. Most debt securities also make periodic coupon payments. Each of these coupon payments may be viewed as a partial maturity of the instrument. Each such payment is part of the entire promised cash flow of the security.

The greater the proportion of the return coming from the coupon, the more of the debt security's promised cash flows will be paid prior to its final maturity. Thus, a higher coupon is somewhat akin to a shorter maturity. The owner of such a security will receive a higher proportion of his or her promised return in the form of coupon interest prior to the return of principal at maturity.

Bonds with coupons close to market yields sell near par. Others, having coupon rates that are very low or very high compared with market rates, will be priced far from par. Computed yields to maturity will have somewhat different implications for each such issue.

On the one hand, a high coupon reduces vulnerability to adverse interest rate moves. At least the coupon payment of such a bond can be reinvested as received. On the other hand, high coupon payments cannot, in a period of falling yields, be reinvested at rates as high as the bond's initial yield. Thus, for equivalent maturities, a high-coupon bond is less exposed to adverse interest-fluctuations but has greater exposure to reinvestment risk than one with a lower coupon. At the opposite extreme, a zero-coupon instrument will exhibit the highest degree of price volatility (interest rate sensitivity) given a change in interest rates, assuming other variables are constant.

The concept of duration is designed to allow the investor to make an appropriate adjustment for different maturities and coupon rates. Duration is defined as the weighted average time (measured in years) to full recovery of principal and interest payments. The weight of each of the promised payments is based on its present value relative to the sum of the present values of the payment stream. That is, each weight equals the present value of that payment divided by the bond's market price. The total of the present values equals the bond's market price. In this way, duration captures the impact of differing payback rates. The formula for duration (D) is:

$$\frac{\sum_{t=1}^{n} \frac{C_t(t)}{(1+i)^t}}{\sum_{t=1}^{n} \frac{C_t}{(1+i)^t}}$$

where:

t   =   payment period (beginning with period one) of coupon or principal

C_t =   payment in period t

i   =   market yield

n   =   number of periods to maturity

Now consider the durations of two bonds maturing in five years. Bond A has a 14% coupon; bond B has a 4% coupon. Table 9.4 reports the results of computing durations of both bonds using a 14% discount rate.

Table 9.4
Duration Computation Example

			BOND A		
1	2	3	4	5	6
Year	Cash Flow	PV at 14%	PV of Flow	PV as Proportion of Price	1 x 5
1	140	.877	122.78	.12278	.12278
2	140	.769	107.66	.10766	.21532

3	140	.675	94.50	.09450	.28350
4	140	.592	82.88	.08280	.33152
5	1140	.519	<u>591.66</u>	<u>.99948</u>	<u>.95830</u>
Sum (Market Price of Bond)			999.48	.99948	3.91142
Duration = 3.91 years					

BOND B					
1	40	.877	35.08	.05348	.05348
2	40	.761	30.44	.04641	.09882
3	40	.675	27.00	.04116	.12348
4	40	.592	23.68	.03610	.13440
5	1040	.519	<u>539.76</u>	<u>.82285</u>	<u>4.11425</u>
Sum (Market Price of Bond)			655.96	1.00000	4.52443
Duration 4.52 years					

Thus, bond B's lower coupon corresponds to a duration that is about a half-year longer than that of bond A. For equivalent maturities, the lower the coupon, the longer is the duration. In fact, the duration for a zero coupon instrument is exactly equal to its time to maturity. The sensitivity of bond price movements to interest rate changes vary proportionately with duration. Thus, a bond's duration reflects its sensitivity to interest rate changes considerably more accurately than does the bond's time to maturity. Duration also provides a better measure of the wait to payoff than does time to maturity.

Other Factors Affecting Bond Prices and Yields: The characteristics already discussed (general interest rate levels, risk of default, maturity-duration, coupon effect, tax status) constitute the principal price/yield determinants of specific bonds. Somewhat less important characteristics include: marketability, seasoning, call protection, sinking fund provisions, me-first rules, usability, industrial classification, condition of collateral, and listing status.

The vast majority of bond trading takes place in high-volume markets with narrow spreads and deep supply and demand. Many lower-volume issues, however, trade in thin markets with spreads of five and even 10 points. A quote of 70 bid to 80 asked implies a 10 point, or 14%, spread. Trading such an issue may be extremely costly. Limit orders are only likely to be effective on bonds that are listed on an exchange. Other things being equal, the less marketable the issue, the higher will be the yield required to make the bond attractive to investors.

Seasoned issues are those that have become established in the marketplace. They have been traded for at least a few weeks beyond completion of the initial (offering) sale. As with new stock issues, new issues of bonds seem to be priced a bit below equivalent seasoned issues. Several authors, however, contend that the apparent yield differences can be explained by the existence of tax, call provision, and other issuer-specific factors.

Call protection varies appreciably from issue to issue. Some bonds are callable when sold. Many others may not be called for the first five or 10 years of their life. Callable issues that are reasonably likely to be redeemed (high yields) should be evaluated on their yield to earliest call, rather than on their yield to maturity. In marginal cases, both yield figures should be computed and compared. Call protection tends to lead to an increase in a bond's price, but the market may well overvalue call protection. Thus, callable issues may be superior investments.

The sinking fund's presence increases demand slightly and reduces the probability that refinancing the issuer's debts will burden the issuer. Thus, a sinking fund generally adds modestly to the value of a bond. Providing for a sinking fund in the bond indenture does not appear to reduce the debt issuer's ex-post cost, however. Me-first rules are designed to protect existing bondholders. Such rules prevent their claims from being weakened by the issuance of additional debt with a priority higher than or equivalent to theirs. Such rules significantly enhance the market values of the protected bonds.

Usable bonds can be employed at their par values in exercising the firm's outstanding warrants. If such bonds sell for less than par, using them at par is a cheaper way of exercising the warrants than using cash. If the stock price is near or below the point where exercising is attractive, the usability feature may add to the bond's value. The price impact of usability depends primarily on two factors: (1) the relative magnitude of the bond's straight-debt value versus its value in exercising the warrant and (2) the relative supply of usable bonds and warrants outstanding.

Boardman and McEnally, who exhaustively studied the factors that affect bond values, found that (1) industrial and transportation issues tend to command higher prices than otherwise-equivalent utility issues; (2) the status of collateral affects values especially when the issue would otherwise have a low rating; and (3) listing has little or no price impact. Table 9.5 summarizes the various factors affecting bond yields.

Table 9.5
Factors Affecting Bond Yields

General Credit Condition	Credit conditions affect all yields to one degree or another.
Default Risk	Riskier issues require higher promised yields.
Term Structure	Yields vary with maturity, reflecting expectations for future rates.
Duration	The average wait until payback is calculated using the duration formula: A measure of interest sensitivity.
Coupon Effect	Low-coupon issues (if issued near par) offer yields that are partially tax sheltered.
Seasoning	Newly issued bonds may sell at a slight discount to otherwise-equivalent established issues.
Marketability	Actively traded issues tend to be worth more than otherwise-equivalent issues that are less actively traded.
Call Protection	Protection from an early call tends to enhance a bond's value.
Sinking Fund Provisions	Sinking funds increase demand and reduce the risk of refinancing, thereby tending to enhance a bond's value.
Me-First Rules	Bonds protected from the diluting effect of additional firm borrowings are generally worth more than otherwise-equivalent unprotected issues.
Usability	Bonds usable at par to exercise warrants tend to be worth more than otherwise-equivalent issues.
Industrial Classification	Industrial and transportation issues tend to command higher prices than otherwise equivalent utility issues.
Collateral Status	Well-maintained collateral tends to enhance bond values relatively to less well-maintained collateral.
Listing	Exchange listing appears to have little or no impact on bond yields.

THE ELIMINATION OF TRADITIONAL COVENANTS

The junk bond era was characterized by an unprecedented rush to achieve maximum yield at all costs. This led to a significant increase in the absence of traditional covenants. An article in *The Business Lawyer* (McDaniel, Bondholders and Corporate Governance) 41 *Business Lawyer* 413 (1986) showed that at the zenith of the era in 1986, only 26% of the indentures of leading corporations had limitations on the borrower incurring other unsecured debts, 32% had limitations on paying dividends, and 84% had limitations incurred on secured debt (negative pledges). The absence of these provisions meant that the bonds, in most cases subordinated, were potentially subordinated to an unlimited amount of debt, causing the bonds to become worth less and less and lead to more and more critical default situations, hence, more bankruptcies. Clearly, the rationale behind most of these traditional provisions was to insure the collectibility of the bonds in question at some future date. Their elimination, in the interest of achieving higher yields, has helped exacerbate the predicted disaster in the junk bond area.

Assembling and Managing a Bond Portfolio: Diversified bond portfolios should be managed to meet their owner's needs. A half-dozen different bond issues are usually sufficient to achieve relatively effective diversification of a portfolio of bonds. Bonds should also be selected to produce the desired level of maturity/duration, default risk/quality rating, coupon/price appreciation, etc. Moreover, bonds are usually part of a larger overall or master portfolio that also includes stocks and perhaps some other types of assets. Thus, bonds should usually be viewed as providing liquidity, dependable income, and so on, in the larger context of the portfolio.

Bond Swaps: Portfolio managers frequently finance a bond purchase with the funds freed by liquidating another position. Such bond swaps may be designed to increase yield to maturity or current yield, to adjust duration or risk, or to establish a tax loss or gain.

The separate transactions involved with many swaps are not executed simultaneously. Thus, swap traders risk making one side of the swap (say the sell) only to encounter an adverse price move before the other side is accomplished. Moreover, transaction costs absorb some of what would otherwise be the expected benefits of the swap. Nonetheless, a variety of circumstances make swaps attractive. For example, a low-coupon, deep-discount issue might be sold and the proceeds used to purchase a higher-coupon issue. The sale would normally generate a tax loss. Presumably, the purchased issue is acquired in order to capture a higher yield. On the other hand, the swap would probably increase both the call risk and the reinvestment risk. In addition to increasing current income, swaps of this type also require a "pay-up," or the infusion of additional cash in order to purchase a par amount equal to that sold.

In another type of swap, an investor might sell one issue that had been held at a loss and then purchase another very similar issue. Such a pure tax swap establishes a tax loss while leaving the portfolio's basic character unchanged. In yet another type of swap, a bond originally purchased as a long-term issue may have moved much closer to maturity. Swapping it for a longer-term bond would restore the desired maturity and duration level and possibly enhance yield as well (if long rates are above short rates). Possible bond swaps are illustrated with the help of the quotes in Table 9.6.

Table 9.6
Selected Bond Quotations

			December 31, 1981			
Issuer (S&P)	Rating	Coupon	Maturity	Price	Current Yield	Yield to Maturity
AT&T	AAA	3 7/8	1990	69 1/2	5.6%	9.4%
AT&T	AAA	10 3/8	1990	98 7/8	10.5	10.6
AT&T	AAA	8.80	2005	79 5/8	11.1	11.3
GMAC	AA+	11 5/8	1990	101 3/4	11.4	11.3
GMAC	AA+	11 3/4	2000	97	12.1	12.2

			December 31, 1987			
AT&T	AA	3 7/8	1990	90 7/8	4.3%	8.0%
AT&T	AA	8.80	2005	91 1/2	9.6	9.8
GMAC	AA-	11 3/4	2000	104 1/2	11.3	11.1

			December 31, 1999			
AT&T	AA-	6	2009	90 1/8	6.66%	6.81%
AT&T	AA-	8 1/8	2022	101	8.04	8.04
GMAC	A	6 3/8	2008	93 3/8	6.83	7.03

			August 10, 2006			
AT&T	A	6	2009	100.96	5.94%	5.60
AT&T		8 1/8	called			
GMAC	BB	6 1/2	2008	94.29	6.89	9.34

Investors owning the AT&T 3 7/8s of 1990 at the end of 1981 could have greatly increased their current yield with a swap into the 10 3/8s of 1990 (10.5% versus 5.6%). The yield to maturity would also have risen (10.6% versus 9.4%). To be effective, a tax swap requires a switch to a different bond issuer. Thus, one holding the AT&T 3 7/8s or 10 3/8s of 1990 at year-end 1981 could have swapped them for the GM Acceptance 11 5/8s of 1990. The maturities are similar and the GMAC quality was only slightly below that of AT&T (AA versus AAA). Maturity swaps could have been made between either AT&T 1990 issues and the 8.80s of 2005 or between the GMAC 11 5/8s of 1990 and the GMAC 11 3/4s of 2000.

Six years later, new prices and yields were obtained for this group of bonds. The changes are interesting. First, two of the bonds are no longer listed. Unfortunately for those who owed them, they were called by the issuer and the outstanding borrowings refinanced at a lower interest rate. Second, the remaining three bonds have all been downgraded. The ratings of the AT&T issues were down to AA (year-end 1987), compared with AAA on the earlier date. The divestiture of AT&T's operating companies had increased the bonds' risks. Similarly, the GMAC bond was (year-end 1987) rated AA', unchanged from its AA' at the earlier date. General Motors' share of the auto market had slipped, as had its profitability. Fourth, notwithstanding the ratings downgrades, each of the bonds was priced higher on the later date. Market interest rates had declined.

Similar bond swaps are possible with the more recent bond quotes. For example, the investor could execute a maturity/yield swap between the AT&T 3 7/8s and the 8.80s. Tax swaps are possible between the AT&T and GMAC issues.

Other Aspects of Bond Portfolio Management: Managing a bond portfolio effectively can involve much more than the simple types of swaps mentioned above. The investor might, for example, speculate on a bond upgrade by buying an issue that the market views pessimistically. Margin borrowing may be used to magnify potential gains and/or to leverage a high yield. Some bonds may have higher promised long-term yields than the current cost of margin money. Whether such apparently attractive yield spreads should be exploited depends on both the likelihood that they will persist and the default risk of high-yielding issues. If market interest rates rise, the margin borrowing rate will increase and bond prices will decline.

Still more complicated maneuvers involve the use of interest futures and hedges between a company's bonds and its other securities. For example, a long bond position in a company with a high default risk might be hedged with a short position in the company's stock. If the company goes bankrupt, the stock could become almost worthless, while its bonds are likely to retain some value in a reorganization or liquidation. If the company avoids bankruptcy, the bonds will continue to pay their coupon and eventually repay their principal. The stock, in contrast, may not perform well unless the company prospers. Finally, portfolio managers can trade on the basis of their interest rate forecasts. If interest rates are expected to fall, portfolio maturities should be lengthened. An expected rise should cause the manager to shift toward near-cash securities. Such a strategy assumes that the manager can accurately forecast interest rate changes, however.

Transaction Costs for Bonds: As with stocks, investors in bonds need to be aware of the costs associated with trading such securities. The costs can vary enormously depending upon the nature of the trade. In addition to the basic price of the debt security, bond traders need to be aware of three charges: commissions, spreads, and accrued interest.

Compared with stocks, commissions on bond trades tend to be relatively low. A trade of 10 bonds or more will typically incur a commission of $5 per bond. A large trade or large trader is likely to qualify for a discount from this rate. Five dollars per bond amounts to 0.5% of a $1,000 face value. Retail commissions on stock trades, in contrast, average closer to 3%. Thus, (compared with stocks) trading bonds that sell near to their par values will normally incur rather modest commissions.

Two circumstances in which the commissions may be of concern are very small trades and bonds that sell for a small fraction of their par value. Most brokers have a minimum commission charge that overrides their per bond formula. Thus, an investor who purchases three bonds may be charged a $50 commission because $50 is the brokerage firm's minimum. Similarly, a trade involving deep-discount or zero-coupon bonds may incur a high commission relative to the dollar value of the trade. That is, $5 per bond is a much higher percentage of the money involved for a bond trading at 20 (2.50%) than one trading at 95 (0.53%).

Bid-ask spreads are another important consideration in bond trading. Spreads on actively traded bonds tend to be quite narrow. For example, the spreads on most governments are measured in 32nds. . A spread of 3/32 on a $1,000 bond amounts to $0.9375, which is less than 0.1% of the price. On the other hand, less actively traded issues may have much wider spreads. For example, a small inactively traded corporate bond might be quoted 80-85. A five-point spread on a bond with a bid of 80 corresponds to a spread of 6.25% of the bid price.

The spreads can be even wider. An inactively traded deep-discount bond might be quoted 30-40. Such a quote corresponds to a spread of 33% of the bid.

The final matter for bond traders to consider is the accrued interest assessed of the buyer. Between coupon payments dates, bonds may be seen as building up an accrual for the forthcoming interest payment. A bond with an 8% coupon will make a semiannual payment of 4% of its par ($40 on a standard $1,000 face value bond). Midway between coupon payments the bond will have accrued half of the coupon ($20). According to standard trading practice, a buyer of the bond at that point would pay the seller the price of the bond plus the amount of accrued interest. When the next coupon is paid, the new owner will receive the entire payment and thereby recoup the accrued amount advanced to the seller. Not all bonds are traded this way, but most are. The remainder are traded flat, which means no allowance is made for accrued interest. Bonds are likely to trade flat only if they have defaulted on a prior coupon payment, if the amount of the interest payment is uncertain (income bonds and floating rate notes, for example) or if the issuer has announced that it does not expect to make the scheduled payment. Two potential concerns with the accrued interest component of a bond's cost should be borne in mind. First, the buyer earns no interest on the amount of the accrued interest advance. The seller receives his or her share of the coupon payment at settlement, while the buyer is not reimbursed until the next coupon is received. Thus, the accrued interest is analogous to an interest-free loan from the buyer to the seller. Normally, the amounts advanced are relatively small so this concern is rarely a major consideration. Moreover, the market price paid for the bond may take the impact of accrued interest into account. The buyer should, however, realize that the cost of the purchase will include this allowance for accrued interest. The trader should be sure of having enough money to cover the full amount due at settlement.

The second concern with the accrued interest advance is potentially more serious. Bonds that default on their interest obligations during a given interest payment period leave the new buyer without any coupon payment and with no recourse to reclaim the accrued interest paid to the seller. Accrued interest on bonds is not returned in the event of a default. Once the bond defaults on a payment, it will begin to trade flat, so accrued interest will no longer be collected from the buyer. During the payment period when the bond defaults, however, the interest will have been accrued and then lost to an investor who bought at that time. The owner will have a claim for interest against the issuer, but that claim goes with the owner of the bond as it continues to trade. Moreover, how much is a claim for back interest worth on a defaulted bond? Normally, bonds default on their interest payment by failing to make the payment and announcing that they are unable to do so. Thus the default action itself frequently occurs at the end of the coupon payment period. Accordingly, a full coupon payment of accrued interest is potentially lost. Because a default on coupon payment generally causes the bond price to fall, the newer buyer of a quickly defaulting bond typically suffers two losses: the bond price decline and the lost accrued interest.

SUMMARY AND CONCLUSIONS

A variety of factors influence bond yields. General market forces affect both the level and term structure of rates. For a given maturity class and market environment, rates differ primarily with default risk. Informal workouts may reduce the impact of technical defaults and near-defaults, while Chapter 11 proceedings are less costly than the more formal Chapter 7 process. Rating agencies assess the default risks of bonds and their issuers' financial strengths.

Various hypotheses attempt to explain the term structure of interest rates. Segmented markets ascribe rates to supply and demand for each maturity class. Liquidity preference asserts that borrowers generally prefer the long end, while lenders prefer the short. The unbiased expectations hypothesis holds that the term structure reflects a contiguous set of short-term interest rate expectations. Investors may use the term structure relationship to identify securities that are potentially mispriced. Moreover, some investors may ride a downward sloping yield curve that is expected to remain approximately stable.

Duration, the weighted average term of the payment stream, is a more accurate measure of repayment timing than is length to maturity. Investors and portfolio managers may utilize the duration concept in a strategy designed to immunize their portfolios from reinvestment risk. Specifically, they may minimize the potentially adverse impacts of being unable to reinvest coupons at attractive rates by assembling a portfolio with durations equal to their planning horizons.

Prices tend to be higher for more marketable, seasoned issues with sinking funds, me-first rules, and call protection. Usable bonds may also command higher prices. Industrial classification, condition of collateral, and listing status may have some minor price impacts.

INVESTMENT INFORMATION SOURCES

Effective investment analysis requires access to and evaluation of significant amounts of relevant information. No one knows more about a particular company than the company itself, and a great deal of what it knows must be disclosed.

Over the last two decades, first personal computers and then the Internet have radically transformed how such information can be retrieved, stored and studied. Most forms that a company files with the SEC, as well as news releases it issues, are readily available over the Internet.

These forms and news releases are generally available directly from the company, on its Web site or by calling its investor relations office. The filings (though not the news releases) are also available from the SEC's EDGAR system (http://www.sec.gov/edgar.shtml), at no charge (EDGAR is an acronym for electronic data gathering and retrieval). Various online subscription-only services, such as 10K Wizard (www.10kwizard.com) or Edgar Online Pro (www.edgarpro.com), offer the same documents in a somewhat easier-to-find and easier-to-use format, and also allow you to perform text searches, receive alerts when particular companies or forms are filed and build your own databases. These services typically start at about $200 a year and range well upward.

Brokerage firms, other financial institutions and a great many financial advice and investing sites allow you to register, build a portfolio, track its changes and receive automatic notification of every document a company files with the SEC and every news release it issues. Many of these sites and services are offered at no charge; others, which offer sophisticated investors extremely advanced tools for comparing and analyze investments, have monthly or yearly charges.

If you seek help, you will find that many reference librarians at public libraries and at university libraries you might have access to are trained in Web searching and retrieving documents from EDGAR.

Among the company documents that you'll want to read and study are these:

Table 9.7
Principal Company-Issued Reports and the Nature of Their Contents

Annual Report	Financial statements, letter from the CEO, auditor's report, management analysis
10K	Annual report containing detailed financial data, required by the SEC and the listing exchange, if any of the firm's securities are listed
10Q	Quarterly report containing detailed financial data, required by the SEC and the listing exchange, if any of the firm's securities are listed
Prospectus	All relevant facts relating to a proposed action
Proxy Statement	All relevant information relating to any item requiring a shareholder vote
8K	Information on major developments
	News Releases Descriptive material on newsworthy events

The company files an annual report with the SEC, known as the **10K**, and a report each quarter, the **10Q**, that contain basic financial statements and a variety of additional descriptive information. Among the sections that should be most closely reviewed at Management's Discussion and Analysis, Litigation and Related Party Transactions, as well as the audit footnotes. Keep in mind that the 10K is audited, the 10Qs are not.

Prospectuses are required whenever a company makes any major financial move requiring shareholder approval or notification. For example, a prospectus should be produced and made available if the firm publicly sells or repurchases a nontrivial amount of its securities, proposes a significant acquisition or divestiture, or begins a dividend reinvestment plan. The preparers of the prospectus (the company's lawyers, accountants, and management) are legally obligated to reveal all relevant and material information regarding the proposal. Most prospectuses are, therefore, quite carefully written and detailed. Including information that is not required is safer for the preparer than excluding information that a court might later determine should have been revealed.

The Proxy Statement also contains interesting information about what shareholders will be asked to vote on at regularly scheduled or specially called shareholder meetings. These meetings provide the vehicle for electing directors, approving auditors, and acting on a number of other matters requiring stockholder approval, such as increasing the authorized number of shares or changing the company's legal form. Accordingly, a proxy (ballot) accompanied by relevant information on the issues (proxy statement) must be distributed to the shareholders. Proxy statements typically contain names and holdings of the company's principal shareholders (over 5% of outstanding shares), biographical information and company holdings of nominees to the board of directors, information on committees of the board, and executive and director compensation, as well as information relating to any issue to be voted on. As with a prospectus, the preparers of a proxy statement are liable for any damages resulting from incomplete disclosure.

Whenever some significant new development occurs that is not reflected in the earlier filings of the company, it may file an **8K** report on the matter. For example, a firm that wins or loses a major court suit or buys or sells a substantial property is likely to file an 8K to report on the matter.

News releases often report additional bits of company information. Unlike the official filings, no stringent standards or set forms apply to news releases. Until such information, if material, is made public, knowledgeable insiders are legally barred from trading the stock (except under very restricted circumstances such as trades with other insiders).

Owners of 5% or more of the stock of a public company are required to file a **13D** report with the SEC, listing exchange, and the company itself. This form must be filed within 10 days of crossing the 5% threshold for any class of equity or convertible debt security. Rights to acquire stock through options, warrants or convertibles count toward reaching the 5% level. The document must reveal the extent of the holdings, purpose (investment, takeover, etc.), source of their funds, and any relevant agreements (such as those with other investors). The 13D must be amended whenever a material change requires an update of the prior filing. One such material change would be a change of ownership by the filer of 1% or more. Because the holdings and intentions of large shareholders often affect share values, 13D filings are another useful information source.

In addition to all these primary documents, an enormous amount of financial news, commentary and advice is available on cable television, radio, local and network television programs, magazines and newspapers. Many of these entities have their own Web sites, as well. In many ways, the greatest challenge is not finding information but sorting through all that is available.

GLOSSARY

abnormal rate of return: The amount by which an asset's return departs from its expected rate of return, where that expected return is based on the market's rate of return and the security's relationship to the market.

absolute priority of claims principle: The general rule in bankruptcy law that requires each class of liability claims to be repaid in full before the next highest priority category can receive even a partial payment.

accelerated depreciation: The writing off the recorded balance sheet values of assets at a more rapid rate than proportional to their pro rata life expectancy. See *straight line depreciation*.

acceptance: See *banker's acceptance*.

accrued interest: The amount of the pro rata interest obligation on a bond or other debt instrument that has accumulated since the last (typically semi-annual) payment date. Most bonds trade at a price that reflects their net market price plus accrued interest. Defaulted and certain other bonds, however, trade "flat." See *flat*.

acid test ratio: Cash and accounts receivable divided by current liabilities; used as an index of short-term liquidity. Also called the quick ratio.

actuarial tables: Data tables containing statistics on the probabilities of death for members of a particular age groups; based on past experience, with separate tables for men and women and certain hazardous occupations. An actuarial table might indicate that at age 25 a male would have 1 chance in 750 of dying within the next year and is expected to live 50 more years (to age 75). A 65-year-old male's chance of dying in the next year might be reported as 1 in 50 and his future life expectancy as 16 years (to age 81).

adequate protection: Not specifically defined in the Bankruptcy Code. Generally refers to the concept of protecting a creditor's interest in property owned by the debtor. Several non-exclusive methods for providing adequate protection for creditors are specified including periodic cash payments to a lien creditor equal to a decrease in the value of the creditor's interest in the collateral. Another example would be an additional lien or substitute lien on other property to protect against a decline in value. An additional concept would be to provide a secured creditor with the "indubitable equivalent" of its bargain with the debtor.

adjusted gross income (AGI): An interim figure that is reached on the way to computing a taxpayer's tax liability; consists of total income less allowed adjustments, which include such items as moving expenses, IRA and Keogh contributions, alimony payments and employee business expenses (above a defined threshold). Taxable income is obtained by subtracting deductions and the allowance for exemptions from adjusted gross income. See taxable income.

administrative priority: A claim incurred after a company has filed for bankruptcy. The claim must be paid before prepetition unsecured claims holders receive a distribution.

ADR (American depository receipt): A U.S.-traded security representing ownership of stock in a foreign corporation.

advisor's sentiment index: A technical market indicator based on a composite of investment advisors' forecasts; index users believe that bullish (bearish) advisors sentiment forecasts a market decline (rise).

affiliate: An entity that directly or indirectly owns control or holds power to vote 20% or more of the debtor or an entity that operates the business or substantially all of the property of the debtor under a lease agreement.

after-tax cash flow: The difference in the actual cash income and outgo for an investment project after taking account of (subtracting) the tax impact.

after-tax return: The rate of return an investor receives on an investment after adjusting for its associated tax liability. Thus, for example, a fully taxable 10% return corresponds to a 7.5% after-tax return for one in the 25% marginal tax bracket.

agency security: A debt security issued by a U.S. federal government agency such as GNMA. Such securities may or may not be backed by the full faith and credit of the U.S. treasury.

agent: A person who acts on behalf of one or more of the principals involved. The agent may, for example, be an investment banker or an attorney representing the debtor or one of its creditors.

air rights: The right to build and occupy a structure over someone else's property as, for example, the right to build an office complex above a downtown railroad switching yard.

all-or-nothing order: An order to purchase securities that must either be immediately executed in its entirety or if that is not possible, not at all.

allowed claim: A claim that has been both (1) timely filed (see *bar date*) and (2) agreed to in amount by the debtor and the creditor. If such a claim has not been agreed to, it is referred to as "disputed." See *disputed claim*.

alpha: The intercept term in the market model; provides an estimate of a security's return for market return of zero. Also used as a performance measure for portfolio managers.

alternative minimum tax (AMT): A special tax liability computation that may be applicable to those with large amounts of otherwise sheltered income (preferences) such as accelerated depreciation deductions; applies when the AMT tax liability computed (after disallowing these preferences) exceeds the liability when the tax is computed the normal way.

amalgamation: A merger-like transaction combining more than two firms into a single company.

American Association of Individual Investors (AAII): Organization designed to help and promote the interests of small investors.

American option: An option contract (put or call) that can be exercised at any time over its life up until it expires. See *European option*.

American Stock Exchange Index: A value-weighted index of AMEX stocks.

Americus Trust certificate: A type of security that divides the ownership of certain stocks into two categories of instruments: the primes receive dividends and are entitled to a liquidation value equal to the price of the stock at termination or a predetermined value, whichever is lower; the scores are entitled to the remaining termination values. (if any)

AMEX (American Stock Exchange): The second largest (in terms of primary security listings) U.S. stock exchange (after NYSE); occasionally abbreviated as ASE; listed firms tend to be of medium size compared with the larger NYSE issues and the typically smaller OTC issues. AMEX lists a disproportionate number of energy stocks.

amortization: The process of periodically writing down (for accounting purposes) an asset's or liability's stated book value, particularly a paper asset or liability.

annual percentage rate (APR): The yield to maturity on a fixed income investment or the interest rate charged on a loan; computed using a compounding factor reflecting the balance still due.

annual report: A yearly report to shareholders containing financial statements (balance sheet, income statement, changes in financial position statement, and funds statement), auditor's statement, president's letter, and various other information about the firm.

annuitant: One who holds an annuity. See *annuity*.

annuity: An investment-like asset that provides a payment stream to its owner. The annuity usually promises to pay a fixed amount periodically for a predetermined period, although some pay a sum for an individual's lifetime (life annuity); certain annuities' values are variable thereby depending upon the issuer's investment experience. Most annuities are sold by insurance companies.

anomalies: Security price relationships that appear to be inconsistent with the efficient market hypothesis. Examples include the January effect, size effect, Value Line enigma, etc.

antidilution clause: A provision in a convertible bond or other security's indenture restricting the issuance of new shares.

anxious trader effects: Short-run price distortions caused by sales or purchases of impatient large traders.

appreciation: Increases in the value of an asset over time.

appreciation mortgage: A mortgage in which the lender is assigned the rights to a percentage of any price appreciation that is realized when the property is sold. In exchange for giving up part of this profit potential, the borrower usually is charged a more attractive interest rate (lower) than that charged on a standard loan.

arbitrage (pure): Simultaneously buying in one market and selling equivalent assets in another for a certain but usually modest profit. See also *risk arbitrage*.

arbitrage pricing theory (APT): A competitor to the capital asset pricing model that introduces more than one index in place of (or in addition to) CAPM's market index. See *CAPM*.

ARM (adjustable rate mortgage): A type of mortgage in which the interest rate charged by the mortgage holder is periodically adjusted to reflect changes in market interest rates.

arrearage: An overdue payment, as in passed preferred dividends; if the dividends on the senior security are cumulative, arrearage must be made up before common dividends are allowed to be resumed.

arithmetic mean return: The simple average return found by dividing the sum of the separate per period returns by the number of periods over which they were earned. See *geometric mean return*.

ask: The lowest price at which a security is currently offered for sale; may emanate from a specialist (exchange), market maker (OTC), or unexercised limit order.

asset: Any item of value; often income producing; appears on the left side of the balance sheet.

asset allocation: A compromise or more balanced approach to market timing (as compared to pure market timing). The asset allocator divides his or her portfolio among a number of categories such as stocks, bonds, and cash. The percentage of the portfolio invested in each of these categories is varied depending upon whether the asset allocator's outlook on that asset class is positive or negative.

asset class: Securities that have similar characteristics. Examples include stocks, bonds, options, futures, cash etc.

asset divestiture: Disposition of an asset by a company. Frequently companies will divest an asset that is not performing well, not vital to the company's core business, worth more either to a potential buyer or as a separate entity than as part of the company, or in order to raise cash to fund continuing operations.

asset play: A firm whose underlying net assets are worth substantially more (after deducting the firm's liabilities) than the market value of its stock.

assets under management (AUM): The total market value of the assets managed by an investment manager.

at-the-close order: An order that must be executed at or near the time of that day's close.

at-the-money: an option for which the exercise price and the market price of the underlying asset are identical.

at-the-opening order: An order that must be executed at that day's market opening.

auditor's statement: A letter from the auditor to the company and its shareholders in which the accounting firm certifies the propriety of the methods (GAAP) used to produce the firm's financial statements. See *GAAP*.

automatic stay: When a company files for bankruptcy protection, the code automatically provides a stay which prevents secured creditors from seeking to foreclose on the debtor's assets or otherwise enforce their liens. Such a stay is integral to the debtor's rehabilitation process. It may only be lifted through a judicial process, after the creditor has shown it would otherwise suffer damage.

average tax rate: A taxpayer's total tax liability divided by his or her total income.

avoidance: The debtor in a bankruptcy proceeding has the ability to set aside, or "avoid", certain transactions. If for example a transaction of questionable merit involving insiders had occurred just prior to the company's filing for bankruptcy, the court might avoid (reverse) the transaction, and force rescission.

backwardated: A set of futures market prices in which the current contract price is less than the current spot price for the underlying asset. Thus the cost of carry is negative. See *cost of carry*.

backtesting: Simulating a proposed investment strategy on historical data in order to determine if it would have been profitable to employ in the past. Successful backtesting does not necessarily prove that the tested rule will work (be profitable) in the future; the past experience may not reflect the future market environment.

balanced fund: A mutual fund that holds both stocks and bonds in its portfolio; may own both common and preferred shares as well as bonds.

balance of payments: The difference between a country's international payments and its international receipts.

balance of trade: The difference between a country's expenditures on imports and its revenues from exports.

balance sheet: A financial statement providing an instant in time picture of a firm's or individual's financial position; lists assets, liabilities, and net worth as of the date of the statement.

balloon payment: A final large principal payment on a debt instrument whose interim payments either did not amortize or only incompletely amortized the initial principal.

banker's acceptance: A money market instrument which usually arises from international trade; made highly secure by a bank's guarantee or acceptance. Also called acceptance.

Bankruptcy Code: The body of laws (as modified by court interpretations) that governs bankruptcy proceeding for businesses, individuals and government entities. The relevant sections for most corporations, are chapter 11 (governing reorganizations) and chapter 7 (governing liquidations).

bankruptcy proceeding: A legal process under Title 11 of the United States Code for dealing formally with an entity seeking protection from creditors; may result in a liquidation (chapter 7) or reorganization (chapter 11).

bankruptcy remote vehicle: Secure creditors are frequently unable to collect on amounts due from a bankrupt debtor. See *automatic stay*. In response, attorneys and investment bankers have devised structures that seek to get around the bankruptcy laws. For example a company could sell receivables to a newly formed subsidiary. This subsidiary could then borrow money secured by the receivables. The proceeds could be upstreamed to the parent. If the parent seeks bankruptcy protection at a later date, the secured creditors lending to the newly formed subsidiary would expect that their legal rights to the receivables would be unaffected by the parent's bankruptcy – hence "bankruptcy remote".

bankruptcy trustee: generally, a representative of the estate. The filing of a bankruptcy petition, leads to the creation of an estate consisting of all of the non exempt property of the debtor as of the time of the bankruptcy filing. This estate is a separate legal entity and the Trustee is the representative of this entity.

bar chart: In technical analysis, a type of graph that contains plots of the price over time; typically contains data on the high, low and closing prices as well as the volume of trading.

bar date: To assert a claim in a bankruptcy, creditors must file a proof of claim before a deadline set by the court – the "bar date". Claims asserted after the bar date are automatically disqualified (unless allowed by the court as late claims).

Barron's: A major weekly investment periodical published by Dow Jones Inc.

Barron's Confidence Index: A technical market indicator series based on the yield differential between high-grade and average-grade corporate bonds, with a small differential signifying confidence in the future and a large differential signaling a lack of confidence.

basis (commodity): The difference between the spot price and the futures price of the asset underlying a futures contract.

basis (taxable): The acquisition cost of an asset as adjusted for any capital distributions, depreciation, amortization, etc. The taxable gain equals the difference between the basis and the sale proceeds.

basis point: A unit of measurement equal to one-hundredth of one percentage point; primarily used with interest rates.

basis risk: The risk that the basis of a commodity contract will move adversely.

bear: One who expects a declining market.

bearer bond: An unregistered bond whose ownership is determined by possession of the bond certificate

bear market: A declining market.

bear raid: An attempt (often by a group of short sellers) to drive prices down by selling short.

before-tax return: The gross return on an investment prior to any adjustment being made for the impact of income taxes.

behavioral finance: The analysis of various psychological traits of investors or managers of businesses and how these traits affect how they act.

benchmark error: An error that results from using an inappropriate or incorrect benchmark to compare and assess portfolio returns.

benchmark portfolio: A comparison standard of risk and assets referenced in the policy statement and similar to the investor's risk preference and investment needs; can be used to evaluate the investment performance of the portfolio manager.

benefactor: A person named to receive property or other resources as in a will or insurance policy.

Bernhard, (Arnold) and Company: The firm that owns over 80% of the stock of the investment periodical Value Line. See *Value Line*.

best interest of creditors test: Bankruptcy code rule which requires that any departure from absolute priority be such that all creditors none the less receive a distribution that is worth at least as much as they would have received in a liquidation.

beta: A parameter that relates stock performance to market performance; for a z% change in the market, a stock's price will tend to change by (beta) z%.

bid: The highest currently unexercised offer to buy a security; may emanate from a specialist (exchange), market maker (OTC), or limit order. See *ask*.

Big Board: A popular term for the New York Stock Exchange, the largest U.S. stock exchange.

bills: Government debt securities issued on a discount basis by the U.S. Treasury for periods of less than one year.

Billy Martin indicator: A whimsical technical market indicator which hypothesized that any time the New York Yankees name Billy Martin to be their manager, the stock market would decline. Inoperative since the death of Mr. Martin.

binomial option pricing model: An option valuation equation based on the assumption that the price of the underlying asset changes through a series of discrete upward or downward movements.

black knight: A potential acquirer who is opposed by existing management and to which management would prefer to find an alternative (i.e., a white knight).

Black/Scholes formula: An option valuation formula based on the assumption that a riskless hedge between an option and its underlying stock should yield the riskless return; thus an option's value is a function of the stock price, striking price, stock return volatility, riskless interest rate, and length to expiration.

blind pool offerings: Bonds issued, the proceeds of which are to be used for some as-yet-to-be-stated purpose.

block trade: A stock trade involving 10,000 or more shares; the transaction is usually handled by a block trader.

block trader: One who, for a fee, assembles the passive side of a block trade in order to facilitate the transaction for the active side.

Bloody Monday: October 19, 1987, when the stock market experienced its worst one-day decline in its history; the Dow Jones Industrial Average dropped by 508 points, which corresponded to a 23% decline.

blue chip stock: Shares of a large, mature company with a steady record of profits and dividends and a high probability of continued healthy earnings.

blue sky laws: State laws designed to protect investors from securities frauds.

Blume adjustment: A method for adjusting estimated betas toward unity in an effort to improve their general accuracy and reliability.

boiler room operations: High-pressure selling programs often associated with investment scams such as Ponzi schemes; characterized by aggressive sales forces utilizing banks of telephones and cold callers in order to extract "investments" from unsophisticated individuals for risky and often worthless ventures. See *Ponzi scheme*.

bond: A debt obligation (usually long term) in which the borrower promises to pay a coupon rate which is almost always fixed (not variable) until the issue matures, at which time the principal is to be repaid; sometimes secured by a mortgage on a specific property, plant, or piece of equipment.   See also *collateral trust bond, debenture, equipment trust certificate, variable rate note, zero coupon bond.*

bond rating: An estimated index of the bond's investment quality and default risk. See *Fitch, Moody's, Standard & Poor.*

bond swap: A procedure utilized in the managing of a bond portfolio that involves selling some bonds and using the proceeds to buy others; may be designed to achieve benefits in the form of taxes, yields, maturity structure, or trading profits.

book value (of common shares):   The total accounting value of the assets of an enterprise minus its liabilities, minority interests, and the par value of any preferred stock, divided by the number of outstanding common shares.

borrower life insurance: An insurance policy on the borrower's life having coverage equal to the outstanding loan principal and naming the lender as the beneficiary.

Boston Consulting Group (BCG):   A strategic planning consulting firm famous for its growth-share matrix (BCG matrix) and learning curve concepts.

bottom up approach: An approach to fundamental analysis that begins with the individual investments (e.g. the firm and its stock) and then examines the relevant environment (economy).

box spread: A type of option position in which the investor assembles a vertical spread with calls and a similar but offsetting vertical spread with puts.

Brady Commission: One of a number of commissions that studied the causes for the stock market crash of October 19, 1987; set up by the U.S. Congress and named after Nicholas Brady, former New Jersey senator.

breakeven: The period of time required for an investor to recoup the amount of the conversion premium from the coupon income on a convertible instrument.

breakup fee: a penalty payment that one side to a negotiated merger agreement must pay to the other side in order voluntarily to exit from the deal.

breakup value: The sum of the values of a company's individual assets, if sold separately.

broker: An employee of a financial intermediary who acts as an agent in the buying and selling of securities (or other types of assets). A broker, unlike a dealer, never owns the securities that he or she trades for his or her customers.

brokerage firm: A firm that offers various services such as access to the securities markets, account management, margin loans, investment advice, and underwriting.

broker call-loan rate: The interest rate charged by banks to brokers for the loans that brokerage firms utilize in order to fund their margin loans to their own customers.

bull: One who expects a rising (usually stock) market.

bullion: Gold, silver, or other precious metals in the form of bars, plates, or certain coins minted to contain a specific unit of weight (bullion coins).

bull market: A rising market.

burn rate: The rate at which a firm with negative cash flow is using up its available cash.

business cycle: The pattern of fluctuations in the level of economic activity.

Business Week: A popular business periodical published weekly by McGraw-Hill Inc.

business risk: The variability of operating income arising from the characteristics of the firm's industry. Sources include sales variability and operating leverage.

butterfly spread: A type of option spread in which two call contracts are sold at one striking price and one call contract each is purchased at striking prices above and below the striking price for the contracts that were sold; or a similar configurations with puts.

buying power: The dollar value of additional marginable securities that can be purchased with the current equity in the customer's account.

buy-and-hold strategy: A portfolio management strategy in which securities are bought and held until maturity if bonds, or held for a lengthy period of time, if stock or other asset.

call: An option contract to buy stock or some other asset at a pre-specified price over a pre-specified time period. The standard contract size for a call is 100 shares.

callable: The characteristic of certain securities which allows the issuer to redeem them prior to maturity. See *call right*.

call market: A market for individual stocks in which trading only takes place at specific times. All of the available offers to buy and sell are assembled. The market administrators can then specify a single price designed to clear the market at that time.

call premium: The amount in addition to a bond's face value that the issuer must pay to bondholders in order to retire a callable bond prior to its stated maturity.

call-loan rate: See *broker call-loan rate*.

call price: The price at which a bond, preferred stock, warrant, or other security may be redeemed by the issuer prior to its maturity; the call price usually starts out at a significant premium over the face value; the premium then declines as the instrument approaches its stated maturity. Also called the redemption price.

call protection: An indenture provision preventing a security (usually a bond or preferred stock) from being redeemed earlier than a certain time period after its issue; for example, a 20-year bond might not be callable for the first five years.

call right: A feature in the indenture of a bond or preferred stock. An option that allows the issuing company to repurchase the securities at a set price over a pre-specified period (prior to maturity).

call risk: The danger to the holder of a callable bond or preferred stock that the security will be redeemed early (called) by the issuer.

cap agreement: A contract that on each pre-specified settlement date pays the holder the greater of zero or the difference between the reference (interest) rate and the cap rate.

capacity effect: The tendency of inflationary pressures to accelerate when the economy approaches the full employment level.

capital asset: Virtually any asset held as an investment. To qualify as a capital asset (and thus be subject to the advantages, if any, of long-term capital gains treatment) an asset must be held as an investment rather than in inventory as an item of trade.

Capital Asset Pricing Model (CAPM): A theoretical relationship that is designed to explain returns as a function of the risk-free rate, market risk and the return on the market portfolio.

capital distribution: A dividend paid out of the firm's capital rather than from its earnings. Such distributions are not taxable when received but do have the effect of reducing the investment's basis.

capital gains (losses): The difference between the basis of an investment asset and its sales price.

capitalizing of expenses: Placing on the business' balance sheet as assets sums expended for current business expenses. Such "asset" values can then be written off over time rather than expensed all at once, thereby spreading out their cost impact for accounting purposes.

capital market line: The theoretical relation between an efficiently diversified portfolio's expected return and risk derived from the capital asset pricing model.

capital preservation: An investment objective in which the investor seeks to limit the risk of loss even at the sacrifice of some upside potential.

capital structure: The composition of the ways in which a firm has obtained the capital needed for its business activities (short term debt, long term debt, common equity and preferred equity).

carry: The cost of holding and maintaining a physical commodity until it becomes deliverable under the terms of a futures contract; the primary components of the carry are storage and financing costs. Also called cost of carry.

cash cow: A company subsidiary or division of a company that, in the normal course of its operations, throws off a substantial cash surplus.

cash flow: Reported profits plus the sum of the non-cash expenses of depreciation, depletion, and amortization.

cash flow bond: A debt instrument whose coupon payments rise if the reorganized company produces better earnings.

cash management account: An individual financial account that combines checking, credit card, money fund, and margin accounts. Funds and liabilities are swept from account to account in order to maximize returns and minimize interest charges on transaction balances.

cash market: A market in which physical commodities (spot) are bought and sold for immediate (as opposed to future) delivery.

cash surrender value: The accumulated savings element of a life insurance policy. Under the terms of the policy, this cash value can be recovered by canceling the policy. The policy's cash value can also be borrowed against at an interest rate specified in the policy's contract.

cause of action: A fact pattern that gives rise to the owner of the cause of a c - tion the right to file a law suite.

CBOE (Chicago Board Options Exchange): The largest of the option exchanges; originator and promoter of organized options trading.

CBT (Chicago Board of Trade): The largest of the commodity exchanges; lists futures contracts on a variety of physicals including wheat, corn, oats, soybeans, plywood, silver, stock indexes, GNMA, and long-term bonds.

CD (certificate of deposit): Special redeemable debt obligation issued by a bank or other depository institution.

CEA (Commodity Exchange Authority): A former government agency that once had regulatory authority over agricultural futures markets; now regulated by the CFTC.

Central Certificate Service: An organization that allows clearing firms to effect security deliveries with computerized bookkeeping entries.

central market: A Congressionally mandated concept for a complete linkup of the various markets in which securities are traded; the development was underway but incomplete as of 2005.

central unemployment rate: The unemployment rate for males in the 25 to 45 age group or the unemployment rate for some similar high-employment component of the labor force.

CFTC (Commodity Futures Trading Commission): The federal agency that regulates the futures markets.

changes in financial position statement: An accounting statement that contains reports on a firm's cash inflows and outflows. Formerly called source and application of funds statement.

Chapter 7 bankruptcy: Provides for a liquidation of a debtor under the Bankruptcy Code.

Chapter 11 reorganization: Contemplates a rehabilitation and restructuring of a debtor under the Bankruptcy Code.

Chapter 22: A term for companies that return to the bankruptcy court once they fail after being reorganized the first time.

characteristic line: The relationship between a security's expected return and the market return; defined by the security's á (intercept) and â (slope parameter).

chart reading: A method of attempting to forecast stock price changes using charts of past price and volume data.

Chicago Mercantile Exchange (the Merc): The second largest of the U.S. commodity exchanges; lists futures contracts on a variety of physicals including cattle, hogs, pork bellies, fresh broilers, lumber, stock indexes, currencies, and debt securities.

chicken (strategy): A negotiation tactic where one negotiator takes and aggressive and potentially self destructive position and waits for the other side to blink first.

churning: Overactive trading of customer accounts designed to generate commissions for the manager/broker without necessarily benefiting the customer.

circuit breakers: A procedure calling for the suspending of trading when a market move reaches a prescribed threshold; for example, stock trading might be halted for 30 minutes whenever the DJIA moved 150 points during a single day.

claim: A right to seek payment.

classified common stock: Different categories of common stock, some of which may be nonvoting and others nondividend receiving.

clearing house: An organization that keeps track of and guarantees fulfillment of futures contracts or options contracts.

Clifford Trust: A device for shifting tax liability on income, usually from parent to dependent child; trusts set up since the Tax Reform Act of 1986 do not achieve the desired tax shifting goal.

CLOB (consolidated limit order book): A composite book of limit orders that could be executed in any market where a security is traded; a feature of the proposed central market. See *central market*.

closed-end fund: A type of investment company that is organized as a public corporation with its stock traded in the same markets as other stocks; its market price may vary appreciably from the fund's net asset value.

closing costs: Costs associated with obtaining a real estate loan and completing the purchase; may include the costs of a title search, points, transfer taxes, and various other fees.

Coffee, Sugar and Cocoa Exchange: A commodity exchange located in New York City that lists futures contracts for coffee, sugar, and cocoa.

coincident indicators: A set of economic variables whose values tend to reach peaks and troughs at about the same time as the aggregate economy.

cold call: An unsolicited call (by phone or in person) by someone who is trying to sell something to a targeted individual who may very well have no interest in even hearing the seller's pitch.

collateral: Asset pledged by the borrower to assure repayment of debt to the lender; the lender may take ownership of the collateral (foreclose) if the loan is not repaid as promised.

collateral trust bond: A secured bond; for example, an equipment trust certificate secured by such collateral as railroad rolling stock or airplanes.

collar merger offer: A takeover offer in which the consideration is in the form of stock in a ratio to be determined by the average price of the acquiesces shares shortly before the transaction closes.

Collateralized Mortgage Obligation (CMO): A debt security based on a pool of mortgages that provides a relatively stable stream of payments for a relatively predictable term.

combination security: An asset combining characteristics of more than one type of security; includes convertible bonds, convertible preferred stocks, hybrid convertibles, equity notes, commodity-backed bonds, and stock-indexed bonds.

commercial paper: Short-term, usually low-risk debt instruments issued by large corporations with very strong credit ratings.

commingled real estate fund (CREF): In effect a self-liquidating unit investment trust with a managed portfolio of real estate.

commissions: Fees charged by brokers for handling investment transactions such as those involving the buying and selling of securities or real estate.

commodity: In general, any article of commerce; in investments, any of a select group of items traded on one of the commodity futures exchanges either spot (for immediate delivery) or in the futures market (for delivery at a pre-specified future date).

commodity board: An electronic sign in the trading room of a commodity exchange that displays current market statistics.

commodity option: A put or call option to purchase or sell a futures contract.

common stock: Security that represents proportional ownership of an incorporated enterprise; common stockholders are the residual claimants for earnings and assets once all creditors and holders of preferred stock have received their contractual payments.

company analysis: Evaluating the strengths and weaknesses of a firm and its investment appeal vis-à-vis its markets and competitors. Also called firm analysis. Step three of the three-step-top-down-approach of fundamental analysis. See *three-step-top-down-approach.*

competitive bid: An underwriting alternative wherein an issuing entity specifies the type of security to be offered and characteristics of the issue. The issuer solicits bids from competing investment banking firms. The issuer agrees to accept the highest bid from the bankers.

completeness fund: A specialized index used to form the basis of a passive portfolio. Its purpose is to provide diversification to a client's total portfolio by excluding (including) those segments in which the client's active managers (do not) invest.

composition of creditors: a contract between a debtor and two or more creditors in which the creditors consent to take a specified partial payment in full satisfaction of their claims. This arrangement is generally arrived at outside of the bankruptcy law and is frequently referred to as a "formal workout"

compound interest: Interest earned on prior interest payments as in a result of reinvesting one period's income to earn additional income in the following period. For example, $100 earning 9% compounded annually, will yield a payment of $9 the first year. The investor will, therefore, start the second year with $109. The 9% yield will be applied to $109 for a return of $9.81 in year two. In the third year the principal will have grown to $118.81 (100 + 9 + 9.81) and another 9% yield applied for that sum will earn about $10.62. This process continues with the interest rate being applied to a larger and larger principal.

compound value: The end-period value of a sum earning a compounded return.

COMPUSTAT Data Tape: A data source containing balance sheet, income statement, and other financial information on a substantial number of companies for the most recent 20 years.

concentrated position: A margined portfolio having a disproportionate amount of its value represented by one or a few securities; such a concentrated position account may be assigned a higher margin maintenance percentage than that set by brokerage firms for more diversified accounts.

conditional forecast: A prediction based upon some exogenous factor such as a stock performance forecast relative to market performance.

Conference Board: An organization that compiles quarterly capital appropriations statistics and reports them in *Manufacturing Industrial Statistics*.

confirmation: To be consummated, a plan of reorganization must be "confirmed" by the bankruptcy court. The confirmation hearing occurs after the voting process has been completed. The court must determine that the claims and interests have been appropriately classified, that the voting process met certain technical requirements and that the requisite number of claims (by both dollar amount and number of creditors voting) and interests (by number of shares voting) approved the plan. The courts must also find that the plan is "feasible" that creditors receive more than they would under a hypothetical chapter 7 liquidation, and that no creditor receives value for more than 100% of its claims.

conflicts of interest: The company's former advisors and principals may have their own selfish agendas, such as limiting any liability they may have for the organization's demise. Moreover, certain professionals and other participants in the case may have relationships with other entities also in the case. These agendas and relationships can cause an individual or firm to have conflicted loyalties to the debtor and its best interests. To deal with these "conflicts of interest", the participants in the case must disclose their conflicts. The court then determines whether a firm or individual may continue to be engaged in the case.

conglomerate: A company with a diversified portfolio of business units; particularly one formed through a merger of a diverse array of formerly independent companies.

consideration: The payment made in exchange for an asset, claim or interest. Such a payment may be in the form of cash, debt, stock or other form of currency.

consol: A perpetual debt instrument that pays a set coupon each period but never matures and thus never returns the original borrowed principal.

consumer credit: Personal debt as represented by credit card loans, finance company loans, or similar debts.

consumer durables: Long-life consumer assets such as furniture or appliances.

Consumer Price Index (CPI): A monthly cost of living index prepared by the Bureau of Labor Statistics, U.S. Department of Labor. One of the primary indices used to measure the rate of inflation.

Consumer Reports: A periodical publication that (among other things) frequently contains personal finance oriented articles.

consumption expenditures: Spending by individual consumers on final goods and services.

contango: A price structure in the futures market in which the later delivery futures contract price is greater than the underlying asset's current spot price.

contingent deferred sales load: A mutual fund that imposes a sales charge when the investor sells or redeems shares. Also referred to *redemption charges*.

contingent liability: A potential claim against a company or other entity; for example, an unresolved lawsuit seeking to recover damages would represent a contingent claim against the defendant.

contrarian: An investor who attempts to buy (sell) securities on which the majority of other investors are bearish (bullish).

contrary opinion: An investment approach that concentrates on out-of-favor securities; contrarians assert that what is not wanted today may be quite desirable in the future. The approach is similar to buying Christmas ornaments in January.

convenience yield: An adjustment to the theoretical forward or futures contract delivery price that reflects the preferences which consumers have for holding spot positions in the underlying asset.

conversion: A complicated set of security market transactions in related assets. Specifically a conversion involves purchasing options, shorting the underlying stock, and reinvesting the sale proceeds; a technique used by brokerage firms which is designed to earn substantial returns when option and stock prices are not in line with their theoretical relationship.

conversion premium: The amount by which the price of a convertible (bond or preferred) exceeds the corresponding market price of the package of underlying instruments into which it is convertible.

conversion price: The face value of a convertible bond divided by the number of shares into which it is convertible.

conversion ratio: The number of common shares into which a convertible bond or preferred stock may be converted.

conversion value: The market price of the underlying stock referenced in a convertible bond or convertible preferred stock times the number of shares for which the convertible may be exchanged. In other words, the value of the stock embedded in the convertible security.

convertible: A bond or preferred stock that may be exchanged for a specific number of common shares.

convertible debenture: A debenture bond that may, for the bond's life, be exchanged for a specific number of shares of the issuing firm's common stock.

convertible preferred: A preferred stock that may be exchanged for a specific number of shares of the issuing company's common stock.

convexity: The degree to which a bond's price-yield relationship departs from a straight line. The characteristic reflects a bond's price variability for a given change in yields.

corner: The act of acquiring a large, often controlling, interest in a security issue or other specific type of asset that restricts supply and thereby pushes the market price to a very high level; corners can be especially damaging to short sellers who may need to cover their short positions at very disadvantageous prices. Corners are generally illegal.

corporate bond fund: A mutual fund holding a diversified portfolio of corporate bonds.

corporates: Corporate bonds; Bonds issued by incorporated enterprises.

correlation coefficient: A measure of the co-movement tendency of two variables, such as the returns of two securities. See *covariance*.

cost of carry: The cost of holding an asset in inventory; including financing, storage and insurance costs.

country fund: A type of mutual fund which assembles and manages a portfolio of securities that were issued by enterprises located in a single country, such as the Japan Fund or the Mexico Fund.

coupon: The sum of money paid on a fixed-income instrument as interest or preferred dividends. The coupon is generally stated as an annual rate (i.e., 10%). It may be payable annually, semi-annually, quarterly or otherwise.

coupon bond: A bond with attached coupons that the owner must periodically clip and send to the issuer in order to receive the scheduled interest payments.

coupon clipping: Claiming income on coupon bonds by detaching each physical coupon and presenting it to the issuer for payment when due.

coupon-effect: The price impact of differential yield components derived from coupon versus price appreciation as a bond moves toward maturity. Thus a deep-discount, low-coupon bond will offer a yield to maturity that includes a substantial component of tax-deferred capital gains; such a bond's price will usually be affected favorably by the coupon effect.

coupon-equivalent yield: Yield calculation for an investment that provides a discount yield (e.g. a T-bill) computed to correspond with (make it comparable to) a bond that pays a semiannual coupon.

coupon rate: The stated dollar return of a fixed-income investment. For example a coupon rate of 6% on a $1,000 bond implies an annual coupon rate of $60.

counterparty: A participant (buyer or seller) in a derivative transaction.

country risk: Uncertainty of future investment values due to the possibility of major political or economic change in the country or region where an investment is located. Also called *political risk*.

coupon reinvestment risk: The component of interest rate risk due to the uncertainty regarding the future level of market interest rates at which coupon payments can be reinvested.

covariance: The covariance of variables x and y is: Cov = E[x-E(x)][y-E(y)] where E(z) is the expected value of z. If x and y tend to be above their means simultaneously and below their means simultaneously, the covariance is positive. If one is above, when the other tends to be below, the covariance is negative. If they are independent, the covariance is zero.

covenants: Legally binding pledges between bond issuers and bondholders contained in indentures.

covered interest arbitrage: a trading strategy involving borrowing money in one country and lending it in another in an effort to exploit deviations from the parity interest rate.

covered writing: Writing options against existing stock holdings. Or writing options against an existing position in other similar but more senior options.

covering: Repurchasing securities or other assets such as options or future contracts that have been sold short.

crack: Combination future market trade in which the trader buys crude oil futures and sells corresponding amounts of heating oil and gasoline futures. See *reverse crack*.

cram-down: The acceptance by the bankruptcy court of a reorganization plan when less than every class of creditors votes in favor of the plan. Certain additional requirements exist that must be satisfied, including (a) at least one impaired class of claimants has accepted the plan; (b) the plan does not discriminate unfairly; and (c) the plan is fair and equitable.

Crash of 1987: The largest one-day decline in stock market history; on October 19, 1987, the Dow Jones Industrial Average dropped 508 points, which corresponded to 23% of its value as of the previous close.

crawling peg approach: A technique whereby a protective stop loss order is entered on a stock position and as the stock's price rises, the threshold on the stop loss order is also raised.

credit: In this context "Credit" is used as a synonym for "Company" or "High Yield Issuer."

credit analysis: A type of bond analysis used to facilitate a type of active bond portfolio management strategy which is designed to identify bonds that are expected to experience rating changes (upgrades or downgrades).

credit balance: A positive balance, as in a brokerage account.

Credit Derivative: A Type of option which provides a guarantee against default loss for specified debt investment.

credit union: A cooperative association offering many banking-like services in which the members' pooled savings are made available for loans to the membership.

creditor: Entities that have a debt claim against a debtor.

creditors' committee: An organized group of people that the United States Trustee is instructed to appoint; composed of the largest unsecured creditors willing to serve. This committee consults with the Trustee or debtor in possession and investigates the debtor's acts and financial condition as well as participates in the formulation of the plan of reorganization.

Creditwatch: One of several short-term credit analysis services. A bond in danger of being downgraded would be likely to be placed on S&P's Creditwatch list once some degree of trouble is spotted.

CREF: See *commingled real estate fund*.

CRISPE data tape: A data source containing daily stock price information.

cross-border: A transaction involving entities from various countries.

cross hedge: A set of trading positions in which the price volatility of a commodity or security position is hedged with a forward or futures contract based on a different underlying contract.

crown jewel option: Anti-takeover defense in which the most sought after subsidiary of a target firm is spun off thereby making its takeover unattractive.

crown loan: An interest-free loan, usually from a parent to dependent child, designed to shift taxable income from a high- to low-bracket individual. The Tax Reform Act of 1986 ended the tax advantage of this type of transaction.

crush: A combination trade involving futures contracts, especially a commodity trade in which soybean futures are bought and corresponding amounts of soybean oil and meal futures are shorted.

cum-rights period: The time prior to the day of record that determines when shareholders receive a rights distribution; securities that sell cum-rights will reflect the imputed value of the rights to be distributed. See *ex-rights period*.

cumulative preferred: A preferred stock for which any unpaid dividends in arrears are accumulated and must be paid before common dividends can be resumed.

cumulative voting: A method of voting for corporate directors that assigns each shareholder votes equal to the product of the number of shares held times the number of director slots; allows a group of shareholders with a substantial but minority position to concentrate their votes on one or a few candidates and thereby elect their proportional share of directors.

Curb exchange: The American Stock Exchange, which until 1953 was called the New York Curb Exchange. Relates back to the time when the predecessor to the AMEX was an outdoor trading vehicle.

currency: Any form of money accepted by a country and in actual use within that country as a medium of exchange.

currency swap: An asset or liability swap transaction in which the cash flows, that can be either fixed or variable, are denominated in different currencies.

current assets: Assets that are expected to be converted into cash within the next year or next operating period, whichever is longer; primarily cash, accounts receivable, and inventory.

current income: A return objective in which the investor prefers to generate spendable cash income rather than earn capital gains.

current liabilities: Liabilities that are scheduled to become due and payable in the next year or the next operating cycle, whichever is longer; includes accounts payable, short-term bank loans, the current portion of long-term debt, and taxes payable.

current ratio: The ratio of a company's current assets to its current liabilities; a measure of short-term liquidity.

current yield: A bond's coupon rate divided by its current market price or in the case of a stock, its indicated dividend rate divided by its current per share price.

cyclical change: An economic trend arising from the business cycle.

cyclical company: A firm whose earnings tend to rise and fall largely with the general level of economic activity.

day of record: The date on which ownership is determined for deciding to whom to pay that quarter's dividends or for the issuance of some other distributions such as rights.

day order: An order that is canceled at the day's end if it is not executed sometime during the day that it was entered.

day trader: A commodity trader who closes all of his or her positions by the end of each day, thus all day trader transactions are opened and closed on the same day.

dead cat bounce: A small rise in the market following a major decline and followed by a further decline.

dealer: A security trader who acts as a principal rather than as an agent; thus, a specialist or a market maker would be a dealer but a broker would not (brokers are agents).

death benefit: Payment to a beneficiary upon the death of the annuity owner, usually the greater of the annuity value or the payments for the annuity. Also, payment to the beneficiary of a life insurance policy.

death spiral preferred: An instrument issued by a company in financial distress. Such a security may be convertible into the underlying common stock of the issuer at a price fixed at issuance. If however, the price of the company's stock subsequently drops, the conversion price would be reduced in accordance with a formula based on the lower stock price. This security could ultimately be convertible into virtually all of the company's pro formula equity if the stock price fell sufficiently.

debenture: A long-term debt obligation that, unlike a collateralized bond, only provides the lender with a general claim against the borrower's assets. In a default the debenture holder has no claim against any specific assets.

debit balance: A negative balance (debt) in a margin account.

debt: A liability or a claim.

debt-equity ratio: The ratio of total debt to total equity.

debt capacity: The maximum debt that can be issued by a firm or secured by a specific asset.

debt securities: Bonds and similar securities that call for the payment of interest until maturity and principal at maturity. A firm that defaults on its interest or principal obligations is likely eventually to be forced into bankruptcy, unless it quickly cures the default.

debtor: A person concerning which a case under the Bankruptcy Code has been commenced.

debtor in possession (DIP): The party in bankruptcy that is operating the bankrupt estate under the supervision of the court.

decreasing term: A type of term insurance in which the dollar value of protection decreases with the insured's age. Typically the annual premium payment remains constant.

dedication: An investment management technique in which the dollar value of the portfolio's cash flows are structured so that they can be directly used to retire a set of liabilities over time.

deduction: In a tax computation, an amount that is to be subtracted from the taxpayer's adjusted gross income in order to determine his or her taxable income, if the taxpayer itemizes. Deductions include: state income taxes, charitable contributions, mortgage interest expenses, and certain other expenses.

deep-discount bond: A bond selling for substantially less than its par value.

default: Failure to live up to any of the terms in an agreement, especially a debt contract (indenture).

default risk: The risk that a debt security's contractual interest or principal will not be paid when due.

defeasance: The process whereby a debtor offsets the cash flow impact of a portion of its debt by purchasing high-quality debt instruments (usually governments) whose payments are structured to cover the payment obligations of the debt issue.

defensive recapitalizations: A form of leveraging a company where the majority of historical equity ownership is maintained. Assets are not generally written up to fair market value for balance sheet purposes.

deferred annuity: A contract which provides that the annuitant will not begin receiving income payments until some specified time the future.

deferred compensation plan: A procedure whereby employees are permitted to set aside and thereby defer the income tax liability on a portion of their wages and salaries. The funds set aside are then paid into qualified investment plans.

defined benefit pension plan: An employee benefit plan in which the company contributes a certain sum each year for the benefit of each employee. That account (pension fund) provides employees with an income after they retire based on factors such as workers' age, salary and time of employment.

defined contribution pension plan: An employee benefit plan in which worker benefits are determined by the size of employees' contributions to the plan and the returns earned on the fund's investments.

delisting: The act of removing a security from the list of securities authorized to trade on an exchange.

delta: The change in the price of the option with respect to a one dollar change in the price of the underlying asset; the hedge ratio; the number of units of the underlying assets that can be hedged by a single option contract.

derivative security: An instrument whose market value depends upon (or is derived from) the value of a more fundamental investment vehicle (the underlying asset). Examples include options and futures contracts.

deflation: An increase in the purchasing power of the dollar or some other currency unit; the opposite of inflation.

depletion: The writing off (for accounting statement purposes) of the book valuations of assets as they are exploited, particularly mineral assets such as oil or natural gas,.

Depository Trust Company: A financial services firm that facilitates securities trading between exchange members' by using bookkeeping entries rather than physically delivering the stock certificates.

depreciation: A sum deducted from a firm's revenues in the process of producing its reported income. Depreciation allocates the acquisition costs of fixed assets over the course of their useful lives for the purpose of computing per period income.

depression: An economic collapse during which unemployment rises to a high level and economic growth turns very negative.

dilution: Issuing additional shares of a corporation and thereby reducing proportional ownership of existing shareholders.

DIP financing: Funds obtained by a bankrupt debtor. The Bankruptcy Code provides incentives for lenders to provide new capital. These incentives include "super-priority" status. The new DIP loan can be repaid before any other unsecured claim. The DIP financer may even obtain a senior interest in the collateral of the estate.

disability insurance: Insurance protection designed to provide an offset to a potential income loss from a health condition that reduces or ends the insured's ability to earn an income.

discharge: A release from and forgiveness of certain debts of a debtor taking place in a bankruptcy proceeding. Certain debts (e.g. tax liens, environmental liabilities, etc.) are not dischargeable as part of a bankruptcy proceeding. In general a discharge protects a debtor from any further personal liability on account of the debts that are discharged.

disclosure statement: As part of reorganization process, the debtor issues a prospectus-like document, called the Disclosure Statement. It is supposed to contain all material information needed for a claimant or interest holder to make an intelligent decision whether to support or oppose the plan. The statement must include historical and forecasted financial information, a description of the business, history and prospects, and a summary of the Plan. Prior to its dissemination, the court must find the disclosure in the document to be "adequate".

discount bond: A bond selling at a price below its face value

discount brokers: Brokers who charge below-retail commission rates and usually offer a more limited set of investment services than do full service brokerage firms. See *internet brokers*.

discount loan: A short term loan from the Federal Reserve System to a member bank. The loan is extended in order to cure or avoid a temporary reserve deficiency. The fed emphasizes for the borrowing bank that it's access to discount loans is a privilege, not a right to the borrower.

discount rate (for Fed members): The interest rate charged by the Federal Reserve System on discount loans to member banks.

discount rate (for income stream): The interest rate applied to an actual or expected income stream that is used in estimating or calculating its present value. The appropriate discount rate will vary with the level of the expected income stream's risk.

discount yield: A yield computation in which the return is based on the final value of the asset; thus a Treasury bill that sells for 100 minus x and matures in one year for 100 has a discount yield of x%.

discounted cash flow analysis (DCF): The method of discounting a projected stream of cash flows in order to compute its present worth. Similar to interest operationing in reverse. A method for determining the worth of dollars to be received in the future in terms of their present worth.

disinflation: A slowing in the rate at which prices increase. A slowing down of the inflation rate.

disinterested: The opposite of "conflicted".

disintermediation: The movement of funds out of intermediaries and into direct investments. An example is the tendency of high market interest rates to draw funds out of thrift institutions and therefore away from the mortgage market.

diversifiable risk: Firm-specific or industry-specific risk as opposed to overall market risk; diversifiable risks tend to offset one another and thus average out in an efficiently diversified portfolio.

diversification: A technique used to reduce portfolio risks by assembling an investment portfolio with components spread out over different industries, companies, investment types, and risk levels; used to reduce risk by not having "all of your eggs in one basket."

dividend capture: A strategy in which an investor purchases dividend paying stocks timed so as to own them on the day of record and then quickly sells them; designed to capture the dividend payment but avoid the risk of a lengthy holding period.

dividend discount model: An approach to stock valuation that is used to evaluate stocks on the basis of the present value of their expected stream of dividends; the basic formula is $P = d/(r - g)$ where: P = stock price, d = next year dividend, r = appropriate discount rate, and g = expected growth rate in the dividend.

dividend exclusion: An amount of qualifying dividends that an individual could at one time have excluded from taxable income. The Tax Reform Act of 1986 ended this exclusion.

dividend reinvestment plan (DRIP): A company program that facilitates the dividend payments to its shareholders being reinvested in additional shares of the dividend paying company. The shares distributed to the participants are often newly issued by the company and may be sold to the shareholders at a discount from the current market price. Some plans also provide an option for additional share purchases with cash.

dividend restriction: The limitation placed on dividend payments in a bond indenture.

dividends: Payments made by companies to their stockholders out of the company's assets; usually financed from after-tax profits.

divisor: The number which is divided into the sum of the prices of the Dow Jones 30 stocks in order to calculate the value of the Dow Jones Industrial Average. Whenever a DOW component stock is split, the divisor is adjusted to preserve time series consistency.

dollar averaging: A formula-investment-plan requiring periodic (such as monthly) fixed dollar amount investments. This practice tends to "average" the unit purchase costs of an investment program made over time. A greater number of units are purchased when asset prices are lower thereby reducing the average cost per unit.

DOT (designated order transmission): A system on the New York Stock Exchange in which orders are routed electronically to the trading posts where the securities are traded; often used by program traders to effectuate their index arbitrage trades.

Dow: See *Dow Jones Industrial Average*.

Dow Jones Inc.: The firm that publishes *The Wall Street Journal* and *Barron's* and also compiles Dow Jones stock indexes.

Dow Jones Industrial Average: The most commonly referred to index of stock prices; computed as the sum of the stock prices of 30 leading industrial firms divided by a divisor that is adjusted to reflect splits of its components. Dow Jones indexes are also computed for utilities and transportation companies. Also called simply the Dow. See *divisor*.

Dow Theory: A charting theory originated by Charles Dow (Dow Jones Inc.). According to Dow Theory a market uptrend is confirmed if the primary market index (such as the Dow Jones Industrial Average) reaches a new high that is soon followed by a high in the secondary index (such as the Dow Jones Transportation Index). A downtrend is signaled in a similar fashion for down moves in the indexes.

downtick: A price decline in a transaction price from the pervious transaction price

draft: A check-like instrument that calls for payment upon receipt.

dual fund: A type of closed-end investment company that divides its returns between two classes of fund holders: (1)dividend-receiving fundholders and (2)capital gains-receiving fundholders.

dual listing: A security listed for trading on more than one exchange.

due diligence: The process of investigating the risks, merits, prices and overall potential of an investment opportunity.

Dun & Bradstreet: A firm that evaluates and then rates the creditworthiness of many borrowers and generates benchmark financial ratios for many in-dustry groups.

Dupont Equation: A profitability relationship that relates return on equity to several components; ROE = ROS x Sales/Assets x Assets/Equity. In words return on equity equals the product of margin, turnover and leverage.

duration: The weighted average rate of return of a bond's principal and coupon payment; a superior index of the payback rate. The length to maturity, in contrast, ignores the impact of payments received prior to principal re-payment.

Dutch Auction: A type of exchange or tender offer in which the company does not set a specific tender price. Rather the holders are encouraged to sub-mit offers to the company indicating the amount of securities and price that they would be willing to accept. The company then notifies the holders which securities will be purchased, and at what price.

earnings per common share (EPS): The net income of a company, minus any preferred dividend requirements, divided by the number of outstanding common shares; provides the investor or potential investor with informa-tion relevant to the sustainability of the dividend rate and capital gains potential; is considered one of the most important determinants of the value of common stock.

earnings momentum: A portfolio management strategy which identifies and selects stocks of firms with rising (accelerating) earnings

earnings surprise: an earnings announcement that differs from analysts' expecta-tions

EBIT: "Earnings Before Interest and Taxes," a measure of profit. It is used as a base to derive values for the "enterprise value" of the company.

EBITDA: "Earnings Before Interest, Taxes, Depreciation and Amortization," a measure of profits, sometimes called "pretax cash flow". EBITDA is often viewed as an estimate for how much money (in the very short term) a com-pany can afford to pay for debt service. Both EBIT and EBITDA are used to derive estimates for the "enterprise value" of the company.

econometric model: A model based on an analysis of economic data; particularly models of the economy.

econometrics: The statistical analysis of economic data.

economic analysis: An evaluation of a firm's investment potential within its economic setting.

economic value added:(EVA) a management performance measure which compares net operating profit to the total cost of capital. Reflects how profitable company projects are as a sign of management performance.

efficient frontier: A set of investment portfolios with risk-return trade-offs, each of which offers the highest expected return for a given level of risk.

efficient market hypothesis: The theory that the market correctly prices securities in light of the known relevant information. In its weak form the hypothesis implies that past price and volume data (technical analysis) cannot be profitably used in stock selection. The semistrong form implies that superior valuation analysis which utilizes only public data is impossible; thus such data cannot be used to improve stock selection over what is possible through random selection. In the strong form of the hypothesis even inside (nonpublic) information is thought to be reflected accurately in prices.

efficient portfolio: A portfolio on the efficient frontier of the capital asset pricing model. Such a portfolio offers the highest expected return for that risk level.

election-year cycle: The alleged tendency for the stock market to reach a peak about seven months after a presidential election and then fall to a low about 11 months later.

enhanced death benefit: An increased death benefit for which an annuity owner pays an extra fee.

enterprise value: The aggregate value of the financial debt and equity, net of cash on the balance sheet. It represents the value of owning all of the financial interests of the company.

equipment trust certificate: A type of bond collateralized by equipment, particularly railroad rolling stock or airplanes.

equity: See *net worth*.

equity accounting: Partially consolidating (on a pro rata basis) income and equity of affiliates that are 20% or more owned by the parent firm.

equity buyback: When a company repurchases its own stock.

equity capital: That part of a business's assets, financed by the owners as opposed to the part financed by the creditors.

equity kicker: A sweetener (such as warrant) designed to make a debt issue more attractive by giving its owner an opportunity to benefit from the borrower's success (if any).

equity notes: Debt securities that are automatically converted into stock on a pre-specified date at a specific price or at a price level based on a formula that is pre-specified. Also called mandatory convertible notes.

equity security: A share of ownership in a corporation whether or not transferable; common or preferred stock, or a similar security.

ERISA (Employee Retirement Income Security Act): A 1974 federal law that protects pension benefits which have been promised by employers to their workers.

escrow account: In general, an account designed to hold a sum of money for a specific purpose; in a real estate transaction, the fund is normally set up for monthly deposits of the expected pro rata amount of real estate taxes.

ESOP (Employee Stock Ownership Plan): A federally sanctioned program in which a corporation contributes newly issued company stock worth up to 15% of employee payrolls into what amounts to a tax-sheltered profit sharing plan.

estate: A person's total worth as determined by his or her vested interests in property and other assets, exclusive of any liabilities. Also the business of a debtor in a bankruptcy proceeding.

estate tax: A progressive tax on the assets left by deceased parties. Also called the "death tax".

Eurobonds: Bonds that may be denominated in dollars or some other currency but must be traded internationally.

Eurodollars: Dollar-denominated deposits held in banks based outside of the United States, mostly in Europe, but some are deposited in Asian and other area banks.

Euromarkets: Financial markets that operate outside of any national jurisdiction and deal in securities that may pay relatively high interest rates. The securities are usually based on deposits of large, international corporations or governments of nations involved in extensive foreign trade.

European option: an option contract which can be exercised only on its expiration date (not before). See *American option*.

examiner: A court-appointed individual that the United States Trustee selects who (does not run the debtor's business) examines certain facts concerning the debtor and files a report on the investigations.

ex ante: Before the fact; thus a procedure that consistently identifies attractive investments ex ante would generally facilitate a profitable trading strategy. See *ex post*.

ex-dividend date: The day after the day of record. Buyers who completed their purchase on or after the ex-dividend date do not receive that period's dividend even if the stock is held on the payment date.

exchange offer: An out-of-court restructuring attempt. The debtor may offer to swap cash or newly-issued common stock or bonds in exchange for outstanding indebtedness.

exchange rate risk: uncertainty due to the pricing of an investment in a foreign currency.

exclusivity: The chapter 11 debtor has the exclusive right to file a plan of reorganization for a period of months after bankruptcy filing.

executor: The person appointed to carry out the provisions of a will.

exempt property. See *reaffirmation agreement*.

exemptions: In tax laws a dollar sum per dependent that may be subtracted from the taxpayer's adjusted gross income in order to compute the individual's taxable income. note that the tax benefit of exemptions is subject to phase out as the taxpayer's income level rises.

exercise value (put): The striking price of a put less the market price of the associated stock, if positive. Defined as zero if the difference is negative. Also called intrinsic value.

exercise value (warrant, call, or right): The market price of the associated stock less the striking price of the option, if positive. Defined as zero if the difference is negative. Also called intrinsic value.

exordium clause: The introductory portion of a will or other legal document.

expected rate of return: The expected return that analysts' calculations suggest a security should provide based on the combined impact of the market's rate of return during the period and the security's market risk

expected value: The sum of the probabilities multiplied by their associated outcomes; the mean or average value.

expense deferral: An accounting technique whereby, for the purpose of computing reported income, expense recognitions are spread over time.

explanatory notes: Additional information in the form of footnotes; keyed to stock and bond quotations by letter symbols.

ex post: After the fact; thus a procedure that identifies attractive investments but relies on ex post data to do so would not, by itself, facilitate a profitable trading strategy. See *ex ante*.

ex-rights period: The time period subsequent to the day-of-record for a rights distribution.

extraordinary gain (loss): An unusual nonrecurring gain (loss).

face value: The maturity value of a bond or other debt instrument; sometimes referred to as the bond's par value.

fairness opinion: "Fairness" is a financial concept that applies to a variety of negotiated transactions, including both mergers and reorganizations. Fairness addresses the question of whether the consideration received by a given constituency is sufficient.

FASB (Financial Accounting Standards Board): An accounting organization that establishes rules for preparing financial statements.

FDIC (Federal Deposit Insurance Corporation): A federal agency that insures deposits at commercial banks and thrifts. The insurance provides protection of up to $100,000 per depositor per institution.

Fed: See *Federal Reserve System*.

Fed call: A type of margin call that the Federal Reserve requires be issued when a margin borrower's equity falls below 25% of the borrower's account value. See *house call, margin call*.

Federal Funds Market: The market in which banks and other financial institutions borrow and lend immediately-deliverable reserve-free funds, usually on a one-day basis.

Federal Reserve Board of Governors: The governing body of the Federal Reserve System, comprised of seven members appointed by the President for long and staggered terms.

Federal Reserve System: The federal government agency that exercises monetary policy through its control over banking system reserves. Also called the Fed.

fee only financial planner: An investment advisor who, for a fee, assists individuals with their financial planning but does not generate his or her compensation by recommending investments that would produce a commission for the planner.

FHA (Federal Housing Administration): A federal government agency that insures home mortgages for qualified borrowers.

fiduciary: A person who supervises the investment portfolio or manages the property of a third party and makes decisions in accordance with the owner's wishes and objectives.

FIFO (first in, first out): An inventory valuation method. With FIFO items taken out of inventory are, for accounting purposes, assumed to have cost the amount paid for the earliest unused purchase. See *LIFO*.

fill-or-kill order: A type of security market order that must be either filled immediately or canceled.

filter rules: Any mechanical trading system, such as a rule to buy stocks when their PE ratios fall below some predetermined level or to trade whenever a particular price pattern is observed.

financial ratio: A ratio such as the debt/equity or times-interest-earned ratio; designed to reflect a firm's long-term financial strength.

financial risk: The variability of future income arising from the firm's financing costs. Fixed financial costs which magnify the effect of changes in operating profit on net income and earnings per share

firm analysis: See *company analysis*.

fiscalists: A group of economists who believes that fiscal (rather than monetary) policy is the economic tool having by far the greatest impact. See *monetarist*.

fiscal policy: Government tax and spending policy that affects the level of economic activity.

Fitch Investors Service: A bond rating service; respected but somewhat less well known than Moody's or Standard & Poor's.

fixed asset value: The present value of the free cash flows expected to be generated by a business, plus the residual asset value.

fixed assets: Tangible assets with relatively long expected lives (greater than a year) which are not intended for resale and that are used in the operations of the business; includes plant and equipment but not inventories or accounts receivable.

fixed costs: Costs of operating a business that do not vary with the firm's level of output, in the short run.

fixed-income security: Any security that promises to pay a periodic nonvariable sum, such as a bond paying a fixed coupon amount per period.

fixed rate: An interest rate that does not vary during the life of the loan.

fixed rate mortgage: A mortgage having a constant interest rate for the life of the debt.

flat: Term used to describe a type of bond trade; bonds trading for a net price that is not adjusted to reflect any accrued interest are said to trade flat. See *accrued interest*.

flight away from quality: A market that becomes increasingly tolerant of risk and, as such, is willing to price lower quality debt instruments at a smaller premium yield over higher quality instruments than had heretofore been the case. See *flight to quality*.

flight to quality: A market that finds high quality debt instruments such as governments increasingly attractive relative to lower quality debt instruments. The result is a growing spread in their yields. See *flight away from quality*.

flipping: The act of quickly selling a recently acquired investment; thus an investor, who subscribes to a new issue IPO and then sells the shares in the immediate aftermarket, would be described as a flipper.

floating rate notes: A type of debt security whose coupon rate varies with market interest rates (e.g. treasuries).

floating rate preferred: A type of preferred stock whose indicated dividend rate is determined by a formula which varies its payment rate with moves in market interest rates.

floor agreement: a contract that, on each settlement date, requires the maker to pay the holder a sum determined by the difference (if positive) between the floor interest rate and the reference interest rate. Otherwise no payment is made.

floor trader: One holding a seat on an exchange who trades for his or her own account. Also called RCMM.

Florida land boom: A speculative real estate boom that took place in the 1920's and was followed by a crash in the price of Florida property.

flower bonds: Government bonds that may be used at their par value for estate tax payments.

flowthrough: A method of handling the reporting of investment tax credits in which benefits are taken into and reflected in the income statements as they are incurred rather than spread over the acquired asset's life (normalization).

FNMA (Federal National Mortgage Association): A financial corporation that was previously government-owned, but now privately owned by its shareholders. FNMA operates a secondary market in mortgages. FNMA issues its own debt securities to finance its mortgage portfolio.

focal point: A round number value that is generally agreed upon or recognized by market participants as such. For example, a price of $20 would likely by viewed as a focal point whereas a number such as $19.83 would not.

footnotes (to a financial statement): Notes that explain or expand upon entries; an integral part of a financial statement.

Forbes: A twice-monthly popular investment periodical famous for, among other things, its Forbes lists, such as the list of loaded laggers.

foreclosure: The process by which secured lenders seize the collateral underlying their loans. The "automatic stay" provision of the Bankruptcy Code initially prevents such foreclosures. If, however, the court later determines that the secured lenders are not receiving "adequate protection", the court may lift the automatic stay in favor of the secured lenders.

Form 10K: A detailed annual report that must, in a timely manner, be submitted to the SEC, to the listing exchange, and to any shareholders who request it.

Form 10Q: A detailed quarterly report that must, in a timely manner, be submitted to the SEC and the listing exchange and may be sent to shareholders who request it.

Form 13D: A required SEC filing of any individual or group owning 5% or more of any public corporation; to be properly filed the form must disclose a number of matters including the filer's actual ownership percentage, its cost, the intentions of the owner and any relevant agreements of the owner with any other party.

forward contract: An agreement between a buyer and a seller that calls for the delivery of an asset at a pre-specified price, amount, time and place. Unique one-of-a-kind contract; not traded on an exchange. See *futures*.

forward rate: a short-term yield (interest rate) for a future holding period implied by the spot rates of two different maturity securities.

four-nine position: A holding of approximately 4.9% of the outstanding shares of a company; about the limit for a quiet holding. At 5% the holder must file a Form 13d with the SEC revealing his or her position.

fourth market: The market for direct trading of listed securities between institutions.

franchise factor: A unique competitive advantage that facilitates a firm earning excess returns on its capital. These excess returns tend to cause the firm's stock price to have a PE ratio above its base PE ratio.

fraudulent conveyances: Defined differently by the several uniform state statutes and the Federal Bankruptcy Statutes. All have their origin in the statute of 13 Elizabeth enacted in 1570 that provided that "Covinous and fraudulent feoffments, gifts, grants...devised and contrived of malice, fraud, coven, collusion or guile, to the end, purpose and intent, *to delay, hinder or defraud creditors* and others...shall be utterly void...."

Freddie Mac (The Federal Home Loan Mortgage Corporation): A government agency that assembles pools of conventional mortgages and sells participations in a secondary market.

free cash flow: The amount of cash flow remaining after funding required levels of capital expenditures.

front-end loading: Taking a large portion of the sales fee on the purchase from the early payments on that long-term purchase contract.

front running: An illegal trading strategy in which the trader (usually an employee of a brokerage or specialist firm) learns that a large order to trade is about to be entered (usually placed by a substantial customer) and runs ahead of that trade to place an order at the then current market price just prior to the time that the market learns of the large trade intention. If the large order causes a major price change, the position established by the front runner can, shortly thereafter, be reversed at an attractive profit. The front runner is (illegally) trading on inside information (knowledge of the forthcoming trade).

full employment: The unemployment rate that is thought to be the minimum sustainable level which can be reached before inflationary pressures accelerate and the maximum level that the public will view as reasonable. Opinions on this level have over time varied from around 4% to 6%.

full faith and credit: The promise backing a debenture or other type of uncollateralized debt instrument; the borrower promises to pay and pledges its full faith and credit (best efforts).

full replication: a technique for constructing a passive index portfolio where all of the components of an index are purchased in proportion to their weights.

fundamental analysis: The evaluation of the stocks or other assets and their investment-attractiveness based on their underlying financial, competitive, earning, and managerial position or similar evaluation of other types of investments.

fundamental betas: Betas calculated from the firm's fundamental characteristics such as its operating leverage, sensitivity to market interest rates, etc.

fundamental indexing: Creates a set of index weights, based on same non-market fundamental yardstick such as sales. Proposed as an attenuation way of constructing as index fund.

futures. Deferred delivery commodities contracts.

GAAP (Generally Accepted Accounting Principles): A set of accounting principles that are supposed to be followed in preparing audited accounting statements.

gambler's ruin: The wiping out of an individual's original capital by one or a series of adverse events. Often used in the context of the risk of gambler's ruin.

gamma factor: The number of years of above-average growth at a rate equal to that of the recent past which is necessary to justify the current multiple on a high PE growth stock.

general unsecured creditor: A creditor whose loan is not secured (is uncollateralized) by any specific assets; debts are evaluated based only on the creditworthiness of the borrower.

general mortgage bond: A bond having a generalized claim against the issuing company's property.

general obligation: A municipal bond secured by the issuer's full faith and credit but without any specific collateral or claim to a stream of tax payments.

geometric mean return (GMR): The computed average return that, if earned over the entire set of periods, produces the same ending compound value as the separate per period returns applied period by period; mathematically the value obtained by taking one minus the nth root of the product of one plus each of the n per period returns;

GIC (Guaranteed Interest Contract): An investment sold by insurance companies that offers high yields plus the opportunity to earn similar returns on additions to the investment plan.

gift tax: A progressive tax on gifts; now integrated with estate taxes.

gilt-edge security: A very secure bond or other security.

gilts: Debt securities issued by the government of the United Kingdom.

give up: A now-prohibited practice whereby brokers making trades for the portfolios of mutual funds were directed by the fund to pay a portion of their commission fees to brokers who had sold the fund's shares.

Glass-Steagall Act: A 1933 (depression era) federal act that required the separation of commercial and investment banking. Now largely repealed.

GNMA (Ginnie Mae) (Government National Mortgage Association): A government agency that provides special assistance on selected types of home mortgages; securities are backed both by GNMA mortgage portfolios and by the general credit of the government.

go-go fund: A type of mutual fund which was popular in the late 1960s. Such funds sought short-term trading profits. Also called a performance fund.

going concern: The concept of a firm continuing in business. Conversely if a firm cannot continue as a going concern, it may need to liquidate. A company capable of continuing in business is usually (but not always) more valuable than one in liquidation mode.

going private: The process by which a heretofore public company buys back all of its publicly held stock so that ownership rests with a few owners and it thereby becomes a privately held company.

going public: The process by which a start-up or heretofore private firm sells its shares in a public offering and thereby becomes a publicly traded company.

golden handcuffs: An employment agreement that makes the voluntary departure prior to normal retirement age of upper level managers very costly to such managers; these managers may lose attractive deferred compensation and unvested stock options, if they leave prematurely.

golden handshake: A provision in a preliminary merger agreement in which the target firm provides the acquiring firm with an option to purchase its shares or assets at attractive prices or to receive a substantial bonus if the proposed takeover does not occur.

golden parachute: A very generous provisional termination payment that is paid to upper management if control of their firm's ownership shifts to another group (a takeover).

good till canceled order (GTC): A type of security market order (buy or sell) that remains in effect until it is either executed or canceled.

goodwill: The amount by which a firm's going concern value exceeds its book value.

governments-only fund: A type of money market mutual fund that invests exclusively in very short term U.S. government securities.

governments: U.S. Government bonds issued by the Treasury Department and backed by the full faith and credit of the federal government.

grace period: Time period (e.g. 30 days) in which offensive action (e.g. foreclosure or bankruptcy) is stayed thereby providing a defaulting debtor with an opportunity to cure the default.

Graham and Dodd approach: A type of securities analysis that stresses the importances of an investment's current fundamentals as opposed to its future prospects. Its originator, Benjamin Graham, coauthored the investment text that dominated the college investments course market from the 1930s to 1950s. Also called Graham approach.

grantee: The individual receiving property under a grantor deed.

grantor: The conveyor of property under a grantor deed; the one who transfers property to another.

Gray approach: An investment timing technique that seeks to identify over and undervalued market phases on the basis of interest rates relative to market PE ratios.

Great Crash: 1929 stock market decline which proceeded the great depression of the 1930s.

greater-fool theory: The tongue-in-cheek view that a still "greater fool" will come along to bail out a foolish investor's foolish investment.

greenmail: The practice of acquiring a large percentage of a firm's stock and then threatening to take over the firm in an effort to have the company buy the greenmailer out at a premium

gross income: Total income, either actual or estimated.

gross margin: The net sales of an enterprise minus its cost of goods sold.

Gross Domestic Product (GDP): The sum of the market values of all final goods and services produced annually in the country, valued at their market prices.

growth fund: A common stock mutual fund which seeks to achieve price appreciation by assembling a portfolio of growth stocks.

growth share matrix: A relationship popularized by the Boston Consulting Group (BCG) that relates interfirm profit differences to the combined impacts of market share and growth.

growth stock: The shares of a company that is expected to achieve rapid growth; often carries above-average risks and PE ratios.

guarantee bond: A bond having a guarantee from a company other than the issuer.

guarantee preferred: A preferred stock having a guarantee from a company other than the issuer.

haircut: An economic concession suffered by a creditor in connection with a restructuring. The "haircut" may be implemented through a reduction in principal and/or interest owed, a "stretched out" payment schedule or other mechanisms.

head and shoulders price formation: A technical pattern of historical stock prices that looks like a human head and shoulders (small price rise then a decline then a larger rise followed by a second decline and finally a second small rise followed by a decline: left shoulder, head, right shoulder) and is said to forecast a price decline.

hedge: a trading strategy in which derivative or other securities are used in an attempt to reduce or completely offset a counterparty's risk exposure to an existing asset position.

hedge fund: A type of investment company that operates with wide latitude in the management of its portfolio. This wide latitude permits the hedge fund to do things that standard investment companies such as mutual funds are generally not permitted to do: sell short, buy and sell futures and options, take a large concentrated position in a single company, take an active role in management, etc. Only sophisticated investors are allowed to purchase and hold units of these types of funds.

hedging: Taking opposite positions in related securities or other assets (e.g. common stock and bonds convertible into the same common stock) in an attempt to profit from relative price movements (risk hedging) or to reduce exposure to an existing risk (pure hedging).

hemline indicator: A whimsical technical market indicator that forecasts stock market moves on the basis of women's hemlines. The higher the hemline, the higher the market level. For, example in the 1920's hemlines were high and the market was rising. In the 1930s hemlines and stock prices fell.

high-yield bond: a bond that is rated below investment grade (below BBB).

highest and best: In considering among alternatives (such as choosing the best bid), debtors, creditors and the court need to consider a variety of factors. Bids frequently include a package of consideration, including equity and debt instruments each of which need to be valued. Some bids may be unconditional. Others may be highly conditional due to financing and other contingencies. Under these circumstances, the highest nominal bid may not necessarily be the best. The parties will consider factors such as the need for cash vs. speculative value, and the ability to close quickly vs. needing to satisfy various conditions. Certainty of closure and consideration may be more valuable than nominal amount of consideration. As a result, the winning bid is frequently referred to a "highest and best", rather than just the "highest".

highest and best use: The use of an asset to which the highest value attaches. For example, land used for farming may achieve its highest and best use if homes are built on it.

histogram: A discrete probability distribution display.

hockey stick: Projections depicting increasing profits after years of flat or declining performance. The graph of such trends is in the shape of a hockey stick.

holding company: A company that is set up to maintain voting control over other business enterprises.

holding period return (HPR): The rate of return over some specific time period.

holding period return relative (HPRR): The end period compound value for a specific holding period.

holdouts: In out-of-court restructurings, where consenting creditors agree to significant economic concessions, other creditors have a major incentive to hold out. They not only avoid having to take "haircuts", but they benefit from having a more creditworthy company (brought about by the other creditors' concessions).

horizontal integration: The process of a business buying or building from scratch a business that is complementary in nature to its existing lines of business.

horizontal spread: Short and long option positions on the same security with the same strike price but different expiration dates.

house call: A margin call in which the margin borrower's equity falls below the brokerage firm's minimum. This minimum is typically set at 35% but some brokerage firms may set the minimum as low as 30%. See *Fed call*, *margin call*.

Hulbert Financial Digest: A publication containing ratings of investment advisory services.

hypothecation: The pledging of securities as loan collateral.

immediate annuity: An annuity contract that provides for income payments to the annuitant to begin immediately upon its purchase

immunization: The process of buying bonds with durations equal to one's investment horizon or using interest futures to accomplish the same purpose. Such a program is designed largely to eliminate the risk inherent in the fluctuations of market interest rates.

impaired: A claim that is paid in full or is reinstated on its original terms will generally be deemed to be "unimpaired". Otherwise, the claim will be "impaired". Impaired claims are entitled to vote on its treatment in a plan of reorganization.

inactive post: NYSE trading post for inactively traded securities. See *post*.

in and out: The purchase and subsequent sale of the same security within a short time period.

income anticipation: An accounting practice in which a profit is reflected on the income statement before the corresponding revenues are received.

income approach: Valuing real estate or some other type of asset as the discounted value (present value) of its expected income stream.

income bond: A bond on which interest is paid if and only if the issuer has sufficient earnings.

income fund: A common stock mutual fund holding and managing a portfolio of stocks paying high dividends.

income statement: A financial statement of interim earnings; provides a financial accounting of revenues and expenses during a specified period, i.e., three months, one year, etc.

income stock: A stock with a high indicated dividend rate.

incorporation: The forming of a business enterprise into a legal body endowed with various rights and duties. Once formed, the corporation limits the exposure of its owners to the amount invested in the enterprise.

increasing rate notes: Bond issues whose coupon rates automatically increase by some predetermined amount at predetermined times.

indenture (bond): The statement of promises under the Trust Indenture Act that the company makes to its bondholders, including a commitment to pay a stated coupon amount periodically and return the face value (usually $1,000) at the end of a certain period (such as 20 years after issue). An indenture trustee, such as a bank, is charged with overseeing the issuing firm's commitments. See *indenture trustee*.

indenture trustee: The trustee named in the debt instrument's indenture who is charged with acting for the benefit of the holders of the debt represented by the indenture. This trustee represents the bondholders' interests in dealing with the bond issuer. See *indenture*.

independence (statistical): The relationship between two variables in the situation where knowledge of one's value does not help explain the other's value. Thus, if IBM and AT&T stock returns are totally unrelated, knowing that AT&T stock returned x% over the most recent 12 months would not help explain IBM stock's return over the same period.

indexing: a passive bond or stock portfolio management strategy that seeks to match the performance of a selected market index.

index arbitrage: A (program) trading strategy involving the simultaneous undertaking of offsetting positions in stock index futures contracts and the underlying cash market securities (stocks making up the index). If, for example, the index futures contract is priced above the stocks making up the index, the arbitrageur would buy the stocks and sell the futures contract on the index. If, in contrast, the index was priced below its corresponding stocks, the arbitrageur would short the stocks and buy the index contract. The index arbitrage positions would be reversed at contract expiration.

index fund: A mutual or closed-end fund that attempts to duplicate the performance of a market index such as the S&P 500.

industry analysis: The evaluation of an industry's position and prospects as they relate to its component firm's investment attractiveness.

inflation: The rate of increase in the price level; for example, if on the average $1.06 will buy what $1 would buy a year earlier, inflation equal to 6% has occurred.

inflation hedge: An investment asset whose value varies directly with its price level.

informal workout: An approach to dealing with a troubled firm that seeks to avoid the problems and costs of a formal bankruptcy proceeding by obtaining sufficient lender concessions to allow the obligor to continue to function outside of the jurisdiction of the bankruptcy court.

initial public offering (IPO): A new issue of stock offered by a firm that has no prior public market or public trading of its stock.

in play: The status of being an actively pursued target takeover candidate.

input-output model: A mathematical model in the form of a grid that relates various industries' outputs to their derived demands for inputs from other industries.

insider trading: The buying or selling of traders having access to relevant nonpublic information relating to the company in question. Such trading is illegal.

insolvency: Can be defined in several different ways depending upon the particular statute to be applied. One common classification is a simple balance sheet insolvency (liabilities exceeding assets). A second test is the inability of a debtor to pay its debts as they become due.

installment sale: In general, any sale that calls for payments to be made over time rather than upon the closing of the transaction; in real estate transactions, an installment sale may reduce and postpone the seller's tax liability if the payments are stretched out over a sufficiently long period.

Instinet: An automated communications network among block traders.

institutional investor: A type of organization that invests the pooled assets of others; includes pension funds, mutual funds, bank trust departments, insurance companies, and investment companies.

intercorporate dividend: Dividend payment from one corporation to another; 70% of such dividends are not subject to the corporate income tax for the recipient.

interest: The amount a borrower pays for the use of a lender's funds; frequently expressed as an annual percentage of the principal balance outstanding; may be compounded on a monthly, quarterly, annually or on some other periodic basis.

interest futures: A futures contract calling for the delivery of a debt security such as a T-bill or long-term government bond.

interest rate anticipation: An active bond portfolio management strategy designed to preserve capital or take advantage of capital gains opportunities by predicting the direction of interest rates and their effects on bond prices.

interest rate collar: The combination of a long position in a cap agreement and a short position in a floor agreement, or vice versa.

interest rate parity: In an efficient market the relationship that must exist between two countries' spot and forward foreign exchange rates and those two countries' respective interest rates.

interest rate risk: The risk to an investor that a market interest rate rise will take place, thereby reducing the market value of fixed income securities. Or the risk that market interest rates will decline thereby reducing the return on coupon payments that are to be received and reinvested.

interest rate swap: An agreement calling for the periodic exchange of cash flows based on an interest rate that remains fixed and one that is linked to a variable-rate index.

interest-on-interest: Income from reinvestment of interest payments. See *compound interest*.

interest spread: The cost of carry, measured in percentage points.

internal liquidity (solvency) ratios: Financial ratios that measure the ability of the firm to meet future short term financial obligations.

Internal Rate of Return (IRR): The discount rate at which the value of the expected cash outflows of an investment are equal to those of the expected cash inflows.

international fund: A mutual fund that invests in securities of firms based outside the fund's home country.

International Monetary Market: A futures exchange associated with the Chicago Mercantile Exchange. It lists futures contracts on gold, T-bills, Eurodollars, CDs, and several foreign currencies, stock index futures and options on futures.

internet brokers: Brokerage firms that implement securities trade orders entered on the internet and usually charge very low commission rates (e.g. $7 a trade).

in-the-money option: An option whose striking price is more favorable to optionholders than the current market price of the underlying security. For a call (put) the strike price would be below (above) the underlying stock's prices.

intraday dependencies: Nonrandom price movements of transactions taking place over the course of a single day.

intrinsic value (option): See *exercise value*.

intrinsic value (stock): The underlying value that a careful evaluation would produce; generally takes into account both the going concern value and the liquidation or breakup value of the company. An efficient market would always price stocks at their intrinsic values. An inefficient market would not necessarily do so.

inverted market: A futures market in which the futures price on a particular asset exceeds its corresponding spot price.

inverted yield curve: A market in which short term interest rates are above long term interest rates.

investment: The current commitment of dollars for a period of time in order to derive future payments that are expected to compensate the investor for the combined impact of the time the funds are committed, the expected rate of inflation, and uncertainty.

investment banker: A financial firm that (among other things) organizes a syndicate to underwrite or market a new issue of securities.

Investment Companies: Periodical that reports on mutual funds; published by Weisenberger.

investment company: A company that manages pooled portfolios for a group of owners; may be either a closed-end company, whose fixed number of shares outstanding are traded like other shares, or an open-end company (mutual fund), whose shares outstanding change by the net amounts bought and sold.

Investment Company Institute: Organization of mutual funds and other institutional investors; publishes *Mutual Fund Forum*.

investment grade (bond): A bond rated BBB or higher.

investment management company: A company, distinct from the investment company (e.g. mutual fund), that manages the portfolio and performs administrative functions for the fund.

investment manager: One who manages an investment portfolio.

Investor's Daily: A national business newspaper that competes with *The Wall Street Journal*.

involuntary bankruptcy: A bankruptcy petition filed by the creditors of a debtor that is designed to force the commencement of a case under chapter 11 or 7 of the Bankruptcy Code.

IRA (Individual Retirement Account): A retirement plan that allows employees to set aside up to $3,000 annually (2005) in a tax-sheltered investment instrument. Earnings in the retirement fund are not taxed until they are withdrawn. The contributed sum is also deductible from taxable income if the individual is not covered by a company pension or has a relatively low income. See *Roth IRA*.

itemizing: One of two basic options available to those filing income tax returns; involves taking deductions for specific allowed expenses rather than taking the standard deduction. Itemized deductions are subtracted from adjusted gross income in the process of computing taxable income. Taxpayers are permitted either to itemize or take a standard deduction amount. Itemizing is preferred when the total for itemizes deductions exceeds that for the standard deduction. See *deduction*.

January effect: An empirical anomaly in which risk-adjusted stock returns (particularly of depressed stocks) in the month of January are significantly higher than those in any other month of the year. See *anomalies*.

January indicator: A technical timing device based on the assertion that as January goes so goes the year. Empirical evidence is not supportive.

junk bonds: High-risk bonds (rated below investment grade, below BBB) usually promising a very high indicated return coupled with a substantial default risk.

Kansas City Board of Trade: A futures exchange that lists contracts for the trading of wheat and Value Line stock index futures.

Keogh account: A retirement account that allows self-employed individuals to set aside (2005) up to $40,000 or 20% of their self employment income (whichever is lower) in a tax-sheltered fund. Neither the contribution nor the accounts earnings are subject to tax until the funds are withdrawn.

key person life insurance: Life insurance on key employees naming their employer as the beneficiary; designed to assure creditors, suppliers and customers that the firm would survive the loss of the insured.

kickers: Investors sometimes seek additional return beyond the rate promised through the interest rate on a bond. They negotiate with the issuer for additional securities to provide such returns. These instruments, called "kickers", may take the form of warrants or other equity securities that provide the investor with an upside reward if the company is successful.

Krugerrand: A South African gold coin containing exactly one ounce of gold. The coin is often used as an investment vehicle by gold investors and speculators.

kurtosis: The degree to which a distribution departs from the normal distributions. See also *leptokurtosis* and *platokurtosis*.

lagging indicators: A set of economic variables whose values tend to reach peaks and troughs after the aggregate economy has already done so.

law of one price: The principle that, whenever two assets offer equivalent payoff matrices, their prices must be identical.

leading indicators: Government-compiled data series whose movements are identified as tending to precede turns in the overall economy.

leap: A long term option contract (put or call).

leakages: Spendable funds that, rather than being spent on domestically produced goods or services, "leak" into savings, import purchases, or taxes during each round of stimulatory spending or tax-reduction, reducing each spending round relative to its prior level thereby reducing the power of fiscal policy to stimulate the economy.

learning curve: A relationship popularized by the Boston Consulting Group which hypothesizes that manufacturers are able to reduce per unit costs substantially as they increase their cumulative volume; in one formulation, costs are said to decrease by 20% with each doubling of cumulative volume.

legacy costs: Expenses that will need to be paid in the future to current and past employees for their current and past service (pension, medical, etc.) or other future costs such as for environmental cleanup that firms are liable for resulting from prior operations. In other words future costs that existing companies are saddled with because of their history of past operations. A new startup company would not be saddled with these types of costs.

legal lists: Lists of stocks authorized by various states for investing by fiduciaries.

leg on: The process of assembling an option spread trade or other combination investment position one side at a time.

lender liability: Claims against pre bankruptcy lenders relating to the lender group's inappropriate and actionable activities that contributed to the company's failure.

leptokurtosis: The characteristic of a population distribution which differs from the normal by having a greater amount of its probability in the peak and tails and less in the two intermediate zones.

lettered stock: Newly issued stock sold at a discount to large investors prior to a public offering of the same issue; in accordance with SEC Rule 144, buyers agree not to sell their shares for a pre-specified period after purchase.

leverage: Using borrowed funds or special types of securities (warrants, calls) to increase the potential return relative to the amount invested; usually increases both the risk or loss and the expected return.

Leveraged Buy Out (LBO): The takeover of a company financed largely through the use of debt that is secured by the acquired firm's own assets.

liabilities: Debts; appear on right side of a balance sheet.

LIBOR: London Inter-Bank Offered Rate. It is a floating rate contained in many borrowing arrangements. It is frequently offered to borrowers as an alternative to the prime rate. Typically, companies borrow at a spread over LIBOR. Weaker credits pay higher spreads.

lien: A charge against or interest in property designed to secure payment of a debt for performance of an obligation.

life annuity: An annuity that pays a fixed income for the life of the annuitant.

LIFO (last in, first out): An accounting method that, for income reporting purposes, values items taken out of inventory at the most recent unused invoice cost. See *FIFO.*

limited liability: Property that, under most circumstances, protects shareholders from exposure to their corporation's debts in a bankruptcy.

limit order: An order to buy or sell an asset at a pre-specified price (or better).

linear model: A method for estimating portfolio risks that requires only alpha and beta estimates of the components.

line of credit: A prearranged agreement from a lender to supply up to some maximum loan amount at pre-specified terms.

liquidation: The process of selling all of a firm's assets and distributing the proceeds according to the priority of their claims first to creditors beginning with the highest priority and then any residual to shareholders (first preferred, then common).

liquidation value: The total value of a going concern's assets (in excess of its debts) if those assets are sold piecemeal.

liquidity: The ease with which an investment can be converted into cash for approximately its original cost plus its expected accrued interest.

liquidity preference hypothesis: The term structure of interest rates hypothesis which asserts that most borrowers prefer to borrow long and most lenders prefer to lend short; implies that long term interest rates generally exceed short term interest rates. See *segmented markets hypothesis* and *unbiased expectations hypothesis.*

liquidity ratio: A ratio (e.g., current or quick) designed to reflect a firm's short-run financial situation.

liquidity risk: The degree to which an asset's holding period return varies with interest rate moves in the market place.

listed bonds: Bonds authorized for trading on one or more exchanges.

listed stocks: Stocks authorized for trading by one or more of the stock exchanges.

listing: The act of obtaining exchange approval for trading on that exchange.

listing requirements: The criteria that a company must meet in order to have its securities listed for trading on an exchange.

load: The selling fee applied to a load mutual fund purchase; typically 6% of the amount invested.

loaded lagger: A stock of a company whose assets, particularly its liquid assets, have high values relative to the stock's market price.

load fund: A type of mutual fund sold through agents who receive fees. Such fees are typically 6% on small purchases and somewhat less on investments above $10,000.

lock-up agreement: An agreement between an acquirer and its intended takeover target that is designed to make the target unattractive to any other acquirer; similar to a golden handshake. Usually, both the target and would-be acquirer commit to use their best efforts to obtain approval of the merger agreement. If either side fails to do so, it agrees to pay the other side a substantial sum of money: the breakup fee.

long interest: The number of futures or options contracts outstanding (owned and sold). For such contracts, long interest equals short interest.

long position: The ownership of stocks or other securities as opposed to a short position, in which the investor has sold securities that he or she does not own.

long-term assets: See *fixed assets*.

long-term capital gain (loss): Gain (loss) on a capital asset held for at least a year.

long-term liabilities: Liabilities for which payment is not due for at least year or until the end of the next operating period, whichever is shorter; usually includes outstanding bonds, debentures, mortgages, and term loans.

loss: Net revenues minus costs when costs exceed revenues. See *profit*.

low load fund: A mutual fund that imposes a small front-end sales charge; typically 2% to 4%. See *load fund, no load fund*.

low PE stocks: Stocks whose price-earnings ratios (PEs) are well below the market average; sought out by value-oriented investors.

LTM: Last Twelve Months or the four most recent quarters of operating results.

LYON: A complicated type of zero coupon convertible debt security that is both callable and redeemable at prices that escalate through time.

M1: The basic money supply; includes checking deposits and cash held by the public.

M2: A broader based money supply definition than M1; includes everything in M1 plus most savings and money market deposit accounts. See *M1*

M3: A still broader based money supply definition than M2; includes everything in M2 plus large certificates of deposit and money market mutual funds sold to institutions. See *M1 & M2*.

M&A: Abbreviation for "mergers and acquisitions".

MAC: Acronym for "material adverse change".

maintenance capital expenditures: The amount a business must spend in order to do no more than preserve the efficiency and appearance of plant and equipment. No net additions to plant and equipment are contemplated.

maintenance margin: The required proportion that the investor's equity value must be in relation to the total market value of the portfolio in order to avoid a margin call. The investor will receive a margin call if the percentage drops below this level (typically 35%). See *margin call*.

management control: A situation in which no investor group owns enough of the firm's stock to exercise control and thus control is abdicated to the company's senior managers.

management fee: The compensation paid to the investment management company for its services to the fund. The average annual fee for a mutual fund is about 0.75 percent of assets for actively managed funds and 0.20 percent for index funds.

management-oriented company: A firm that is operated largely in the interest of management as opposed to that of the shareholders.

mandatory convertible notes: See *equity notes*.

manufactured call: A call-like position generated by a combination of a put and a long position in the underlying stock; position with a similar payoff matrix to a call.

manufactured put: A put-like position generated by a combination of a call and a short position in the underlying stock; position with a similar payoff matrix to a put.

margin (borrowing): Borrowing to finance a portion of a securities purchase; regulated by the Fed. For example, if a 60% margin rate is set, $10,000 worth of stock may be purchased with up to $4,000 of borrowed money. Only securities of listed and some large OTC companies qualify for margin loans.

margin (sales): profit as a percentage of sales revenues.

marginal tax rate: The percentage that must be paid in taxes on the last increment of taxable income.

margin call: A demand by a brokerage firm for additional collateral or cash needed to support existing margin debt; such a call is issued when the borrower's equity position falls below a preset percentage (e.g., 35%) of the value of margined securities. See *fed call* and *house call*.

margin maintenance: The minimum percentage of equity that a margin account must maintain in order to avoid triggering a margin call (e.g. 35%).

margin rate: The minimum percentage of the cost of a purchase of marginable securities that must be paid for with the investor's own money. Currently (2005) set at 50%.

market: The means by which buyers and sellers are brought together to trade goods and/or services for money.

marketability: The ease with which an investment can be bought or sold without appreciably affecting its price; for example, blue chip stocks are usually highly marketable because they are actively traded.

market approach: Estimating the value of properties (particularly real estate)
based on what similar properties have been selling for in the marketplace.

market clearing price: The price at which quantity supplied for an item equals
its quantity demanded. At that market clearing level no unsatisfied seller is
available at or below the market price and no unsatisfied buyer is available
at or above that market price.

market indexes: An average of security prices designed to reflect overall market
performance. The Dow-Jones Industrial Average, the best known and most
closely followed, is calculated by adding up the market prices of 30 leading industrial companies and dividing by a divisor; the divisor is changed
periodically in order to offset the impact of stock splits. Dow Jones Inc.
also compiles averages for utility and transportation stocks. Standard &
Poor's investor service, the NYSE, NASD, and AMEX all compute their
own indexes. Indexes are also compiled for bonds, commodities, options,
and various other types of investments (e.g. art work).

market indicator: See *technical market indicator*.

market maker: One who creates a market for a security by continuously quoting
a bid and asked price. Most market makers are members of NASD.

market model: Relating the price of individual security returns to market returns with a linear equation of the form: $R_{it} = á_i + â_i R_{mt}$ where R_{it} = return
of security i for period t; R_{mt} = market return for period t; and $á_i$ and $â_i$ are
firm i parameters.

market-on-close order: An order that is to be held until just before the close of
the market and then executed.

market order: An order to buy or sell an asset at the current market price;
requires immediate execution at the best currently available price.

market portfolio: A hypothetical portfolio representing each investment asset in proportion to its relative weight in the universe of investment assets.

market price: The current price at which willing buyers and willing sellers will
transact. Determined by the interplay of supply and demand.

market risk: The return variability associated with general market movements;
not diversifiable within the market. Also called systematic risk.

market risk premium: The increment of expected return above the risk-free rate
that investors demand from the market as compensation for accepting
exposure to systematic risk.

mark to market: The practice of re-computing the equity percentage in a margin account (stock or futures) on a daily basis.

master limited partnership (MLP): A type of business organization that combines some of the advantages of a corporation with some of the advantages of a limited partnership. Shares of ownership trade much like corporate stock yet the MLP is taxed like a partnership; that is, the partnership's pro rata profits are imputed to its owners and taxed only once.

matched and lost: Term applied to the outcome for the loser when two traders simultaneously arrive at the relevant trading post with equivalent orders, only one of which may be filled within the current market situation; they flip a coin to determine whose order is to be filled.

maturity: The length of time left until a security (e.g. bond or derivative) must be redeemed by its issuer.

maturity date: The date at which a security's principal must be redeemed.

mean: The average or expected value of a sample or distribution.

me-first rules: Restrictions in a bond's indenture that limit a firm's ability to take on additional debt with similar standing to that of the bonds in question.

merger: The act of combining two firms into a single company.

MGIC (Mortgage Guarantee Insurance Corporation): One of a group of companies that, in exchange for a fee, guarantee the timely payment of a portion of certain mortgages' obligations.

middle-of-the-road fund: A mutual fund that assembles and manages a balanced portfolio of stocks (some blue chips and some more speculative).

MIS: Management Information System. The computing resources that hold and allow access to the information owned by an organization.

mode: The high point or most likely outcome of a distribution; for a symmetrical distribution the mode and mean (average value) are identical.

modern portfolio theory (MPT): The combination of the capital asset pricing model, efficient market hypothesis, and related theoretical models of security market pricing and performance.

Monday-Friday stock pattern: The observed (if weak) tendency of stock prices to decline on Mondays and rise on Fridays.

monetarists: A group of economist who emphasizes the powerful role of monetary (as opposed to fiscal) policy in its influence over the level of economic activity. See *fiscalist*.

monetary asset: An investment that is denominated in dollars.

monetary policy: Government policy that utilizes growth in the money supply to affect the level and direction of economic activity; implemented by the

Fed through its control over bank reserves and required reserves, especially though the use of open market operations.

money fund: See *money market mutual fund.*

money illusion: Failure to take account of inflation's impact; thus an individual who received a 10% raise and thought his or her financial situation had improved in spite of the fact that prices had risen by 20% would suffer from money illusion.

Money Magazine: A monthly personal finance periodical published by Time Inc.

money market: The market for high-quality, short-term securities such as CDs, commercial paper, bankers acceptances, Treasury bills, short-term tax-exempt notes, and Eurodollar loans.

money market account: A type of bank or thrift institution account that pays money market rates and seeks to compete with money market mutual funds.

money market mutual fund: A type of mutual fund that invests in and holds a portfolio of short-term highly liquid securities. Also called a money fund.

money multiplier: The ratio of a change in reserves to the change in the money supply; thus a money multiplier of five would imply that a $1 billion increase (decrease) in reserves would result in a $5 billion increase (decrease) in the money supply.

money supply: Generally defined as the sum of all coin, currency (outside bank holdings), and deposits on which check-like instruments may be written. See *M1, M2,* and *M3.*

monkey with a gun (strategy): A negotiation tactic where one very aggressive party to the negotiations attempts to convince the other parties that he or she is so irrational that unless his or her demands are met, he or she will do something that hurts everyone.

mood indicators: Technical market indicators designed to reflect the market's degree of pessimism or optimism.

Moody's Industrial Manual: An annual publication containing detailed historical information on a very large number of publicly traded firms.

Moody's Investor Service: A firm that publishes manuals containing extensive historical data on a large number of publicly traded firms. Moody's also rates the riskiness of bonds and assigns ratings (e.g. AA).

mortgage: A loan collateralized by property, particularly real estate; the lender is entitled to take possession of the property if the debt is not repaid in a timely manner.

mortgage-backed security: A debt instrument representing a share of ownership in a pool of mortgages (e.g., GNMA passthroughs) or backed by a pool of mortgages (e.g., FNMA bonds).

mortgage bond: Debt security for which specific property is pledged as collateral.

mortgagee: The lender under a mortgage loan. See *mortgagor*.

mortgages — secured claims: The law governing real property mortgages and mortgages on chattel; are governed by various laws and different statutes in various jurisdictions. No central federal bankruptcy law exists on the subject.

mortgagor: The borrower under a mortgage loan. See *mortagagee*.

multiplier: The ratio of the change in the level of government spending to the resulting change in the level of GNP.

municipal bond fund: A mutual or closed-end fund holding a portfolio of municipal bonds.

municipals: Bonds issued by state and local governments. Most such bonds pay interest that is tax free to the recipient.

multi-index model: A method for estimating portfolio risk that utilizes a market index as well as indexes for various market subcategories.

mutual fund: A pooled investment in which managers buy and sell assets for a common portfolio. The portfolio's income and gains and losses accruing to the owners; may be either load (with sales fee) or no-load (no sales fee); stands ready to buy back its shares at their net asset value (sometimes less a redemption fee) on a continuous basis.

mutual fund cash position: A technical market indicator based on mutual fund liquidity; high (low) fund liquidity is said to be associated with a subsequent market rise (fall).

naked option writing: Writing call options without owning the underlying shares; if it is exercised the naked writer satisfies the contract with the optionholder by buying the required shares on the market.

NASD (National Association of Securities Dealers): The self-regulator of the OTC market. The NASD sponsored the NASDAQ trading system. These two, NASD and NASDAQ, are now separate organizations.

NASDAQ (National Association of Securities Dealers Automated Quotations): An automated information system that provides brokers and dealers with price quotations on securities that are traded OTC. See *NASD*.

NASDAQ Composite Index: A value-weighted index of OTC issues.

NASDAQ National Market System List: The primary list of OTC issues carried in most newspaper stock quotations. Membership is determined by criteria similar to the AMEX listing.

National Association of Investment Clubs (NAIC):   Organization that fosters and assists in the setting up of and operating of investment clubs.

NAV (Net Asset Value):   The per share market value of a mutual fund's portfolio.

NBER (National Bureau of Economic Research):   A private nonprofit research foundation that establishes the dates for business cycles and sponsors economic research.

near money: Assets such as savings accounts and Treasury bills that can quickly and easily be converted into spendable form.

net equity value: The stated accounting value of a firm obtained after subtracting the value of its outstanding debt obligations.

net-net: A stock whose market price is very low relative to the value of its liquid assets; more specifically, stock whose per share price is less than the company's net per share liquid assets where net liquid assets equals gross liquid assets less the pro rata amount of both short- and long-term debt.

net present value (NPV):   A measure of the value of the excess cash flows expected from a potential investment project. NPV is equal to the present value of the cash inflows from the project, discounted at the investment's required rate of return, minus the present value of the investment's cash outflows also discounted at the investment's required rate of return.

net worth: The dollar value of assets minus liabilities; the stockholders' residual ownership position. Also called equity.

new issue: An initial stock sale, usually of a company going public; also an initial sale of a bond issue.

new listing: A stock that has recently been listed on an exchange; may be the company's first listing on the particular exchange or first on any exchange.

New York Curb Exchange: The name which was once applied to the stock exchange that is now called the American Stock Exchange.

nifty fifty: A list of about 50 companies, with high current PE multiples and rapid recent growth rates that were preferred by many institutional investors in the 1970's.

noise trader: One who buys and sells securities without having any specific knowledge or superior analysis relating to its underlying value (an uninformed trader).

no-load (mutual) fund: A mutual fund whose shares are bought and sold directly from the fund at its NAV. Unlike a load fund, no agent or sales fee is involved.

non-market risk: Individual risk not related to general market movements; the total risk of an investment may be decomposed into that associated with the market (market risk) and that which is not (non-market risk). Also called unsystematic risk.

non-normal distribution: A distribution, such as a skewed distribution of returns, that differs from the normal shape. See *kurtosis, leptokurtosis, platokurtosis,* and *skewness*.

nonparticipating insurance: A type of insurance policy sold by a stockholder-owned company as opposed to participating insurance, which is sold by an insurance company owned by its policyholders (mutual).

normal distribution: A population distribution corresponding to the precisely defined normal bell shaped curve.

normal yield curve: A bond market in which bond yields to maturity rise with their terms to maturity.

normalization: Spreading the benefits of investment tax credits or other types of credits across the life of the asset that produced the credits. See also *flow- through*.

notes: Intermediate-term debt securities issued with maturity dates of one to ten years.

notional principal: The principal value of a swap transaction, which is used as a scale factor to translate interest rate differentials into cash settlement payments.

NOW (negotiable orders of withdrawal) accounts: A special type of deposit account that earns interest and allows check-like instruments to be written against it.

NYFE (New York Futures Exchange): A futures exchange associated with the NYSE; lists futures and option contracts on the NYSE Composite Index.

NYSE (New York Stock Exchange): The largest U.S. stock exchange. The vast majority of large U.S. companies list their stocks on the NYSE.

NYSE Composite Index: A value-weighted index of all NYSE-listed securities.

odd-lot short ratio: A technical market indicator based on relative long-short trading by small investors; when such trading is heavy, the market is said to be near a bottom.

odd-lotter: One who trades shares of stock in odd lots.

odd lot trade: A transaction involving less than one round lot of stock; usually 100 shares, although a few stocks are traded in 10-share lots.

off-board trading: Trading that takes place off an exchange, particularly OTC trading in NYSE-listed securities.

one-decision stocks: A now largely discredited concept popular the early 1970s that certain high-quality growth stocks should be bought and held; supposedly, the only decision necessary was to buy (like the old saying: "Buy but do not sell Manhattan real estate").

open-end investment company: A mutual fund or other pooled portfolio of investments that stands ready to buy or sell its shares at its NAV or NAV plus load if the fund has a load.

open interest: The number of option or commodity contracts outstanding; analogous to the number of shares outstanding for a stock.

open market committee: The Federal Reserve committee that decides on open market policy; consists of all seven of the Federal Reserve Board Governors plus five of the presidents of the regional Fed Banks including the president of the New York bank.

open market operations: Fed transactions in the government bond market (treasury bills). These operations are designed to affect bank reserves and thereby influence the money supply, interest rates, and economic activity.

optimal portfolio: The portfolio that has the highest utility for a given investment. It lies at the point of tangency between the efficient frontier and the curve with the investor's highest possible utility.

operating company: A firm with active ongoing business activities.

option: A put, call, warrant, right, or other security giving the holder the right but not the obligation to purchase or sell a security or other asset at a set price for a specific period.

Options Clearing Corporation (OCC): A company whose job is to guarantee performance of, monitor margin accounts for, and settle exchange-traded option transactions.

ordinary least squares: A method of estimating regression parameters by choosing linear coefficients that minimize the squares of the residuals.

organizational slack: Wasted firm resources resulting from managerial deadwood, lack of aggressiveness, carelessness, and so on.

OTC (Over the Counter): The market in unlisted securities and off-board trading in listed securities.

out-of-the-money option: An option whose striking price is less attractive than the current market price of its underlying stock. For a call (put) the strike price is above (below) the stock price.

overbought: An opinion that the market has risen too high too rapidly and is therefore poised for a downward correction.

oversold: An opinion that the market has fallen too far too rapidly and is therefore poised for an upward correction.

Pac Man defense: Tactic designed to avoid a takeover by attempting to acquire the attacking firm. Named after a video game.

paper: See *commercial paper*.

paper loss: An unrealized loss.

paper profit: An unrealized gain.

par (bond): The face value at which the bond issue matures.

par (common stock): A stated amount below which per share equity (net worth) may not fall without barring any future dividend payments.

par (preferred stock): The stated value on which the security's dividend and liquidation value is based.

parking: The illegal practice of holding a security in the name of one (sham) owner for the benefit of another (true owner) in an attempt to conceal the beneficial owner's true identity. Sometimes stock is parked during the period prior to launching a takeover attempt.

Par ROI equation: An empirically estimated profitability equation of the Strategic Planning Institute.

participating bond: Bond that may pay an extra coupon increment in years in which the issuing firm is especially profitable.

participating life insurance: Life insurance sold by a mutual company, which is owned by and shares its profits with its policyholders.

participating preferred: Preferred stock that may pay an extra dividend increment in years in which the issuing firm is especially profitable.

passed dividend: The omission of a regular dividend payment.

passthrough: A share of ownership in a mortgage pool whose interest and principal payments are flowed through to the owners.

payback period: The length of time until the amount originally invested in a project is recaptured via earnings from the project.

payout ratio: Dividends per share as a percentage of earnings per share.

payment default: A failure to make scheduled payments of interest or principal that are due on a debt obligation.

PE (price earnings ratio): The stock price relative to the most recent 12-month's earnings per share (or sometimes relative to the company's next 12 months forecasted earnings)

penny stock market: A market for low-priced stocks (under $1 per share); especially active in Denver.

penny stocks: Low-priced stocks usually selling for under $1 per share; normally are issued by small speculative companies.

pension: A periodic or lump sum payment to a person following retirement from employment or such a payment to surviving dependents of a deceased former employee.

PE ratio model: An empirical model designed to explain price earnings ratios as a function of various fundamental factors.

pennying: Entering a limit order (either to buy or sell) with a threshold price a penny better than the best current offer level.

percentage order: A market or limit order that is entered once a certain amount of stock has traded.

performance fund: See *go-go fund*.

per period return (PPR): The return earned for a single period.

physical: The underlying physical delivery instrument for a particular futures contract.

PIKs (payment in kind securities): Securities whose yields are, at the issuer's option, payable in additional securities of like kind to the existing securities; thus a preferred stock may choose to pay the dividend in additional preferred shares.

pink sheets: Quotation source for most publicly traded OTC issues, especially non NASDAQ issues.

pink sheet stocks: OTC stocks not traded on the NASDAQ system; issued by very small, obscure, and often speculative companies.

pit: The name of the physical location where specific commodity contracts are traded.

planning horizon (portfolio management): The time frame in which a portfolio is managed.

platokurtosis: The characteristic of a distribution which differs from the normal by having less of the distribution concentrated at the peaks and tails. See *kurtosis, leptokurtosis*.

point (stocks and bonds): Pricing units; for stocks, a point represents $1 per share; for bonds, a point is equivalent to $10.

point and figure chart: A technical chart that has no time dimension. An x is used to designate an up move of a certain magnitude while an o denotes a similar size down move. The xs (os) are stacked on top of each other as long as the direction of movement remains up (down); a new column is begun when direction changes.

points (real estate): A fee charged for granting a loan, especially for a mortgage on real estate. One point represents one percent of the amount of the loan.

poison pill: Anti-takeover defense in which a new diluting security is issued if control over some pre-specified percentage of the firm (e.g. 20%) is about to shift.

policy statement: A statement in which the investor specifies investment goals, constraints, and risk preferences for the benefit of the manager.

Ponzi scheme: An investment scam promising high returns that are secretly paid out of the money coming in from "investors"; usually exposed when incoming funds are insufficient to cover promised out payments. The scam depends upon fresh investor money being brought in to pay its promised return.

pooling of interest accounting: A type of merger accounting in which an acquired firm's assets and liabilities are transferred to the acquiring firm's balance sheet without any valuation adjustment.

portfolio: A set of investment asset holdings in an investment like account by a single owner (institution or individual).

portfolio insurance: An investment service in which the "insurer" endeavors to place a floor under the value of the "insured" portfolio. If the portfolio's value falls to a pre-specified threshold level, the portfolio insurer attempts to neutralizes it against a further decline by purchasing an appropriate number of index puts or selling an appropriate number of index options.

portfolio risk: Risk that takes account of the diversifying impact of portfolio components.

position trader: A commodity trader who takes and holds futures position for several days or more (as opposed to a day trader).

post: One of eighteen horseshoe-shaped locations on the NYSE floor where securities are traded. Also called trading post.

postponable expenditures: Purchases of long-term assets such as consumer durables.

preemptive rights: Shareholder rights to maintain their proportional share of their firm by subscribing proportionally to any new stock issue. Such rights are reserved for the shareholders of some publicly traded companies but many companies do not provide preemptive rights to their shareholders.

preferences: In general, a transfer of the debtor's property to or for the benefit of a creditor on account of an antecedent debt at a time in which the debtor was insolvent, the purpose or result of which was to facilitate the creditor receiving more than the creditor would receive in a bankruptcy proceeding.

preferred habitat: One of four hypotheses, designed to explain the term structure of interest rates based on a tendency for borrowers and lenders to gravitate toward their preferred loan lengths.

preferred stock: Shares of equity in a corporation whose indicated dividends and liquidation values must be paid after creditors but before common shareholders receive any dividends or liquidation payments.

premium (bond): The amount by which a bond's market price exceeds its par value.

premium (option): The market price of an option; confusingly, the term is also sometimes used to refer to an option's time value.

premium over conversion value: The amount by which a convertible's market price exceeds its conversion value.

premium over straight-debt value: The amount by which a convertible bond's market price exceeds its value as a nonconvertible debt security.

prepackaged bankruptcy: A bankruptcy proceeding in which the debtor and major creditors have worked out the terms of the reorganization plan prior to the bankruptcy filing so that the legal process can move along quickly.

prepayment penalty: The fee assessed for early liquidation of an outstanding debt if so provided in the loan agreement.

pre-petition: Referring to events or the status that existed pre-bankruptcy; that is before the bankruptcy petition was filed.

present value: The value today of a dollar to be received at some future point in time, using appropriate discount rates.

present value factor: The number used when deriving the present value of a future cash flow. For the first year, it is calculated as one divided by one plus the discount rate, or $\{1 / (1 + \text{Discount Rate})\}$. For subsequent years, it is calculated as one divided by one plus the discount rate raised to the power of the year in question. For example, in year five the present value factor would be $\{1 / ((1 + \text{Discount Rate})^5)\}$.

price dependencies: Price movements that are related to (correlated with) past price movements.

price floor: The support level of a convertible bond provided by its straight-debt value.

price momentum: A strategy in which an investor acquires stocks which have enjoyed above-market stock price increases.

price stability: The absence of inflation or deflation.

primary distribution: The initial sale of a stock or bond (new issue).

primary market: The market for the initial sale of a security; subsequent trades of the security are said to take place in the secondary market.

prime: One of the two component securities created when appropriate shares are deposited into an Americus Trust. The prime receives the stock's dividends and up to some pre-specified liquidation payment at the termination date; the score receives any value in excess of the amount assigned to the prime.

prime rate: The interest rate that banks advertise as the best (lowest) rate that they will charge their very good/excellent credit worthy customers. Some very secure borrowers may, however, be able to borrow at a still lower super prime rate.

principal (in a trade): The person or institution for whom the broker acts as an agent.

principal (of a bond): The face value of a bond.

priorities: Certain claims such as claims for back taxes, debtor in possession financing and the costs of administering a bankrupt estate are paid ahead of the general claims of other creditors, all as particularized in the Bankruptcy Code.

private equity: Investing in entire companies (not public) or divisions purchased from other companies. The exit for such investments is often to take them public after enhancing their value.

private market value: The value that a private buyer would pay for an entire company in order to control the disposition of it's cash flow. Determined using discounted cash flow analysis.

private placement: A direct sale of a security issue to a small number of large qualified buyers.

probability distribution: A display of possible events along with their associated probabilities.

professional corporation pension plans: Pension plans as a means to shelter income from taxes; set up by professionals such as doctors, lawyers, and architects after organizing their businesses as corporations. The 1982 tax act severely limited the amount of tax-sheltered contributions that may be put into such plans.

profit: Net revenues minus costs when revenues exceed costs. See *loss*.

profitability models: Models designed to explain company profit rates.

profitability ratio: A ratio such as return on equity and return on sales designed to reflect the firm's profit rates.

profit and loss statement: See *income statement*.

programs: The actual trades instituted by a program trader. Market watchers might, for example, see a series of large trades in stocks making up the S&P 500 and conclude that programs are moving the market in a particular direction.

program trading: A type of mechanical trading in large blocks by institutional investors; usually involves both stock and index futures contracts as, for example, in index arbitrage or portfolio insurance. Also called programmed trading.

proof of claim: A document that creditors seeking to participate in the distribution of the proceeds of a bankrupt estate must file with the Court within the time periods provided in order thereby to be eligible to receive a payment and distribution from the bankrupt estate.

proprietorship: The condition of ownership of a business entity, usually referring to sole ownership.

prospectus: An official document that all companies offering new securities for public sale must file with the SEC prior to proceeding with the offerings; spells out in detail the financial position of the offering company, what the new funds will be used for, the qualifications of the corporate officers, and any other material information.

protective put: A strategy in which a put option is purchased in order to protect a long position in an underlying asset or portfolio of assets.

proxy: A shareholder ballot.

proxy fight: A contest for control of a company.

proxy material: A statement of relevant information that the firm must supply to shareholders when they solicit proxies. See *proxy*.

public offering: A security sale made through dealers to the general public and registered with the SEC.

pump and dump: A market manipulation strategy (illegal) wherein a trader, who has accumulated a substantial position in a stock or less often another security, recommends an investment in it to others (pump) while quietly unloading his or her position (dump).

purchase accounting: An accounting procedure used to consolidate the financial statements of two merged companies in which the net assets of the acquired firm are entered on the books of the acquiring firm at amounts that sum to the firm's acquisition price. As opposed to the "pooling of interest" method of accounting for a business combination, the purchase method allows assets to be written up to their fair market values. Under the pooling method, assets of the acquired firm continue to be carried over to the books of the acquiring company at their historical basis. Earnings under the purchase method are included only from the date of acquisition, whereas under the pooling method they are restated as far back as necessary. See *pooling of interest accounting*.

pure arbitrage: An arbitrage trade that involves no element of risk. See *arbitrage*.

pure hedge: A hedge whose purpose is to reduce the risk on an existing position. See *hedge*.

pure risk aversion: A desire to avoid risk and willingness to trade off expected returns in order to reduce risk.

pure risk premium: The portion of the promised yield in excess of the riskless rate which is due to pure risk aversion as opposed to that which reflects the expected default loss.

put: An option to sell a specified amount of stock or other asset at a specified price over a specified time period.

put bond: A bond with an indenture provision allowing it to be sold back to the issuer at a pre-specified price.

put-call parity: A theoretical relationship between the value of a put and the value of a corresponding call on the same underlying security with the same strike and expiration date.

quarterly earnings: Interim profits, usually per share profits, for a three-month period.

quarterly report: A report to shareholders containing three-month financial statements and certain other information.

quick ratio: See *acid test ratio*.

raider: A hostile (unfriendly to present management) outside party that seeks to take over control of a target company.

rally: A brisk general rise in security prices.

random walk: The random motion of stock prices, analogous to the movement of a drunk who at any time is as likely to move in one direction as another; implies that the next price change is as likely to be up as down regardless of past price history. This type of behavior is called Brownian motion in the physical sciences.

rate of return: The profit rate on an investment that takes into account both dividends and capital appreciation (increases in the price of the security); for example, a 9% rate of return implies that the owner of $100 worth of stock will earn a total of $9 in dividends and capital appreciation over the forthcoming year.

rating (bond): A credit quality or risk evaluation assigned by a rating agency such as Standard & Poor's or Moody's.

ratio analysis: Balance sheet, income statement and other types of financial analysis that utilize ratios of financial aggregates.

reaffirmation agreement: An agreement by a debtor to pay a debt that would otherwise have been dischargeable in a bankruptcy proceeding. Under state law and the bankruptcy code, all pre-bankruptcy property of the debtor generally becomes property of the estate. However, an individual is permitted to exempt certain properties. These properties are called "exempt property". Property designated through certain exemption statutes cannot be reached by creditors through judicial collection efforts.

RCMM (registered competitive market maker): See *floor trader*.

real estate limited partnership (RELP): A type of investment vehicle that is organized as a limited partnership and invests directly in real estate properties.

real estate sales company: A firm that sells property, especially at marketing events such as complimentary dinners; the property is often in a distant location (Florida, Arizona) and part of a projected retirement or vacation development.

real options: Options embedded in a firm's real assets that provide managers with valuable decision-making flexibility, such as the right to abandon an investment project rather than sink more money into it.

real return: A return calculation adjusted for the impact of changes in the price level; for example, if the nominal rate of return was 7%, a 3% inflation rate would correspond to a real rate of return to 4% (7-3 = 4).

real risk free rate (RRFR): The basic interest rate with no reflection of inflation or uncertainty. The pure time value of money.

realized capital gains: Gains that result (and generally become taxable) when an appreciated asset is sold.

realized yield: The expected component yield on a bond that is sold assuming the reinvestment of all cash flows at an explicit rate.

rebate: The return of a portion of a payment.

receivership: A prejudgment collection remedy that exists outside of the Bankruptcy Code. The court appoints a receiver as an equitable remedy in order to prevent the deterioration or impairment of the value of the property of a debtor.

recession: An economic downturn categorized as a recession by the National Bureau of Economic Research (NBER); historically, two successive quarters of decline in real (in noninflationary dollars) GNP have signaled the start of a recession.

record date: The shareholder registration date that determines who is to receive that period's dividends. Or a similar date for a bond and its coupon payment.

red chip stocks: Stocks of intermediate quality. See *blue chip stock, white chip stock*.

Red Herring: See *registration statement*.

redemption fee: A charge (typically 2%) that is assessed of those who cash in their shares of certain mutual funds.

redemption price: See *call price*.

refinancing: The selling of new securities in order to finance the retirement of others that are maturing or being called.

registered bond: A bond whose ownership is determined by registration as opposed to possession (bearer bond).

Registered Competitive Market Maker (RCMM): See *floor trader*.

registered representative: A full-time employee of a NYSE member firm who is qualified to serve as an account executive for the firm's customers.

registered trader: An exchange member who trades stocks on the exchange floor for his or her own account (or account in which he or she is part owner).

registrar: A company such as a bank that maintains the records of share ownership.

registration statement: A form that must be filed with the SEC before a security can be offered for sale; must contain all materially relevant information relating to the offering. A similar type of statement is required when a firm's shares are listed for trading. Referred to in the trade as a "Red Herring" due to the disclaimers written in red ink on its cover. Describes the terms of the bond issue, business operations of the company and other relevant information required by the SEC.

regional exchange: A U.S. stock exchange located outside New York City.

regression: An equation that is fitted to data by statistical techniques; computers are generally used to perform the calculations. In the simplest case a regression will have one variable to be explained (dependent variable) and one variable to explain it (independent variable) and would take the form: $x_t = a + by_t$ (where x_t = dependent variable; y_t = independent variable; and a and b are parameters determined by the computer that best fits the data). Graphically one can envision a scatter diagram relating x_t and y_t with a line drawn through the points close to line on the average) as the regression line. The "a" is the intercept and "b" the slope coefficient of this line. More complicated multiple regression equations of the form $x_t = a + by_t + cz_t + dw_t + ev_t$ ... containing more than one explanatory variable may also be estimated. Again the computer can be used to select the best values for a, b, c, etc.

regression toward the mean: The tendency of many phenomena to migrate toward their average values over time.

regulated investment company: A company such as a mutual fund or closed-end fund that qualifies for exemption from federal corporate income tax liability as a result of meeting the requirements set forth in Subchapter M of the Internal Revenue Code.

Regulation Q: A Fed rule that at one time limited interest rates that banks and thrifts could pay on certain types of deposits/investments; rendered inoperative by deregulation.

Regulation T: A Fed rule that governs credit to brokers and dealers for security purchases.

Regulation U: A Fed rule that governs margin credit limits.

reinvestment risk: The risk associated with reinvesting coupon payments at unknown future (market determined) interest rates. The yield to maturity on a bond is generally computed under the assumption that coupons will be reinvested at the same rate as the bond's current yield to maturity; if, however, market interest rates decline prior to the bond's maturity, the reinvested coupons will not generate the expected return and the actual realized yield to maturity will be lower.

REIT (real estate investment trust): Companies that buy and manage rental properties and/or real estate mortgages and pay out more than 95% of their income as dividends; no corporate profit taxes are due on their income.

relative strength: A technical analysis concept based on an assumption that stocks whose market prices have risen relative to the overall market exhibit "relative strength", and this relative strength tends to carry them to still higher price levels. Tests of the concept are largely negative.

release: A canceling of litigation claims, frequently granted pursuant to the plan of reorganization to various entities involved in the case.

REMIC (Real Estate Mortgage Investment Conduit): A type of mortgage-based debt security that restructures the payment streams of a portfolio of mortgages into bond-like components. Thus the short-term REMICs receive most of the initial cash flows in a pattern similar to a short-term debt security. Similarly, the longer term REMICs are promised a cash flow much like a long-term bond. The uncertain portion of the cash flow stream is left largely with a residual security called the resid.

reorganization: Restructuring a firm's capital structure and operating facilities in the face of a default, near-default, or bankruptcy.

replacement cost approach: The valuing of real estate or other asset on the basis of the cost of producing equivalent assets.

repo: See *repurchase agreement*.

repurchase agreement (repo): A type of investment in which a security is sold with a prearranged purchase price and date designed to produce a particular yield.

required rate of return: The expected return that is designed to compensate investors for the passage of time, the expected rate of inflation, and the uncertainty of the return.

reserve requirement: The percentage of reserves that each bank is required to maintain on deposit with the Fed relative to each increment of demand or time deposits.

resid: The residual security left as the various cash flows are assigned to the various term REMICs.

residual asset value: The present value of the amount in which the assets of a business are to be sold at some specified future date.

resistance level: A price range or level that, according to technical analysis, tends to block or at least restrict further price rises.

retained earnings: An entry on the income statement equal to annual after-tax profits less dividends paid; also an entry on the balance sheet, the sum of annual retained earnings to date.

re-trade: When a buyer of assets takes advantage of the vulnerability of a distressed seller to insist on new more advantageous terms, at the last minute, for a deal already agreed to. Or more generally when one party to a negotiation seeks to alter the terms of an agreement to the disadvantage of the other party.

return on assets (ROA): Profits before interest and taxes as a percentage of total assets. Also called return on investment (ROI).

return on equity (ROE): Profits after taxes, interest, and preferred dividends as a percentage of common equity.

return on investment (ROI): Profits before interest and taxes as a percentage of total assets. Also called return on assets (ROA).

return on sales (ROS): Profits as a percentage of sales; also called sales margin.

revenue bond: A municipal bond backed by the revenues of the project that it finances.

reverse crack: A commodity trade involving buying heating oil and gasoline and selling an equivalent amount of crude oil.

reverse crush: A commodity trade involving buying soybean oil and meal and selling a corresponding amount of soybean futures.

reverse merger: An acquisition structure whereby the acquirer first acquires control of the target by, for example, purchasing majority ownership of its stock. Then the acquirer causes the target to merge the acquirer into the target. This transaction is typically accomplished to take what is currently a shell corporation (the target) that has a prior history as a public company and use it as a vehicle for turning the acquirer (a here to for private company) into a public company without the expense of an IPO. The surviving company usually goes forward with the name and history of the target.

reverse mortgage: A type of mortgage in which the mortgagor uses his or her home as a vehicle to obtain a periodic (e.g. monthly) income. Typically a relatively old person (e.g. 65 years or older) owns his or her home and has no outstanding mortgage. This person pledges the home in exchange for a promise of a monthly income for as long as the homeowner continues to live in the home. A debit balance is built up against the house. When the house is sold, the maker of the reverse mortgage receives the balance due from the proceeds of the sale.

reverse split: A security exchange transaction in which each shareholder exchanges his or her existing shares for a reduced number of shares but retains the same proportional ownership; thus a 10-for-1 reverse split would exchange 10 new shares for each 100 old shares. Reverse splits are generally motivated by a desire to raise the company's pre share market price.

revolving credit facility: Similar to working capital facilities but may be used for other corporate purposes. Similar in nature to credit cards in that they typically provide for some minimum repayment schedule.

riding the yield curve: A bond portfolio management strategy which seeks to take advantage of an upward sloping yield curve by purchasing intermediate term bonds and then selling them as they approach maturity.

right: A security allowing shareholders to acquire new stock at a pre-specified price over a pre-specified time period, generally issued proportional to the number of shares currently held; normally exercisable at a specified price that is usually below the current market price. Rights generally trade in a secondary market after they are issued. Some rights are not transferable and as such they do not trade.

risk: The variance of the expected return, i.e., the degree of certainty associated with the expected return. See also *systematic* and *unsystematic risk*.

risk arbitrage: An investment strategy in which offsetting positions in the securities of an acquisition target and its would-be acquirer are taken when the combined position is computed to show a profit if the merger takes place at the announced terms.

risk averse: The property of preferring security and demonstrating a willingness to sacrifice some amount of expected return in order to achieve a more secure yield.

risk-free rate: The interest rate on an investment, such as a Treasury bill, that is viewed by investors as devoid of risk.

risk hedge: A hedge position undertaken from scratch that is designed to profit from relative price moves in the underlying positions; option spreads are an example.

riskless investment: An investment having an expected return which is certain to be realized; that is, if a riskless asset is expected to yield 6%, the probability of its earning exactly a 6% return is 100%.

risk neutral: The property of preferring the highest expected return available without regard to risk; indifference to risk.

risk premium: The expected return in excess of the risk-free rate reflecting an extra increment of return to compensate for the investment's risk.

risk return trade-off: Tendency for more risky assets to be priced to yield higher expected returns than less risky assets.

risk-reward ratio: A measure of the amount of risk assumed in seeking a specific level of profit.

risky asset: An asset whose future returns are uncertain.

Robert Morris Associates: An organization of bankers that compiles averages of financial ratios for various industry groups.

rollover: A change from holding one investment asset in the investor's portfolio to holding another. For example, replacing a maturing bond with a new bond.

rollup: An amalgamation of a group of failed firms into a newly reconstituted entity shorn of its component's legacy costs.

Roth IRA: A type of IRA for which the contributions deposited into the account are in the form of after-tax dollars (no tax deduction) but the funds that are withdrawn, emerge without a tax liability attached. Thus all of the account's earnings are tax free. See *IRA*.

round lot: The basic unit in which securities are traded; usually 100 shares although some stocks trade in 10-unit lots.

Rule 144: An SEC rule restricting the sale of lettered stock.

Rule 390: A NYSE rule restricting members of the exchange from off-board trading (trades not taking place on an exchange).

Rule 415: An SEC rule allowing shelf registration of a security, which may then be sold periodically without separate registrations of each part.

Rule of 20: A market timing rule based on the proposition that the sum of the Dow Jones Industrial Average's PE and the inflation rate generally tend toward a value of 20; thus, according to those who advocate the validity of this rule, departures in either direction tend to forecast a market move.

run: An uninterrupted series (usually daily) of an price increases or an unintercepted series of price decreases.

Sallie Mae (Student Loan Market Association): A federal government agency that facilitates education lending and raises funds by selling notes backed by government-guaranteed student loans.

Sarbanes-Oxley: Reform legislation requiring CEOs to vouch for the fairness and accuracy of the firm's financial statements.

saturation effect: The impact on profits and revenues when a heretofore rapid growth firm or industry largely satisfies what had been the market's pent up demand.

savings bonds: Low-denomination Treasury issues designed to appeal to small investors. Such securities do not trade in a public market.

scalper: A commodity trader who seeks to profit from very short-run (intra day) price changes.

scorched-earth defense: An anti-takeover tactic in which the defending company's management engages in practices designed to reduce the firm's value to such a degree that it is no longer attractive to the potential acquirer.

S Corporation: See *Subchapter S corporation*.

seasoned equity issues: New equity shares offered for sale by firms which already have publicly traded stock outstanding.

seasoning: The process by which new issues of securities acquire market acceptance in their post-issue trading.

seat: A membership on an exchange.

SEC (Securities and Exchange Commission): The government agency with direct regulatory authority over the securities industry.

secondary distribution: A large public securities offering that is made outside of the usual exchange or OTC market. Such an offering is used in order to sell a larger quantity of the security than those making the offering believe can be easily absorbed by the market's usual channels. A secondary offering facilitates spreading out the period for absorption.

secondary market: The market for already-issued securities. May take place on the exchanges or OTC market.

secondary stocks: Relatively obscure stocks not favored by institutional investors, thus individual investors are the principle market for these stocks; secondary stocks may trade on the AMEX, NASD, regional exchanges or be among the smaller companies listed on the NYSE market. See *tertiary stocks*.

second mortgage: A mortgage debt secured by a property's equity but subordinated to the first mortgage holder's claim on the property.

Section 341 Hearing: An organizational meeting early in a bankruptcy case involving unsecured creditors, the U.S. Trustee and the company.

Section 363 Sale: A bankruptcy auction sale. Debtors can sell assets two ways – through a plan and through the exemptions provided under Section 363. Sales are allowed pursuant to Section 363 if certain tests are met – such as if the asset's value is sinking rapidly or the company will not be able to afford the cash burn through consummation of a Plan.

Section 382: A Tax Code provision in relation to cancellation of indebtedness (COD) income. When a company pays off prepetition debt at the discount (a common event in a bankruptcy), the haircut can be recognized as taxable gain. The company often will have incurred net operating losses, or "NOLs", over a period of years. Such NOLs can be utilized to offset the gains from discharge of indebtedness. Section 382 limits the use of such NOLs to shelter COD income if a "change of control" of the company's equity has occurred.

sector fund: A type of mutual fund that specializes in a narrow segment of the market; for example, an industry (chemicals), region (Sunbelt), or category (small capitalization).

sector rotation strategy: An active investment strategy that involves investing in the stocks of companies that operate in specific industries or stocks with specific characteristics (low P/E, growth, value) that are anticipated to outperform the market. Then shifts in sector concentrations occur as their relative attractivenesses changes.

secured (senior) bond: A bond backed by a legal claim on specified assets owned by the issuer.

security: A financial instrument, such as indebtedness, common stock, preferred stock, rights or warrants.

securities: Paper assets representing a claim on or interest in something of value. Examples include stocks, bonds, mortgages, warrants, rights, puts, calls, futures contracts, and certain warehouse receipts (e.g. ADRs).

Securities Amendment Act of 1970: An act restricting the front-end loading fees that mutual funds can charge their investors.

securitization: The process of turning the ownership of an asset with relatively poor marketability into a security with substantially greater market acceptability; for example, a portfolio of mortgages can be turned into a security that looks like a standard bond but is derived from real estate mortgage loans, auto loans, or credit card balances.

security agreement: An agreement that creates or provides for a security interest (e.g. collateral).

security interest: A lien created by an agreement.

security market line: The theoretical relationship between a security's market risk and its expected return.

segmented markets hypothesis: A theory designed to explain the term structure of interest rates as due to the supply and demand of each maturity class. See *liquidity preference* and *unbiased expectations hypotheses*.

self-tender: A firm tendering for the purchase of its own shares; sometimes used as an anti-takeover defense. A self-tender may be used as an alternative to paying a dividend.

seller financing: A procedure in which the real estate seller finances part of the property's purchase price by accepting the buyer's note as partial payment.

selling short: The act of selling a security that belongs to someone else and is borrowed; the short seller covers his or her short position by buying back equivalent securities and restoring them to the original owner. The short seller hopes that the securities prices will fall while he or she is short.

selling short against the box: Selling short securities which the seller already owns. Usually done to defer a gain for tax purposes.

semistrong form of the efficient market hypothesis: The view that market prices quickly and accurately reflect all public information; implies that fundamental analysis applied to public data is a useless waste of time.

semi weak form of the efficient market hypothesis: The view that market prices cannot be successfully forecast with technical market indicators.

senior obligation: A claim that is not subordinated to another claim. Such obligations may come behind secured obligations.

SEP (Simplified Employee Pension Plan): Pension plan in which both the employee and the employer contribute to an Individual Retirement Account (IRA).

serial bond: A bond issue portions of which mature at stated time intervals rather than all at once.

serial correlation: Correlation between adjacent time series data.

shark repellent: Anti-takeover provisions such as a poison pill.

shelf registration: An SEC provision allowing the preregistration of an amount of a security to be sold over time without specific registration of each sale; permitted by SEC Rule 415.

short against the box: The short selling of stock that the short seller also owns; usually employed as a tax device for extending the date of realizing a gain.

short covering: Buying an asset to offset an existing short position.

short interest (futures and options): The number of futures or options contracts written and outstanding for a particular contract. For these contracts, short interest always equals long interest.

short interest (stocks): The number of shares sold short.

short position: To have sold an asset that is not owned with a promise to repurchase it later, hopefully at a lower price.

short sale: The sale of borrowed securities with the intention of repurchasing them later at a lower price.

short-short fund: A type of bond mutual fund holding a portfolio of very short term debt instruments (but longer than that of a money market mutual fund).

short squeeze: The result when powerful forces driving up the price of a stock have the effect of squeezing a substantial short interest. The squeezed shorts are forced to cover by buying in the shares that they have sold short, usually at inflated prices, thereby driving prices still higher.

short-swing profit: A gain made by an insider on stock held for less than twelve months; such gains must be paid back to the company.

short-term gains (losses): Gains (losses) on capital assets held for less than six months.

short-term trading index: A technical market indicator based on the relative percentage of advancing versus declining stocks.

short-term unit trust: A unit investment trust made up of an unmanaged portfolio of short-term debt securities; usually self-liquidating within six months of issue.

simple interest: Interest paid and computed only on the principal. No compounding takes place.

single-index model: A method of estimating portfolio risk that utilizes only the market index and market model as opposed to the full variance-covariance matrix.

single-premium deferred annuity contract: An annuity with a defined future value; sold by insurance companies.

sinking fund: An indenture provision calling for a specified portion of a bond issue to be redeemed, periodically; required by many bond indentures in order to provide that all of the issue's outstanding debt will not come due at one time but rather will be spread out over a number of years.

SIPC (Securities Investors Protection Corporation): A federal government agency that guarantees the safety of brokerage accounts up to $500,000, no more than $100,000 of which may be in cash.

skewed distribution: A nonsymmetrical distribution; it's probabilities are spread out more on one side of its mode than the other.

skewness: The degree to which a distribution is nonsymmetrical.

skunk at the picnic (strategy): An approach in a negotiation where one party is extremely aggressive in seeking to gain an advantage vis-a-vis the other parties to the negotiation.

SMA (special miscellaneous account): A sum associated with a margin account; normally equal to the account's (margin) buying power. The SMA account is increased when stock is sold and decreased when stock is purchased. At times the SMA of an account can become inflated (above the account's buying power) when the equity of the account is near or below the minimum for margin maintenance.

Special Purpose Acquisition Company (SPAC): A blind pool investment company that plans to acquire one or more companies for investment purposes.

small-firm effect: An empirical anomaly in which risk-adjusted stock returns for companies with low market capitalization tend to be above those returns generated by high market capitalization firms.

smokestack companies: Companies in basic industries (e.g. steel, chemicals, paper, etc.) whose profits and sales revenues tend to move cyclical with the economy.

social responsibility fund: A type of mutual fund that avoids investments in companies whose activity it views as socially undesirable. For example, those involved with tobacco, alcohol, pollution, defense, guns, and so forth would likely be avoided by such a fund.

social irresponsibility fund: A type of mutual fund that assembles a portfolio of the stocks of the very types of companies that social responsibility funds avoid.

source and application of funds statement: An accounting statement reporting a firm's cash inflows and outflows. Now called changes in financial position statement.

S&P (Standard & Poor's Corporation): A major firm in the investment area that rates bonds (level of risk), collects and reports financial data, and computes market indexes.

S&P 500 Index: A value-weighted stock index based on the share prices of 500 large firms. Many index funds select this representative index as their benchmark.

specialist: An exchange member who makes a market in assigned listed securities on an exchange.

specialized dependencies: Predictable return patterns related to some specific type of event such as a new issue or tax-loss trading.

special offering: A large block of stock offered for sale on an exchange with special incentive fees paid to the brokers whose customers are purchasers. Also called a spot secondary.

speculating: The act of committing funds for a short period of time at high risk in the hopes of realizing a large gain.

split: An exchange of securities whereby each shareholder ends up with a different number of shares (usually more but sometimes less) but the new number of shares represents the same percentage of the firm's ownership as before the split. In a two-for-one split a shareholder with 100 old shares would receive an additional 100 shares. See *forward split, reverse split*.

spot market: The market for immediate delivery of some commodity such as wheat or silver.

spot secondary: See *special offering*.

spread (bid-ask): The difference between the bid and the ask price.

spread (interest rate): The different between two market yields such as the spread between BB (Junk) bond yields and that of equivalent maturity governments.

spread (trade): A type of hedge trade such as a vertical or horizontal spread (options) or some comparable combination trade in the futures market; offsetting positions taken in similar securities in the hope of profiting from relative price moves.

stalking horse: In connection with an auction sale, sellers generally find a "stalking horse", or "lead bidder" to be beneficial. Such a stalking horse provides a minimum price that the company will receive for its asset in the sale.

standard deviation: A measure of the degree to which the distribution of a random variable is compact or spread out. For a normal distribution about two times out of three the variable's actual value will be within one standard deviation on either side of the mean value; about 19 out of 20 times it will be within two standard deviations. One standard deviation is the square root of the variance. See also *variance*.

Standard & Poor's Corporation Reports: An investment periodical containing quarterly updated analyses of a large number of publicly traded firms.

Standard & Poor's Encyclopedia: A book published periodically that contains analyses of S&P 500 stocks.

Standard & Poor's Investor Service: A major firm in the investment area that rates bonds (risk level); also computes market indexes, compiles investment information, and publishes various investment periodicals.

Standard & Poor's Stock Guide: A monthly publication with a compact line of data containing information on most publicly traded corporations.

standstill agreement: A reciprocal understanding between a company's management on one side and an outside party that owns a significant minority position in the company's stock on the other side. Each party gives up certain rights in exchange for corresponding concessions by the other party.

For example, the outside ownership group may agree to limit its owner-ship position to some pre-specified level. In exchange management may agree to allow some minority board representation by the outside group.

stays: A restraining of creditors (in a bankruptcy proceeding) from taking action to collect on their claims against the debtor and enforce security interests against the debtor or the debtor's property.

Stein estimators: Statistical techniques for estimating a variable that assumes a regres-sion toward the mean tendency and makes a corresponding adjustment in the estimated value of the variable.

Stock Clearing Corporation: A NYSE subsidiary that clears transactions for member firms.

stock dividend: A distribution to shareholders paid in the form of additional shares of stock; similar to a stock split although usually proportionately fewer new shares are distributed. Stock dividend payments do not alter each stockholder's percentage of ownership.

stock exchange: An organization established for trading a specific list of securi-ties during specific trading hours usually at a single location.

stockholder-oriented company: A company whose management is particularly responsive to the interest of its stockholders; a large ownership group may exercise effective control or management itself may own a large block of the company's stock.

stock split (forward split): The division of a company's existing stock into more shares (say, 2 for 1, or 3 for 1); usually undertaken in order to reduce the price per share with the objective of improving the shares' marketability. See also *reverse split*.

stock split (reverse split): See *reverse split*.

stop-limit order: A type of securities market order which turns into a limit order when (if) the market price reaches a certain pre-specified threshold level where the market price is moving adversely.

stop-loss order: An order to sell or buy an asset (usually stock) at the current market price immediately after a certain pre-specified threshold price is reached where the market price is moving adversely.

straddle (in commodities): Another name for a spread, where offsetting positions are taken in similar contracts such as adjacent expirations of the same physical.

straddle (in options): A combination put and call on the same stock at the same striking price.

straight debt: Bonds without a conversion feature or other equity-like features.

straight-debt value: The underlying value of a convertible bond if it were to be stripped of its conversion feature and thus was valued only as a straight-debt (nonconvertible) bond.

straight-line depreciation: A method of writing off the recorded balance sheet values of long-lived assets at a constant dollar rate over their estimated lives.

stranded costs: Previously incurred costs for plant and equipment that, while still carried on the books, are no longer useful and now need to be written off.

stangle: Combination put and call position where the two options have different strike prices.

strap: A combination of two calls and one put each having the same strike and expiration date.

street-name: Securities held in customer accounts at brokerage houses but registered in the brokerage firm's name.

strike: See *striking price*.

striking price: The amount that an option holder (call) is required to pay in order to exercise an option. For a put the price that the put writer must pay in order to purchase the stock if the put holder exercises his or her option to sell. Also called strike, strike price or exercise price.

strip: A combination of two puts and one call each having the same strike and expiration date.

strip bond: A coupon bond with its coupons removed. A strip bond returns only principal at maturity and thus is equivalent to a zero-coupon bond.

strong form of the efficient market hypothesis: The view that market prices quickly and accurately reflect all public and nonpublic information; implies that inside information is useless in security selection.

style analysis: An effort to explain the variability in the observed returns of a portfolio in terms of the movements in the returns to a series of benchmark portfolios designed to capture the essence of a particular security characteristic such as its size, value, and growth.

Subaccounts: Stock, bond and money market funds used as part of a program to invest money in an annuity.

Subchapter M: The section of the Internal Revenue Code that sets forth the criteria which must be met in order to qualify as a regulated investment company.

Subchapter S: The section of the Internal Revenue Code that sets forth the criteria which must be met in order to qualify as a Subchapter S corporation. See *Subchapter S corporation*.

Subchapter S corporation: A classification whereby a corporation may be taxed as a partnership under the provisions of the Internal Revenue Code. See *Subchapter S*.

subordinate (junior) bonds: Bonds that, in case of default, entitle holders to claims on the issuer's assets only after the claims of holders of more senior creditors (bank debt senior debentures and mortgage bonds) are satisfied in full.

subordination provisions: Bond indenture provisions that assign a bond issue a lower priority than other (senior) bond issues.

sum of the years' digits depreciation: A method of calculating accelerated depreciation that each year assigns depreciation charges equal to the ratio of the number of years remaining in the asset's estimated useful life to the total of the years in the asset's estimated life.

Super Bowl indicator: A whimsical technical market indicator whose signal is based on whether the Super Bowl (football) is won by a former member of the old American Football League (AFL) or the National Football League (NFL). An NFL victory forecasts an up market for the coming year; an AFL victory forecasts a down market. No forecast is derived from an expansion team win.

Super Dot System: See *DOT*.

superNOW account: An interest-bearing checking account.

support level: A floor price that, according to technical analysis, tends to restrict a stock's downside price moves.

surrender charges: A penalty assessed for withdrawing money from a annuity prior to the pre-specified time allowed for withdrawals.

Survey Research Center: Research institute located at the University of Michigan that surveys consumers and publishes statistics on consumer sentiments.

swap fund: A type of mutual fund that allows investors to purchase its shares using the shares of other companies as currency; valuing those exchanged shares at their market prices.

sweep account: A type of bank account that sweeps the portion of the balance exceeding some pre-assigned minimum into a money market account on a daily basis.

syndicate: A group of investment bankers organized to underwrite a new issue or secondary offering.

systematic risk: See *market risk*.

tactical asset allocation: A portfolio strategy that adjusts the investor's mix of stocks, bonds, and cash by increasing (decreasing) the allocation to the asset class that is believed to be relatively undervalued (overvalued).

takeover bid: A tender offer designed to acquire a sufficient number of shares to achieve working control of the target firm.

tangible investments: A broad group of assets that includes precious metals, gemstones, artifacts, and some types of collectibles.

tangibles: See *tangible investments*.

taxable income: adjusted gross income less deductions and allowance for exemptions; The income figure on which one's income tax liability is computed.

tax basis: The cost of capital assets that is subtracted from the selling price in order to determine the gain or loss for tax purposes.

tax credit: Sums derived from various types of activities (e.g. purchase of solar energy equipment) that can be applied to offset computed taxes on a dollar-for-dollar basis thereby reducing the amount of taxes otherwise due.

tax-loss carry forward: Unutilized prior-period reported losses that may be employed to offset the tax liability of subsequent income.

tax-loss trading: Year-end selling of depressed securities designed to establish a tax loss.

tax-managed fund: A type of investment company that sought to convert dividend income into capital gains; prior to IRS rulings disallowing the practice, such funds organized themselves as corporations rather than as mutual funds and reinvested their portfolios' dividends.

tax shelter: An investment that produces deductions which can be applied against the investor's other income with a resulting savings in income taxes. The Tax Reform Act of 1986 severely restricted most types of tax shelters.

tax swap: A type of bond swap in which one bond issue is sold in order to yield a tax loss and replaced with an equivalent (similar but not identical) bond issue.

T-bill: See *Treasury bill*.

TEBF (Tax-Exempt Bond Fund): A mutual or closed-end fund that invests in municipal bonds, thereby providing tax-free income to its holders.

technical analysis (broad form): A method used for forecasting general market movements with technical market indicators.

technical analysis (narrow form): A method used for evaluating securities' investment attractiveness based on past price and volume behavior; largely debunked by evidence favorable to the weak form of the efficient market hypothesis.

technical default: A default related to a breach of a financial covenant or other such promise as distinct from an actual payment default, where the company fails to make a principal or in interest payment.

technical market indicator: A data series or combination of data series said to be helpful in forecasting the market's future direction. Also called a market indicator.

Templeton approach: A fundamental approach to investment analysis named after renowned mutual fund manager John Marks Templeton; emphasizes a world view to finding undervalued issues.

tender offer: An offer to purchase a large block of securities made outside the general market (exchanges, OTC) in which the securities are traded; often made as part of an effort to take over a company.

term insurance: A type of life insurance, not having a savings feature; unlike whole life where annual premium rates are fixed, premiums rise with the age of the insured in order thereby to reflect the greater probability of death. See also *whole life insurance.*

term loan: Bank loans that are generally of a longer term nature (several years) than most bank loans and have preset amortization schedules and a stated maturity.

term structure of interest rates: A pattern of yields for differing maturities (risk controlled). See also *liquidity preference, segmented markets, unbiased expectations hypotheses.*

term to maturity: The length of time until the maturity (final payment date) of a debt instrument.

tertiary stocks: The most obscure classification of stocks; much less popular than even the secondary stocks; often trade only in the Pink Sheets. See *secondary stocks.*

testator: See *testor.*

testimonium: The concluding portion of a will.

testor: A person who leaves a will in force at his or her death. Also called testator.

thin market: A market in which trading volume is low and transactions relatively infrequent.

third market: The over-the-counter market in listed securities.

363 Motion: Section 363 of the Bankruptcy Code allows companies in chapter 11 to sell all or a significant portion of their assets in a bankruptcy auction sale. The court can give buyers assurances regarding clear title.

three step top down approach: A type of approach to fundamental analysis that focuses on: (1) economic, (2) industry and (3) firm factors, performed in that order.

thrifts: Bank like depository institutions other than commercial banks that accept savings deposits, especially savings and loan associations, mutual savings banks, and credit unions.

tick: The minimum size price increment on a futures contract.

ticker symbols: Symbols for identifying securities on the ticker tape and quotation machines; listed in *S&P Stock Guide* and several other publications.

ticker tape: A device for displaying relevant information on stock market trading.

Tigers (Treasury Investment Growth Receipts): Zero-coupon securities assembled by Merrill Lynch and backed by a portfolio of Treasury issues.

tight money: Restrictive monetary policy.

times-interest-earned ratio: Gross (before-tax, before-interest) profit relative to a firm's interest obligation.

time value (option): The excess of an option's market price over its intrinsic value.

time value (present value): The value of a current as opposed to a future sum.

title search: A process whereby the validity of a title to a real estate parcel is researched and evaluated.

TIPS: Treasury Inflation Protected Securities. Government bonds whose values are adjusted twice a year to offset the effects of changes in the consumer price index.

TOLSR (Total Odd-Lot Short Ratio): A technical market indicator that relates odd-lot short sales to total odd-lot trading.

top down approach: an approach to fundamental analysis that begins with economic analysis, then industry analysis and finally company analysis. See *three step top down approach.*

top-tier stocks: Established growth stocks preferred by many institutional investors.

total return: Dividend return plus capital gains return (stocks). On an analogous concept for other types of investments such as bonds.

total risk: The sum of market and non-market risk.

tracking error: The difference in returns between an active investment portfolio and its benchmark portfolio.

trade creditor: A supplier or vendor who has provided goods, services or raw materials to a company and has not yet been paid.

trading post: See *post.*

trading rule: A formula approach used to decide whether or not to undertake a particular transaction based on relationships observed in historical data.

transaction cost: The cost of executing a trade; includes, commissions and the impact of the bid-ask spread.

transfer agent: The agent who maintains the records for and keeps track of changes in security holder ownership.

transfer: Every mode, direct or indirect, absolute or conditional, voluntary or involuntary, for disposing of or parting with either property or an interest in property.

transfer tax: A New York State tax applied to the transfer of equity securities.

Treasury bill: Government debt security issued on a discount basis by the U.S. Treasury. Also called a T-bill.

Treasury bond: A U.S. government bond issued with an initial maturity greater than 10 years.

Treasury note: A U.S. government bond issued with an initial maturity of 1 to 10 years.

treasury stock: Previously issued stock reacquired by the issuing company.

trust: A property interest held by one person for the benefit of another.

trustee: See *bankruptcy trustee*; also under an indenture, a bank or other third party that administers the provisions of a bond indenture. See also *indenture trustee*.

turnover: Trading volume in a security or the market as a whole.

Turov's Formula: A formula for computing the amount by which a stock price must change in order to produce returns equivalent to the returns on its call options.

12b-1 fund: A type of mutual fund that does not charge an upfront load but does withdraw a selling fee from the fund's assets on an annual basis.

two-tier tender offer: A takeover tactic in which an initial offer is made for a controlling interest in the target (usually cash) and a second, generally less attractive offer, (usually securities) is made for the remainder. Such an offer structure is designed to put pressure on hold out shareholders to take advantage of the front end of the offer.

ugly duckling: A business unit whose surface characteristics make it unattractive – but which can become very valuable (become a swan) under certain circumstances.

unbiased expectations hypothesis: A theory designed to explain the term structure of interest rates as reflecting the market consensus of contiguous forthcoming short rates. See *liquidity preference* and *segmented market hypotheses*.

underwriter: An investment banker who agrees to buy part or all of a new security issue with the expectation of selling the securities to the public at a slightly higher price. Or an investment banker who performs a similar function for a tender offer.

underwriting fee: The underwriter's selling fee earned as the difference between the price paid to the seller of an underwritten issue and the price paid by the buyer.

unemployment rate: The percentage of those members of the labor force who are actively seeking employment but are currently out of work.

United Shareholders of America (USA): A shareholder rights organization that was sponsored by T. Boone Pickens; USA advocated such issues as equal voting rights for all classes of stock, secret proxy votes, and prohibition of poison pills. Established in 1986. Dissolved in 1994.

United States Trustee: An employee of the Department of Justice who attends to certain administrative functions in the administration of bankruptcy cases. This person is different from a bankruptcy trustee who is an individual assigned to manage and run a debtor's estate and an indenture trustee who is charged with enforcing the rights of the bondholders.

unit investment trust: A self-liquidating unmanaged portfolio in which investors own shares and receive distributions.

universal life: A type of life insurance policy in which the cash value varies with the policyholder's payments and the company's investment returns.

Unlisted Market Guide: An investment periodical that covers small companies which are not reported on by larger periodicals such as Value Line and Standard and Poor's.

unlisted security: A security that trades only in the OTC market.

unrealized capital gains: Paper gains that reflect the price appreciation of currently held unsold assets.

unsecured obligation: A claim against the firm that is not backed by any specific collateral interest.

unsystematic risk: See *non-market risk*.

uptick: A transaction that takes place at a higher price than the immediately preceding price.

uptick-downtick ratio: A ratio of the number of uptick block transactions relative to the number of downtick block transactions.

urgent selling index: A technical market indicator based on the volume of advancing relative to declining issues.

usable bond: A bond that may be utilized at its face value in order to exercise corresponding warrants of the issuing firm.

VA (Veterans Administration): A federal government agency that is concerned with the affairs of veterans and among other things, guarantees mortgage loans for qualifying veterans.

Value Line: A finance/investments periodical that publishes quarterly analyses on about 1,700 firms and compiles the *Value Line Index*; owned by Arnold Bernhard and Company.

Value Line Index: An equally weighted broadly based stock price index.

value oriented investor: A type of investor who seeks to assemble and own a portfolio of stocks that sell at low prices relative to their tangible underlying values; that is, a low price relative to their earnings, cash flows, book values, breakup values, and liquid asset values.

value stock: The stock of a company whose market price is low compared to earnings, net worth, sales and other fundamental characteristics.

variable annuity: An investment vehicle similar to a mutual fund but sold by insurance companies.

variable life: A type of life insurance policy in which the cash value varies with the return on the policyholder's portfolio.

variable rate mortgage: A mortgage in which the interest rate applied to the mortgage is structured to vary with market interest rates.

variable rate note: A bond whose coupon rate is reset periodically according to a formula based on the current level of market interests rates.

variance: The expected (average) value of the square of the deviation from the mean; variance of $X = E(X-\bar{X})^2$ where $\bar{X}$ is the mean of X and E is the expected value operator.

variance-covariance model: A method of estimating portfolio risk that utilizes the variances and covariances of all of the potential components.

Vasicek adjustment: A method of adjusting estimated raw betas based on the uncertainty of the mean and specific raw beta estimates.

venture capital: Risk capital extended to start-up or small going concerns.

venture capital fund: An investment company that invests in venture capital opportunities.

versus purchase order: A type of sales order used to identify the specific purchase date and price of securities to be delivered for sale. Used to minimize the current tax liability of the transaction.

vertical integration: The process of a business either buying or building from scratch a further stage of the production process: supplier or customer.

vertical spread: Short and long option positions on the same security with the same expiration but different striking prices.

vested benefits: Pension benefits that are retained by the employee even if the individual leaves his or her employer.

volume: The number of shares traded in a particular period (e.g. day).

WACC: Weighted Average Cost of Capital. A company's cost for its blend of debt and equity. The WACC rate may be used to discount a company's future cash flows back to the present value.

wallpaper: Worthless securities that can be more effectively used for wallpapering one's house.

Wall Street Journal, The: A widely read business/investments newspaper published five (now six) days a week by Dow Jones Inc.

Wall Street Week (WSW): A popular and long-running weekly business news television program. Carried by the public broadcasting corporation.

warrants: Certificates offering the right to purchase a specified amount of stock (or in rare cases bonds) in a company at a specified price over a specified period. If exercised, to be satisfied by the issuance of additional shares of the warrant issuing company.

wash sale: A sale and repurchase made within 30 days, thereby failing to establish a reportable loss for tax purposes.

weak form of the efficient market hypothesis: The theory that market prices move randomly with respect to past price-return patterns; implies that technical analysis, as practiced by the chart readers, is useless.

Weighted Average Life (WAL): A measure of a bond's maturity. It takes into account principal payments made over time, so that a bond making interim principal payments will have a WAL shorter than the actual maturity. See *duration*.

Weisenberger: A major publisher of mutual fund investment information, including *Investment Companies*.

whack-up: The process of allocating the finite pie of a restructuring firm's value among the various constituencies.

when-issued trading: Trading in as yet unissued securities that have a projected future issue date. Payment is due upon issuance.

white chip stock: A stock of low quality. See *blue chip stock, red chip stocks*.

white knight defense: Finding an alternative and presumably more friendly acquirer (the white knight) than the immediate takeover threat.

white squire defense: Finding an important ally who will acquire a substantial minority position of the firm now controlled by existing management but threatened by an outside group; presumably the white squire will oppose and hopefully help block the efforts of the outsider to take control of the vulnerable company.

whole life insurance: A type of life insurance policy that couples life insurance protection with a savings program. Annual premiums are established and fixed at the time of the initial purchase. A surplus account is built up in the policy's early years for the purpose of meeting claims that exceed premiums when the policyholders are older and death rates are higher.

will: A legal document stating a person's intentions with regard to the disposition of his or her property or estate at the time of death.

Wilshire 5000 Index: A value-weighted stock index based on a large number of NYSE, AMEX, and OTC stocks.

winnowing: The process of eliminating certain potential buyers who have expressed interest in specific assets or properties that may be for sale. This is done in an attempt to maximize the efficiency of the sale process and to eliminate the merely curious.

wire house: An exchange member electronically linked to an exchange.

withholding tax: A portion of an employee's income withheld by the employer as partial payment of the employee's income tax liability.

working capital (gross): The sum of the values of a firm's short-term assets.

working capital (net): The difference between the values of a firm's short-term assets and its short-term liabilities.

working capital facilities: Those portions of a company's bank credit agreement usually reserved for the acquisition of working capital such as to finance its inventory or accounts receivable.

working control: The ownership of a sufficient number of shares to elect a majority to the company's board of directors.

work-out: Another term for a restructuring (usually undertaken out of court).

writer (of an option): One who sells and thereby assumes the short side of a put or call contract and therefore stands ready to satisfy the potential exercise by the long side.

Yankee bonds: Bonds denominated in U.S. dollars but issued by a foreign firm or government.

yield: The return on an investment expressed as a percentage of its market value.

yield (current): Current income (dividend, coupon, rent, etc.) divided by the price of the asset.

yield curve: The relationship between yield to maturity and term to maturity (or duration) for equivalent risk debt securities.

yield curve note: A type of debt security whose coupon rate is structured to move inversely with market rates; thus when the market interest rates decline the coupon rate on the yield curve notes will rise, and vice versa.

yield spread: The difference between the promised yields of particular bonds or classes of bonds at a given time relative to yields on Treasury issues of equal maturity.

yield to earliest call: The holding-period return under the assumption that the issue is called as soon as the no-call provision in the bond's indenture expires.

Yield-to-maturity: The yield calculation that takes proper account of both the coupon return and the principal repayment at maturity.

yield-to-worst: The lowest of (1) the current yield, (2) the yield-to-maturity and (3) the yield-to-call.

zero-coupon bond: A bond issued at a discount from its par or face value that matures at its face value.

zero tick: A transaction immediately preceded by a transaction at the same price.

zone of insolvency: A financial situation in which the company's position has deteriorated to the point where creditors may be adversely affected. Bankruptcy is possible but not certain.

INDEX

A

2005 Amendments, 11, 13, 16–17
Administrative Office of U. S. courts, 4
Allegheny International, 19
Allied Chemical, 178
Amerco, 20
American Association of Individual Investors, 222
American Stock Exchange (AMEX) Index, 222, 241, 274
Andrew Fastow, 63
Arbitraging, 186–188, 204

B

Bankruptcies, investing in
    and creditors' committee, 5–6, 18, 35, 38, 41, 91, 94, 100–101, 104, 240
    disclosure statement, 7, 13–16, 19, 22–24, 26, 41– 43, 50, 67, 69, 71–72, 74, 76–77, 110, 126–127, 132, 244
exclusivity period, 6, 13, 39, 96
Bankruptcy Act, 1
Bankruptcy Code, v, vi, 1, 2, 11–11–17, 19, 22–23, 26, 44–46, 52–54, 57–58, 72–73, 78–79, 220, 225, 227, 232, 242, 244, 253, 264, 281, 283–284, 300
    tax issues, 25
Bankruptcy procedure, 3, 18
Bankruptcy trustee, 2–6, 226, 302–303
Bankruptcy values estimation
    bankruptcy filing, 9, 24, 28, 35, 54, 87, 103, 113–114, 116–118, 120, 192, 194–197, 200, 226, 250, 280
Bankruptcy/reorganization examples
    MGF Oil Corporation, 70–73
    Storage Technology Corporation, 65–69
Bond ratings and performance, 201–202
Book value per common share, 146

Braniff Airways, 20, 76–79
Broker-based buyouts, 157–158
Business Lawyer, 211
Business Week, 229
Busted Converts, 177

C

Call protection, 191, 193, 208–210, 216, 230
Calls, 37, 114, 184–186, 192, 202, 229, 246, 254, 262, 266, 291, 297
Cash flow, 51, 59, 114, 127, 135–138, 140–142, 146–148–153, 156–158, 195, 206–207, 221, 229, 231, 241–243, 245, 247, 252, 254, 263, 274, 280–281, 284, 286–287, 304
Cash flow per share, 146, 148
Chapter 11, 1–11, 13, 15–17, 19–22, 24–29, 31–32, 34–35, 39, 41, 44–45, 52, 56–60, 62–63, 65, 70, 72–73, 79, 82–83, 96, 98, 110, 114, 117, 123–125, 191, 216, 225, 232, 250, 264, 300
    disclosure statement, 7, 13–16, 19, 22–24, 26, 41– 43, 50, 67, 69, 71–72, 74, 76–77, 110, 126–127, 132, 244
    exclusivity period, 6, 13, 39, 96
    prepackaged, 15–16, 280
Chapter 15 (international cases), 1–2
Chapter 7, 1–4, 6–9, 11, 14, 16, 41, 45–46, 48, 50, 92–93, 96, 101–102, 111, 123–125, 133, 191, 216, 225, 232, 236
Chase Manhattan Bank, 64
Citicorp, 168
Commercial paper, 83, 85–86, 92–93, 163, 189, 234, 272, 277
Commodity-backed bonds, 173, 178–179, 189, 234
COMPUSTAT, 235

Convertible preferreds, 173, 182–183, 189
Corporate bond funds, 168, 189
Crystal Oil, 42

D

Debt securities, 28, 42, 79–80, 114, 152,
    162–164, 172–173, 176–177, 179, 181,
    187–189, 191, 204, 206, 227, 233, 242,
    249, 253, 256, 275, 293, 306
  and bankruptcy, 227
  money market, 162–164, 168, 189, 225, 257,
    268, 272, 293, 297,
Debt security default risk
  bankruptcy filings, 24, 195–196
  bond ratings, 191, 198, 201
  exchange offers, 195–196
  indenture provisions, 49, 125, 177, 190–194,
    298
  informal reorganization, 194–195
  term structure of interest rates, 202–203, 216,
    267, 279, 292, 300, 302
Defensive recapitalization, 141, 157–158, 243
Delphi, 113, 118, 194
Digital Equipment, 184
Doskocil, Inc., 21

E

Earnings per share (EPS), 145, 148, 252, 277
Enron (In re Enron Corp., et al.), 17, 52, 62–65,
    113, 194, 202
Equity Funding, 40, 201
Equity notes, 173, 178–179, 189, 234, 249, 269
Eurobonds, 164, 168, 171–173, 189, 249
Exide Technologies, 21

F

Fallen angels, 157–158
Finance, 24, 38, 51–52, 70, 83–84, 86, 92, 104,
    116, 128, 139, 141, 146, 158, 163, 200,
    211, 226, 236, 244, 246, 248, 253, 266,
    269, 272, 284, 287, 303, 306
Financial indenture covenants, 154
  elimination of, 211–216
Fitch Investors Service, 198, 252
Forbes, 200, 253
ForcEnergy Company, 17

Fortune, 137
Fully diluted EPS, 146

G

General American, 178
General Foods, 159
Global Marine Inc., 73–76
GM Acceptance, 213

H

Hedging, 186–190
High-yield securities, qualitative aspects of
  financial indenture covenants, 154
High-yield securities, quantitative analysis of
  profitability and efficiency ratios, 138,
    144–145, 147
  ratio analysis, 137–145
HRT Industries, 20

I

IBM, 159, 261
Income bonds, 164, 196, 215
Internet, 32, 34, 217, 244, 263
Investment Company Institute, 264
Itel Corporation, 20

J

JPMorgan study, 20

K

Keogh accounts, 170
Kodak, 159

L

Limited partnerships, 183–184, 187
Liquidity ratios, 138, 147
LTV Energy Products, 19

M

Magellan Health, 20
Magma Copper, 17
Merrill Lynch, 170, 178, 301
Mesa Limited Partners, 184
Mesa Petroleum, 178
MGF Oil Corporation, 70–73

N

National Association of Investment Clubs, 274

National Association of Securities, 273
Dealers Automated Quotations, 273

New York Stock Exchange (NYSE)
Composite Index, 275

Northwestern Corp., 21

O

Options, 27–28, 59, 61, 103, 127, 177, 179–180, 184–187, 219, 224, 232–233, 237, 239, 243, 257–258, 263–264, 268, 270, 273, 276, 279, 284, 292, 295–297, 302

P

Pacer system, 34

Pacific Stock Exchange, 186

Penn Central, 10, 201–202

Petro Lewis, 179

Preferred stock, 27, 42, 56, 58, 64, 71, 75, 77, 114, 117, 126, 128, 129–130, 132, 142, 164, 173, 179–182, 187, 189–190, 195–196, 228, 230, 234, 237, 240, 1249, 253, 278–279, 291

Procter & Gamble, 159

Prospectus, 7, 41, 172, 218–219, 244, 282

Protective covenants, 155

Proxy materials, 282

Puts, 153, 183, 184–186

R

Refinement International, 179

Revere Copper and Brass, 19

Risk hedges, 188

S

Securities and Exchange Commission, 290

Seitel, 20

Sinking fund, 80, 115, 191–193, 208–210, 293

Storage Technology Corporation, 65–68

Strategic acquisitions or financings, 157–158

T

Textron, 178, 184

Trade creditors, 33, 44, 46, 49, 66–67, 91, 116, 123–124, 128, 197

Treasury bills, 161, 163, 169, 272, 274, 276

Trump Hotels and Casino Resorts, 58–62,

Trust Indenture Act, 16, 195, 261

U

U.S. Savings Bonds, 169

UAL, 56–58, 113, 194, 201–202

Uniform Fraudulent Transfer Act and Uniform Fraudulent Conveyance Act, 22

United Airlines (In re UAL Corporation, et al.), 56–58, 113, 194, 201–202

United Merchants and Manufacturers, 40

United Shareholders of America, 303

Unlisted Market Guide, 303

US Airways, 21

V

Value Line, 200, 223, 227, 265, 303–304

Venture capital, 180, 184, 304

Vinson & Elkins, 65

W

Wall Street Journal, The, 246, 264, 305

Wall Street Week, 305

Warrants and rights, 184–185

Working capital, 61, 138–139, 141–142, 149, 151, 194, 196, 200, 288, 306

WorldCom, 17, 113, 194, 202

Z

Zeta Services, 201

www.ingramcontent.com/pod-product-compliance
Lightning Source LLC
Chambersburg PA
CBHW021029210326
41598CB00016B/960